THE BIBLE AS BOOK
THE MANUSCRIPT TRADITION

THE BIBLE AS BOOK
THE MANUSCRIPT TRADITION

Edited by

JOHN L. SHARPE III AND KIMBERLY VAN KAMPEN

THE BRITISH LIBRARY
& OAK KNOLL PRESS

*in association with The Scriptorium:
Center for Christian Antiquities*

1998

FOR ROBERT AND JUDITH VAN KAMPEN

First published 1998 by
The British Library
96 Euston Road
St Pancras
London NW1

Reprinted 2002

Published exclusively in North and South America by
Oak Knoll Press
414 Delaware Street
New Castle
DE 19720

in association with
The Scriptorium: Center for Christian Antiquities
926 Robbins Road, Suite 183
Grand Haven
Michigan 49417

British Library Cataloguing-in-Publication Data
A CIP Record is available from The British Library

Library of Congress Cataloging-in-Publication Data
The Bible as book: the manuscript tradition / edited by
John L. Sharpe III and Kimberly Van Kampen.
p.   cm.
Collection of papers based on a conference and sponsored by
the Scriptorium, Center for Christian Antiquities.
Includes bibliographical references and index.
ISBN 1-884718-38-8
1. Bible – Manuscripts – Congresses.   I. Sharpe, John L.
(John Lawrence)   II. Van Kampen, Kimberly.
BS4.5.B53   1998
220.4'046 – DC21   97-2700   CIP

ISBN 1-884718-38-8 (Oak Knoll)
ISBN 0-7123-4522-1 (British Library)

Designed by John Trevitt
Typeset in England by Norman Tilley Graphics, Northampton
Printed in England by Bookcraft, Midsomer Norton, Bath

CONTENTS

Contents

CONTRIBUTORS

CHRISTOPHER CLARKSON, *West Dean College*

CHRISTOPHER DE HAMEL, *Sotheby's, London*

STEPHEN EMMEL, *Yale University*

LUCY-ANNE HUNT, *University of Birmingham*

ANDREW LOUTH, *Goldsmith's College, London*

SCOT MCKENDRICK, *The British Library*

MARTIN MCNAMARA, *The Milltown Institute of Theology and Philosophy*

RICHARD MARSDEN, *University of Leeds*

SYLVIE L. MERIAN, *The Pierpont Morgan Library, New York*

JENNIFER O'REILLY, *University College, Cork*

T. S. PATTIE, *formerly of The British Library*

GABRIELLE SED-RAJNA, *Paris*

JOHN SHARPE, *University of North Carolina*

EMANUEL TOV, *Hebrew University*

BASTIAAN VAN ELDEREN, *Vrije Universiteit, Amsterdam*

KIMBERLY VAN KAMPEN, *The Scriptorium Center for Christian Antiquities*

CHRISTINA VON NOLCKEN, *University of Chicago*

CHRISTOPHER VEREY, *London*

LIST OF ILLUSTRATIONS

(reproduced between pages 228 and 229)

List of Illustrations

FOREWORD

IN 1994, two American foundations were established. The first, Van Kampen Foundation, exists as an entity to maintain and develop the growing collection of rare bibles belonging to Robert and Judith Van Kampen of western Michigan. The second takes the form of an institution. The Scriptorium: Center for Christian Antiquities, the home of the Van Kampen Collection, is equipped to initiate and stimulate research within the fields which apply to the items within the collection and to the periods it represents. Both foundations are active in the USA and Britain.

The first academic event sponsored by the Scriptorium was a conference in May 1995 which bore the same title as this volume. Hampton Court, Herefordshire, provided a serene and intimate setting for the delegates who gathered to investigate the transmission and veneration of the biblical text by early Christian communities. The papers fostered an approach to biblical scholarship which regards codicological elements as evidence of textual evolution, as well as an attestation to the devotional practices of historical Bible readers.

The Bible is actually a text, but bibles are books which have had manifold uses and have occupied divers positions of prominence throughout history. This present volume gathers together many traditions – both Jewish and Christian – as a tribute to the scholars, artists, and readers of the handwritten Bible, and as a representation of the textual ancestry of modern Scripture. Both encyclopedic and theoretical, this body of research will prove an enlightening tool in the hands of all who are interested in how manuscript evidence speaks to the legacy of a given text, particularly the Bible – the most important medieval text.

I should like to thank especially the following friends and colleagues for their assistance in the production of this work as a whole: Scott Carroll, Beverly Van Kampen, Andrea Masvero, and Susan Grant of the Scriptorium; John Sharpe, my partner in this project; Joanne Sharpe and Scott and Karla Pierre for their help with the organization of the conference; Ellen Middlebrook for assembling and editing the bibliography; David Way, Scot McKendrick, and the support staff of The British Library; Richard Marsden; and, of course, all the contributors.

KIMBERLY VAN KAMPEN

7 August 1997

xi

INTRODUCTION

John Sharpe, Scot McKendrick, and Kimberly Van Kampen

WHATEVER ITS FORM – scroll, codex, or tablet – a book is amassed cultural evidence. Like agglutinated archeological layers that, separated one from the other and analysed, reveal layers of distinctive civilizations and cultures, every book is a witness to its time. Nowhere is that more evident than in the forms and shapes that the Bible has taken over the centuries since the first scribe wrote down the first words. Unlike any other book, the Bible as an object embodies its own message: that of a culturally transcendent text contained within the artistic handiwork of the cultures to which it is relevant. Whatever the time period or the society which produced it, every Bible bears the imprint of its ancestry.

The theme of the first Hereford Conference, sponsored by the Scriptorium: Center for Christian Antiquities, was 'The Bible as Book: the Manuscript Tradition'. The aim was to examine the ways in which the Bible as a manuscript was given shape in terms of text, decoration, materials, and construction, and thereby given identity by the particular community of believers which produced each manuscript. The theme of the conference was admittedly a broad one, the subtitle of which could have been 'Imaging the Word from Qumran to the Lollards'.

Long before technological innovation transformed a gathering of leaves into a codex, the ancient Mesopotamians produced bas-relief images of dutiful servants standing with pens raised in one hand and in the other a tablet on which to write the spoken words.[1] A statue of the Egyptian scribe in the Louvre – found at Saqqarah belonging to the Fifth Dynasty – continues to sit cross-legged, attentive, with right hand poised, ready to transcribe the next word on the sheet of papyrus spread across his lap. Although the pen is no longer in his hand, his gaze and posture mark the value of the place occupied by those who transform the spoken word into graphic symbols to be recalled, remembered, and used when memory has failed.

The Word, spoken or read, takes on meaning beyond what it simply says. While it is impossible that the entire content of the Covenant between God and the Children of Israel could have been written on the two tablets of stone which Moses brought down from the mountain, the responsibilities of each party to the contract were summarized in the Decalogue, or the 'Ten Words' – ultimately representing the entire Covenant made between Yahweh and his people. The object itself represents what it contains: the Ten Commandments finally were distilled by the rabbis into the summary of the Law, meaning the responsibilities of the relationships between God and His people, to 'love God and love your neighbour' – a summary of the total responsibility between God and man that could be recited while standing on one foot. Even though one can read the Torah from an edition such as that produced by Kittel,[2] the object itself as a scroll occupies the place of honour in the tabernacle in the synagogue. Likewise the Four Gospels lie on the holy table in the Orthodox Church; and among Protestants, the Bible

I

holds the position of honour on the pulpit. Whether prepared for an opulent Romanesque or Byzantine court, for the simple desert communities of Egypt and the Middle East, or for the remote monasteries of the northern reaches of the Roman Empire, the Bible as a book, perhaps more than any other written object, is easily recognized as a 'Holy Book' by its outward appearance. The materials and method of decoration, illumination, and binding not only caused the reader to have a greater veneration for the text; they also encouraged those unable to read it to admire the Bible as a sacred and beautiful object.

Throughout its history, the Bible has functioned as both 'book' and 'image': as a book in all that it contains – histories, prophecies, songs, stories, letters, in essence, the revelation of God; and as an image in what it means to a people or community and how they expressed that meaning. In this sense, the biblical text was 'reincarnated', that is, its life and message were renewed and reaffirmed, with each new generation of scribes, artists, binders, and printers. Drawing on their own historical repertoire of talent and experience, each gave new expression, new shape, and new importance to the age-old realities contained within it. In the process of transmitting the text, each generation of artisans from the earliest of the biblical recorders has produced another cultural artifact and illustration of the devotion with which they carried out their work. With each new generation, a new image of the Word was born.

The pervasive theme of this collection of papers is that of the relationship between the form or shape of the Word and its contents, as expressed by the scribe, illuminator, binder, translator, or theologian. By 'the manuscript tradition' we imply, of course, the vast period of time of written transmission of the biblical text prior to printing. For our purposes, this period spans from approximately the time of Christ to the fifteenth century. The scope of this volume, chronologically and culturally, is vast, beginning with an examination of the methodology of the scribes who produced the Dead Sea Scrolls and concluding with the late-medieval propagation of the Scriptures. Like the conference which initiated these proceedings, this study is innovative in bringing together scholars of different disciplines and time periods to investigate a single text. The unifying thread, however, is strong: that of the prominence of the biblical text itself in these various eras and societies, combined with the universal practice of reproducing the text with the finest of book-making skills. In sum, *The Bible as Book: the Manuscript Tradition* investigates the abstract topic of textual transmission through the tangible application of codicology, a critical technique which is gaining credibility with scholars of history and literature. No text is better suited for such an investigation than the Bible, and no text has enjoyed such broad popularity, as evidenced by the various manuscripts discussed in this volume. In this way, the sum of these studies produces an important contribution to the present understanding of this ancient, ageless text and its prominence throughout time.

The earliest form of the book addressed in this volume is that of the scroll and it is represented by the library of the Qumrān community. This was indeed the quintessential scroll community – a reclusive Jewish group who preserved their written tradition in a form that was, for the time, the only way a book could look: written on the hair side of tawed skin, in narrow columns in black carbon ink, and rolled. Emanuel Tov, in 'Scribal Practices Reflected in the Dead Sea Scrolls', identifies the procedures and materials that shaped the written form of Scriptural texts within the traditions of the first-century Qumrān community: scrolls of skin (leather or a form of alum-tawed parchment) and specially made inks were utilized according to the methods of the scriptorium. Rules of production were probably drawn from a larger reading and writing community but were then adapted and applied to the transcription of holy words. The materials acquired liturgical, even talismanic, power that guaranteed the sanctity of the materials that carried the letters, of the ink which gave them visibility, and of the copying rules of the scriptorium that guarded and verified the accuracy both in doctrine and in the form of the letters. From there developed individual approaches to certain types of texts, not only exegetical, but also poetical and historical.

According to Professor Tov, his large corpus of manuscripts, written in different periods and localities, reveals that hardly any distinction was made by scribes between the writing of sacred and non-sacred texts. Yet a particular look, or form, was expected of a particular kind of document. While most Qumrān scrolls were written on leather, papyrus was used for personal copies or non-biblical composition. Papyrus copies of biblical books were indeed forbidden by the Rabbis: 'If it was written with caustic, red dye, or *copperas*, or on paper (papyrus), or *diftera*, he had not fulfilled his obligation; but only if it was written in Assyrian writing, on parchment and with ink.'³ The published document was expected to have a particular appearance – a particular colour of ink, layout, line length, and column height – as prescribed first by convention and later by rules of the scriptorium that developed for theological and liturgical reasons.

Changes in the look and form of the book were beginning as early as the first century of this era. The evolution of the scroll to the leaf book was certainly accomplished by the middle of the fourth century; however, the forces at work in this change remain the subject of debate. Was it the Christians who wanted a form of book that was distinct from that employed by the Jewish community? Was it the Chinese-folded accordion-leaf format or classical influences which became the inspiration for the first gatherings of stacked leaves? It is likely that many factors contributed to the innovation of the codex format.

The best preserved early codices come from Egypt. Stephen Emmel, in 'The Christian Book in Egypt: Innovation and the Coptic Tradition', considers the contribution of the Coptic communities to the development of the book. The conviction of these early Egyptian Christians that the leaf book is 'the way a book should look' is investigated by Emmel as he interweaves the stories of Coptic language, monasticism, and book reproduction. In his own words, 'As in the case of the creation of the literary codex, we cannot know who took the first steps toward creating the Coptic alphabet. But it was likely the Christians who standardized the new writing system [i.e. the codex format] and maintained it. And certainly Coptic literature reached its maturity nurtured by the Christian church and the allied monastic movement.'

The form standarized by the Egyptian Christians consisted of a single-signature papyrus-leaf book, made up of single leaves that were usually cut from a papyrus roll. The stack of papyrus leaves, folded and sewn down the centre, were provided with a light cover of leather wrapped around several of the outer leaves that had been pasted together to form a kind of papyrus paste board. Collections of these codices that were hidden from sight in remote parts of Egypt until earlier this century are the subject of Bastiaan Van Elderen's 'The Great Christian Libraries'. He explores the treasures that have become an essential part of the literary scholarship of early Christian studies, the most remarkable of them are those discovered at Nag Hammadi. The contents of these libraries are presently scattered between Geneva, Cairo, and New York, but are catalogued here as a single archive.

The transition to the multi-quire codex using papyrus was unsuccessful because of the friability of papyrus. With the availability and acceptance of parchment as a writing surface, the multi-layered codex was born. By the fourth century, parchment – a washed, stretched, and polished skin – was the popular medium for book production. Folded, and gathered into groups of eight leaves, it presented a far more practical alternative to the single-leaf books of frail papyrus. Parchment gatherings could be sewn together, one to the other, and the whole enclosed in a cover. A much larger book, in both format and number of pages, was now a possibility.

This innovation in the technology of book production – a triumph of Christianity – made possible the large-format codices that we know as Codex Sinaiticus, Codex Alexandrinus, and Codex Vaticanus – the subjects of 'The Creation of the Great Codices' by T. S. Pattie. In AD 331 Emperor Constantine wrote to Eusebius of Caesarea and ordered fifty Bibles for his new churches in Constantinople. The books he ordered were parchment codices, the acceptable standard for the church book by this time. But the elegance and quality of the materials used for the three monumental manuscripts here described by Pattie introduced a new era in book-making.

The Bible now achieved an imagistic value. The change in scale alone affected the way the book was viewed and used. Ornamentation was derived from the imagery of the culture in which it grew and was transferred to the leaf of a manuscript – images that were often copied from the walls of the church buildings. Having made the transition from the wall to the page, these previously fixed decorative elements were easily transmitted by way of the portable codex from Egypt to Latin Rome, and from there throughout Europe to the farthest reaches of the empire. The three following papers discuss imported trends as well as native influences on the Insular Bible.

In exploring the name of Christ in the Book of Kells, Jennifer O'Reilly in 'Gospel Harmony and the Names of Christ: Insular Images of a Patristic Theme' considers how ornamentation and text are integrated. The Lord's final command to his followers was to teach and baptize all peoples to the ends of the earth. The western isles on the northern horizon of the Roman world were the farthest known limits of civilization. As far as St Patrick was concerned, his mission to the Irish in the fifth century fulfilled that scriptural injunction.[4] With the conversion of the Anglo-Saxons, Bede vigorously asserted the achievements of an insular monastic life and culture fully within the universal Church.[5] Incorporation into the church also meant embracing its learning and therefore its images which would be translated into the vernacular of these northern regions. The Codex Amiatinus and Bede's scholarship, along with studies of such scholars as Columbanus, Cummian, and Adomnan of Iona, testify to the wide variety of resources from the Mediterranean world that were available to the Northumbrian monastic community. On the other hand, their distinctive script and decorative motifs adapted from native metalwork and the highly stylized use of figures seem to set apart the Insular gospel-books and, according to O'Reilly, mark them as barbaric works that would never be mistaken for works from the sixth-century Mediterranean world. The bridge between the two cultures may be the book of Kells, which combines the conventions and images of the Insular gospel-book tradition and a range of figural Mediterranean motifs.

At the centre of the worshipping community, regardless of culture, has always been the Psalter, whether for Jew or Christian. In its many manifestations within different communities, no less the Irish monastic community, it takes on the aspects of the culture in which it is produced – illustrations, commentary, text, arrangement, supplementary material. In 'The Psalms in the Irish Church' Fr Martin McNamara brings to light the origins of the Psalter of Charlemagne by exploring all aspects of that manuscript from the arrangement of its text to its illustration. The unique combination of factors in its make-up and association with other manuscripts reveal the context of its creation. Whether written somewhere on the Rhine or in Belgium or eastern France, the Psalter of Charlemagne clearly depended on an Insular original.

Distinguishing and identifying characteristics that sort manuscripts into groups and families – particularly textual characteristics that may be used to prove a geneaological connection – are the foundation of the work of Christopher Verey on the Cambridge–London Gospels in 'A Northumbrian Gospel Text Family'. Verey's textual analysis is fitting in this collection of articles which primarily considers the non-textual 'portable' properties of manuscript Bibles. Verey argues that 'any discussion of that most portable of features, namely the text, all too often becomes a side-show or is ignored'. He concludes that there was a distinct Anglo-Saxon role in the transmission of the Latin gospels. Verey's textual comparison is groundbreaking in its revelation that the Cambridge–London gospels, the Durham Gospels, and Durham A.II.16 had their origins in a Northumbrian text tradition derived from an archetype closely akin to the text found in a seventh-century Italian uncial gospel-book (Bodleian Auct. D.2.14). This tradition is complementary to but distinct from the Italo-Northumbrian gospel tradition, as well as from the influence of the Irish tradition. The prefaces in the Cambridge–London gospels, however, maintain a textual affinity to Irish exemplars.

In a broader context of the textual and artistic influence of the portable book, Lucy-Anne Hunt, in 'Cultural Transmission: Illustrated Biblical Manuscripts from the Medieval Eastern Christian and Arab World', demonstrates how the content and form of biblical manuscripts played a key role in the cross-fertilization and interaction between eastern and western societies in the Middle Ages, as well as within the cultural and intellectual lives of the individual Christian communities that first produced them. She identifies imported influences on several major communities which are evident in their book production: the link between Christian Egypt and the British Isles in the fourth to eighth centuries; the interplay between indigenous Syrian and Mesopotamian Christian communities between the sixth and thirteenth centuries; and medieval Christian-Muslim co-existence under the domination of Islam.

Excepting a period of reversal to Byzantine rule between the later tenth and eleventh centuries, and the period of the Crusades between the later eleventh and thirteenth centuries, the Holy Land and much of Syria remained in Muslim hands from the early seventh century. Although it is a common assumption that the Christian churches in these regions (Palestine, Egypt, and Mesopotamia) were therefore isolated from mainstream theological developments in the Latin and Greek churches, the manuscript evidence suggests a very different picture. Textually and artistically, the manuscripts reveal traditions that were shared by both individuals and institutions. Hunt illustrates how the image of the Word in the eastern traditions, not to mention those of the strange and remote regions of northern Europe, took shape and was propagated by the conveniently portable codex book.

Despite Christopher de Hamel's curiosity, even amusement, in the topic assigned to his conference paper, his contribution beautifully illustrates his title, 'Books of Hours: Imaging the Word'. The story of Scripture is one of giving verbal form to the revelation of the Creator to His creation. As remote as was the medieval world from the land and times of the Bible, medieval readers were able to 'image the Word' by a repeated encounter with the Scriptures in the cyclical movement of their daily lives – the sanctification of every hour in every day, whether waking or sleeping, working or resting. The Book of Hours, while ever lacking the whole counsel of God and, at the same time, full of additional helps for the daily Christian life, contained 'all the little pieces of the Bible needed for salvation'. De Hamel emphasizes that the 'Book of Hours, as the first mass-distributed sacramentary, had an efficacious value because it used the very words of the Scriptures'. Their use evolved into a symbol of the devotion, as well as the affluence, of their owners. As objects, Books of Hours, the most plenteous of extant medieval books, are witnesses to medieval piety.

Two papers are dedicated to examinations of the place of the manuscript Bible within two specific eras and cultures in medieval England: the Anglo-Saxon period and that of the Wycliffite Rebellion. Richard Marsden, in 'Ask what I am Called: the Anglo-Saxons and the Bibles', examines the place of the Latin Scriptures in England during the entire period of Anglo-Saxon Christianity. He begins with one of their characteristically enigmatic riddles, which not only specifies the process of book production in the tenth century but also suggests the people's perspective of the benefit of the text, portrayed in the language of popular Germanic heroism:

If the sons of men will make use of me, they shall be the sounder, the more sure of victory, bolder in mind, blither in spirit, wiser in heart, and shall have more friends, dear ones and close, true and noble, good and faithful, who will surround them with grace and clasp them in the firm embraces of love.

Marsden considers the Bibles of the Anglo-Saxons by first examining their own writings concerning the Book, and then by describing the surviving manuscripts themselves. He divides Anglo-Saxon history into early and later periods, and investigates the place and use of the Bible in each. The vernacular Scriptures which emerged in the late tenth century, an innovation unique to England in that period, are addressed as a separate category since the Vulgate, in several versions, was the primary text for the Bible that circulated in the British Isles and the Continent. Marsden appends to his contribution the first list of all Bibles of Anglo-Saxon origin, an essential tool for scholars of the period.

The story of the vernacular Bible in England is continued with Christina von Nolcken's consideration of the first complete translation of the Scriptures into English in 'Lay Literacy, the Democratization of God's Law, and the Lollards'. As von Nolcken explains, the followers of Wyclif explicitly directed their translation at 'alle men in oure rewme, which God wole haue sauid'. Coming to life in the language of the people, the Word acquired both a new usage and a new power. Often circulating as small, palm-sized books which could be easily slipped inside a robe or under a cushion, the Wyclif

Introduction

Bible survived the fierce persecution and censorship brought about by the 1408 Constitutions of Oxford to the extent that over two hundred and fifty biblical manuscripts are extant today. Although deemed heterodox, even heretical, by the established Church, the biblical versions of the Lollards were created with a precision and foreknowledge of translation theory unprecedented in England before the sixteenth century. The ideological stamina behind the work of the Lollards was the philosophical realism of Wyclif which affirmed the legitimacy of the vernacular tongue, and a determined Biblicism with Scripture as the ultimate authority. The surviving Wyclif manuscripts themselves are symbols of the efficacy of the Word when borne on the common tongues of people.

The changing form of the book, from the papyrus roll to the lavish Book of Hours, was made possible in practice by those craftsmen who prepared and constructed the written leaves in monastic workshops, near the scriptoria, or on the side streets of a university city. The progressive story of how the materials of the book were prepared, from the manufacture of parchment to the attaching of boards, is recounted by Christopher Clarkson in 'Some Representations of the Book and Bookmaking, from the Bamburg Codex through Jost Ammon'. Likewise and in consideration of one particular tradition known for its exquisite bindings, Sylvie Merian describes 'The Armenian Bookmaking Tradition in the Christian East'. She explains through illustration how the Armenian Christians adapted their own craft traditions – leatherworking, woodworking, illumination, stamp design and arrangement – to a unique presentation for the book which is distinct from that of the other regions of the eastern littoral of the Meditteranean.

As illustrated throughout the contributions to this volume, theology and codicology are often indivisible in the manuscript tradition of the Bible. Gabrielle Sed-Rajna expounds the iconographic commentary found in medieval Hebrew codices in 'The Image as Exegetical Tool: Paintings in Medieval Hebrew Manuscripts of the Bible'. Dominant exegetical trends of the period are reflected in the unique decoration of these manuscripts (what she calls 'the visual complements') which, she explains, serve to interpret for the medieval reader the text they accompany. She explores the symbolic value of the traditional Hebrew tools of worship as they are represented on the pages of the manuscripts, such as the candelabrum, tongs, censers, instruments, and amphorae, in light of the commentaries of Maïmonides and Rashi. Illustration therefore develops a pedagogical function. Iconography illuminates text.

The most direct parallel between the Word made flesh – as in the incarnation of Christ – and the Word expressed in 'syllables and letters' is made in the final chapter, 'The Theology of the Word Made Flesh' by Andrew Louth. Invoking the thoughts of Maximus the Confessor, Louth says, 'When he [i.e., the Word] is present to human beings, ... he converses in a way familiar to them in a variety of stories, enigmas, parables, and dark sayings, then he becomes flesh.' The Word becomes flesh not simply in the physical incarnation but also through the immortality of His words. Scripture itself – at the heart of which are the words of the Word, and other words helping us to understand and encounter Him – and the incarnation are in this way juxtaposed. Hereby divine spiritual reality is put within reach of material beings of flesh and blood.

Both Scripture and the created order – the *kosmoi* – point to and express the transfiguration of the Word in its fleshly form, the final theophany. Louth summarizes the discussion of 'imaging the Word' succinctly in the final paragraph of his paper in which he describes the Byzantine understanding of Scripture: 'It is ... multi-faceted: embracing both the interlocking pattern of meanings of the words of the Word and also its relationship to the Word revealed in the created order and in the human person – all of which revelations are summed up in the Word made flesh.'

'Imaging the Word', therefore, is a way to describe how many cultures and traditions, eras and civilizations, have assimilated, propagated, and venerated the Bible within their own societies and beyond. For Copt as well as Lollard, the Word of God is both perpetual and timely in its message. 'Imaging the Word' is what each new generation of scribes, illuminators, scholars, and binders did when taking the transmitted text into their hands. The shape given to it by each community is universally recognizable – the Word appearing in terms and in a form in which it may be understood and honoured by the generation which has received it.

NOTES

1 David Diringer, *The Hand-Produced Book* (New York: Philosophical Library, 1953), 80ff., esp. fig. III-1.
2 *Biblia Hebraica*, ed. by R. Kittel & P. Kahle (Stuttgart & New York: The American Bible Society and the Württembergische Bibelanstalt, 1965).
3 See *m. Meg.* 2:2 (cf. *V. Meg.* 1:17d).
4 D. Connelly, *The Letters of St Patrick* (Maynooth: An Sagart, 1993), Confessio, 41, 70.
5 Letter of Columbanus to Pope Boniface IV, 613: G. S. M. Walker, ed., *Sancti Columbani opera* (Dublin: Institute for Advanced Studies, 1970), Ep. 5. 38-9.

SCRIBAL PRACTICES AND PHYSICAL ASPECTS OF THE DEAD SEA SCROLLS

Emanuel Tov

I. GENERAL

1.1. *Purpose and nature of the description*

THE DOCUMENTS FROM THE JUDAEAN DESERT constitute the largest corpus of texts in non-lapidary scripts providing information about scribal habits in early Israel relating to biblical and non-biblical texts. These practices should be compared with other contemporary and earlier material in Hebrew and Aramaic in non-lapidary texts; that is material from the period prior to the third century BCE, involving, among others, the Elephantine papyri and other Aramaic documents from the fifth and fourth centuries BCE. These two groups of texts are very significant as comparative material for the present analysis, but at the same time they provide only limited relevant information, as they may reflect the local Egyptian tradition. The Egyptian Aramaic corpus is significant because it is extensive and ancient. The corpus of documents from the Judaean Desert is larger and thus constitutes the largest corpus for our knowledge of scribal habits for Hebrew and Aramaic texts from ancient Israel prior to the early Middle Ages, from which time the first documents from the Cairo Genizah derive. Comparison of these practices with scribal habits of earlier cultures in the ancient Middle East and with contemporary Greek practices is mandatory, but, because these texts were written in different languages and often on different materials, such a comparison is only partially relevant.

The description of scribal practices as seen in the documents from the Judaean Desert is as complete as possible at present, especially the Qumran documents, since this corpus provides the greatest amount of relevant information. The coverage of the published documents is greater than that of the unpublished texts, although many of the latter are also covered.[1] Since not all the texts have been published and analysed, and details concerning the individual scribal practices have not been dealt with in monographic treatments, the present survey can only begin to describe the issues at stake. In fact, each of the scribal features to be mentioned below deserves a special analysis, so treatment of these features cannot be exhaustive in the present article. Use is made of some previous analyses, but these are incomplete and often based on only very few texts.[2]

The description pertains to technical aspects of the copying of the texts, many of which have implications for wider areas, such as the provenance of the scrolls, the

9

relation between individual manuscripts of the same composition, the composition and contents of the texts, and their textual transmission. In due course, when all the relevant data on the scribal practices has been recorded, it is likely that conclusions may be drawn on such general matters as scribal schools, and the background of many of the scrolls found in the Judaean Desert. In the meantime, we have to content ourselves with partial conclusions and practical results of limited scope. For example, on the basis of a study of the inter-columnar margins we may conclude that the large margin before the first column in 4QS^d indicates that this fragment (starting with the text which runs parallel to 1QS V, 1-21) constituted the beginning of that manuscript. We note that the great majority of the marginal notes are in the nature of corrections, and not variant readings, that certain words were often joined with other words, and that some of the Qumran writings included markings in the Cryptic A script. We learn about the approaches of scribes to certain types of texts, and we learn about exegetical aspects of the work of the scribes. One of the characteristics of the exegetical dimensions of scribal activity is that of the sense divisions within the text, but exegetical activity is also visible in the content itself.

1.2. Background of the documents

A description of the scribal practices reflected in the documents found in the Judaean Desert is more encompassing than the name of the geographic area implies. Many of the documents found in the Judaean Desert had been copied elsewhere in Israel, so that the documents and scribal practices reflected in them are representative not only of the persons who lived and wrote in the Judaean Desert but, to an even greater extent, of the scribes of Palestine as a whole.[3] At the present stage of research this is a mere assumption, which may be supported in the future by research into either the content of the documents or their physical components, that is the parchment, sinews, and ink.

Some of the letters found in the Judaean Desert mention localities in Judaea, but for the largest segment of the documents, the Qumran texts, we have no clue with regard to their geographic origin. Furthermore, with the exception of the dated documents from Murabbaʿat and Naḥal Ḥever, the dates of the documents also remain hypothetical, although palaeography and carbon-14 examination provide an ever-increasing probability about their dating (the latter procedure applied to a select number of texts only).[4] The dates for the Qumran and Masada documents (the *terminus a quo* for the Masada documents has not yet been determined) range from the third century BCE until 70 CE, and until the middle of the second century CE for the texts from Wadi Murabbaʿat, Naḥal Ḥever, and Seʾelim. One of the documents, however, a palimpsest papyrus (Mur 17), was dated by its editor, J. T. Milik, to the eighth century BCE and by F. M. Cross to the second half of the seventh century BCE.[5]

These documents reflect a variety of scribal systems. The languages involved are in the first place Hebrew, in the second place Aramaic, and further Greek and Latin, as well as combinations of these languages, namely Hebrew-Aramaic and Greek-Aramaic in documentary texts. Among the scripts represented are the square and palaeo-Hebrew scripts for Hebrew documents, the square script for Aramaic, as well as the Greek and Latin scripts for Greek and Latin documents, and the Nabatean script and three different cryptic scripts which include palaeo-Hebrew and Greek letters.[6] The Copper Scroll

(3Q15) written in the square script contains clusters of several Greek letters. The discussion which follows focuses on the Qumran documents, written in different places in Israel, but it also treats documents found at the other sites in the Judaean Desert. The scribal practices of the Nabatean, Greek, and Latin documents from Masada, Naḥal Ḥever, and Murabbaʿat are, as a rule, excluded from this analysis. Since there is hardly any distinction between the writing of sacred and non-sacred texts at the scribal level, both are included in the present article. Furthermore, since the documents were written in different periods and in different localities, they reflect a variety of scribal practices. For the present purpose, however, these different groups of documents are described as one large, somewhat artificial, corpus, whose common practices are described in the main section of this paper.

1.3. Local production of texts in Qumran and Masada?

If it can be proven that locus 30 at Qumran served as a room in which documents were written (a scriptorium in medieval terminology), the assumption of a Qumran scribal school would receive further support, but the reliability of the evidence pointing to the existence of such a scriptorium is questionable.[7] As for scribal activity at Qumran, it is irrelevant whether or not locus 30 was a scriptorium, because in either case most scholars now believe that some, many, or all of the documents found in Qumran had been copied locally. Indeed, most scholars now assume that some of the texts found at Qumran had been written in situ, while the major part of the texts were imported there, even though the proportions of the two groups remain unknown.

Stegemann holds a maximalistic view on this issue, assuming that most Qumran scrolls were written on the spot. According to him,[8] one of the main occupations of the Qumran community was the preparation of parchment and leather for writing and the mass-production of written texts. These texts were offered for sale by the Qumran community to the outside world, and Stegemann pinpoints the places in the community buildings in which the scrolls were manufactured, stored, and offered for sale. Golb (see note 7), expressing a minimalistic view, claimed that none of the Qumran documents were written locally (Golb does not express himself with regard to the other documents from the Judaean Desert).

Accordingly there is no consensus regarding the locality or localities of the copying of the Qumran documents, but since most scholars believe that at least some, if not many, of the texts from Qumran were written locally, it remains correct to refer to the texts found in Qumran as the Qumran corpus, as long as the necessary reservations are kept in mind. Similar reasoning applies to the texts found at the other sites in the Judaean Desert, although few have claimed that texts were actually written at Masada, in Murabbaʿat, or Naḥal Ḥever.

As a result of this analysis, it appears that the scribes of the texts found in the Judaean Desert remain as anonymous today in identity and origin as they were two generations ago. A generation ago, the corpus of the Qumran documents as well as their scribes were automatically identified with the Qumran community; today, this claim is not made, although undoubtedly some of the texts were copied by that community. By the same token, the documents found at Masada should not be identified with the people who occupied that site. These documents, too, reflect the work of scribes from all of Israel, possibly including some local scribes. This pertains also to the letters found in Naḥal Ḥever and Wadi Murabbaʿat.

2. WRITING MATERIALS

2.1. *Leather, papyrus, copper, ostraca, wood*

The majority of the documents from the Judaean Desert were written on leather and papyrus.[9] In addition, a large number of ostraca were found in several places, especially Masada, and a sherd (an abecedary), or possibly three sherds, were found in Ḥirbet Qumran. A single text was written on copper (the Copper Scroll), and a single one on a wooden table (5/6Ḥev54=p. Yadin 54). The great majority of texts found in the Qumran caves were written on leather, and a minority on papyrus, and this pertains also to the finds at Masada, which in addition include a large number of ostraca. On the other hand, the great majority of the documents from the other sites in the Judaean Desert were written on papyrus.

This use of different materials at the various sites in the Judaean Desert is related to the content of the documents. Most of the texts of literary content were written on leather, which accounts for the contents of the corpora of texts from Qumran and Masada, while papyrus was used for personal documents such as letters and documentary texts, found at the other sites.

At the same time, it is less clear why some of the copies of literary works were written on papyrus. Papyrus was less expensive, and it was therefore probably used for some personal copies of literary compositions,[10] at Qumran mainly for non-biblical compositions, sectarian and non-sectarian, but also for some biblical books. While most of the Qumran biblical scrolls were written on leather, a few were written on papyrus, viz., 4QpapIsa[p], 6Q3 (Deuteronomy?), 6Q4 (Kings), 6Q5 (Psalms?), 6Q7 (Daniel), and 4Q483 (4QpapGen or papJub).

Such papyrus copies of biblical books were not permitted by the Rabbis, see *m. Meg.* 2:2 (cf. *y. Meg.* 1:71d):

If it was written with caustic, red dye, gum, or copperas, or on paper (papyrus), or *diftera*, he has not fulfilled his obligation; but only if it was written in Assyrian writing, on parchment and with ink.

Accordingly, the Qumran texts written on papyrus apparently derived from a different milieu in which such copies were allowed. In view of this situation an examination of the textual character of the papyrus fragments is in order. While several of the fragments are too small to determine their character, the larger fragments of 1-2 Kings and possibly also Daniel may be characterized as non-Masoretic, more specifically as independent, which could mean that these texts did not derive from Pharisaic circles.

Wise, 'Thunder in Gemini', pp. 131 ff. lists the several hundred papyrus copies of non-documentary texts found at Qumran. Compositions found at Qumran in multiple copies are often represented by one or two copies on papyrus. Thus of the six copies of MMT, 4QpapMMT[e] (4Q398) is on papyrus. Of the sixteen calendrical documents, 4QpapCalDoc C[e] (4Q324b) is on papyrus; of the eleven copies of the Community Rule, two are on papyrus, namely 4QpapS[a,c] (4Q255, 4Q257); and of the eight copies of the Damascus Document, 4QpapD[h] (4Q273) is on papyrus.

Scribal Practices and Physical Aspects of the Dead Sea Scrolls

All the texts from Qumran written in palaeo-Hebrew characters are contained in leather scrolls. On the other hand, the enigmatic Masada text pap paleoMas 10 (Mas1039-320), is written on papyrus, inscribed on both sides.

2.2. *Nature of the leather and its preparation*

Additional research is needed in order to determine from which animal skins the Qumran texts were prepared. According to examinations in 1958 and the beginning of the 1960s by M. L. Ryder and J. Poole & R. Reed,[11] the parchment fragments found at Qumran were made mainly from skins of sheep and goats.[12] A report published by Freedman & Mathews about 11QpaleoLev[a] ascribes that scroll to a kid (young goat) rather than a hairy sheep, but the latter is not excluded.[13] DNA examination of 11QT[a] determined some fragments of this scroll to have been made of goatskin, and others of ibex.[14]

At present little is known about the stages of preparation, locally and elsewhere, of the leather and papyrus fragments found in the Judaean Desert. It is not impossible that the skins from which some of the Qumran documents were prepared were immersed in basins in Ein Fashkha.[15] According to Stegemann the refined preparation of these parchments took place in Qumran, but there is no solid evidence in support of this assumption.[16] The tanning techniques applied to the texts found at Qumran were discussed by Haran, who considered the Qumran scrolls 'basically parchments, but with moderately tanned surface to facilitate writing'.[17] According to Pedley, the table, of which remnants were found in locus 30 in Qumran, served for all the activities in connection with the scrolls for which a long surface was needed, such as the sewing together of the sheets of which the scrolls were composed, treating them with oil, rolling them out,[18] but there is no supporting evidence for his view.

Upon preparation, most skins were inscribed on the (hairy) outside, while 11QT[a] was inscribed on the inside of the skin.

It stands to reason that, before the writing, the length of the composition was roughly calculated, so that the required number of sheets and their size could be planned. The single sheets were then ruled and inscribed and only afterwards stitched together. The fact that some sheets were numbered probably indicates that they were indeed inscribed separately, to be joined in accordance with these numbers. One further indication for the existence of separate sheets is the different nature of the two sheets of 1QpHab: above the text of the second sheet of 1QpHab, containing cols VIII-XIII, one clearly recognizes one, two, or three uninscribed ruled lines, which do not appear on the sheet containing the previous columns (I-VII). Since the top margin consists of ruled lines, and since all known sheets have an unruled top margin, by implication the manufacturer of this scroll used for the second sheet an existing ruled sheet of larger score than he needed for this scroll, and he subsequently cut it for the size required for the present purpose, cutting off the unruled top margin of that sheet.

Outside Qumran there is some evidence for the existence of rolls of glued sheets from which the required number of sheets was detached, but this evidence pertains to papyrus scrolls only.[19] The calculation of the sheets needed for the copying of a composition could never be precise, so that often a ruled column was left uninscribed after the last inscribed column of a sheet.

2.3. Sheets of parchment

Short documents were written on single sheets. For example, letters and other documentary texts written on papyrus and 4QTest written on parchment were included in single sheets. The shape of some documents is irregular; they probably were mere remnants left over after large sheets of straight geometric shapes had been cut from the hides. This pertains to the scraps of leather which now contain the lists in 4Q339 ('List of False Prophets') and 4Q340 ('List of Netinim'). The irregular shape of 4QList of Proper Names (4Q341) is obvious, and it required the scribe to adapt the writing of the last lines to the slanting bottom margin. Likewise, *tefillin* and *mezuzot* were written on pieces of parchment of irregular shape, which were probably remnants of leather (see especially 4QPhyl J where the shape of the leather necessitated the writing of long lines in the beginning and very short lines at the end).

Longer texts were written on scrolls which were composed of sheets of parchment or papyrus sewn together horizontally. Only one document is known in which tiny pieces of parchment were stitched together vertically, namely 4QIncantation (4Q444).[20] The holes left by these stitches as well as the threads used for stitching are clearly visible in many fragments – codices were not yet in use in this period.

On the other hand, papyrus sheets were glued together with some kind of adhesive, as described in the edition of 4Qpap paraKings (4Q382) frg. 10 and 8ḤevXIIgr cols XVII-XVIII.

2.4. Scrolls of parchment and papyrus

Documents comprising more than one column were usually contained in scrolls composed of sheets of parchment or papyrus. These scrolls were of different dimensions. They could be rolled easily, and on completion of the reading they were usually rolled back to the beginning, so that the first sheet of the scroll or its uninscribed handling sheet always remained the external layer of the scroll, which was therefore more susceptible to damage than the inside of the rolled scroll. On the other hand, if the scroll was rolled with its beginning sections on the inside, the middle and end of the scroll were more likely to be damaged. This was the case with several scrolls from caves 1 and 4.[21]

Parchment scrolls were closed or fastened in three different ways:

(1) Many scrolls were fastened with thongs tied around them. These thongs were connected to reinforcing tabs stuck to the scroll itself. Many such reinforcing tabs have been found in some of the Qumran caves, detached from the scrolls themselves, see *DJD* VI (Oxford, 1977), pl. V. In fact, in cave 8 archaeologists discovered 68 such reinforcing tabs, usually of coarse leather, together with remains of only 4 manuscripts.[22] Since each reinforcing tab was attached to a single scroll, this cave probably contained a leather workshop or depository (unless it originally contained an equal number of scrolls and reinforcing tabs and many scrolls subsequently disintegrated). In only two cases have scrolls with attached reinforcement tabs been preserved, namely, 4QApocr. Psalm and prayer (4Q448) and 4QD^a (olim 4QD^b).[23] A similar system of binding scrolls was referred to by Catullus 22:7, who mentions a 'lora rubra', a red thong tied around the scroll.[24]

(2) Some scrolls were covered with linen wrappings. A part of one such scroll was

found in cave 1 with its wrapper still around it (see *DJD* I [Oxford, 1955] pl. I, 8-10), but according to the description by G. Lankester Harding on p. 7 there, upon the opening of the wrapping, the material of the scroll was seen to have corroded to a solid black mass. Some of the linen fragments found in the same cave probably derived from such wrappings.[25] The linen fragments from this cave are both dyed and non-dyed, and both with and without rectangular patterns. Crowfoot mentioned some parallels from the classical world for the use of linen wrappings for scrolls. Similar references are found in *m. Kil.* 9:3 and *m. Kel.* 28:4 (both מטפחות (ה)ספרים, wrappers for scrolls). The latter reference is particularly interesting as it mentions wrappers with figures portrayed on them (מצוירות); the rectangular patterns and the blue elements in some of the linen fragments found in cave 1 may constitute precisely such wrappers.

(3) In a combination of the two aforementioned systems scrolls were wrapped with a linen wrapping which was tied with a leather thong. One of the linen fragments from cave 4 (Israel Museum photograph X94.920) was attached to such a leather thong and must have covered the scroll together with the leather thong reflecting a system which had not been described previously in the literature.[26]

Little is known about the storage of scrolls. Caves 1 and 3 at Qumran held large numbers of jars for storing scrolls. Although it is not known which scrolls were stored in these jars, the jars in cave 1 probably contained the scrolls which remained rather well intact, namely, 1QIsa[a], 1QM, 1QS, and 1QH[a]. The scrolls in cave 4 were probably stored on shelves attached to the walls, for which there is some archaeological evidence.

The writing of scrolls followed certain conventions regarding sheets, columns, ruling, margins, and spacing.

2.5. Ink

To date insufficient research has been conducted into the ink used in the documents found in the Judaean Desert, but two types of ink have been assumed and partially identified, although the pattern of their distribution in the scrolls is not clear:

(1) carbon ink, based on lampblack or soot,[27] described by Vitruvius, *De Architectura*, VII:10,2 and Dioscorides, *De Materia Medica*, V: 162;

(2) iron-gall ink, consisting of copperas (green vitriol), treated with a decoction of oak-nut galls.[28]

In *m. Shabb.* 12:4 various types of writing liquids are mentioned, partly coinciding with the composition of the ink assumed for the Qumran writings: סם (arsenic [caustic]), סקרא (red chalk), קומוס (gum), קנקנתום (sulphate of copper [copperas]).[29] In addition, in the next verse in the Mishna additional liquids are mentioned which disappear after the writing: liquids, fruit-juice, dust of the roads, and writer's sand.

On the basis of examinations carried out on undetermined fragments from cave 4 in 1995, Nir-El & Broshi (see n. 28) concluded that no iron ink was used in writing the Qumran scrolls.[30] These scholars assumed that the copper elements in the ink used for the papyrus and parchment fragments derived from copper inkwells used by the scribes, and that the ink used was carbon-based. A similar suggestion was reached earlier by H. J. Plenderleith for the texts from cave 1,[31] by the editors of 4QpaleoExod[m],[32] and by Haran on the basis of theoretical observations.[33] According to Haran metal-based ink was used only from the second century CE onwards.

That different types of ink were used is clear from the differing states of preservation of the manuscripts. While in most cases the ink has been preserved extremely well, on some scrolls it has corroded and eaten through the leather, often creating the impression of a photographic negative. This is the case with 1QapGen, 4QExod-Lev^f, 4QLev^d. According to F. M. Cross, *DJD* XII (Oxford, 1994), p. 133, the ink has etched the leather 'presumably because of some residual acid in the ink from its storage in a metal inkwell'. On the other hand, according to Nir-El & Broshi (see n. 28), this deterioration was caused by the binding agents of the carbon-based ink, such as 'vegetable gum, animal size, oil or honey'.

Two inkwells were found by de Vaux in locus 30 of Qumran, the so-called scriptorium, one made of ceramic and one made of bronze (both are exhibited in the Jordan Archaeological Museum in Amman).[34] A third one, ceramic, also found by de Vaux, came from locus 31,[35] a fourth one, found by Steckoll, came from an unspecified place at Qumran,[36] while a possible fifth one is mentioned by Goranson, 'Inkwell', who summarized the known data about the inkwells. Dried ink has been left in two of these inkwells.

Little is known about the pens used for writing the texts found in the Judaean Desert, as these have not been preserved. The pens used were probably of the *calamus* (κάλαμος, קולמוס) type, made from reed (קנה, κάννα, κάννη, canna).[37]

3. TECHNICAL DATA

Some aspects of the technical data have been studied for many scrolls, but most aspects still need to be studied in detail.

3.1. *Ruling*

Ruling of lines was the normal practice for most literary texts written on parchment in Semitic languages and Greek,[39] as it was in earlier times in lapidary Semitic inscriptions. In some inscriptions these lines were often not clearly visible, while in others they were written very distinctively, almost for ornamental purposes, especially in the Samaritan inscriptions of later periods (but also in some of the early Aramaic inscriptions and in the ossuary of Simon, 'builder of the temple' written in the palaeo-Hebrew script in the first century CE).[40]

On the other hand, the Qumran texts written on papyrus were not ruled (e.g., 4QpapMMT^e, 4QpapJub^h and the Greek texts 4Q120 and 4Q127).

The technique of ruling is also mentioned in Talmudic sources according to which the ruling of the lines was called *syrtwt* (*b. Shabb.* 75b; *b. Meg.* 18b). In Palestinian texts it is referred to as *msrglyn bqnh*, 'one rules with a reed' (*y. Meg.* 171d; *Sof.* 1.1).

Most Qumran parchment texts written in the square script (*not* the *tefillin*) and in the palaeo-Hebrew script were ruled horizontally (indicating lines) as well as vertically (indicating the beginnings and often also the ends of columns) – thus also most medieval copies of the Sam. Pent.[41] Only a few of the Qumran documents were not ruled, and as a consequence in these documents the distance between the lines is irregular and the lines are not straight.

For examples of unruled literary texts (that is, texts for which there is no evidence of ruling), see 4QJer^c, 4QCant^b, 4QFlor, 5QLam^a, 5QLam^b, 5QDeut.[42] It remains unclear what these texts otherwise have in common. For examples of texts ruled only horizontally, see 4QDan^b, 4QQoh.

A unique example of ruling is the recto of the palaeo-Hebrew text pap paleoMas 10 (Mas1039-320) in which the text was ruled with a double horizontal ruling for the top and bottom lines of letters in the text (which was, incidentally, not carefully adhered to by the scribe).

The most frequently used system of vertical ruling pertains to both the beginning (right side) and end (left side) of the column. The horizontal line at the end of a column together with the line to the right of the next column thus created an effect of double ruling and an exact indication of the intercolumnar margin. For examples of this double ruling, see 1QIsa^a, 1QIsa^b, 1QS, 1QapGen, 1QH^a, 1QM, 1QpHab, 1QMyst. In texts written in the palaeo-Hebrew script the adherence to the left margin could be more stringent because of the splitting up of words between two lines.

The ruling may have been executed by the scribes themselves, but more likely it was inserted, often with the aid of guide dots (see below), by the persons who prepared the parchment. The so-called blind ruling was usually performed with a pointed instrument, probably of bone, making a sharp crease in the parchment. There are several indications that sheets were ruled before the scribe knew exactly how many columns would be inscribed with text, or before the scribe even knew which text would be inscribed on the parchment:

a. The presence of ruled columns after the last column of several compositions.

b. The uninscribed handling sheets at the ends of compositions were ruled.

c. 4QRP^c (4Q365) frg. 7 has three uninscribed dry lines at the bottom of *both* columns in the middle of the composition.

d. 4QMMT^f has 12 ruled, but only 11 inscribed lines.

e. The first sheet of 4QDeutⁿ has 8 inscribed lines, but 15 ruled lines.

In several Qumran texts written in the square and palaeo-Hebrew scripts single guide dots (*points jalons*) were drawn in the space between the right edge of the sheet and the beginning of the first column of the sheet (usually close to the right side of the column) and in the space between the last column and the left edge of the sheet, guiding the drawing of dry lines. These dots are also somewhat rarely drawn in the middle of a sheet: 4QRP^c (4Q365) frg. 12a; 4QpHos^a; 4QShirShabb^f. These guide dots occur at the beginnings and/or ends of the sheets in sixteen biblical scrolls, among which: 4QGen-Exod^a, 2QpaleoLev, 4QpaleoExod^m, 4QXII^c, 4QPs^b, 4QPs^f. While the great majority of the biblical Qumran texts reflect the MT, only one of the aforementioned texts in which the guide dots are found belongs to this group. As a result, this custom must have been used in particular outside the circle of the Masoretic texts. In the non-biblical texts, guide dots are found almost exclusively in texts written in the Qumran practice: 1QMyst, 1Q36, 2QSir, 4QShirShabb^f, 4QpHos^a, as well as in twelve other texts.

In 2QpaleoLev and 4QpaleoExod^m small diagonal strokes guided the ruling of the lines, in the latter case at the end of the sheet (col. I), but not at the beginning of sheets (cols II, XIX, XLV). Since the guide dots are found almost exclusively in non-biblical texts written in the Qumran practice, this system displays one of the special features of the scroll production by the Qumran scribes.

The system of indicating guide dots (or strokes) resembles that of pinpricking in

Emanuel Tov

manuscript codices of later periods. For example, see the elaborate pricking system of codex S of the LXX.[43]

3.2. Opistographs

Most parchment and papyrus texts were written on one side only, while several of the documents from the Judaean Desert (mainly papyri) were inscribed on both sides (οπιστογραφ, *opistographs*) – see the list by Wise, 'Thunder in Gemini', p. 133. Also the enigmatic palaeo-Hebrew text pap paleoMas 10 (Mas1039-320) was inscribed on both sides, in different handwriting.

Writing on both sides sometimes implies that the texts on the recto and verso are somehow related. For example, 4QpapCryptA MSM (4Q249) and 4Q250 (unknown work) are both written in the Cryptic A script. Likewise, the two sides of 4Q417 both contain sapiental works, and different segments of 4QpsMoses C are contained in the two sides of 4Q377. However, more often the content of the two sides is not related,[44] with the verso used simply because of the scarcity of writing material. For example, 4Q460, temporarily named 'pseudepigraphic work', has an account of cereal in Greek on its verso (4Q350). Two opistographs from Qumran and many of the ones from Egypt are of this type: a literary text on the recto and a documentary text of some kind on the verso. Likewise, a large collection of different compositions and different copies of one composition is found on the two sides of a papyrus containing on the recto 4QpapPrFêtes^c (4Q509), 4QpapDibHam^b (4Q505), and again 4QpapPrFêtes^c, and on the verso 4QpapM^f (4Q496) and 4QpapDibHam^c (4Q506).

Likewise, phylacteries were usually inscribed on both sides. On contracts the signatures were written on the verso.

3.3. Length of scrolls

Almost all Qumran fragments constitute parts of scrolls of parchment or papyrus. Insufficient information is available on the length of these scrolls, since only very few complete scrolls have been preserved. Compositions written on single sheets are rare: 4QTest (one-column sheet), 4QList of False Prophets (4Q339), 4QList of Netinim (4Q340), 4QList of Proper Names (4Q341). The latter three texts were written on fragments of leather.

Several small scrolls are known from Qumran, and the evidence shows that scrolls of limited size were written in columns of small dimensions. Such small scrolls contained compositions of limited size or small biblical books (the Five Scrolls), and excerpted biblical books of various types: scrolls meant for liturgical purposes (4QDeut^n probably containing mere selections of Deuteronomy, 4QDeut^q containing Deuteronomy 32, and 4QPs^g containing Psalm 119). In his discussion of excerpting in classical antiquity. Birt noted that some texts were excerpted because they were too long; travellers wanted to take smaller editions with them.[45] In the case of the Qumran scrolls, it was probably their liturgical character which dictated the small, and hence more practical, dimensions of the scrolls.

Such small scrolls measured between 1.5 and 2.5 metres, although even smaller scrolls may have existed as well (possibly 4QApocr. Psalm and Prayer [4Q448] and some of the Calendrical documents).

18

Scribal Practices and Physical Aspects of the Dead Sea Scrolls

Medium-sized scrolls are 1QS and 1QM, measuring 3 metres, and 1QH[a], measuring 4.2 metres.[46]

Longer compositions naturally required longer scrolls, but it is unclear what the maximum length of the scrolls was. In *b. B. Bat.* 13b large scrolls containing all the books of the Torah, Prophets, or Writings are mentioned, but the Qumran evidence neither supports nor contradicts the existence of such large scrolls. There is possible evidence for a complete Torah scroll (Genesis-Exodus and possibly Numbers), as well as evidence for the following combinations of books of the Pentateuch in different scrolls: Genesis-Exodus, Exodus-Leviticus, and Leviticus-Numbers. See Mur 1 (Genesis, Exodus, and possibly Numbers), 4QGen-Exod[a], 4QExod[b] (preceded by a blank indicating the existence of the book of Genesis), 4QpaleoGen-Exod[l], 4QExod-Lev[f], 4QLev-Num[a]. It therefore stands to reason that several of the scrolls found in Qumran contained all of the Pentateuch, and thus probably measured 25-30 metres.

The only solid evidence for much smaller, yet still sizeable, scrolls pertains to 1QIsa[a] (7.34 m) and 11QT[a] (8.148 m – the reconstructed length for the whole scroll is 8.75 m), while the reconstructed length of 8HevXIIgr is more than 10 metres, and that of 4QRP 22-27 metres.[47] Three of the Jeremiah scrolls are reconstructed as 9.5 metres (2QJer, see *DJD* III [Oxford 1962] 62), 7.9-8.5 metres (4QJer[a]), and 16.3-17.6 metres (4QJer[c]; for the latter two see *DJD* XV [Oxford 1997]).

3.4. Sheets

The width of most sheets is between 25 and 90 cm. The natural limitations of the sizes of animal hides determined the different lengths of these sheets within each scroll: 1QIsa[b] (between 26 and 45 cm),[a] 11QT[a] (37-61 cm), 1QH[a] (56-62 cm), MurXII (62 cm), 1QpHab (62-79 cm), 11QpaleoLev[a] (63 cm), 1QM (47-89 cm), and 11QPs[a] (72-87 cm). Papyrus scrolls have not been found in the Judaean Desert.

In accordance with their differing widths, sheets contain different numbers of columns of written text, usually three or four (e.g., 1QIsa[a] and 11QT[a]). At the same time, the sheets in 1QH[a] contain four columns; 1QM has three, four, six, and five columns; and 11QPs[a] contains four, five, and six columns. 1QSa and two sheets in 1QIsa[a] (cols XXVI-XXVII, LIII-LIV) contain merely two columns, while other scrolls contain as many as seven (1QpHab with two sheets of seven columns [the last column of the second sheet was uninscribed], 1QapGen). One-column sheets are a rare exception (1QS col. XI, 4QDeut[n] col. I). The latter are forbidden in *y. Meg.* 1:71d and *Sof.* 2:10 according to which one should not write fewer than three columns of scripture or more than eight.

According to rabbinic prescription, sheets of scrolls are to be joined by sinews of ritually clean cattle or wild animals. Cf. *Sof.* 1:1.

It is an oral prescription delivered to Moses at Sinai that <all these> shall be written on the skins of ritually clean cattle or ritually clean wild animals, and be sewn together with their sinews. ...

On the other hand, Poole & Reed,[48] on investigation of stitching material, claim that these were all of vegetable origin and most probably derived from flax. It is not known, however, which texts were examined for this purpose. In his edition of 4QNum[b], N. Jastram likewise concluded that the unraveling of the thread before col. xv suggested that it consisted of flax rather than sinews.[49] Also Pfann, '4Q298', 208 describes the stitching material of 4Q298 as flax. The stitching material in 1QIsa[a] was described by Burrows[50] as 'linen thread'. A thorough investigation of the stitching material should be carried out, in order to find out which items were made of animal sinews and which of flax, in the latter case in disagreement with rabbinic custom. The two scrolls quoted above which deviate from the rabbinic custom are non-Masoretic: 4QNum[b] and 1QIsa[a].

3.5. Columns

The great majority of the texts from the Judaean Desert are arranged in blocks of writing that cover the greater part of the surface of the leather or papyrus, leaving margins on all sides of the inscribed surface. In some types of texts, however, a maximal use of the material is made (*tefillin, mezuzot*), only occasionally leaving room for such margins. Usually the inscribed surface has the shape of a column, certainly in literary compositions; and in texts consisting of more than one column, these columns follow one another. Only on rare occasions is a different arrangement devised. Thus in 4QApocr. Psalm and Prayer the small fragment preserves three columns of which col. A is written as the uppermost writing block preceded by a large indentation, while columns B and C are more or less written under column A, although B protrudes much to the right because of the large indentation of A.

The sizes of the columns differ in accordance with the number of columns per sheet, the measurements of the sheets and the traditions of the scroll manufacturers. The different parameters of the columns pertain to their width and length as well as to the margins around the columns (top and bottom margins as well as the margins between the columns).[51]

In many Qumran texts the length and width of the columns are generally consistent, while in others the measurements vary from sheet to sheet. For example, the width of some columns in 1QM and 4QLam differs as much as 50 per cent from other columns in the same scroll. A certain regularity in these differences between the columns is noticeable. Usually the available space in a sheet was evenly divided between the columns, but the different sizes of the sheets did not always allow for such unity. (The columns which are unusually wide or narrow are generally found in the beginning or end of sheets.) The larger columns often occur at the beginning of the sheets (cf. e.g., the second sheet of 1QIsa[a] [cols IV-VII] with columns of 123, 115, 119, and 114 mm), without regard to or plan for available writing space. By the same token, the narrow columns were often at the ends of sheets (e.g., sheet XIII of 1QIsa[a] [cols XLI-XLIII] with columns of 157, 163, 129 mm; sheet XVI [cols L-LII] with columns of 133, 140, and 88 mm), when the scribe had to content himself with the space that remained. Conversely, narrow columns are often drawn at the beginning of the sheets in anticipation of conserving space, but wider columns often appeared at the end (e.g., sheet XV [cols XLVII-XLIX] with columns of 142, 148, and 163 mm) to fill out the empty space.

The average column for Qumran scrolls consists of 20 lines or 14-15 cm in height (including the margins). Small scrolls contained merely 4-14 lines and their size was likewise small – as, for example, in all the known copies of the Five Scrolls (copies of Canticles, Lamentations and Ruth have been preserved). Large scrolls contained 25-60 lines.

For comparison note the numbers of lines in columns presented in *Sof.* 2.6: 42, 60, 72, and 98. Medieval codices of the MT usually have 42 lines. Note further that codex Vaticanus (B) of the LXX has 42 lines as well. Codex S(inaiticus) of the LXX has 48 lines per page.

The lines of the calendrical documents are extremely narrow, often containing merely a single word per line (for example, the first fragment of 4QMMT[a] [4Q394]. 4QApocr. Psalm and Prayer (4Q448) contains nine lines of 1-3 words. 4QNon-Canonical Psalms A (4Q380) is also written in narrow columns.

Usually scrolls were written with the same number of lines per column throughout the different sheets, or at least in the same sheet, but in some scrolls there are slight variations (for example, 4QNum[b] with 30-32 lines, 1QIsa[a] with 28-32 lines, 1QS with 26-27 lines, and 8HevXIIgr with 42-45 lines). More substantial differences are visible in 11QT[a], in which almost all columns contain 22 lines, except for cols XLIX-LX containing 28 lines.[52] 4QTohA (4Q274; PAM 43.309) is written in columns of 9 lines until the end of the first sheet, while the next sheet (still attached) starts with a densely written column (12 lines extant, 14 lines reconstructed).

Since the number of lines differs in most cases it is to be expected that identical compositions were written with different layouts, so that every copy would not start each line with the same words. In those instances in which these data can be examined, no similar layouts have been detected, and only in one case is a similar layout visible. In the overlapping sections of 4QDan[a] and 4QDan[b] (Dan 8:1-4), four lines have an identical layout and two lines approximately the same layout.[53]

In the Qumran scrolls the upper margin of the columns is usually smaller than the bottom margin. In a detailed research of the measurements of the margins of a single scroll, Yadin (*Temple Scroll*, I, pp. 15-17) found that the measurements usually agree with the prescriptions of the Talmud. Further details on other scrolls were provided by W. Fields. For example, for the top and bottom margins of the following texts these figures were listed by Fields: 1QIsa[a]: 2.0-2.8 cm and 2.5-3.3 cm; 4QDan[a]: 1.2 and 1.7; 4QJer[a]: 2.2 and 2.6; 4QpaleoExod[m]: 2.7 and 4.3.[54]

Different sizes of the upper and bottom margins were likewise prescribed by *b. Menah.* 30a:

The width of the margin below shall be one handbreadth, above three fingerbreadths, and between one column and the other the space of two fingerbreadths [in all the books of the Bible]. In the books of the Torah the margin below shall be three fingerbreadths, above two fingerbreadths, and between one column and the other the space of a thumb-breadth.

Different measurements were prescribed in the following sources, in which there is likewise a difference between the top and bottom margins: *y. Meg.* 1.71d and *Sof.* 2.5 prescribe for the books of the Bible, except for the Torah, a margin of two fingerbreadths above the text and three below. The discussion in these places also mentions the view of Rabbi prescribing for the Torah of three fingerbreadths above the text and a handbreadth below the text.

3.6. Lines

Most literary texts from the Judaean Desert were ruled not only to determine column width but also to guide the lines of the text. In the majority of these texts, the letters were suspended below the ruled lines. At the same time, in a few Qumran texts the letters were sometimes consistently written slightly below those lines as, for example, in 4QHodayot-like text (4Q440), while in other texts scribes disregarded the guidance of the lines. In 4QText with a citation from Jubilees (4Q228) and 4QWork with Place Names frg. 8 (= 4Q522; 'Rock of Zion'), for example, the letters are written irregularly between the lines, on and under the lines, and also through them. In 1QMyst (1Q27) the words are more frequently written on the lines than under them. In the palaeo-Hebrew text pap paleoMas 10 (Mas1039-320) some of the words were written through the lines. These examples show that scribes received sheets of leather previously ruled by others, and that these lines were sometimes disregarded by (less skilled?) scribes. Because of the ruling, the distance between the lines is usually more or less equal, but there are exceptions.

Most texts were ruled also with a vertical line guiding the right margin of the writing surface and some texts were ruled with a left vertical line to mark the line end and the width of the column. Because of these vertical rules, the right margin is usually straight, but the left is not, even when it is ruled. Since the scribes left more or less equal spaces between the words in texts written with square characters, it was virtually impossible to maintain a straight left margin. However, in texts written in the palaeo-Hebrew script it was relatively easy to adhere to the left margin, since in these texts words were divided at the end of a line (split between lines). For example, in 11QpaleoLev^a col. III the following words are broken up at the ends of lines: יהו/ה, יש/ראל, ב/נ, ל/א, א/תו. As a result of dividing words, almost straight left margins could be obtained, e.g., in 4QpaleoExod^m cols I, VI, IX and in all columns of 11QpaleoLev^a (cf. Freedman & Mathews, *Leviticus*, p. 9, cited at note 13 below). A similar system was used in the medieval manuscripts of the Sam. Pent. (see below). On the other hand, in all texts written in square characters several lines either fall short of or exceed the vertical rule at the left edge of the column, whether it was drawn or existed in the scribe's mind.[55] In any event, the prescription of *Sof.* 2:3 for the number of letters which one may write beyond the vertical margin is not adhered to in most texts written in square characters:

It is permitted to insert between columns [part of] a word of five letters. One may not write two letters within the column and three beyond [the column]; but this is not the case with a short word. If [the part of a longer word forms] a short word of two letters on its own, it is forbidden [to insert it between the columns].

In his study, Herbert analysed the level of adherence of scribes to the left margin. While Martin[56] stressed the scribal disregard of the ruled margin, Herbert found that scribes often adhered to the ruled margin, but also to a 'notional' margin, that is, a margin which they had in mind. This margin was either to the left (1QIsa^a, 1QS) or to the right (1QpHab) of the ruled margin, for example, 3.75 mm to the left of the ruled margin in cols I-XXVII of 1QIsa^a, and 5.25 mm to the left in cols XXVIII-LIV of that scroll.[57] Sometimes scribes slightly exceeded the margin in order to keep parts of a phrase together.

As a rule, vertical rules at the left side of the block of writing helped the scribes to obtain a neatly written column, but the adherence to the left margin was not a major concern for scribes writing in square characters. There are, however, exceptions. For example, the scribe of 4QNum^b, which has left margin vertical rules, often left extra spaces between the words towards the end of the line, so that the line of text would be written to the left of, but flush with, the vertical rules. This phenomenon is noticeable in several columns (I,9,13; XII,26; XVIII,27; XIX,29; XXXI,12,14,15), and probably was the rule for this scroll (XVI,14 is an exception). This practice is also known, in a much more developed way, from the medieval Samaritan manuscripts, and it is therefore not coincidental that the content of this scroll is close to the Samaritan Pentateuch. In those manuscripts, the last letters of the line were similarly pressed against the vertical left rules, at the cost of leaving spaces elsewhere in the line, both between words and within the words.

Among the scrolls, some scribes adhered more to the left margin than others. As a rule, however, they accommodated the text to the margins by means of one of several devices:

1. Leaving extra spaces in the middle of the line so that the ends of the lines would be flush with the left marginal line, as in 4QNum[b].

2. Use of line-fillers.

3. Writing parts of words at the end of the line, to be repeated in full in the next line (thus 1QIsa[a] cols II,11-12 and XLI,10-11; Mur 42, line 5 [not erased as transcribed in *DJD* II (Oxford, 1961, p. 156)]. These letters were probably written beyond the vertical rule at the ends of the lines. When the scribe realized that his writing would extend too far beyond the vertical line, he repeated the word on the next line, for some reason not erasing the letters on the previous line.

4. Dividing words between lines in texts written in paleo-Hebrew characters, so that their margin was straighter than that of texts written in square characters in which words were not split between lines.

5. Writing single letters or words under the last word in the line. For an example of a single letter, see 4QD[a] frg. 10 i, l. 6 והשופטי.

3.7. Beginnings and ends of scrolls

The beginnings of several biblical and non-biblical scrolls have been preserved. Among the biblical texts are: 4QGen[b,g,k], 4QLev[c], 4QDeut[h], 5QKings, 1QIsa[a], 4QIsa[a,b,j], 4QXII[d], 6QCant, 4QRuth[a]. 4QLam. Non-biblical texts: 1QM, 1QS, 1QSa, 1QSb, 4QD[b], 4Qproverbs (?) ar (4Q560), and probably also 3QpIsa. The beginning of Exodus has also been preserved in 4QpaleoGen-Exod[l], but this was not the beginning of the scroll, which started with Genesis.

The beginnings of only a few of the Qumran texts have been preserved, probably because they were rolled up with their beginning inside. In other cases, when a scroll was rolled up with its ends as the innermost section, that part has often been preserved. Yet there are no fixed patterns for the preservation of beginnings and ends of scrolls, since in rare cases both ends were preserved (as in 4QD[b], 4QIsa[b] and 1QIsa[a], the latter stored in a jar). The ends of the following scrolls have been preserved: biblical texts: 11QpaleoLev[a], MasDeut, 4QJudg[b], 1QIsa[a], 4QIsa[b], 4QIsa[c]; non-biblical texts: 1QpHab, 4QText with a citation from Jubilees (4Q228), 4QD[a] (olim 4QD[b]), 4QD[b], 4QD[e], 4QMMT[f], 4QHodayot-like text (4Q440), 4Qps-Dan[c] ar, 11QPs[a], 11QtgJob, 11QT[a], 11QApPs[a], MasDeut, and MasPs[b]. Among the other scrolls that preserve sections near the end are 1QpaleoLev, 4QpaleoGen-Exod[l], 4QNum[b], 1QpaleoNum,

MurNum, 1QDeut^b, 4QDeut^l, 4Qpaleo-Deut^r, 4QSam^a, 6QpapKgs, 5QLam^a, 2QRuth^a.

Special arrangements were made for handling the scrolls, in order to avoid touch by the users of the inscribed area in sacred as well as non-sacred texts, both at the beginnings and the ends. This was done in two ways:

Beginnings of scrolls:

(1) The scribe left an uninscribed and ruled or unruled surface, the width of one or more columns, before the first column of text: 1QM, 4QGen^b, 4Qproverbs (?) ar (4Q560), 6QCant, and Mur 3 (Isaiah). (Although ruled, the space before the beginning of 3QpIsa probably presents a handling area at the beginning of the scroll.) This system was imitated in the Copper Scroll (3Q15) in which the first column was preceded by a handling area of 6 cm.

(2) A separate uninscribed handling sheet was attached to the scroll at the beginning. Such beginning sheets were also known from the tradition of the Greek and Latin manuscripts from antiquity as *protocollon*. See 1QS, 1QSa, 4QGen^g and 4QGen^k (for these, also see 3.9), as well as the uninscribed fragment photographed on PAM 41.656. The stitches before the first column of 1QIsa^a indicate the existence of such a separate sheet which Archbishop Samuel reportedly saw still connected to the scroll itself.[58]

In the case of 5QKings, the two systems were combined, as the scribe left a space of 7 cm to the right of the text, and further attached a separate handling sheet before the beginning of the scroll (see 3.9).

Ends of scrolls:

The last column of the text was usually ruled beyond the last inscribed line of the composition: 1QpHab, 1QIsa^a, 4QText with a citation from Jubilee (4Q228), 11QtgJob, 11QPs^a. This column was often followed by an uninscribed surface, which was either unruled (MasPs^b, 4QD^a), or, more frequently, ruled. In the latter case the scroll contained an additional column which was ruled because the precise contents of the surface needed for writing could not be calculated: 1QpHab, 4QMMT^f, 4QHodayot-like text (4Q440), 4QD^c, 4QpsDan^c ar, 11QTgJob, 11QpaleoLev^a, 11QPs^a. A separate ruled uninscribed handling sheet was preserved at the end of 11QT^a, 11QApPs^a (PAM 43.988), and MasDeut, and was probably also attached to 1QS and 11QpaleoLev^a after the stitches in the last columns. Note the high frequency of texts from cave 11 in this group.

The existence of end-sheets is mentioned in *m. Yadayim* 3:4. There is scanty evidence for the existence of wooden bars (*'amudim*), viz., 11QapocrPs. The handling sheets and empty surface served the same purpose.

In scrolls containing more than one biblical book, all but the first books usually started in the middle of a column[59] after several blank lines (4QGen-Exod^a, 4QExod^b, 4QpaleoGen-Exod^l, 4QRP^c[60]).[61] Similarly, all the biblical books in MurXII started in the middle of the column after three blank lines, but MurXII is a special case since the Minor Prophets were considered a single book. *y. Meg.* 1.71d prescribes the layout: '[In the Torah] one has to finish in the middle of a page and to commence in the middle of the [same] page. In the Prophets one finishes at the end and begins at the top of a page, but in the Dodekapropheton this is forbidden.'

3.8. Titles

Insufficient information is available on the existence of titles or name tags denoting the contents of the compositions since the beginnings of most scrolls have been lost. There is some evidence for the use of two systems which could have been used concurrently for the same scroll:

(1) The title was written (in non-biblical scrolls) as the first item, as part of the running text: 1QSa (זה הסרך לכול עדת ישראל), 1QM (partly reconstructed), 4QS[a] (?). Likewise, the title in Jer 23:9 'Concerning the prophets. My heart is crushed within me ...' is now part of the running text.

(2) The title was written opposite the beginning of the scroll in such a way that when the scroll was rolled, the title was visible on the outside. When the scroll was rolled up with its beginning on the outside, the title would be visible if it had been written on the verso, even when the scroll was tied with a thong. If the title was written on the recto, the scroll had to be slightly opened. If the scroll was rolled up with the beginning on the inside, such titles would not be visible. A title was written on the recto of the scroll in 1QS (סר[ך] היחד ומן[ )[62] and likewise on a fragment 4QGen[h-title] (4Q8[c]) (ברשית), now detached from the main manuscript which has not been found.[63] The title was written on the verso in 4QDibHam[a] (דברי המֵאֹרֹת)[64] and 4QpapCryptA MSM (4Q249) (מדרש ספר מושה). Although the latter scroll contained a composition written in Cryptic A writing, its title was nevertheless written on the verso in the square script for purposes of identification.[65] A similar system of writing titles is known for Greek compositions.[66]

3.9. Damage, Patching, and Stitching

Upon their preparation, some scrolls were of good quality while the surface of other scrolls was sometimes uneven, often showing scar tissue.

Poor tanning or scar tissue forced the scribes to leave uninscribed certain areas, for example:

a. In 4QRP[e] (4Q367) frg. 3 a great part of the middle section of the lines was left uninscribed in eight consecutive lines because of such surface problems.

b. Segments were left uninscribed in 1QM[67] and 11QPs[a].[68]

c. The scribe of 4QDeut[n] col. IV avoided writing on lines 1-4, 7-8.

Patching. There is evidence of wear and tear in scrolls in antiquity. At times a segment of a scroll was replaced with a patch which was stitched onto it. Most of these were not inscribed, while there is some evidence for inscribed patches. 11QT[a] was patched in places with uninscribed repair patches (see col. XXVII). In 4QpaleoExod[m 69] an inscribed round patch once attached to col. VIII,[70] displays a script and orthography different from the remainder of the scroll ('*hrn* is spelled defectively on the patch, but *plene* in the main text of the scroll). The patch was sewn on the back of the manuscript, as is clear from the partially written words on the patch written within the stitching and blank rims of the patch. These partially written words were continued in the main text of the manuscript. This is the only known inscribed patch from Qumran, while similar ones are known from the scribal tradition of the Samaritan Pentateuch.[71] The writing on such attached patches was not acceptable according to the main view in *Sof.* 2:11: '... nor is it permitted to write on a patch' but it was acceptable according to the view of R. Simeon ben Eleazar[72]:

R. Simeon b. Eleazar said in the name of R. Meir: [A torn sheet] may be joined with glue and it is permitted to write on the patch. It is forbidden, however, to do the sewing on the written side, but it must be done on the outside.

It is therefore relevant to note that the one text in which an inscribed patch has been spotted does not belong to the family of the MT: 4QpaleoExod^m (pre-Samaritan).

The evidence is unclear as to whether a complete sheet of a scroll was replaced as a whole when damaged beyond repair. This assumption is invoked, however, by J. Strugnell for the first sheet of 4QDeut^n which according to him was a correction sheet incorrectly sewn to the right of what now constitutes the second sheet.[73] Likewise, in their edition of 4QJub^a, VanderKam & Milik suggested that the first sheet of that scroll, written by a different scribe from the one who wrote the next sheet, was worn and replaced with a new one.

Stitching. When a scroll was rent, it was often stitched both before and after the writing. Stitching done prior to the writing in a scroll made it necessary for the scribe to leave open segments, often as much as complete lines. Stitching done after the writing made some of the words illegible. Accordingly, when the stitching was done in the middle of an inscribed area it can often be determined whether it was done before or after the writing. When the stitching was done in the uninscribed margins, as in most instances, it cannot be determined when the scroll was stitched.

a. Several rents in 1QIsa^a were stitched before the writing (for example, col. XVII line 4 from bottom) or after the leather was inscribed (for example, col. XVI and col. XII, in the latter case with stitches in the full length of the column).

b. Rents in 4QJer^c were stitched both before (cols IV, XXI and XXIII) and after the writing (for example, col. XXIII). It is not possible to know when the stitches in col. XVI were inserted. Note also stitches in the bottom margins of 4QCant^b frg. 1 and of 4QLev^c frg. 5 (with the preservation of parts of the threads).

c. 4QGen^g was stitched in the middle of the text before Gen 1:20 prior to the inscription of the leather. According to *b. Menah.* 31b such stitching of an already inscribed scroll was permitted in the following case:

R. Zeira said in the name of R. Hananel who said it in the name of Rab. If a rent [in a scroll of the Law] extended into two lines it may be sewn together; but if into three lines it may not be sewn together.[74]

See also the aforementioned *Sof.* 2:11 (for the view of R. Simeon see above):

[A tear in a parchment sheet of a Torah scroll] may not be joined with glue, nor is it permitted to write on a patch, nor may [the sheets] be sewn together on the written side.

Since the rabbinic texts refer to the Torah scroll as an existing unit, and not to the sheets before they were joined, the stitching before the writing may have been permitted, while there were limitations to the stitching after the writing. According to *Sof.* 2:11, 'A space should be left [unstitched] at the top and at the bottom [of the sheets] in order that the scroll be not torn [in use].' Cf. *b. Meg.* 19b. Accordingly, some sheets were stitched following the rabbinic prescriptions, not at the very end of the parchment but somewhat before the top edge or above the bottom edge: 4QNum^b col. XV; 11QT^a cols IL, LIII, LVII, LXI, LXIV, LXVII. On the other hand, in 1QIsa^a and 1QS the stitching extends to the very end of the parchment. A more detailed study of this practice is in order.

Scribal Practices and Physical Aspects of the Dead Sea Scrolls

Repair. According to the description by F. M. Cross, papyrus strips were attached in antiquity to the back of the leather of 4QSam[a] in order that its sheets would not fall apart.[75]

Re-inking. The last column of 1QIsa[a] was probably damaged in antiquity because of extensive use of that scroll. The ends of lines 1-4, 6, 7, 9, 10 had become so faint that they were re-inked. Likewise, *b. Meg.* 18b mentions broken letters (אותיות . . . מקורעות) and letters which have become faint (מטושטשות).

CONCLUSION

The present article, mainly descriptive, is not meant to propose a specific theory. Rather, it offers a description of many aspects of the scribal practices and physical features of the Hebrew and Aramaic texts copied between the third century BCE and the second century CE and found in the Judaean Desert. It is only known where these texts were found, and not where they were copied. Written both in the Judaean Desert and in various other places in ancient Israel, these texts provide useful insights into the transmission and copying of the Hebrew and Aramaic texts in Israel in the last three centuries BCE and the first two centuries CE. Some of the traditions of copying noted here continue earlier practices connected with the Aramaic texts written in the fifth century BCE. At the same time they reflect contemporary Greek traditions from the last centuries BCE. The latter aspect demonstrates the cross-cultural influences of the transmission of texts in antiquity.

ABBREVIATIONS

ASOR	*American Schools of Oriental Research*
BA	*Biblical Archaeologist*
BAR	*Biblical Archaelogy Review*
BASOR	*Bulletin of the American Schools of Oriental Research*
DJD	*Discoveries in the Judaean Desert* (Clarendon Press: Oxford)
DSD	*Dead Sea Discoveries*
ErIsr	*Eretz Israel*
HUCA	*Hebrew Union College Annual*
IEJ	*Israel Exploration Journal*
JJS	*Journal of Jewish Studies*
JNES	*Journal of Near Eastern Studies*
JQR	*Jewish Quarterly Review*
JSOT	*Journal for the Study of the Old Testament*
OBO	Orbis biblicus et orientalis
PEQ	*Palestine Exploration Quarterly*
RB	*Revue biblique*
RevQ	*Revue de Qumran*
SBL	Society of Biblical Literature
VT	*Vetus Testamentum*

NOTES

1 For bibliographical references relating to the published and unpublished documents the reader is referred to E. Tov with the collaboration of S. J. Pfann, *Companion Volume to the Dead Sea Scrolls Microfiche Edition*, 2nd rev. edn (Leiden: Brill, 1995). See further the indexes in E. Ulrich, 'An Index of the Passages in the Biblical Manuscripts from the Judean Desert (Part 1: Genesis-Kings)', *DSD* 1 (1994), 113-29; 'An Index ... (Part 2: Isaiah-Chronicles)', *DSD* 2 (1995), 86-107; J. A. Fitzmyer, *The Dead Sea Scrolls, Major Publications and Tools for Study, Revised Edition* (SBL Resources for Biblical Study 20; Atlanta: Scholars Press, 1990), 205-37.

2 Especially helpful are the following monographs: C. Kuhl, 'Schreibereigentümlichkeiten – Bemerkungen zur Jesajarolle (DSIa)', *VT* 2 (1952), 307-33; M. Martin, *The Scribal Character of the Dead Sea Scrolls* I-II (Bibliothèque du Muséon 44, 45; Louvain, 1958) – although this study is extremely detailed and helpful, it is based only on the major texts from cave 1; H. Stegemann, ΚΘΡΙΟΣ Ο ΘΕΟΣ ΚΘΡΙΟΣ ΙΗΣΟΘΣ – *Aufkommen und Ausbreitung des religiösen Gebrauchs von ΚΘΡΙΟΣ und seine Verwendung im Neuen Testament* (Habilitationsschrift, Bonn 1969); J. P. Siegel, 'Final *Mem* in Medial Position and Medial *Mem* in Final Position in 11QPs^a – Some Observations', *RevQ* 7 (1969), 125-30; Siegel, 'The Employment of Palaeo-Hebrew Characters for the Divine Names at Qumran in the Light of Tannaitic Sources', *HUCA* 42 (1971), 159-72; Siegel, *The Scribes of Qumran: Studies in the Early History of Jewish Scribal Customs, with Special Reference to the Qumran Biblical Scrolls and to the Tannaitic Traditions of Massekheth Soferim*, Unpubl. Diss., Brandeis University, 1971 (Ann Arbor: University Microfilms, 1972); J. M. Oesch, *Petucha und Setuma, Untersuchungen zu einer überlieferten Gliederung im hebräischen Text des Alten Testament* (OBO 27; Freiburg/Göttingen 1979); Oesch, 'Textgliederung im Alten Testament und in den Qumranhandschriften', *Henoch* 5 (1983), 289-321.

3 Thus also M. O. Wise, 'Thunder in Gemini, and Other Essays on the History, Language and Literature of Second Temple Palestine' (*Journal for the Study of the Pseudepigrapha*, Suppl. Series 15; Sheffield, 1994), 103-57 (137): 'Thus the most satisfactory explanation for the scribal phenomena of the DSS is to regard them as the product of the wider Hebrew and Aramaic book culture'.

4 G. Bonani, M. Broshi, I. Carmi, S. Ivy, J. Strugnell, W. Wölfli, 'Radiocarbon Dating of the Dead Sea Scrolls', *Atiqot* 20 (1991), 27-32; A. J. T. Jull, D. J. Donahue, M. Broshi, E. Tov, 'Radio-carbon Dating of Scrolls and Linen Fragments from the Judean Desert', *Radiocarbon* 37 (1995), 11-19.

5 J. T. Milik in 'Les grottes de Murabba'at' by P. Benoit and others (*DJD* II, 1961), 93-100 and pl. XXVIII; F. M. Cross, 'Epigraphic Notes on Hebrew Documents of the Eighth-Sixth Centuries B.C. II. The Murabba'at Papyrus and the Letter Found near Yabneh-Yam', *BASOR* 165 (1962), 34-42.

6 Cryptic A, B, and C. For an initial analysis of Cryptic A (4QHoroscope [4Q186], 4Q249, 4Q298, 4Q317 as well as the more fragmentary texts: 4Q250, 4QCal. Document C^f [4Q324c], and 4Q313 [unclassified frgs.]), see S. J. Pfann, '4Q298: The Maskîl's Address to All Sons of Dawn', *JQR* 85 (1994), 203-35.

7 In this room archaeologists found a 5-metre long table, small tables, and a number of inkwells (cf. PAM 42.865), which were situated either in this room or on a second floor which according to some scholars was situated above this room. See J. B. Humbert & A. Chambon, *Fouilles de Khirbet Qumrân et de Aïn Feshkha*, I (Novum Testamentum et Orbis Antiquus, Series Archaeologica 1; Fribourg-Göttingen, 1994), pl. 114-20. However, doubts have been raised with regard to this identification. Several scholars have claimed that the height of the table, 40 cm, was too low for writing: see B. M. Metzger, 'The Furniture of the Scriptorium

at Qumran', *RevQ* 1 (1958), 509-15; K. G. Pedley, 'The Library at Qumran', *RevQ* 2 (1959), 21-41 (35); K. W. Clark, 'The Posture of the Ancient Scribe', *BA* 26 (1963), 63-72. This claim was also made by A. Lemaire, 'L'enseignement', who suggested that in this room the intellectual life of the members of the community took place. The most detailed disagreement with the assumption of a scriptorium is provided by N. Golb. According to him, that no remnants of scrolls were found in the room also proves that it was not used for the purpose of writing: 'The Problem of Origin and Identification of the Dead Sea Scrolls', *Proc. Am. Phil. Soc.* 124 (1980), 1-24; 'Who Hid the Dead Sea Scrolls?' *BA* 48 (1985), 68-82; 'Khirbet Qumran and the Manuscripts of the Judaean Wilderness – Observations on the Logic of Their Investigation', *JNES* 49 (1990), 103-14; *Who Wrote the Dead Sea Scrolls – The Search for the Secret of Qumran* (New York: Scribner, 1994). Similar doubts, though in less detail, had been voiced before Golb by H. E. del Medico, *L'énigme des manuscrits de la Mer Morte* (Paris: Plon 1957); K. H. Rengstorf, *Hirbet Qumrân und die Bibliothek vom Toten Meer* (*Studia Delitzschiana* 5; Stuttgart, 1960). The theory of Golb was refuted in detail by F. García Martínez & A. S. van der Woude, 'A "Groningen" Hypothesis of Qumran Origins and Early History', *RevQ* 14 (1990), 521-41, but the doubts about the relevance of the artifacts found in locus 30 remain. For a more recent analysis, see M. O. Wise, 'Thunder in Gemini', 120.

8 H. Stegemann, *Die Essener, Qumran, Johannes der Taufer und Jesus: Ein Sachbuch*, 4th edn (Freiburg im Breisgau: Herder, 1994), 77-82.

9 It is not clear what the main writing material was in ancient Israel before the period attested by the documents from the Judaean Desert. According to M. Haran, 'Book-Scrolls in Israel in Pre-Exilic Times', *JJS* 33 (1982), 161-73, although no biblical texts have been preserved from the First Temple period, various allusions in the Bible make it reasonable to assume that papyrus served as the main writing material during this period. Jer 51:63 mentions the binding of a stone to a scroll so that it would sink in the Euphrates River. It seems that this scroll was made of papyrus, since a leather scroll would have sunk even without a stone. Another allusion to the employment of papyrus is found in Ezek 2:10, where a scroll written on 'both the front and the back' is mentioned, a feature which, according to Haran, is more suited to papyrus than to leather. Note, however, *tefillin* and *mezuzot*, and other opistographs, which are written on both sides of the leather. An argument in support of such an assumption is the fact that during the First Temple period papyrus was used in the countries surrounding Israel. Haran (ibid.) remarks on the Egyptian influence on Canaan which brought in its wake Egyptian scribal customs, the low price of papyrus in contrast to leather, and the biblical use of the root *ḥ'jm*, a verb signifying the erasure with water of a text written on papyrus. According to Haran, at the beginning of the Second Temple period scribes started to use leather when the need was felt to use materials capable of containing longer texts. However, there is also evidence of the use of papyrus for long texts, viz., the 'large' Harris papyrus of 'The Book of the Dead' from the eleventh century BCE (in Egyptian) which is 43 metres long.

10 Thus Wise, 'Thunder in Gemini', 125ff.

11 M. L. Ryder, 'Follicle Arrangement in Skin from Wild Sheep, Primitive Domestic Sheep and in Parchment', *Nature* 182 (1958), 1-6; J. Poole & R. Reed, 'The Preparation of Leather and Parchment by the Dead Sea Scrolls Community', *Technology and Culture* 3 (1962), 1-26; Poole & Reed, 'A Study of Some Dead Sea Scroll and leather Fragments from Cave 4 at Qumran: Part II, Chemical examination', *Proceedings of the Leeds Philosophical and Literary Society*, Scientific Section 9/6 (1964), 171-82.

12 Ibid., Part I, 'Physical Examination', 1-13 (8).

13 D. N. Freedman & K. A. Mathews, *The Paleo-Hebrew Leviticus Scroll* (11QpaleoLev; Winona Lake, Ind.: Eisenbrauns, 1985), 3.

14 Oral communication, April 1995, by Ms. Gila Kahila.

15 Thus R. de Vaux, 'Fouilles de Feshkha', *RB* 66 (1959), 225-55 (230-7). This view was contradicted by J. B. Poole & R. Reed, 'The "Tannery" of 'Ain Feshkha', *PEQ* 93 (1961), 114-23. For the data, see Humbert-Chambon, *Fouilles de Khirbet Qumrân*, 251ff. and photographs PAM 42.538-543.

16 H. Stegemann, *Die Essener*, 77-82.

17 M. Haran, 'Bible Scrolls in Eastern and Western Jewish Communities from Qumran to the High Middle Ages', *HUCA* 56 (1985), 21-62 (the quote is from p. 38).

18 K. G. Pedley, 'The Library at Qumran', *RevQ* 2 (1959), 21-41 (35-6).

19 Cf. the description of B. Porten & A. Yardeni referring to the Elephantine texts: *Textbook of Aramaic Documents from Ancient Egypt* (Jerusalem: Academon, 1993), 3, p. xiii: 'Fresh, rectangular papyrus sheets were not stored in a pile, but were glued together along their length to make a scroll. In writing a document, the scribe detached from the scroll a piece of required size'. A similar procedure must have existed in the classical world, in which sometimes even single sheets had stitches on both sides.

20 See E. Glickler-Chazon, 'New Liturgical Manuscripts from Qumran', *Proceedings of the Eleventh World Congress of Jewish Studies*, A (Jerusalem, 1994), 207-14.

21 According to Stegemann, *Die Essener*, 92, only in these two caves were scrolls found which had the end of the composition at the outside (1Q22, 1Q27, 1QH, 1QM, 1QS, 4Q2, 4Q174, 4Q401).

22 See J. Carswell, 'Fastenings on the Qumran Manuscripts', *DJD* VI (1977), 23-8 (24).

23 For the former, see E. Eshel, H. Eshel, & A. Yardeni, 'A Qumran Composition Containing Part of Ps. 154 and a Prayer for the Welfare of King Jonathan and His Kingdom', *IEJ* 42 (1992), 199-229, and for the latter see pl. IVa and IVb in *DJD* VI. See further the description by Carswell, 'Fastenings'. The damage of the thongs to the middle section of the scroll in 1QS, 1QSa, 1QSb, 1QIsa^a, and 4Q298 was described by Pfann, '4Q298', n. 11.

24 The reference, together with other ones, is provided by Th. Birt, *Das antike Buchwesen in seinem Verhältniss zur Litteratur* (Berlin: Hertz, 1882), 68.

25 See the publication of this material by G. M. Crowfoot in *DJD* I (1955), 18-38 (24-8, 'The linen textiles'). See p. 24 ibid.: 'It seems probable that all the cloths were made for one of two purposes, either as scroll wrappers or as jar covers'.

26 The linen fragment has been dated to 160-41 BCE in the radiocarbon examination performed by Jull and others (see n. 4), that is, the period of the scrolls themselves. The quoted article also presents a photograph of the linen fragment with the attached thong.

27 That the ink of texts from cave 1 had a carbon base was suggested by H. J. Plenderleith in *DJD* I (1955), 39, and a similar suggestion was made by the editors of *DJD* IX (1992), 18 for 4QpaleoExod^m.

28 The description is by Y. Nir-El & M. Broshi, 'The Black Ink of the Qumran Scrolls', *DSD*, 3 (1996), 157-67. For earlier literature, see S. H. Steckoll, 'Investigations of the Inks Used in Writing the Dead Sea Scrolls', *Nature* 220 (1968), 91-2.

29 The translations are by H. Albeck in his edition of the Mishna, סדר מועד, ששה סדרי משנה (Jerusalem & Tel Aviv, 1958), 48. Alternative translations in brackets are by H. Danby, *The Mishnah* (Oxford, 1964).

30 On the other hand, H. J. M. Milne & T. C. Skeat, *Scribes and Correctors of the Codex Sinaiticus* (London: British Museum, 1938), 79-80 remarked on the ink of that codex: '... the ink was in the main an iron compound, and not the old carbon-and-gum ink which is found almost universally on papyri ... a carbon ink would not stick to the surface of the vellum, whereas a chemical ink held, often only too well'.

31 *DJD* I (1955), 39.

32 *DJD* IX (1992), 18.

33 M. Haran, 'Scribal Workmanship in Biblical Times – The Scrolls and the Writing Implements', *Tarbiz* 50 (1981), 65-87 (Heb.) (81-4).

34 See S. Goranson, 'Qumran: A Hub of Scribal Activity', *BAR* 20,5 (1994), 36-9; 'An Inkwell from Qumran', *Michmanim* 6 (1992), 37-40.

35 R. de Vaux, 'Fouilles au Khirbet Qumran: Rapport préliminaire sur la der nière campagne', *RB* 61 (1954), 206-33 (212 and pl. 5, 6, 10b). For further information on inkwells found in ancient Israel, see Goranson, 'Inkwell', 38.

36 S. H. Steckoll, 'Marginal Notes on the Qumran Excavations', *RevQ* 7 (1969), 33-40 (35).

37 Haran, 'Scribal Workmanship', 76.

38 For an analysis of several valuable technical data on the scrolls, see H. Stegemann, 'Methods for the Reconstruction of Scrolls from Scattered Fragments', in: *Archaeology and History in the Dead Sea Scrolls – The New York University Conference in Memory of Yigael Yadin*, ed. by L. H. Schiffman (*JSOT/ASOR* Monograph Series 2; Sheffield, 1990), 189-220.

39 For a general introduction, see J. Leroy, *Les types de reglure des manuscrits grecs* (Paris, 1976).

40 For a discussion of the evidence, see J. Naveh, 'An Aramaic Tomb Inscription Written in Paleo-Hebrew Script', *IEJ* 23 (1973), 82-91 (89).

41 For a description, see E. Robertson, *Catalogue of Samaritan Manuscripts in the John Rylands Library of Manchester* (Manchester, 1938); S. Talmon, 'Some Unrecorded Fragments of the Hebrew Pentateuch in the Samaritan Versions', *Textus* 3 (1963), 63; T. Anderson, *Studies in Samaritan Manuscripts and Artifacts – The Chamberlain-Warren Collection* (American Schools of Oriental Research Monograph Series 1: Cambridge, MA, 1978), 16.

42 A more detailed study of the frequency of the ruling is in order. The Masada fragments of Leviticus were not ruled: see S. Talmon, 'Fragments of Two Scrolls of the Book of Leviticus from Masada', *ErIsr* 24 (Jerusalem, 1993), 99-110. Likewise, two small lists, 4Q339 ('List of False Prophets'), and 340 ('List of Netinim'), whose original form was probably not much larger than their present fragmentary shape, were not ruled.

43 See Milne & Skeat, *Scribes and Correctors*, 73-4. For investigations on this system, see the detailed bibliography on New Testament manuscripts listed by B. M. Metzger, *The Text of the New Testament* (Oxford: Clarendon, 1964), 8, n. 1. For still later sources, see the description of the pricking in medieval Hebrew manuscripts by M. Beit Arié, 'Some Technical Practices Employed in Hebrew Dated Medieval Manuscripts', *Litterae textuales, Codicologica 2, Éléments pour une codicology comparée* (Leiden, 1978), 79-92 (84-90). See also M. Glatzer, 'The Aleppo Codex – Codicological and Paleographical Aspects', *Sefunot* 4 (1989), 210-15 (Hebrew with English summary).

43 Th. Birt, *Kritik und Hermeneutik nebst Abriss des Antiken Buchwesens* (München, 1913), 349.

44 This was also remarked by I. Gallo, *Greek and Latin Papyrology* (Classical Handbook 1; London: Institute of Classical Studies, 1986), 10.

45 Birt, *Kritik und Hermeneutik*, 349.

46 These data are based on Stegemann, 'Reconstruction', 199.

47 For the former, see E. Tov, 'The Greek Minor Prophets Scroll from Naḥal Ḥever (8ḤevXIIgr) (The Seiyal Collection I)' (*DJD* VIII, 1990), 9, and for the latter see Tov in: H. Attridge & others, in consultation with J. VanderKam, 'Qumran Cave 4.VIII, Parabiblical Texts, Part 1' (*DJD* XIII, 1994), 102.

48 Poole & Reed, 'The Preparation of Leather and Parchment by the Dead Sea Scrolls Community', *Technology and Culture* 3 (1962), 1-26. The quote is from p. 22.

49 *DJD* XII (1994), 217.

50 M. Burrows, *The Dead Sea Scrolls of St. Mark's Monastery* (New Haven: American Schools of Oriental Research, 1950), vol. I, xiv.

51 The precise details for some of the sheets have been listed for 1QIsaᵃ by J. C. Trever in the edition of Burrows, *Dead Sea Scrolls*, 27-8.

52 According to Y. Yadin, *The Temple Scroll* (Israel Exploration Society: Jerusalem, 1983), I, 15, the scribe increased the number of lines at this point in order not to make the scroll exceedingly long, and he decreased them on the realization that he would not succeed in doing so. It is, however, more likely that he was simply given sheets of parchment of identical size but with a different number of ruled lines.

53 See E. Ulrich, 'Orthography and Text in 4QDanᵃ and 4QDanᵇ and in the Received Masoretic Text' in: *Of Scribes and Scrolls, Studies on the Hebrew Bible, Intertestamental Judaism, and Christian Origins Presented to John Strugnell*, ed. by H. W. Attridge & others (College Theology Society Resources in Religion 5; Lanham, Md, 1990), 29-42 (38).

54 W. Fields, 'Qumran Scribal Practices and the Size of the Column Block in the Scrolls from the Judean Desert', Unpublished seminar paper, Hebrew University (Jerusalem, 1987).

55 The amount of marginal observance in the scrolls from Qumran cave 1 was described in detail by Martin, *Scribal Character*, I, 109-17 (cited n. 2 above) and additional texts were described by E. D. Herbert, *A New Method for Reconstructing Biblical Scrolls, and Its Application to the Reconstruction of 4QSamᵃ* (STDJ 22; Brill: Leiden 1997).

56 *Scribal Character*, 112-13.

57 Ibid., 39-40.

58 Reported by J. C. Trever, in Burrows, *Dead Sea Scrolls*, XIII.

59 According to J. T. Milik, *Books of Enoch* (Oxford: Clarendon, 1976), 143, 4QEnᵃ as well as other Qumran texts, left half-blank pages in the first column for easy handling. This is not confirmed, however, for 4QEnᵃ where such spacing is not evidenced, while the list of the 'other texts' still needs to be supplied. Examples such as listed here (books which form part of a multi-book composition) would not be valid examples for this description.

60 In frg. 26,a-b the first verse of Numbers is preceded by what looks like a paraphrastic version of the last verse of Leviticus, followed by an empty line.

61 Note that also in the manuscripts of the Sam. Pent. new books started in the middle of a page, usually at one-third of the way down the page (A. Crown, personal communication).

62 Published as 1Q28 in D. Barthélemy & J. T. Milik, 'Qumran Cave 1' (*DJD* I, 1955), 109. The title was written perpendicular to the writing of the manuscript.

63 J. Davila, *DJD* XII (1994), 63 suggests that the fragment containing the title of the book was a remnant of a handling page.

64 M. Baillet, 'Qumrân grotte 4.III (4Q482-4Q520)' (*DJD* VII, 1982), 138 and pl. XLIX.

65 Likewise, documentary texts, such as Babatha's *ketubba*, had an identifying inscription on the outside of the document.

66 Cf. E. G. Turner, *Greek Manuscripts of the Ancient World*, 2nd edn revised by P. J. Parsons (London: Institute of Classical Studies, 1987), 13-14. See further Carswell, 'Fastenings', 23-8.

67 For examples, see Y. Yadin, *The Scroll of the War of the Sons of Light against the Sons of Darkness* (Clarendon: Oxford, 1962), 249-51 and fig. 18, group A, frg. 19.

68 See J. A. Sanders, 'The Psalms Scroll of Qumrân Cave 11 (11QPsᵃ)' (*DJD* IV, 1965), 14.

69 *DJD* IX (1992), 84-5 and pl. XI.

70 The patch, which has been perfectly preserved, contains a fragmentary text, since the remainder of the text is contained in the beginnings and ends of the lines of the main manuscript which have not been preserved in this case. The patch shares with the main manuscript the length of lines and the distinctive use of the *waw* in the closed sections when the next word would have started with a conversive *waw*.

71 See Anderson, *Studies*, 24.

72 Ibid.

73 This view was quoted and discussed by S. A. White, '4QDtⁿ: Biblical Manuscript or Excerpted Text?' in *Of Scribes and Scribes*, ed. by H. W. Attridge & others (cited n. 53 above), 193-206.

74 In the continuation of this text the Talmud mentions certain circumstances, the relevance of which cannot be examined any more regarding the preserved texts: 'Rabbah the younger said to R. Ashi: Thus said R. Jeremiah of Difti in the name of Raba: The rule that we have laid down, namely, that if it extended into three lines it may be sewn together, applies only to old scrolls; but in the case of new scrolls it would not matter [that is, it may always be sewn together]. Moreover "old" does not mean actually old, nor "new" actually new, but the one means prepared with gall-nut juice and the other means not so prepared'.

75 'Le travail d'édition des fragments manuscrits de Qumrân', *RB* 63 (1956), 49-67. The quote is from p. 57.

THE CHRISTIAN BOOK IN EGYPT

INNOVATION AND THE COPTIC TRADITION

Stephen Emmel

PRINCIPALLY BECAUSE OF THE REMARKABLY DRY CLIMATE south of the Nile Delta, Egypt has been an exceptionally important source of written artifacts from across thousands of years. As a result, the history of the Christian book in Egypt can be studied nearly from its beginning through an abundance of documentation in the form of actual books, or fragments of books, surviving from every century of the Christian Era. The importance of this Egyptian evidence extends well beyond Egypt itself, because it includes the remains of books written in a number of languages – such as Latin, Greek, Syriac, Hebrew, Nubian, Ethiopic, Coptic, and Arabic – and thus contributes to our knowledge of the history of the book in other cultures and countries. At the same time, Egypt happens to provide most of our artifactual evidence for the early history of the book as such, especially during the early Christian centuries, the period of transition from roll to codex as the standard format for the book.

To study this period and the evidence from Egypt raises basic questions, such as: What *is* a book? Who used books in Greco-Roman Egypt? For what purposes? The sea of questions that opens before us is so vast, in fact, that we can do no more than skim over its surface, touching down here and there for a closer look. This paper conducts a brief survey of the history of the Christian book in Egypt in terms of three innovations, each of which had a profound impact on the manuscript tradition of the Bible as a book.

First I will discuss the emergence, in the first Christian century, of the codex, or leaf-book, format, a *technological innovation* within the general history of the book that is particularly well attested by evidence from Egypt and seems to be closely connected with the rise of Christianity. Second, out of the rich linguistic diversity of manuscripts found in Egypt, Coptic manuscripts are of particular interest because they represent a *linguistic innovation* within the general history of the Egyptian language and its literature, another innovation closely connected with the rise of Christianity. Third, the history of the Christian book in Egypt cannot possibly be kept apart from the spread of the communal monastic movement, a *spiritual innovation* within Christianity that brought with it a reverence for books both as texts and as objects, and hence contributed significantly – in Egypt and elsewhere – to the preservation of ancient words, especially the Bible.

At the beginning of the third century of the Common Era, the Roman jurist Ulpian expressed his professional opinion as to what should be understood as comprised by the term 'books' (*libri* in Latin), when it occurs in a will or bequest for example (*Dig.*

35

32.52 praef.).[1] Ulpian's formulation leaves no room for doubt that the only thing he recognized to be self-evidently a 'book' was the scroll (Latin *volumen*), 'whether of papyrus or parchment or whatever other material'. He goes on to acknowledge, however, that also *codices*, 'whether of parchment or papyrus, or even ivory or another material, or waxed wooden tablets', must be included in the legal definition of 'books' (*libri*), even if – as he implies – they are nonetheless not, properly speaking, 'books' (that is, *volumina*).

Ulpian was making a fundamental distinction between the two book formats that are best known to most of us, the roll and the codex, regardless of material (although it is interesting that with respect to the roll he mentions papyrus first, and when he comes to the codex he first mentions parchment). His attitude toward the codex as only dubiously classifiable as a 'book' except in a certain legal sense would have been completely commonplace two hundred years earlier, when the codex was hardly known except as a small stack of waxed wooden tablets or folded parchment sheets tied together at one edge to form a little reusable notebook for ephemeral and entirely pedestrian purposes. But by the beginning of the third century the codex had been improved upon considerably and was increasingly regarded as a perfectly acceptable format for a book. Ulpian's attitude was highly conservative, even old-fashioned. Probably more reflective of the current view at the time was the statement by Ulpian's colleague Paulus, that 'books' (*libri*) legally comprise both papyrus and parchment rolls, and also codices, 'because,' he wrote, 'by the term "books" is meant not (just) papyrus rolls, but any kind of written work that comes to a conclusive end' (*Sent.* 3.6.87). To quote C. H. Roberts and T. C. Skeat, to whose codicological studies we owe so much, with this statement from Paulus, 'the book is ... defined, and well defined, as a self-contained unit, independent of material or format'.[2]

From a structural and practical point of view, the codex of the third century was not essentially different from today's codex, that is, what we call a 'book'. The completeness with which the codex has become the idea of the book in our world is measurable by imagining how customers in a modern bookshop would react to being offered an inscribed roll of papyrus or parchment or even ordinary paper: probably most would not recognize it as a book at all, even if they recognized its contents to be the same as they might find in a real book, that is, in a codex. Format is important.

In the Mediterranean world at the beginning of the Christian Era, a genuine book was universally understood to be a roll, most typically of papyrus but possibly of parchment or leather. Evidence for the use of the codex format as a vehicle for literature begins to appear in the first century of our era and within six hundred years the codex had effectively supplanted the roll as the 'proper' format for a book.[3] Since books in roll format have a history that can be traced back into the fourth millennium BCE,[4] it need hardly be restated that the replacement of this format by the codex during the early centuries of our era is 'the most momentous development in the history of the book until the invention of printing'.[5]

How and why did this development occur? Precise answers to these questions will probably lie forever beyond our grasp, but the available evidence does permit some striking general observations that merit acceptance as established facts, in so far as such things exist in the realm of ancient studies.

It is here that Egypt, with its remarkably dry climate, becomes particularly important. For in contrast to what has been described as 'the extraordinary poverty of our [literary] sources of information' about the early history of the codex, the tens of thousands of manuscript fragments that have survived from Egypt's Greco-Roman period provide us with a kind of statistical basis for investigating the *realia* that underlie our meagre literary references to the format of books and their production in antiquity.[6] Although this database is – for a variety of reasons – not exactly the random sample that we might like to have if we could travel back in time to this period and personally conduct a survey, it is much more like such a sample than we are accustomed to having from antiquity, except in the realm of less eloquent archaeological artifacts like potsherds and bones. The chief drawback here may be that the evidence comes from Egypt, a single province of the Roman Empire. In fact, however, not every manuscript scrap preserved in Egypt was also produced there (although it is a likely presumption that most were), and the much more limited similar evidence from elsewhere tends to confirm the picture drawn for us in the sands of Egypt. Hence it seems reasonable to take the Egyptian evidence as roughly indicative of certain Empire-wide trends, as, for example, the format of books and the habits of book producers.

Of nearly 3,000 Greek papyrus and parchment books that have been recovered from Egypt and are datable to the first five centuries of our era,[7] about 80 per cent are in roll format, and 20 per cent are codices. This simple statistic illustrates the domination of the roll over the codex at the start of the Common Era. Because this is the period of transition from roll to codex as the standard format for a book, it is not surprising that when the numbers are broken down chronologically the weighting of the percentages shifts gradually from an almost complete dominance of the roll over the codex in the first century, to just the reverse in the fifth. One century later the roll effectively disappeared as a vehicle for works of literature.

What is most interesting about this evidence appears only when the numbers are divided according to Christian books and 'pagan' books, that is, between copies of the Christian Bible (Old and New Testaments) and other Christian literature on the one hand, and classical Greek (and Latin) literature on the other. What emerges then is that whereas for classical literature the roll was practically the only book format in use until the third century, and the roll continued to be the dominant format for this literature until the fourth century, for Christian literature, by contrast, the codex was from the beginning practically the only book format in use: Christian books in roll format are scarcely known.

'The birth of the codex' in the first century and the emergence of Christianity at about the same time is a remarkable coincidence that demands a historical explanation. Given the history of Christian and pagan relations, it is reasonable to conjecture that the ultimate triumph of the codex over the roll had something to do with the conflicting religious affiliations of the two formats. It has even been suggested that the initial Christian adoption of the codex format was a deliberate rejection of the traditional book form, the roll, which Christians regarded as stigmatized by its long history of usage by non-Christians, that is, pagans and Jews.

Any thinking along such lines, however, should proceed with caution. There is far too much that we do not know about the early history of the codex. One thing that we do know is that the oldest extant Christian codices are no older than the oldest extant non-Christian codices (second century), a fact that cautions against any over-hasty inclination to credit Christianity with the initial popularization of the codex as a literary book format, or with its invention.[8] Furthermore, as yet we have few clues as to where the literary codex first came into use and how it first spread. That our earliest examples come from Egypt is probably but a sheer accident of preservation. The precise origins of the literary codex are still a complete mystery.

But whatever the circumstances of the invention of the codex, Egypt merits special consideration in the history of its development, because throughout antiquity Egypt was practically the sole source of papyrus, the paper of the ancient world, manufactured from the papyrus plant, which grew abundantly in Egypt, but hardly anywhere else.[9] Papyrus as a manufactured product was produced in single sheets. Nevertheless, it was also a part of the manufacturing process finally to glue a series of sheets together to create a roll. And hence the basic unit of papyrus as a material was – and always was – the roll. If a customer in a stationery shop wanted to purchase a single sheet of papyrus, the stationer simply cut the required length from the end of a roll. We know this because so many of the single-sheet documents that survive from Egypt include a seam (*kollesis*), where two originally separate sheets were overlapped and glued together in the manufacture of the basic roll; over such seams the writing continues perfectly smoothly. Given the millennia-long circumstance of using the roll as the basic material unit for papyrus, the book roll can be seen as the most obvious and economical way of turning the material into a book: simply by using it in the form in which it came from the shop.

By contrast, the codex was both a formal innovation – a change in the book's fundamental shape – and also a technological innovation, involving a much more complex manufacturing procedure. This latter point can be illustrated from one striking characteristic of codices made from papyrus. Given that the fundamental structural unit of the codex is the sheet, or bifolium, we might expect a papyrus codex to have been manufactured out of individual papyrus sheets. But in fact this expectation is not met by the evidence. On the contrary, the bifolia for papyrus codices were made by cutting up papyrus rolls that had themselves been made by carefully gluing single sheets together. That the roll should thus have remained the basic material unit of papyrus even as the codex form was beginning to emerge is not surprising.

What is surprising is the change that took place in roll technology as a result of the development of the codex. The sheets of papyrus used in the manufacture of rolls were typically rather narrow, on the order of 15-20 cm broad, with sheets as broad as about 40 cm, or a little more, occurring only exceptionally. This practice of manufacturing papyrus in narrow sheets provides the strongest evidence that the roll was the basic material unit: because seams were accordingly frequent in the material as it was sold and used, they are frequently still evident even in the most fragmentary papyri that have survived. They are evident also in the leaves of papyrus codices. In fact, in the case of well-preserved papyrus codices it is usually possible to reconstruct the rolls from which the bifolia had been cut.

Such exercises in roll reconstruction on the part of papyrus codicologists led gradually to the discovery that the rolls used in the manufacture of at least some papyrus codices were made out of papyrus sheets reaching well over a metre in length, sometimes even approaching two metres. Since such very broad sheets have not been found in any book rolls, the conclusion is warranted that the manufacture of these broad sheets was an innovation motivated by the invention of the papyrus codex. Broader sheets meant that it required less work to paste together a roll whose only purpose was to be cut back up into sheets to become the bifolia of a codex.[10]

Thus as long as papyrus continued to be used as a writing material, which was at least into the eleventh century, the roll remained the basic material unit, even if it ceased to be thought of as a useful format for a book and served only as the source of bifolia. Cutting a papyrus roll again into sheets was no doubt one of the simpler operations in manufacturing a papyrus codex, a complicated artifact from the technological point of view. The parchment codex is no less complex, with the difference in material involving different sets of technical problems. Nevertheless, Christians from a very early period, at least in Egypt but presumably elsewhere as well, showed a preference for the new codex format, particularly for copying their sacred books, the Greek 'Old Testament' (the Septuagint) and the specifically Christian works that were beginning to take on scriptural authority as the 'New Testament', also written in Greek.[11]

Evidence for this preference for the codex is seen when Christian literature first appears in the native Egyptian language – it is presented almost exclusively in the 'new' book format, the codex. The appearance of Christian Egyptian literature entailed also a linguistic innovation, because, at the time, the Egyptian language effectively had no written form of expression. The spread of Christianity in Egypt brought with it the creation of a new writing system for Egyptian, using primarily the Greek alphabet, supplemented by several characters from the Egyptian Demotic script, as a system for transliterating the sounds of the spoken language. This writing system, which characterizes Egypt's 'Coptic' period, was probably the creation of Christian missionary activity, produced in an effort to win converts among the Egyptian population that knew no Greek. As in the case of the creation of the literary codex, we cannot know who took the first steps toward creating the Coptic alphabet; but probably it was the Christians who standardized the new writing system and then maintained it. Certainly Coptic literature reached its maturity nurtured by the Christian church and the allied monastic movement.[12]

Apart from the so-called 'Old Coptic' magical and astrological texts, the earliest surviving Coptic manuscripts date from the late third century. They are mostly translations of books from the Bible. Throughout its history, Coptic literature was almost entirely Christian, the only major exceptions being several extraordinary hoards of early books of Manichaean, Gnostic, and related literature.[13] But for all this literature, Christian and non-Christian alike, the books are in the form of codices, almost without exception. In fact, a number of nearly intact early Coptic codices, above all the Nag Hammadi Codices, constitute most of our best examples of what leather-bound papyrus codices were like during the earliest centuries of the codex format's use.[14]

The rebirth of Egyptian literature marked by the standardization of a Coptic writing system during the third century and the emergence of Coptic book production on a relatively large scale during the fourth and fifth centuries are noteworthy phenomena in a number of respects. Not the least interesting aspect of this development is linguistic: the representation of dialectal variation in Coptic books. Dialectal variation is a feature of all natural language, but the variation that occurs naturally in speech does not necessarily find expression in writing. Indeed, standardized writing systems are designed partly for the purpose of disguising such spoken variation. But in the case of Coptic, where the writing system produced a phonemic transliteration of the spoken language, sound by sound, the result was that written Coptic tended from the outset to display graphically the kinds of differences in pronunciation and syntax that are characteristic of what linguists identify as 'dialects'. Although written in the same alphabet and according to the same system, we can distinguish easily between a Coptic manuscript written in, for example, the Sahidic dialect and one written in the Bohairic dialect, observing differences on the order of those that can be *heard* between, say, Oxford English and English as spoken in Scotland.

The study of Coptic dialects is a highly specialized and complex area of research, and it entails all the general theoretical issues of dialectology as a whole, such as, for example, defining what is meant by the concept 'dialect'. But in the present context, the main point can be stated rather simply. That more than a dozen dialects are attested in the earliest centuries of the Coptic period witnesses to literary activity in Coptic that extended throughout Egypt, up and down the Nile. Furthermore, in most cases the evidence for these dialects includes translations of books of the Christian Bible, and for some of the more extensively attested dialects it is clear that the entire Old and New Testaments were translated, which was no small undertaking. All this activity represents a remarkable degree of interest in making the Christian Bible and other literature accessible to speakers of Coptic.

Already in the fourth century the so-called Sahidic dialect began to emerge as a kind of national standard. Its status as a Coptic standard is apparent from several sides: there is the sheer quantity of Sahidic manuscripts, which soon almost completely overwhelm manuscripts in the other dialects (in fact, most of the other dialects disappear, as literary vehicles, after the fifth and sixth centuries); and in the fourth century there is already abundant evidence that authors were writing in Sahidic as a kind of 'prestige dialect', and attempting thereby to disguise (more or less successfully) the non-Sahidic features of their native dialects.[15]

That the Sahidic dialect served as the literary standard during the centuries surrounding the Arab Conquest was surely the result of the literary activity of the Christian monastic movement in Egypt. There is some doubt that communal monasticism was a specifically Egyptian or even Christian creation, but within Christianity it was a spiritual innovation, a new expression of the ascetic tendency that was part of Christian spirituality from the first. And even in antiquity, Egypt was regarded as the seed-bed of monasticism throughout Christendom, and a Copt named Pachom was credited with founding the first monastery, early in the fourth century, and composing the first cenobitic rule, which he wrote in good Sahidic Coptic. From the beginning, the Pachomian monasteries established a tradition of requiring all monks to attain at least a certain degree of literacy and knowledge of the Bible based on reading ability, in Coptic.[16] Thus they established a tradition of monastic libraries and scriptoria, a legacy with a profound impact on the history of literature throughout the Christian world.[17]

Coptic literature had an energetic but foreshortened life. The Arab Conquest of Egypt in 641 was a prelude to the relegation of Egyptian Christianity to an increasingly marginal status, and along with this marginalization came a decline of Coptic culture as a whole, including the death of the Coptic language itself as it was gradually superseded by Arabic, beginning in the eleventh century. Some Coptic literature was translated into Arabic, and some knowledge of Coptic was preserved by a series of

Coptic-Arabic lexicons and grammars that were compiled by erudite Copts between the eleventh and fourteenth centuries. But the great wealth of Coptic literature that had been produced by the church and the monastic tradition, partly through translation of selected works from Greek and Syriac, but also through a steady stream of original compositions that began already with Pachom – this wealth of literature was in grave danger of being lost forever during the Middle Ages. It languished in the decaying remains of hundreds of parchment codices that had been discarded and abandoned as no longer useful or even intelligible, in churches and monasteries, many of which were themselves abandoned and falling to ruin. The rescue of this literature, which is still going on as one of the main activities of Coptic studies, was made possible partly by the medieval bilingual Coptic-Arabic manuscript tradition, which facilitated the scholarly recovery of Coptic, and partly by the activities of western antiquarians and book collectors who began in the sixteenth century to hunt down Coptic manuscripts and transport them to Europe for study. The combined result has been that much of Coptic literature has become a kind of codicological puzzle, where rescuing the written works depends on putting back together the now scattered pieces of hundreds of ancient and medieval papyrus, parchment, and paper codices.[18] This work has advanced far enough that there is in Coptic studies a healthy tendency to think primarily in terms not of the accidental modern collections of fragments of diverse provenience, but of 'bibliological units' – the ancient and medieval libraries and collections to which the now scattered books and fragments of books originally belonged.[19] This approach has the salutary effect of bringing us into closer touch with the communities of believers who assembled and used these libraries, making clear the extent to which we owe the survival of Coptic literature to the ongoing liturgical life of the Coptic church, even as Coptic culture and the Coptic language were waning.[20] Reconstructing Coptic literature is an exciting and rewarding task, in which a love and knowledge of the literature must go hand in hand with a love and knowledge of the codex, as an exquisite and endlessly fascinating artifact.

NOTES

1 For the following I rely on C. H. Roberts & T. C. Skeat, *The Birth of the Codex* (London: Oxford University Press, 1983), 30-2. This book is a revision of Roberts's ground-breaking essay, 'The Codex', *Proceedings of the British Academy* 40 (1954), 169-204, with pl. 12 facing p. 169; cf. Skeat, 'Early Christian Book-Production: Papyri and Manuscripts', *The Cambridge History of the Bible*, vol. 2, *The West from the Fathers to the Reformation*, ed. by G. W. H. Lampe (Cambridge: University Press, 1969), 54-79.

2 Roberts & Skeat, *Birth of the Codex*, 32.

3 Roberts & Skeat, 75. Rolls continued to be used, of course, for a variety of purposes, even to the present day (pp. 51-3).

4 J. Černý, *Paper and Books in Ancient Egypt: An Inaugural Lecture Delivered at University College London 29 May 1947* (London: H. K. Lewis, 1952), 11.

5 Roberts & Skeat, 1.

6 Roberts & Skeat, 14. The evidence is clearly and concisely surveyed on pp. 11-34.

7 I rely on the statistics of Roberts & Skeat (35-44), which to my knowledge have not been brought up to date. It is doubtful that more examples will change the general picture very much (although this hypothesis should of course be tested).

8 E. G. Turner, *The Typology of the Early Codex* (Haney Foundation Series 18; [Philadelphia]: University of Pennsylvania Press, 1977), 89-90 and 93; cf. Roberts & Skeat, 40-2 and 71-3.

9 See, e.g., N. Lewis, *Papyrus in Classical Antiquity* (Oxford: Clarendon Press, 1974).

10 J. M. Robinson, 'The Future of Papyrus Codicology', *The Future of Coptic Studies*, ed. by R. McL. Wilson (Coptic Studies 1; Leiden: E. J. Brill, 1978), 23-70.

11 Roberts & Skeat, 45-61 ('Why Did Christians Adopt the Codex?' and 'The Christian Adoption of the Codex'); see also Roberts, *Manuscript, Society and Belief in Early Christian Egypt* (The Schweich Lectures of the British Academy 1977; London: Oxford University Press, 1979). The evidence remains unfortunately and tantalizingly inconclusive.

12 In general on the history of Coptic, including its death and recovery, see Emmel, 'Coptic Language', *Anchor Bible Dictionary* 4.180-8 (with bibliography).

13 I use 'Gnostic, and related literature' to refer to the Nag Hammadi texts (mainly), because I mean to use 'Gnostic' in the restricted sense delineated most recently by B. Layton, 'Prolegomena to the Study of Ancient Gnosticism', *The Social World of the First Christians: Essays in Honor of Wayne A. Meeks*, ed. by L. M. White & O. L. Yarbrough (Minneapolis: Augsburg Fortress, 1995), 334-50.

14 See *The Facsimile Edition of the Nag Hammadi Codices* (12 vols.; Leiden: E. J. Brill, 1972-84); in the *Introduction* volume (1984), see esp. the frontispiece (described on p. 131), pp. 15-102, and pl. 1*. The Coptic component of the Dishna Papers (often misleadingly called 'the Bodmer papyri' and 'the Chester Beatty papyri') is also significant: see J. M. Robinson, 'The First Christian Monastic Library', *Coptic Studies: Acts of the Third International Congress of Coptic Studies, Warsaw, 20-25 August, 1984*, ed. by Włodzimierz Godlewski (Warsaw: Państwowe Wydawnictwo Naukowe, 1990), 371-8; Robinson, *The Pachomian Monastic Library at the Chester Beatty Library and the Bibliothèque Bodmer* (Occasional Papers of the Institute for Antiquity and Christianity 19; Claremont, Calif.: Institute for Antiquity and Christianity, 1990).

15 Important recent work on the evaluation of this phenomenon has been undertaken by W.-P. Funk, 'Toward a Linguistic Classification of the "Sahidic" Nag Hammadi Texts', *Acts of the Fifth International Congress of Coptic Studies: Washington, 12-15 August 1992*, ed. by T. Orlandi & D. W. Johnson (2 vols.; Rome: Centro Italiano Microfiches, 1993) 2, pp. 163-77.

16 See, e.g., P. Rousseau, *Pachomius: The Making of a Community in Fourth-century Egypt* (Berkeley: University of California Press, 1985).

17 A concise survey of the Coptic evidence (with specific reference to the Nag Hammadi Codices) is given by C. Scholten, 'Die Nag-Hammadi-Texte als Buchbesitz der Pachomianer', *Jahrbuch für Antike und Christentum* 31 (1988), 144-72 (esp. pp. 145-57; note the list of general references, p. 153 n. 61); see esp. also W. E. Crum, *Catalogue of the Coptic Manuscripts in the British Museum* (London: British Museum, 1905), ix-xvii; H. E. Winlock, W. E. Crum, H. G. Evelyn-White, *The Monastery of Epiphanius at Thebes* (2 vols.; Publications of the Metropolitan Museum of Art Egyptian Expedition 3-4; New York: Metropolitan Museum of Art, 1926) 1, pp. 186-208 ('Writing Materials' and 'Literature'; around Thebes c. 600); L. Depuydt, *Catalogue of Coptic Manuscripts in the Pierpont Morgan Library* (2 vols.; Corpus of Illuminated Manuscripts 4-5 [Oriental Series 1-2]; Louvain: Peeters, 1993) 1, pp. ciii-cxvi (esp. pp. cxii-cxvi; the Faiyum, esp. Hamuli and the scriptorium at Touton, c. 641-1000); on the library of the 'White Monastery' of Shenute see n. 18 below.

18 See, e.g., T. Orlandi, 'Un projet milanais concernant les manuscrits coptes du Monastère Blanc', *Muséon* 85 (1972), 403-13 (the project is now a part of the Corpus dei Manoscritti Copti Letterari, based in Rome: Orlandi, 'The Corpus dei Manoscritti Copti Letterari', *Computers and the Humanities* 24 [1990], 397-405); Emmel, 'Shenoute's Literary Corpus' (Ph.D. diss.; Yale University, 1993), 1-106.

19 Emmel, 'Recent Progress in Coptic Codicology and Paleography (1988-1992)', *Fifth International Congress of Coptic Studies* 1.41-3.

20 The liturgical character of the bulk of the surviving Coptic manuscripts has been emphasized especially by Orlandi: see, in sum, 'Literature, Coptic', *Coptic Encyclopedia* 5.1458-9; cf. H. Quecke, 'Zukunftschancen bei der Erforschung der koptischen Liturgie', *Future of Coptic Studies*, 194-6.

EARLY CHRISTIAN LIBRARIES

Bastiaan Van Elderen

THE EARLIEST REFERENCE TO A CHRISTIAN LIBRARY is likely to be found in 2 Tim. 4. 13 in the New Testament. In this passage Timothy is requested to bring with him some personal items. These include a cloak and some books. They are described as τὰ βιβλία μάλιστα αἱ μεμβράναι ('the books, above all the parchments' (New Revised Standard Version)). The term τὰ βιβλία is translated 'my scrolls' in the New International Version, a possible translation as in Rev. 6. 14 where τὸ βιβλίον is characterized as 'rolled up' (ἑλισσόμενον). The other term in 2 Tim. 4. 13 is αἱ μεμβράναι which is usually translated 'the parchments'. The Revised English Bible strikingly translates this term as 'notebooks' – as earlier suggested by T. C. Skeat.[1] This is an unlikely rendering inasmuch as parchment is a better grade of writing material and hence more expensive.[2] W. H. Hatch considered these to be 'parchment codices'.[3] In view of the qualifier, μάλιστα αἱ μεμβράναι, the term τὰ βιβλία in this passage must refer to documents that included codices or scrolls of good quality.

There is no indication of the contents of these books. However, given the nature of parchment it appears that the materials especially wanted contained significant literature – possibly biblical books. Undoubtedly these were Old Testament books (most likely in Greek) and perhaps even some earlier New Testament books, if the Pastoral Epistles are dated to the last quarter of the first century. In any case, the reference in 2 Tim. 4. 13 to a library or collection of books (undoubtedly codices) is the earliest allusion to a Christian library.

Tradition reports the origin of Christianity in Egypt in mid-first century through the work of Mark, the author of the second Gospel.[4] Although these details have not been historically verified, it can be safely concluded from some passing allusions in the New Testament that the Christian faith did come to Egypt in the first century. Egyptians were among those present in Jerusalem for the Feast of Pentecost that is reported in Acts 2. A eunuch from Ethiopia became a Christian as he journeyed homeward from Jerusalem and must have passed through Egypt (Acts 8. 26-39). The Alexandrian Jew, Apollos, had a rudimentary knowledge of the Jesus movement before he arrived in Ephesus (Acts 18. 24-6). Hence, it is not surprising that the earliest Christian libraries have been found in Egypt. A significant catalyst for this phenomenon is the dry climate in Egypt in which such materials have been preserved.

This paper will review some fragments of early Christian literature and then describe the three extensive libraries found in the Nile Valley: the Chester Beatty Papyri, the Nag Hammadi Library, and the Bodmer Library. In contrast to the Dead Sea Scrolls, these documents are written on papyrus and are codices. Most of the materials date from the second to the fourth century.

Bastiaan Van Elderen

1. FRAGMENTS OF EARLY CHRISTIAN LITERATURE

Among the thousands of papyri found in the Nile Valley during the past century there are numerous fragments of Christian literature. Portions of the text of the New Testament have been preserved on almost a hundred papyrus manuscripts and fragments,[5] most of which date from the third to the sixth century. In the textual criticism of the New Testament the papyrus witnesses are numbered in the order of their discovery and designated by the letter 'P'; e.g., P[45], P[47], P[75]. Because of their early date these papyri have become very important for the study and establishment of the New Testament text.[6]

A very important small papyrus fragment from Egypt is the John Rylands Papyrus, which is identified as P[52] in the collection of New Testament papyri. This fragment measures 2.5 inches by 3.5 inches in size. It contains a few verses from John 18. 31-3 on the recto and 18. 37-8 on the verso. This clearly indicates that this was a page of a codex. Although acquired in Egypt by B. P. Grenfell in 1920, it was not identified until 1934 by C. H. Roberts and dated by him in the first half of the second century, a date accepted by most palaeographers and textual critics.[7] This fragment is of great interest to students of the New Testament and early Christianity. The presence of the Gospel of John in Egypt in early second century points to a first-century date for the Gospel and the existence of the Christian movement in Egypt by the beginning of the second century. It also indicates the early use of the codex in Christian communities.

Most of these New Testament papyri cannot be identified as part of a library, since many are loose leaves and were acquired in collections of miscellaneous documents. However, two sets of New Testament papyri can be identified as parts of early Christian libraries of biblical literature: the Chester Beatty Papyri and the Bodmer Papyri (these also contain non-biblical documents). There were no biblical documents in a third library, the Nag Hammadi Papyri, which consisted of Gnostic documents.

2. THE CHESTER BEATTY PAPYRI

This important collection of papyrus manuscripts was found in the Nile Valley and purchased by Chester Beatty in the early 1930s. Most of the collection is housed in the Beatty Library and Museum of Oriental Art in Dublin. Thirty leaves of one of the codices (P[46]) are in the Hatcher Library of the University of Michigan in Ann Arbor. The provenance of this collection has not been precisely established. On the basis of his personal investigation in the early 1930s Carl Schmidt suggested that the find-spot was in the vicinity of At'fih (ancient Aphroditopolis) on the east bank of the Nile near Fayyum.[8] On the other hand, C. H. Roberts has suggested that the Beatty papyri are from the same provenance as the Bodmer papyri.[9]

This collection includes portions of eight Old Testament and fifteen New Testament books, two intertestamentary books and a homily by Melito, bishop of Sardis.

Published biblical texts of the Chester Beatty Papyri

Old Testament and related literature
   Genesis – two copies: 961[10] (44 leaves; early 4th century)
                     962 (22 leaves; late 3rd century)
   Numbers and Deuteronomy – 963 (33 leaves and portions of more; 2nd century)

Isaiah – 965 (portions of 27 leaves; early 3rd century)
Jeremiah – 966 (1 leaf; *c.* AD 200)
Ezekiel and Esther – 966 (16 leaves; late 3rd century)
Daniel – 968 (13 leaves; early 3rd century)
Ecclesiasticus – 964 (1½ leaves; 4th century)
Enoch and a homily by Melito – 8 leaves (4th/5th century)

New Testament
Gospels and Acts – P[45] (30 leaves; early 3rd century)
Pauline Epistles – P[46] (86 leaves; *c.* AD 200)
Revelation – P[47] (10 leaves; *c.* late 3rd century)

It is assumed that the materials in Dublin and Ann Arbor derive from a single provenance, possibly a church or monastery. This suggests that this provenance represents an assemblage or library of biblical literature. These manuscripts also indicate that various biblical books were being combined in a single codex. It is calculated that the manuscript of the Gospels and Acts (P[45]) originally consisted of about 110 leaves or 220 pages. P[46] was a single-quire codex consisting of 104 leaves. Interestingly, as a collection of the Pauline epistles it also included Hebrews (between Romans and 1 Corinthians) but did not have space for the Pastoral Epistles.

The Chester Beatty Papyri, given their antiquity, have played a very significant role in New Testament textual criticism since they are about 150 years older than existing New Testament manuscripts (such as Codex Vaticanus and Codex Sinaiticus). Similarly, they also reflect the development of the biblical canon; e.g., the fourfold Gospel collection and the Pauline corpus. A few decades later there was another important discovery which Bruce Metzger suggests was the most important discovery of New Testament manuscripts since the purchase of the Chester Beatty Papyri[11] – the Bodmer Papyri.[12] However, a few years before there was another significant discovery in Upper Egypt which we shall consider first: the Nag Hammadi Papyri.

3. THE NAG HAMMADI PAPYRI

The discovery of the Nag Hammadi[13] Papyri occurred when local peasants were looking for *sabach*, a soil mixture used as fertilizer, in the low desert at the base of the cliff face of the high desert. Mohammed Ali Samman Khalifah, while engaged in such a search in 1945 in the vicinity of Jebel et-Tarif, located east of Nag Hammadi, came upon a skeleton with which was buried a large jar containing thirteen codices. Today they are identified as the Nag Hammadi Library Codices or Gnostic Papyri Library.

As with the Chester Beatty Papyri described above, the route of these documents from Mohammed Ali to the Coptic Museum in Cairo, where they are now housed, was a tortuous one.[14] One codex (Codex I) was unsuccessfully marketed in the United States in 1949 and eventually in 1952 purchased by the Jung Institute, Zürich, Switzerland. As a result, the *Gospel of Truth* became one of the first documents of the collection to be published. In time most of the codices were acquired by the Egyptian Antiquities Organization. The Jung codex was returned to Cairo in late 1976.[15] All the codices have been disassembled and the leaves mounted between plexiglass plates and housed in the library of the Coptic Museum.

Bastiaan Van Elderen

The slow process of publication prompted the organization of the International Committee for the Nag Hammadi Codices in 1970. The work of this committee resulted in the publication of the *Facsimile Edition of the Nag Hammadi Codices.*[16]

In the 13 codices there are over 1150 surviving pages which contain 52 tractates, 6 of which are duplicates. Only 6 of these tractates were known before – hence, the Nag Hammadi Library contains 40 new texts: 30 fairly complete and 10 rather fragmentary. The documents are written in Coptic, although there are indications that some are translations of Greek originals. The library is dated paleographically to the fourth century and on the basis of dated writing on the *cartonnage* (papyrus fragments reused as reinforcement of the covers and spines of a codex).[17] Some archaeological evidence points likewise to the latter part of the fourth century.

Contents of the Nag Hammadi Library

Codex I
  1. The Prayer of the Apostle of Paul
  2. The Apocryphon of James
  3. The Gospel of Truth
  4. The Treatise on the Resurrection
  5. The Tripartite Tractate

Codex II
  1. The Apocryphon of John
  2. The Gospel of Thomas
  3. The Gospel of Philip
  4. The Hypostatis of the Archons
  5. On the Origin of the World
  6. The Exegesis on the Soul
  7. The Book of Thomas the Contender

Codex III
  1. The Apocryphon of John
  2. The Gospel of the Egyptians
  3. Eugnostos the Blessed
  4. The Sophia of Jesus Christ
  5. The Dialogue of the Savior

Codex IV
  1. The Apocryphon of John
  2. The Gospel of the Egyptians

Codex V
  1. Eugnostos the Blessed
  2. The Apocalypse of Paul
  3. The First Apocalypse of James
  4. The Second Apocalypse of James
  5. The Apocalypse of Adam

Codex VI
1. The Acts of Peter and the Twelve Apostles
2. The Thunder, Perfect Mind
3. Authoritative Teaching
4. The Concept of our Great Power
5. Plato, *Republic* 588B-589B
6. The Discourse on the Eighth and Ninth
7. The Prayer of Thanksgiving
8. Ascelepius

Codex VII
1. The Paraphrase of Shem
2. The Second Treatise of the Great Seth
3. Apocalypse of Peter
4. The Teachings of Silvanus
5. The Three Stelae of Seth

Codex VIII
1. Zostrianos
2. The Letter of Peter to Phillip

Codex IX
1. Melchizedek
2. The Thought of Norea
3. The Testimony of Truth

Codex X
1. Marsanes

Codex XI
1. The Interpretation of Knowledge
2. A Valentinian Exposition on Anointing, Baptism, Eucharist
3. Allogenes
4. Hypsiphrone

Codex XII
1. The Sentence of Sextus
2. The Gospel of Truth
3. Fragments

Codex XIII
1. Trimorphic Protennoia (Primal Thought)
2. On the Origin of the World

The various genres represented in the Nag Hammadi Library include gospels (not in the traditional sense, *vide infra*), apocalypses, prayers, acts, and apocrypha. All the documents in varying degrees reflect the Gnostic perspective. As a sizeable collection of Gnostic literature, this discovery has contributed significantly to the limited knowledge of Gnosticism – a heresy which greatly plagued the early Church, as shown by the anti-Gnostic polemic in the church fathers.

Perhaps the most well-known and popular document in the Nag Hammadi Library is the *Gospel of Thomas*. It is a collection of 114 sayings of Jesus. In contrast to the canonical Gospels, there is no narrative material in this document. Some of these sayings (*logia*) are identical with, or similar to, those in the canonical Gospels, while some are known in the literature of the early Church and others are new *logia* attributed to Jesus.[18] Greek papyri, found at Oxyrhynchus in the Nile Valley in the late 1800s and dated to the second century, also contain *logia* of Jesus. *Logia* in *P.Oxy.* 1, 654, and 655 appear in the same order in the Coptic *Gospel of Thomas*, indicating that the Coptic document is a fourth-century translation of a Greek original from about the middle of the second century. An ongoing debate centres on the question of authenticity – to what degree or extent are there authentic *logia* of Jesus in the *Gospel of Thomas*?[19]

Another 'gospel' in the Nag Hammadi Library is the *Gospel of Philip*. This is a collection of 127 *logia* of Jesus, purported to be revelations imparted by Jesus to a group (Hebrews) including Philip. This appears to be a Coptic version of a Greek original from the second century. The Gnostic influence in this document and its esoteric character are much more extensive than in the *Gospel of Thomas*. This is also true of most of the other documents in the collection.

As these documents began to be published, interest in the find-spot and its environment arose. However, political conditions in the Middle East during the 1960s and the early 1970s made the area inaccessible to foreigners. As conditions eased in the middle 1970s it became possible to mount an archaeological excavation in the area. Four seasons of digging in the area were conducted from 1975 to 1980 under the author's direction.[20] The first season concentrated on the area at the foot of Jebel et-Tarif where Mohammed Ali claimed that he made the discovery thirty years earlier. No conclusive evidence pinpointing the find-spot was uncovered. This suggests that the burial containing the codices was an isolated burial and not part of a cemetery or associated with any settlement.[21] Although no hard evidence regarding the find-spot was obtained, there is sufficient indication that the discovery was made in the general area of Jebel et-Tarif.[22]

In the succeeding seasons of the Nag Hammadi Excavations portions of the Pachomian monastic complex on the edge of the nearby village of Faw Qibli (ancient Pabau) were excavated. The remains of a very large fifth-century five-aisle basilica built by the disciples of Pachomius were uncovered. Underneath this structure the ruins of an earlier fourth-century church were identified.[23] The relationship of this Pachomian monastic complex to the Nag Hammadi Gnostic Papyri has been variously evaluated and will be discussed after a description of another major discovery of papyri in this area, the Bodmer Papyri.

4. THE BODMER PAPYRI

This large and very important collection of Greek and Coptic papyri was discovered in Upper Egypt in the early 1950s and subsequently acquired and taken out of the country by Martin Bodmer, who was then the vice-president of the International Red Cross. The Bodmer Library published the first of these papyri in 1954 (two rolls containing the Iliad, Books 5 and 6) and periodically in succeeding years published additional documents.

The term 'Bodmer Papyri' refers to documents now housed in six locations other than the Bodmer Library. Bodmer Papyri are found in the Chester Beatty Library (Dublin), the Palau-Ribes Collection (Barcelona), Duke University, the Vatican Library, the University of Mississippi, and the University of Cologne. It is questioned whether all these papyri in various locations are from a single collection. Some are of classical texts, whereas most are of biblical and Christian texts. The earlier uncertainty regarding the provenance of these documents further complicated any affirmation of their being a single collection. One can at least suggest that the biblical and Christian documents may derive from a single collection. The circumstances of the discovery appear to be similar to those of the Nag Hammadi Papyri – local peasants in search of *sabach* finding a jar in which documents were stored.

However, the provenance of these documents has been a complex problem. In his publication of *P.Bod.* I in 1954 V. Martin gave the provenance as Panopolis (Achmîm) because the two rolls of the Iliad were written on the verso of an administrative register from Panopolis (*P.Bod.* L). This provenance was also given with caution by Turner, later by Roberts, and a few years ago re-affirmed by Van Haelst.[24] However, there is evidence of such reuse of papyri occurring after transfer to another site.[25] Hence the earlier writings would not be an indicator of the provenance of the later writing. In the 1960s a provenance in the region of Thebes (modern Luxor) was suggested on the basis of features of the Coptic employed in some manuscripts. In the early 1970s a provenance near Nag Hammadi was proposed on the basis of information from an antiquities dealer involved in the sale of the collection. In 1984 R. Kasser located the provenance '*en Haute-Egypte, un peu à Assiout (Lycopolis) ou dans les environs immédiats de cette cité importante*'.[26]

New light on the provenance of the Bodmer Papyri came as a 'spin-off' of the Nag Hammadi Excavations conducted from 1975 to 1980 to investigate the find-spot and environs of the Nag Hammadi Papyri (see above). During the course of this work J. M. Robinson (chief investigator) and the author were told that there had been another major manuscript find in the area at about the same time as the discovery of the Nag Hammadi Papyri. Further investigation by Robinson determined that this other find was the Bodmer Collection, and the local informants suggested that the find-spot was located in the Wadi Sheikh Ali near Abu Mana, about seven miles east of Jebel et-Tarif. A survey of the area gave indication of Coptic occupation but no confirming evidence relating to the find-spot of these papyri. Nevertheless, on the basis of data accumulated by Robinson[27] it is evident that the Bodmer Papyri were found in the same general area as the Nag Hammadi Papyri.[28]

The biblical and Christian documents in the Bodmer Papyri form a large collection. This would indicate that this collection was a library in a church or monastery, rather than a private collection. Near the area of the find-spot suggested above is the large monastic complex of Pachomius on the edge of the modern village of Faw Qibli (ancient Pabau). As part of the Nag Hammadi Excavations, mentioned above, the large basilica of this Pachomian monastic complex was partially uncovered in the late 1970s.[29] This complex is located about three miles south-west of Jebel Abu Mana, the area suggested above as the find-spot of the Bodmer Papyri. The correspondence in these papyri involving leaders of the Pachomian monastic complex suggests that the library may have belonged originally to this monastery. Robinson[30] constructs the following scenario of the history of the monastery and its library. Founded in the fourth century, the monastery flourished in succeeding centuries and gave birth to numerous other monasteries in the area. During a period of decline, possibly in the seventh century as suggested by the latest papyri, the Pachomian library was buried (in jars) in the vicinity of Jebel Abu Mana. 'Perhaps these relics were buried for safe keeping in the period of decline following the imposition of Chalcedonian orthodoxy on the traditionally Monophysite order, as the dating of the latest material in the Seventh Century might suggest.'[31] This seventh century date for the burial of the papyri is indirectly supported by the *floruit* and decline of the basilica as shown in the excavation and the pottery chronology. The significance of the association of the Bodmer Papyri with the Pachomian monastery for the *Sitz im Leben* of the Nag Hammadi Papyri will be discussed below.

The Bodmer Papyri comprise a very large collection of manuscripts only part of which has been published. The library includes classical texts,[32] biblical and Christian texts, correspondence of monastic leaders, and documents relating to Panopolis (Achmîm). The list of papyri ranges from *P.Bod.* I to *P.Bod.* L, although they comprise 9 papyrus rolls and 29 codices (at least 22 of them are made of papyrus).

The announced and/or published texts of the Bodmer Papyri[33]

Classical texts (rolls except Menander text and Latin texts)
Iliad (Books 5 and 6) (*P.Bod.* I)
Iliad (fragments) (*P.Bod.* XLVIII)
Odyssey (Books 3 and 4) (Cologne Library)
Odyssey (fragments) (*P.Bod.* XLIX)
Menander, *Dyskolos* (*P.Bod.* IV)
Menander, *Samia* (*P.Bod.* XXV)
Menander, *Aspis* (*P.Bod.* XXVI)
Thucydides, *History* 6.1.1-2.6 (*P.Bod.* XXVII)
Satyr play involving Heracles and Atlas (*P.Bod.* XXVIII)
Latin texts including Cicero, *in Catilinam and Alcestis (Barcelona Codex)*
Achilleus Tatios (Cologne Library)
Scholia to the *Odyssey* (Cologne Library)
Greek grammar and Greco-Latin lexicon (Chester Beatty Library)
Greek grammar and Greco-Latin lexicon (Chester Beatty Library)

Old Testament and related literature
Genesis 1-4.2 (Coptic) (*P.Bod.* III)
Exodus 1-15 (Coptic) (*P.Bod.* XVI)
Deuteronomy 1-10 (Coptic) (*P.Bod.* XVIII)
Joshua 1-11, 22-24 (Coptic) (*P.Bod.* XXI)
Psalms 33 and 34 (Greek) (*P.Bod.* IX)
Psalms 17-118 (Greek) (*P.Bod.* XXIV)
Psalms 31, 26, 2 (Greek) (*P.Beatty* XIV = Rahlfs 2150)
Psalms 72, 76, 77, 82, 85 (Greek) (*P.Beatty* XIII = Rahlfs 2149)
Proverbs (Coptic) (*P.Bod.* VI)
Song of Songs (Greek on parchment) (*P.Bod.* XL)

Isaiah 47-66 (Coptic) (*P.Bod.* XXIII)

Jeremiah 40-52, Lamentations, Epistle of Jeremiah, Baruch 1-5 (Coptic) (*P.Bod.* XXII and Mississipi Coptic Cod.II)

Daniel (Coptic) (*P.Bod.* XLIV)

Daniel (Greek) (*P.Bod.* XLVI)

Jonah (Coptic) (*Crosby-Schøyen Codex*)

Susanna (Greek) (*P.Bod.* XLV)

Tobit 14.13-15 (Coptic) (*P.Bod.* XXI)

2 Maccabees (Coptic) (*Crosby-Schøyen Codex*)

11th Ode of Solomon (Greek) (*P.Bod.* XI)

New Testament

Matthew 14-28 (Coptic) (*P.Bod.* XIX)

Matthew 25f (Greek) (*P.Bod.* L) – P^{73} (7th century)

Luke 3-24 (Greek) (*P.Bod.* XIV) – P^{75} (*c.* AD 200)

Luke, Mark, John (Coptic) (*P. Palau Ribes* 181-3)

John (Greek) (*P.Bod.* II) – P^{66} (*c.* AD 200)

John (Coptic) (*P.Bod.* III)

Acts, James, 1,2 Peter, 1,2,3 John, Jude (Greek) (*P.Bod.* VII) – P^{74} (7th century)

Romans 1, 2 (Coptic) (*P.Bod.* XIX)

2 Corinthians (Coptic) (*P.Bod.* XLII)

1, 2 Peter (Greek) (*P.Bod.* VIII) – P^{72} (3rd century)

1 Peter (Coptic) (*Crosby-Schøyen Codex*)

Jude (Greek) (*P.Bod.* VII) – P^{72} (3rd century)

Christian literature

Protevangelium Jacobi (Greek) (*P.Bod.* V)

Apocryphal Correspondence of the Corinthians and Paul (3 Corinthians) (Greek) (*P.Bod.* X)

Acts of Paul (Coptic) (*P.Bod.* XLI)

Liturgical Hymn (Greek) (*P.Bod.* XII)

Liturgical Hymn (Coptic) (*Crosby-Schøyen Codex*)

Homily on the Passion by Melito (Greek) (*P.Bod.* XIII)

Homily on the Passion by Melito (Coptic) (*Crosby-Schøyen Codex*)

Homily for Easter Morning (Coptic) (*Crosby-Schøyen Codex*)

Apology of Phileas (Greek) (*P.Bod.* XX)

Vision of Dorotheos (Greek) (*P.Bod.* XXIX)

Shepherd of Hermas 1.1-21.4 (Visions 1-3) (Greek) (*P.Bod.* XXXVIII)

Miscellaneous poems about Abraham, Jesus, the Just, the Murder of Abel by Cain (Greek) (*P.Bod.* XXX-XXXVII)

An Apocryphon (Coptic) (*P.Bod.* XLIII)

Psalmus Responsorius (Latin) (*Barcelona Codex*)

Correspondence

Official letters (all rolls except one) written by leaders (Pachomius, Theodore, Horsiensios) of the Pachomian monastic movement (*P.Bod.* XXXIX; others in the Chester Beatty Library and Cologne Library).

Bastiaan Van Elderen

Documents from Panopolis (Achmim)
    Administrative register of Panopolis (*P.Bod.* L)
    Tax receipts of AD 339-47 from Panopolis (Chester Beatty Library)

The textual and literary significance of the Bodmer Papyri is very great. The New Testament manuscripts, especially P[66] and P[75], have had a major influence in the study of the text of the New Testament. These manuscripts are the oldest substantial copies of Luke and John and their general agreement with Codex Vaticanus has enhanced the value of its text tradition.[34] *P.Bod.* XIV (P[75]) occasioned the abandonment of the Westcott-Hort theory of Western non-interpolation in Nestlé-Aland, *Novum Testamentum Graece* (hereafter NA[26]) and Aland et al., *Greek New Testament* (GNT)[2] and continued in NA[27] and subsequent editions of GNT. Being about 150 years older than Codex Vaticanus and Codex Sinaiticus, these manuscripts have supported one or both of them in the omission of some rather familiar passages: the woman taken in adultery (7. 53-8. 11), Jesus's agony in Gethsemane (Luke 22. 43f), and Jesus's prayer on the cross (Luke 23. 34). P[72] is a valuable witness to the text of 1 and 2 Peter and Jude by virtue of its antiquity.[35]

The Bodmer Papyri have also contributed significantly to early Christian literature. In the collection are some much earlier copies of known documents and some new documents. A popular document in the early Church was the *Protevangelium Jacobi* (PJ) which describes the birth and early life of Mary and the birth of Jesus. Most scholars judge that this document originated in the second half of the second century. It had wide circulation in the early Church, especially in Syria and Egypt. Writers, such as Origen, Clement of Alexandria, Justin Martyr, Hippolytus, were acquainted with it. The text of this document is found in about a hundred manuscripts, mostly in Greek and dating from the tenth century to the fifteenth century. In the early 1900s a few older fragments were discovered in Egypt. This document is found in the Bodmer Papyri with the title *Nativity of Mary, Apocalypse of James* (Γενεσις Μαριας, αποκαλυψις Ιακωβ). This manuscript, *P.Bod.* V, consists of 49 pages and is dated to the third century. Most titles of the document associate it with James (Ιακωβ) and he is so identified in it (PJ 25. 1). He is considered to be the (half-) brother of Jesus (cf. Mark 6. 3 = Matthew 13. 55) who perhaps alludes to himself in PJ 17. 2. This pseudonymous document, originating in the second century, had as its chief purpose the vindication and veneration of Mary, the mother of Jesus, and the defence of her (perpetual) virginity. Her innocence, evident in her unusual birth, early life and temple service, is clearly demonstrated in the account of her relation to Joseph and the unusual birth of Jesus that embellishes and amplifies the rather simple and sparse accounts in the New Testament (Matt. 1 and Luke 1 and 2). H. R. Smid describes the author's aim as 'the glorification of the Virgin Mary' from three aspects: the apologetic, the biographical, and the dogmatic.[36]

Another early Christian writing found in the Bodmer Papyri is *The Apocryphal Correspondence of the Corinthians and the Apostle Paul*. This Bodmer manuscript is dated to the third century and is the earliest text of the document. This work is often referred to as '3 Corinthians' and was given canonical status in parts of the Armenian church. It begins with a letter written by the Corinthians to Paul at Philippi in which they ask for advice to deal with certain Gnostic heretics who had come to Corinth. Paul's response is in the form of a letter in which he refutes these false teachings. The discovery of this document with its strong anti-Gnostic motif close to the Pachomian monastic complex and the place where the Nag Hammadi Gnostic Papyri were found has renewed great interest in this literature and the role of Gnosticism in the early church.[37]

Another genre of literature in the early church was martyrologies – documents venerating particular saints and serving as inspiration and models to other Christians. One such martyr was Phileas, bishop of Thmuis, who died between AD 304 and 306. The first Greek version of the *Acts (Apology) of Phileas* was in the Bodmer Papyri (*P.Bod.* XX). It was known in eight Latin manuscripts dating from the ninth to the thirteenth centuries. The Bodmer version is dated to the fourth century. Subsequent to the publication of the *P.Bod.* XX in 1964 by V. Martin, A. Pietersma identified seventeen unpublished papyrus fragments in the Chester Beatty Library in Dublin as part of a codex containing the *Acta of Phileas* (P.Chester Beatty XV). In a study of these Greek versions and the Latin tradition Pietersma observes:

Alongside of P.Bodmer XX we have not only a remarkably stable and homogeneous Latin tradition, but P.Chester Beatty XV now gives us also the Greek *Vorlage* of that tradition, a *Vorlage* which is contemporaneous with the justly famous Bodmer text; and both Greek versions were written within living memory of the death of Phileas bishop of Thmuis.[38]

The codex containing *P.Bod.* XXIX-XXXVIII has been named *Codex Visionum*. The first document (*P.Bod.* XXIX) is a hitherto unknown text, entitled *Vision of Dorotheos*, which has been published by Hurst et al.[39] This is a poem with 343 preserved hexameter verses in Homeric style. The manuscript is dated to the fourth or early fifth century. The narrator reports his vision in a heavenly palace in the presence of Christ, Gabriel, and other angels, where he is judged for having left his post as guard at the gate and entered an inner chamber. Returning to his post after intervention with God by Christ and Gabriel, he is baptized and the poem concludes with some moral lessons. This poem is of unusual interest as a literary production that uses a classical style and meter and as an indication of the moral and theological thinking in the late fourth century. Further poems that follow the *Vision of Dorotheos* are about Abraham (30 verses), the righteous (δικαιοι) (171 verses), the Lord Jesus (25 verses), the murder of Abel by Cain (19 verses), and the Lord (27 verses). There are also a second poem about the murder of Abel (69 verses), another poem (title incomplete) (79 verses), and a fragmentary hymn. The last document in this codex is the *Shepherd of Hermas* (first three visions) (22 pages), published as *P.Bod.* XXXVIII by Carlini and Kasser.[40] This text and the two copies of Melito's *Homily on the Passover* have provided valuable earlier witnesses to these important pieces of early Christian literature and theological reflection.

The above survey of the Bodmer Papyri indicates how important this major library, the largest early Christian library discovered thus far, is for New Testament and early Christian studies. Unfortunately, the full importance of this discovery for these disciplines has not yet been fully realized. This is largely due to the discovery of another library, the Nag Hammadi Papyri already discussed, that took place about the same time and in the same area and to their occupation of the centre stage in these studies that resulted partly from sensational interpretations of some of its documents.

Bastiaan Van Elderen

The Nag Hammadi Papyri and the Bodmer Papyri were therefore discovered in the area east of Nag Hammadi along the cliff face of the high desert abutting the low desert in places about seven miles apart – Jebel et Tarif and Jebel Abu Mana, respectively. In the green belt between the Nile River and the low desert the ruins of the Pachomian monastic complex are located – a few miles directly south of Jebel Abu Mana. Given the size of these libraries and the magnitude of the Pachomian monastic complex, the question arises as to the relationship of these three entities located so near each other.

The size of the Nag Hammadi Library has led some to posit the presence of a large Gnostic movement in Upper Egypt and by extension among Christians in the fourth century. However, such a judgement must be qualified in view of the absence in the area of any community, settlement, or even cemetery that can be identified with such a movement. Others have attempted to identify the Nag Hammadi Papyri with the Pachomian monastery either as a place of production or as part of the library of the monastery and a reflection of its teachings. This debate has centred largely on the interpretation of the contents of the cartonnage of Codex VII,[41] referred to above. The limitations of reused written materials for the determining of the provenance of documents has been noted above. In the light of the orthodox character of the Pachomian movement as reflected in the writings related to it and also illustrated in the association of Pachomius with Athanasius, who at one time hid in the monastery, the Gnosticism of the Nag Hammadi Papyri would hardly have been compatible with the Pachomian movement. This surely would have been true when Athanasius's Pascal Letter of AD 367 limiting the 'canonical' literature reached the monastery. It is possible that thereafter one or more monks with contraband literature were expelled from the the monastery and lived in the nearby desert area. And according to an ancient practice regarding the burial of heretics, their library was buried with them in their grave.

This dissociation of the Pachomian monastic movement from the Nag Hammadi Library is further confirmed by the association of the Bodmer Library with the monastery, as concluded above. The contents of the Bodmer Library are in the orthodox tradition – not only in its inclusion of biblical books but also in its literature with a clear polemic against Gnosticism, for example *The Apocryphal Correspondence between the Corinthians and the Apostle Paul*, which specifically refutes basic tenets of the Gnostics.

The collocation of the Pachomian monastic movement, the Bodmer Library, and the Nag Hammadi Library within a few miles of each other presents an interesting picture of early Christianity and related movements in this area of Upper Egypt and some challenging and significant problems of integration and historical sequence. It certainly urges further investigation of this area of Upper Egypt. Literary sources refer to the presence of numerous monastic communities in this area which developed from the Pachomian centre at Pabau. A *desideratum* is a complete archaeological survey of this area and additional excavation of promising sites. Unfortunately, at present this is hardly possible for security reasons. However, current excavations of early Christian monasteries and churches in Lower Egypt, such as the Wadi Natrun Excavations sponsored by the Scriptorium and Calvin Theological Seminary, should contribute to the larger picture of the development of Christianity and countermovements in Egypt.

5. CONCLUDING OBSERVATIONS

The huge collection of both documentary and literary papyri discovered in the Nile Valley in the past century has illustrated the extensive writing activity in the early centuries of our era. Furthermore, early Christians were involved in extensive literary activity as demonstrated in the three libraries discussed above – the Chester Beatty Papyri, the Nag Hammadi Papyri, and the Bodmer Papyri. They were engaged not only in the copying of biblical books but also in the composing of a new body of literature. Given the distribution of these materials, this literature was undoubtedly circulating in the churches and monasteries throughout Egypt – and obviously in a similar fashion in other parts of the Mediterranean world. The literacy and literary activities of the early Christians have not always been adequately recognized or fully appreciated in the past.

A nagging and intriguing question remains. Are there more libraries as described above to be found? Perhaps. In any event, these discoveries of the past half century have contributed significantly to studies relating to the text of the Bible. As a result, we have made substantial progress in establishing the text of the Bible. Also, our study of early Christian literature has been greatly enhanced both by earlier copies of known documents and by copies of ones hitherto unknown. Thus, both biblical and early Christian studies have been enriched in a way unparalleled in any century before.

NOTES

1 T. C. Skeat, '"Especially the Parchments": A Note on 2 Timothy IV.13', *Journal of Theological Studies* 30 (1979), 173-7.

2 A. T. Hanson, *The Pastoral Epistles* (Grand Rapids: Eerdmans, 1982), 159.

3 Cited in Bauer, Arndt, Gingrich & Danker, *A Greek-English Lexicon of the New Testament and other Early Christian Literature*, s.v., μεμβράνα. Cf. Bauer-Aland[6], s.v.

4 B. A. Pearson ('Earliest Christianity in Egypt: Some Observations' in *The Roots of Egyptian Christianity*, ed. by B. A. Pearson & J. A. Goehring; Philadelphia: Fortress, 1986, 132-57) provides a detailed review and evaluation of this 'Mark legend'.

5 All of these are from codices, except four (P[12,13,18,22]), which are from scrolls (K. Aland & B. Aland, *The Text of the New Testament* (2nd edn; trans. by E. F. Rhodes; Grand Rapids: Eerdmans, 1989), 102).

6 A striking phenomenon is that all the New Testament books are attested on papyrus except 1 and 2 Timothy (perhaps an accident of non-discovery). Of those attested, all except 2 and 3 John are found on 'early' (e.g., prior to the fifth century) papyri (Aland & Aland, *Text*, 85).

7 B. M. Metzger, *The Text of the New Testament* (3rd edn; New York: Oxford University Press, 1992), 38-9.

8 C. Schmidt, 'Die neuesten Bibelfunde aus Ägypten', *Zeitschrift fur dir neutestamentliche Wissenschaft* 30 (1931) 292; 32 (1933) 225.

9 C. H. Roberts, *Manuscript Society, and Belief in Early Christian Egypt* (London: Oxford University Press, 1979), 28, n. 1.

10 This and similar numbers are those assigned in the Rahlfs register of Greek Old Testament manuscripts.

11 Metzger, *Text*, 32.

12 Regarding the Bodmer Papyri, Kurt and Barbara Aland affirm that P[66] 'finally provided the key to a full appreciation of the Chester Beatty Papyri and of the New Testament text in the late second century' and that '[o]ne of the main pillars supporting the dominant theory of

New Testament textual history was ... demolished' with the discovery of P^{75} (Aland & Aland, *Text*, 87).

13 Nag Hammadi is a small city located about 350 miles south of Cairo on the south side (left bank) of the Nile River and about 30 miles north of Luxor (as the crow flies). The sharp bend of the Nile forms a wide stretch of fertile land where the chief crop today is sugar cane. Across the Nile to the east of Jebel et-Tarif is the Dishna Plain and the town of Dishna. Locally, the Bodmer Papyri are often referred to as the Dishna Papers.

14 J. M. Robinson, 'The Discovering and Marketing of Coptic Manuscripts: The Nag Hammadi Codices and the Bodmer Papyri', *The Roots of Egyptian Christianity* (ed. by B. A. Pearson & J. A. Goehring; Philadelphia: Fortress, 1986) 2-25.

15 The binding is now in the collection of Martin Schøyen, Spikkestad, Norway.

16 12 vols (Leiden: Brill, 1972-84). English translations of the texts can be found in *The Nag Hammadi Library in English* (rev. edn; ed. by J. M. Robinson & M. Meyer; San Francisco: Harper & Row, 1990). Some texts with related documents are translated by B. Layton (*The Gnostic Scriptures* (Garden City: Doubleday, 1987)).

17 These materials are published in *The Facsimile Edition of the Nag Hammadi Codices: Cartonnage* (Leiden: Brill, 1979) and in J. W. B. Barns, G. M. Browne, & J. C. Shelton, *Nag Hammadi Codices: Greek and Coptic Papyri from the Cartonnage of the Covers* (Nag Hammadi Studies XVI; Leiden: Brill, 1981).

18 This document must not be confused with the Greek *Gospel of Thomas* which describes the boyhood of Jesus and miracles he performed to demonstrate his divinity.

19 Some, as the members of the Jesus Seminar, have given major status to it, often at the expense of the canonical Gospels and to the neglect of historical data and critical issues relating to the various documents.

20 J. M. Robinson & B. Van Elderen, *Institute for Antiquity and Christianity Report 1972-1980* (Claremont: Institute for Antiquity and Christianity, 1981) 37-44.

21 A complicating factor in this investigation was the fact that Mohammed Ali had not been back to the area for thirty years since the discovery because of a blood-feud between his village and a neighbouring village near Jebel et-Tarif. Given the nature of the terrain and possible changes in the landscape occasioned by wind-erosion and landslides, the topographical features in 1975 could hardly jog his memory. In fact, fifteen years later when he returned to the area with the author he indicated a place about a mile farther east as the findspot.

22 James M. Robinson has conducted extensive interviews with participants in the discovery, with agents in the initial handling and marketing, and with the officials involved in the final acquisition of the papyri by the Egyptian Antiquities Organization. His reconstruction of the course of events can be found in Robinson, *The Facsimile Edition of the Nag Hammadi Codices* (Leiden: Brill, 1984), Introduction Volume, 37-44; 'Discovering', 2-25, although R. Kasser and M. Krause have reservations regarding certain items in this reconstruction (Robinson, 'Discovering', 3, n. 1).

23 *Institute Report*, 38-44.

24 E. G. Turner, *Greek Papyri: An Introduction* (Oxford: Clarendon, 1968) 52-3; Roberts, *Manuscript*, 28, n. 1, 89; J. van Haelst in A. Carlini & R. Kasser, *Papyrus XXXVIII: II Pastore (Ia-IIIa visione) Erma* (Cologny-Geneva: Fondation Martin Bodmer, 1991) 105, n. 5. In view of the evidence discovered by J. M. Robinson (discussed below), Turner later retracted his earlier suggestion that the Bodmer Papyri came from Panopolis (Achmîm) (Robinson, 'Discovering', 2).

25 J. M. Robinson, *The Pachomian Monastic Library at the Chester Beatty Library and Bibliothèque Bodmer* (IAC Occasional Papers 19; Claremont: Institute for Antiquity and Christianity, 1990) 22.

26 Carlini & Kasser, *Papyrus Bodmer XXXVIII*, 105, n. 5.

27 For an account of the serpentine route of the Bodmer Papyri from discoverer to publisher, cf. Robinson, 'Discovering', 2-25; *Pachomian Monastic Library*, 6-16. Kasser, on the other hand, dismisses Robinson's conclusion as '*basée, pour l'essentiel, sur des informations (?) de valeur excessivement faible recueillies sur place (?) quelque trente ans apres les "événements" (anecdotiques) dont elle fait était*' (Carlini & Kasser, *Papyrus Bodmer XXXVIII*, 106, n. 5).

28 The significance of this proximity will be discussed below.

29 Robinson & Van Elderen, *Institute Report*, 37-44.

30 *Pachomian Monastic Library*, 1-6.

31 *Pachomian Monastic Library*, 6.

32 It has been suggested that these classical texts were added to the Christian codices by the discoverers as similar codices (A. Hurst et al., *Papyrus Bodmer XXIX*, 7), whereas J. M. Robinson thinks that they may have come to the library as gifts from the outside, contributed perhaps by prosperous persons joining the monastery where this library was located (*Pachomian Monastic Library*, 4-5).

33 For a detailed inventory of this collection as of 1990, cf. Robinson, *Pachomian Monastic Library*, 19-21. An inventory with bibliography of the Bodmer Papyri can be found in R. Kasser, 'Bodmer Papyri', *Coptic Encylopedia* (ed. by Aziz S. Atiya; New York: Macmillan, 1991) VIII, 48-53.

34 Aland & Aland, *Text*, 87.

35 Aland & Aland, Text, 87-93.

36 H. R. Smid, *Protevangelium Jacobi* (Assen: Van Gorcum, 1965) 14-19.

37 Scholarly opinion is divided on the question of the origin of this document, because it is also found in the *Acts of Paul*. Was it an independent work which was later included in the *Acts of Paul* or was it originally part of the *Acts of Paul* and later separated?

38 A. Pietersma, *The Acts of Phileas, Bishop of Thmuis* (Cahiers d'Orientalisme VII; Geneva: Cramer, 1984) 29.

39 A. Hurst, O. Reverdin, & J. Rudhardt, *Papyrus Bodmer XXIX: Vision de Dorothéos* (Cologny-Geneva: Fondation Martin Bodmer, 1984).

40 *Papyrus Bodmer XXXVIII* (1991).

41 For a summary of the discussion, cf. S. R. Llewelyn & R. A. Kearsley, *New Documents Illustrating Early Christianity* (Macquarie: Macquarie University, 1992) VI, 182-5.

THE CREATION OF THE GREAT CODICES

Thomas S. Pattie

ON 16 FEBRUARY 310 PAMPHILUS WAS MARTYRED IN PALESTINE; three months earlier, on 13 November, Antoninus the Confessor met the same fate. While in prison awaiting their call to martyrdom they corrected against the Hexapla of Origen a manuscript of a Bible which began at 1 Kingdoms (1 Samuel) and ended with Esther, and Pamphilus added autograph notes at the ends of 2 Esdras and Esther. Some two or three hundred years later, presumably in Caesarea in Palestine, parts of the Codex Sinaiticus were collated against the manuscript corrected by Pamphilus and Antoninus.[1] The shorter of these two notes, at the end of 2 Esdras, reads as follows:

Ἀντεβλήθη πρὸς παλαιώτατον λίαν ἀντίγραφον δεδιορθωμένον χειρὶ τοῦ ἁγίου μάρτυρος Παμφίλου ὅπερ ἀντίγραφον πρὸς τῷ τέλει ὑποσημείωσις τις ἰδιόχειρος αὐτοῦ ὑπέκειτο ἔουσα οὕτως Μετελήώμφθη καὶ διορθώθη πρὸς τὰ ἔξαπλα Ὠριγένους Ἀντωνῖνος ἀντέβαλεν. Πάμφιλος διόρθωσα.

The longer note at the end of 2 Esdras adds the details 'in prison', and that the Bible began 'at the first book of Kingdoms and ended at Esther'.

The Bible that Pamphilus and Antoninus knew was not a single volume, but a boxful of smaller books, all codices and not rolls. This explains why the three ancient codices[2] have different contents (Vaticanus [B] has none of the books of Maccabees, Sinaiticus [ℵ] has the first and fourth, and Alexandrinus [A] has all four), in different order (in the Old Testament Vaticanus ends with Ezekiel and Daniel, Sinaiticus ends with Ecclesiastes and the Song of Songs, and Alexandrinus ends with Wisdom and Ecclesiasticus), and their textual value varies from book to book, e.g. Vaticanus is excellent for the Gospels, not so good for the rest of the New Testament, good in Ezekiel and rather disappointing in Isaiah.

The surviving manuscripts of earlier date are generally quite small. The largest could have held the four gospels, and a particularly celebrated one could have been the trigger that ensured the success of the codex.[3] Even an exception such as the Epistle to the Hebrews confirms the rule, because it was written on the back of a roll containing an epitome of Livy in Latin.[4]

It may be convenient at this point to list the surviving contents of B, ℵ and A (hyphenating the Minor Prophets):

B: (Old Testament) Genesis, Exodus, Leviticus, Numbers, Deuteronomy, Joshua, Judges, Ruth, 1-4 Kingdoms, 1-2 Chronicles, 1-2 Esdras, Psalms, Proverbs, Ecclesiastes, Song of Solomon, Job, Wisdom, Sirach, Esther, Judith, Tobit, Hosea-Amos - Micah - Joel - Obadiah - Jonah - Nahum - Habakkuk - Zephaniah - Haggai-Zechariah-Malachi, Isaiah, Jeremiah, Baruch, Lamentations, Epistle of Jeremiah, Ezekiel, Daniel.

(New Testament) Matthew, Mark, Luke, John, Acts, James, 1-2 Peter, 1-3 John, Jude, Romans, 1-2 Corinthians, Galatians, Ephesians, Philippians, 1-2 Thessalonians, Hebrews.

א: (Old Testament) Genesis [], Numbers[], 1 Chronicles, 2 Esdras, Esther, Tobit, Judith, 1 Maccabees, 4 Maccabees, Isaiah, Jeremiah, Lamentations[], Joel-Obadiah-Jonah-Nahum-Habakkuk-Zephaniah-Haggai-Zechariah-Malachi, Psalms, Proverbs, Ecclesiastes, Song of Songs, Wisdom, Sirach, Job.
(New Testament) Matthew, Mark, Luke, John, Romans, 1-2 Corinthians, Galatians, Ephesians, Philippians, Colossians, 1-2 Thessalonians, Hebrews, 1-2 Timothy, Titus, Philemon, Acts, James, 1-2 Peter, 1-3 John, Jude, Revelation of John, Barnabas, Hermas.

A: (Old Testament) Genesis, Exodus, Leviticus, Numbers, Deuteronomy, Joshua, Judges, Ruth, 1-4 Kingdoms, 1-2 Chronicles, Hosea-Amos-Micah-Joel-Obadiah-Jonah-Nahum-Habakkuk-Zephaniah-Haggai-Zechariah-Malachi, Isaiah, Jeremiah, Baruch, Lamentations, Epistle of Jeremiah, Ezekiel, Daniel, Esther, Tobit, Judith, 1-2 Esdras, 1-4 Maccabees, *Psalms, Odes, Job, Proverbs, Ecclesiastes, Song of Solomon, Wisdom, Sirach.
(New Testament) Matthew, *Mark, *Luke, *John, Acts, James, 1-2 Peter, 1-3 John, Jude, 1-2 Corinthians, Galatians, Ephesians, Philippians, Colossians, 1-2 Thessalonians, Hebrews, 1-2 Timothy, Titus, Philemon, Revelation, 1-2 Clement.

*Note that in A Psalms are preceded by the Epistle of Athanasius and Hypotheses to each Psalm, and Mark, Luke, and John are preceded by capitula.[5]

For a thousand years the roll was the acceptable format for 'proper' books, that is for Homer, Plato, Euripides, and Thucydides. The codex was at first considered appropriate only for rough note-books. Thus we learn that Julius Caesar used the codex to write up his campaign notes: it was the proper medium for rough drafts, or for commentaries on Virgil and Homer (and if the motor car had been invented, for car-manuals).[6] Actually several small codices have survived from as early as the second century, including the Paeans of Pindar on papyrus, Demosthenes on parchment, and a large-paged papyrus codex of Lollianus' romance, the Phoinikika,[7] but literary codices are far outnumbered by rolls until the fourth century. Many theories have been put forward for the supersession of the roll by the codex,[8] e.g., a codex was more compendious or easier to consult or to carry or to conceal, or parchment was cheaper than papyrus (but early papyrus codices were well spaced and papyrus was not expensive). T. C. Skeat has written a number of articles demonstrating that the roll was rather more convenient to use than we in our ignorance suppose. It may have been no more than a slow change of fashion in which the Christians were in the van. What is beyond doubt is that the Christians adopted the codex completely and very early.

With the change of format there followed a change of material. Whereas books in roll and codex form used to be written on papyrus – made from the pith of a reed that grew extensively in Egypt, and still grows wild in Uganda – books began to be written on parchment, animal skins washed, stretched, tawed with alum (not tanned like leather), and polished. By the fourth century parchment was an acceptable medium for fine books. It is probably the change from papyrus to parchment that is referred to in Jerome's brief biography of Euzoius. He says that the volumes in the celebrated library of Origen and Pamphilus at Caesarea, which had become damaged, were replaced by copies on parchment (Euzoius ... corruptam iam bibliothecam Origenis et Pamphili in membranis instaurare conatus).[10] Supply was seasonal, as skins did not become available until the autumn when the animals were killed. On the other hand, if the supply of papyrus, which came exclusively from Egypt, was interrupted, parchment could be made anywhere where there was an abundance of animals.

We can catch glimpses of stages in the development of the codex. Some early codices are single-gathering codices, entailing a marked difference in width between the outer folios and the inner folios. Later examples have several gatherings of various numbers of folios, permitting a larger book.[11] Gatherings of eight leaves became the norm and remained so until the introduction of the glued paperback (the so-called 'perfect' binding) in the 1950s.

These changes amounted to a revolution in the technology of book production, which coincided with the triumph of Christianity. After so many Bibles had been burnt in the Diocletianic and other persecutions, in AD 331 the Emperor Constantine wrote to Eusebius, Bishop of Caesarea, ordering fifty parchment Bibles written by skilled calligraphers for his new foundations in Constantinople.[12] And so it was done: Eusebius reports 'we dispatched them in richly worked containers three- and four-fold' ἐν πολυτελῶς ἠσκημένοις τεύεσι τρισσὰ καὶ τετρασσὰ διαπεμψάντων ἡμῶν.[13] It is not clear what three- and four-fold mean: in three or four columns? in three or four volumes? in batches three or four at a time? At any rate this commission encouraged the new technology. Now it was possible to make huge books, books big enough to hold the whole Bible. It was now possible to make very large pages with wide margins, a feature new in parchment but very old in papyrus. We also find Virgil, Cicero, and Homer in fine codices.[14]

Not everything is new. Papyrus manuscripts of some pretension often have narrow columns, and so have two of the three great biblical codices.[15] Whereas Alexandrinus has two columns of 87 mm throughout, Vaticanus has three columns of 53 mm, and Sinaiticus has four columns of 52 mm, except for the 'poetical' books, Psalms, Job, Proverbs, Ecclesiastes, Song of Solomon, Wisdom, Sirach, Psalms of Solomon, and Lamentations, in which Vaticanus has two columns of 88 mm and Sinaiticus has two columns of 115-120 mm. Sinaiticus has more columns than Vaticanus because it has bigger pages: Sinaiticus measures 380 mm high × 340 wide, Vaticanus 270 mm high × 260 mm wide. The nearly square format is a feature of early codices, but is occasionally found in later manuscripts, e.g., the copy of the Utrecht Psalter (London, British Library, Harley MS 603) written in Latin in England at the beginning of the eleventh century which measures about 370 × 310 mm with three columns about 65 mm wide, each containing 18-23 letters. Alexandrinus, which measures 320 × 270 mm, has two columns throughout: perhaps narrow columns had temporarily gone out of fashion. Nevertheless the narrow-column style lasted for centuries in manuscripts of some pretension. A walk round the British Library's gallery of illuminated manuscripts revealed a Latin Gospel lectionary written about 1508 (BL, Royal MS 2 B.xii) with two columns 55 mm wide each containing 13-15 letters. The three-column form is quite rare, and fits a square page rather well. Royal MS 1 D.ii, a Bible containing Ruth, 1-4 Kingdoms, 1-2 Chronicles, 2 Esdras, Esther, Maccabees, and a second Esther, in a Lucianic text, has three columns on fols 81-112.

The earliest codices, on papyrus or parchment, are not ruled: they have no guides for writing. All three of the great codices show a dramatic innovation, perhaps borrowed from Jewish scribal tradition: they are measured off, pricked, and ruled to guide the writing. In all three manuscripts there are single vertical bounding lines delimiting the columns of the writing area. The horizontal lines designed for guiding the lines of the text (the letters are written *on* the line, not pendant, or hanging from the line, as in later Greek minuscule manuscripts) are ruled in more complicated ways. A few fine manuscripts are ruled in such a way that the text is written between two horizontal lines, e.g., the Freer Psalms, 'N' a purple gospels of the sixth century, and Codex Augusteus of Virgil.[16] Sinaiticus and Alexandrinus are ruled from the inner edge (the 'gutter') to the outer margin. One of the ruling types in Vaticanus is said in Gregory's *Textkritik* to do the same, but the facsimile of 1904-7 suggests that the ruling was drawn beyond the vertical bounding lines, but not as far as the edge.[17] This type is not ruled every line, but every other line, with sometimes the first five and the last two lines drawn each line, or other variants. The other type of ruling is ruled every line strictly within the columns. Later manuscripts are ruled in very complicated patterns, as illustrated in Leroy.[18]

Alexandrinus and Sinaiticus are ruled roughly every other line, but the exact pattern varies considerably. The pattern in which the lines are ruled from edge to edge is described by Leroy as 00A2 or 00A4 (the last digit indicates the number of columns). Pages in which alternate lines are ruled would be described as x 00A2, etc., but many of the pages do not fit any pattern that Leroy gives. Other early manuscripts show the same ruling pattern, such as BL, Add. MS 17210 (Homer, fifth-sixth century) and Add. MS 17211 (Luke). Of these, the Homer is ruled in one long column (00A1), the Luke in two columns (00A2) of about 52 mm. Both Homer and Luke are palimpsests, re-used for a Syriac patristic work: Severus of Antioch against the 'impious John Grammaticus'.

Although the majority of the Bible is in prose, and therefore written continuously, a substantial part is in verse, such as Psalms, Proverbs, Job, etc. These books are written in 'verse-units' which are much longer than the short lines of the prose books. In Vaticanus and Sinaiticus the pages of the poetical books are ruled in two columns instead of the usual three or four, but even so a single line is too short for the verse-units, and two extra verticals in each column are ruled for the indented second and subsequent lines of a verse-unit. These extra lines are ruled on the same side of the leaf, but only the left indent is used for each page.

The production of a large fine book on parchment required several hundred animal skins. A gathering of eight folios became the norm as one animal skin produced one gathering of eight folios of an average sized book. This is most clearly demonstrated in a number of much later Latin manuscripts in the Bibliothèque Royale in Brussels, where the gatherings have been incompletely cut after folding.[19] There would be 32 gatherings of eight in a book of 256 average-sized folios, that is, 32 sheep. An average book has many flaws in the parchment when wounds in the skin have expanded when the skin was stretched. Even a fine manuscript like Vaticanus has many flaws of this nature, including a significant number in the text area, that force the scribe to write around the holes. Sinaiticus has many fewer flaws and most were repaired before the text was inscribed. Its pages are very large: even after trimming they measure 380×340 mm, and before trimming perhaps 400×360 mm. A sheet of two folios would then have measured 400×720 mm, and one sheep, smaller than modern domestic sheep, might have produced enough parchment for only one sheet, taking into account the need to trim off the imperfections at the edges. In that case Sinaiticus, which seems originally to have had 730 folios, would require the perfect skins of 365 sheep or goats. The labour involved in the scraping, washing, stretching, and polishing would have been substantial.

THE CODEX VATICANUS

It is unknown where any of the three great codices were written. Vaticanus is thought by some to have been written in Egypt. Certainly its text of the gospels and Acts is closely related to the text found in manuscripts of Egyptian and probably Alexandrian provenance (its closest relative in the gospels is P[75], written in the third century on papyrus and certainly found in Egypt). It first appears in the Vatican inventory of 1475.[20] The fourth century manuscript had by the fifteenth century lost the first 45 chapters of Genesis, some of the Psalms, the beginning of Matthew, the last part of Hebrews, the Pastoral Epistles (1-2 Timothy, Titus and Philemon), and the Revelation. The gaps in Genesis, Psalms, Matthew, Hebrews, and the Revelation were supplied in a fifteenth-century hand, but not the 'Pastoral Epistles'. Fr Šagi shows that the replacement text in Genesis was copied from Vatican Library, Chigi R VI 38, but he was not able to identify the source of the other supplements. He shows also that there is no foundation for a south Italian provenance. The view that it was John Chortasmenos, a well-known scribe of the period,[21] who wrote the supplementary portions of the manuscript cannot be sustained, nor has any other identification been convincing. On the other hand it is agreed that Esther, Wisdom, Judith, and Tobit in Codex Venetus Gr. 6 (Venice, Bibliotheca Nazionale Mareiana, MS 336) were transcribed from Vaticanus (pp. 9-13) and since Codex Venetus Gr. 6 was probably written for Cardinal Bessarion, it seems likely that Bessarion had knowledge of Vaticanus.

The work of writing the Vaticanus was allocated to two scribes, who can be distinguished by the patterns of the decorative tailpiece, or coronis, that they drew at the end of each book of the Bible.[22] The principal title was at the end of each book, a legacy of the roll format. Literary rolls often had such a coronis, as can be seen in the long papyrus roll of Aristotle's Constitution of Athens (BL, Papyrus 131) and a papyrus roll of Homer in the British Library (Papyrus 136).[23] All the scribes were carefully trained in the style of their scriptorium, so differences in their letter forms are hardly distinguishable. However, once identified by their artistic endeavours, they can be distinguished also by their habits in filling up lines or squeezing letters to fit the line and their spelling habits. Their punctuation habits also differ. In Vaticanus Scribe A, who wrote Genesis 46. 28 – I Kingdoms 19. 11 (pp. 41-334) and Psalms – Tobit (pp. 625-944), in the prose books always begins a new paragraph with a new line, projecting the first letter into the margin. The poetical books, written in verse units, have different ruling. Scribe B, who wrote I Kingdoms 19. 11 – II Esdras, Hosea – Daniel, and the New Testament, writes straight on in the historical books, sometimes beginning a new paragraph in the same line after a punctuation space, and sometimes beginning on a new line. In the Prophets he emphasizes the main divisions by beginning a new line, and he does the same at the beginning of the New Testament.

Thomas S. Pattie

There are no original chapter divisions in Vaticanus, but major sections begin with a new paragraph. Our familiar chapters were devised in Paris in the thirteenth century. Our verses first appeared in Stephanus' 1551 Greek-Latin edition of the New Testament printed and published in Geneva, '*inter equitandum*' as he tells us, which has jokingly been interpreted as 'on horseback'; this might explain a number of awkward verse divisions. More likely it is to be interpreted 'between horse rides', during stop-overs as he travelled between Paris and Geneva, fleeing from the doctors at the Sorbonne. The Eusebian sections (355 Matthew, 236 Mark, 342 Luke, 232 John) were added subsequently, with a very rare chapter division: 170 Matthew, 62 Mark, 152 Luke, 80 John. This is different from the standard Byzantine chapter-divisions into capitula or τίτλοι (Matthew 68, Mark 48, Luke 83, John 18), usually associated with a list of chapter numbers and titles before each Gospel.[24]

Some of the prophetical books in B show the influence of Origen's Hexapla. Two of his critical signs are used, the asterisk to mark text in the Hebrew which ought to be added to the Septuagint (LXX), and the *obelos* (a horizontal line, sometimes with two dots like our division sign) marking text not in the Hebrew which ought to be deleted from the LXX. There is, for example, an asterisk against Isaiah 26. 4 (p. 1028 col. 1): ὅτι ἐπὶ σοὶ ἐλπίδι ἤλπισαν κύριε ἕως τοῦ α'ἰῶνος (meaning not in the LXX but in the Hebrew); and asterisks at Zechariah 4. 11, 12. 6, 13. 1, 13. 8 (in ℵ only 13. 1). There are obeloi at Zechariah 1. 13, 17, 19, and 8. 2. A marginal note, ου κ´ π´ εβρ´ or οὐ κεῖται παρ᾽ ἑβραίω (ἑβραίοις) occurs in Malach 1. 7, 3. 3, and a number of places in Isaiah and Jeremiah. Again this means 'not in the Hebrew and therefore ought to be deleted from the LXX'. At Jeremiah 3. 8 the words ὧν καὶ εἶδον περὶ πάντων have been bracketed as well as marked ου κ´ π´ εβρ´ and in addition they were not overwritten by the later scribe whose task it was to revive the faded lettering.

There is even a glossary at the beginning of Proverbs on p. 714, which defines, for example, σοφία as ἐπιστήμη θείων καὶ ἀνθρωπίνων πραγμάτων, the knowledge of divine and human affairs. For some reason the scribe was not alert at the changeover from 1 Chronicles to 2 Chronicles. Perhaps the new book was not clearly marked. At any rate the scribe wrote the first six lines of 2 Chronicles at the end of 1 Chronicles, added an end mark, left the lower half of the column (the third and last) blank, turned over the page and began again with 2 Chronicles. He left this error unmarked, no doubt on the grounds that a correction would be untidy and no confusion was possible. A much later corrector, not earlier than the fifteenth century, delated the superfluous words rather ostentatiously.

It was in the fifteenth century that the gaps in B were filled, and Skeat in his article points out that it is remarkable that Vaticanus was restored at all, and makes the attractive suggestion that it was found in the East, perhaps in Constantinople, and hurriedly completed (the omission of the Pastoral Epistles is not the only evidence of haste) for presentation to the Pope at the Council of Ferrara-Florence in 1438-9. Until further evidence comes to light, this must remain a suggestion, however plausible.

The Codex Vaticanus is at present dis-bound, and there is no trace of its previous binding, which might have given some clue as to its previous history. C. R. Gregory in 1886 saw what looked like chain and wire lines, which might suggest that the manuscript was written on paper, not vellum. Further, on some pages Italian words could be made out, printed back to front, e.g. p. 575. So we deduce that when the manuscript was bound in its binding of 1886 and was to be pressed, current newspapers were put between the leaves to prevent offsetting the old Greek letters.[25] This binding may well not have been the fifteenth century binding, but a binding of the late seventeenth or early eighteenth century.

THE CODEX SINAITICUS

The Codex Sinaiticus is no more informative as to its origins. It is agreed that, at least for the Gospels, its text is Alexandrian. Kirsopp Lake in his facsimile gives the evidence for its provenance, which is inconclusive.[26] It is further discussed by Milne & Skeat.[27] We are left with tentative pointers to Caesarea: the mention of εἰς τὴν Ἀντιπατρίδα instead of εἰς τὴν πατρίδα at Matthew 13. 54, Ἵππον instead of Ἰόππην at 1 Maccabees 14. 5, as there was a town called Hippos on the south-west shore of Lake Galilee. Further, we have the notes at the end of 2 Esdras and Esther in a sixth-century hand, declaring that part of the manuscript had been collated against a Bible corrected by Pamphilus and Antoninus.

Despite the absurd claim by the notorious forger Constantine Simonides that he had copied out the Codex Sinaiticus at the age of 15,[28] there can be no doubt that it was written in the fourth century. The palaeographical evidence points to the fourth century, and there are two features which support that dating.[29] First, the Eusebian sections were added to the Gospels by the original scribes. As Eusebius died in 340, his system of sections must have been formed between 300 and 340, so Sinaiticus could not have been written earlier. Secondly, the system of numerals for the thousands in Maccabees (elsewhere the numerals are written out in full) belongs to an older system which seems to have changed between 338 and 360, so it could not have been much later than 360.[30]

The scribes of Sinaiticus were well trained and skilful, and although Tischendorf identified four different scribes, A, B, C, D, the biblical scholar S. P. Tregelles spent three days examining the codex at Leipzig and confessed that he could see no difference among them. F. H. A. Scrivener suggested that there might be only two scribes – Tischendorf's A+B and C+D.[31] The manuscript's arrival in London in December 1933 allowed Milne & Skeat to make a thorough examination of the question, and they demonstrated convincingly that there were three scribes and that Tischendorf's C should be removed from consideration. The decorative coronis was the crucial distinguishing mark between the scribes.[32] Their individual habits and preferences could then be distinguished with confidence. It was possible to show that the superscriptions (front-titles) and subscriptions (end-titles) were written by the scribes of the main text. The rubrics in the Psalms were written by the main scribe: D wrote Ps 1. 1-97. 3, and A wrote Ps 97. 3 to the end. Each wrote the rubrics in his own section, and D, the supervisor, overwrote A's rubrics. At the beginning of Matthew, A, who wrote the whole of the New Testament except certain cancel leaves, added the Eusebian apparatus to Matthew §1-52. D overwrote the apparatus to Matthew 1-52, and continued as far as Luke §106, and then he too gave up.

What makes working on ancient manuscripts so exciting is that you can feel yourself in the presence of a living text. It is not just that scribes make mistakes and have to correct them, for they make fewer mistakes than we do, but we can see real changes happening. For example, Luke 22. 43-4, omitted in Vaticanus and Alexandrinus, is present in Sinaiticus. The supervisor, D, has put curved brackets in the margin to indicate deletion of these two verses, and a second corrector, C^a, has deleted the deletion marks. Why were these verses challenged in antiquity? To us the picture of Jesus praying with sweat pouring off his face in the Garden of Gethsemane is a reassuring reminder of Christ's humanity, but many were disturbed by an indicator of God's frailty.

In order to answer that question, we have to examine the various correctors. Since the corrections are often only a few letters, our attributions will be necessarily more tentative than the attribution of the main hands. Lake, building on Tischendorf, listed this terrifying series: A^1, A^2, A^4, A^5, A^{obliq}, A^{Herm}, B, B^a, C^a, C^b, C^c, C^{c*}, D, and E. As Milne & Skeat say, 'Such a plethora of original correctors, unexampled in any other manuscript of antiquity, is a priori unlikely (the scriptorium was a business establishment, not a committee of revisers).'[33] They were able to allocate all the A and B correctors to the main scribes A and D. Scribe B had to correct his own work, as clearly the others did not want to touch his work. In 1 Corinthians 13 the passage γέγονα χαλκὸς ἠφχῶν ... ἀγάπην δὲ μὴ ἔχω has been omitted. It has been supplied in the upper margin in a hand using the type of καὶ compendium characteristic of scribe D, and the shape of the letters *kappa* and *mu* also point to a D, as does the upward-pointing arrow-shaped caret with its head separated from the shaft, with a corresponding downward-pointing arrow opposite the place where the supplement is to be inserted. Scribe A uses rounded arrow-heads which are attached to the shaft. Such close examination of the script of the corrections allows us to distinguish the correctors. Features such as spelling also help: a correction of Hermas has three mis-spellings in two lines (χιρι, εινα, ιασεν), which point to scribe B, who wrote the main text of Hermas.

The dismal scribe B was responsible for a nonsense reading at Isaiah 29. 11, ταθτοθτο. Corrector C^a first corrected this to ταθτα, then corrector C^{b2} re-corrected it to τοθτο. Unless B had it completely wrong, we can suppose that the exemplar had both ταθτα and τοθτο, as variants. Corrector C^a is easily recognized. He uses an orange-brown ink and a peculiar script. He has made corrections over all the books of the Bible, except the Epistle of Barnabas. He very seldom erases text that he wishes to replace. Usually he enters a few letters above the lines in the text, and often there is nothing but the context to show whether they represent additions or substitutions. Longer corrections are set in the side-margins and marked with a single wavy caret. He puts a corresponding wavy caret where the correction is to go. Again, it is often ambiguous whether an addition or a substitution is appropriate. He puts longer insertions in the top or bottom margins with caret signs and a pair of arrows, one in the destined place. These arrows point in the same direction, up from the bottom margin, or down from the top margin, quite different from the arrows of the main scribes, which are opposed in pairs, i.e., a passage in the lower margin to be inserted has an upward-pointing arrow, and there is a downward-pointing arrow where the passage is to be inserted.

C^{b2} is the last important corrector. He worked on Genesis, probably Numbers, some of the prophetic books, and the gospels. Some of his corrections have had to be placed in such a way as to avoid corrections by earlier correctors.

The Creation of the Great Codices

THE CODEX ALEXANDRINUS

The Codex Alexandrinus which came into the possession of King Charles I in 1627 was a present from Cyril Lucar, Patriarch of Alexandria and later of Constantinople, who was glad of the support of Sir Thomas Roe, appointed during the reign of James I as the English ambassador to the Sublime Porte, against the attempt by the Pope and the King of France to induce the Orthodox Church to accept the authority of Rome. A letter from Roe to the Earl of Arundel on 20 January 1625 tells us that Cyril thought it was written by Thekla, the companion of St Paul:

By his meanes (i.e., through Cyril Lucar) I may procure some bookes; but they are indeed Greeke to mee; one only he hath given mee, for his majestie, with express promise to deliuer yt; beeing an autographall bible intire, written by the hand of Tecla the protomartyr of the Greekes, that liued in the tyme of St Paul; and he (Cyril) doth auerr yt to be true and authenticall, of his owne writing, and the greatest antiquitye of the Greeke church.[34]

But James I died on 27 March 1625, and the manuscript seems to have been taken back by the Patriarch. In 1627 the Patriarch again sent it to Roe as a New Year's gift for the King of England, now Charles I, and it remained in the Royal Library until it passed to the British Museum in 1757, having survived neglect, rats, and the disastrous fire of 1731 which damaged so many of the Cotton manuscripts, as is dramatically reported in the Report of the House of Commons Committee, 9 May 1732:

Several entire presses, with the books in them, were also removed, but ... several of the backs of the presses being already on fire, they were obliged to be broke open, and the books, as many as could be, thrown out of the windows.[35]

An eyewitness tells of the learned Dr Bentley in 'nightgown and great wig' stalking out of the building with the Codex Alexandrinus under his arm. It is now divided into four volumes, each of which is enclosed within a binding that bears the Royal arms and 'C.R.' (BL, Royal MSS 1 D.v-viii), but Roe's description suggests that it was in one volume when he saw it, and both the Greek and Arabic folio numerations suggest a single volume.

The arrival of such a great manuscript in England stimulated the study of the biblical text, as a result of which Alexandrinus was the first of the great uncials to have its New Testament published, although the Old Testament text of the Vaticanus was published in the Sixtine edition of the Septuagint in 1587. In 1633 Patrick Young, the Royal Librarian, published the newly discovered Clementine Epistles from A, and his notes on Genesis to Numbers 14 were incorporated in volume VI of Walton's Polyglot Bible of 1657. A collation of the principal readings of Alexandrinus in the New Testament were reported in volume V of the same work. The New Testament was collated for Mill's great edition of 1707, and in 1707-20 a complete edition of the Old Testament was produced by J. E. Grabe.

The manuscript's history can be traced back to 1625, when it was in the Patriarchal Library in Alexandria. However, there is no reason to suppose it was originally written there. A fourteenth-century note in Arabic on the fly-leaf, translated by Bentley as '*Memorant hunc librum scriptum fuisse manu Theclae Martyris*', is not to be believed for a minute. From the Arabic note at the foot of the first page of Genesis, which reads in English 'Bound to the Patriarchall Cell in the Fortress of Alexandria. Whoever removes it thence shall be excommunicated and cut off. Written by Athanasius the humble,' it appears that the manuscript was brought to Alexandria by Athanasius II about AD 1308, very likely from Constantinople as he had spent some years there.[36] Athanasius, whose adventurous life is recorded in the History of George Pachymeres, wrote similar notes of presentation, signing himself 'The humble Athanasius, Archbishop of Alexandria' in three manuscripts he gave to the Patriarchal Library of Alexandria, two still there (MSS 12 and 34: notes in Greek) and one in the Vatican Library (Vatican Ottob. 452: note in Arabic).[37]

It is a reasonable guess that the Codex Alexandrinus was in Constantinople before Athanasius II acquired it, but we have no idea where it was originally written. Its gospel text shows some of the corrections that ended in the Byzantine ecclesiastical text, and this may be the explanation of one interesting difference between A and B. According to Hatch & Redpath's *Concordance to the Septuagint*,[38] the Greek word ἀδωναι occurs 89 times in the Septuagint, 88 of them in Ezekiel. It occurs in the phrase 'thus saith the Lord God', and in 86 cases A and its relatives have ἀδωναι κύριος, and twice κύριος ὁ θεός; B has κύριος 74 times, κύριος κύριος 11 times, ἀδωναι κύριος once, and omits the whole phrase twice; and a corrector of B, whom we call B², has ἀδωναι κύριος, once. ℵ does not come into the reckoning here, as it no longer contains Ezekiel. If the LXX was originally a translation into Greek made for the Jews of Alexandria, B's text ('Thus spake the Lord' or 'Thus spake Lord Lord') could represent the original LXX and A's text ('Thus spake Adonai Lord') could be a correction in the direction of the Masoretic text. But A's 'Adonai Lord' is an unusual expression, and a dozen examples in B of 'Lord Lord' make us uneasy with this explanation, and the obvious translation of the Masoretic text 'the Lord God', κύριος ὁ θεός, in fact occurs only a few times here. If on the other hand A's text ('Thus spake Adonai Lord') is original, it will be a peculiarity due to the translator of Ezekiel. Then B's text will be secondary: it will have translated ἀδωναι as κύριος, making κύριος κύριος, and will have simplified the majority of those instances to a single κύριος.[39]

The Codex Alexandrinus was written later than the other two great codices, and has some introductory material which they do not have. The Psalter, which includes Psalm 151, is preceded by the Epistle of Athanasius to Marcellinus, the Hypotheseis or table of contents of the Psalms by Eusebius of Caesarea, and Canons of the Morning and Evening Psalms, and at the end of the Psalter are the fourteen Liturgical Canticles. After Revelation come the 1st and 2nd Epistles of Clement to the Corinthians, and an ancient table of contents prefixed to the whole Bible shows that the apocryphal Psalms of Solomon once came after 2 Clement. As Athanasius died in 373 and Eusebius in 340, Alexandrinus is likely to have been written after those dates. It must also be later than the other two great codices of the Bible because in the Gospels it has, written in the first hand, the standard Byzantine chapter divisions and titles and list of titles (capitula) before each Gospel. It is commonly though to have been written in the first half of the fifth century, but Cavallo emphasizes the early stages of the decorative features fully developed in the early-sixth-century Dioscorides (Vienna, Österreichische National-bibliothek, Med. Gr. 1) and dates it to the third quarter of the fifth century.[40]

The significance of these three great codices of the Bible is twofold. Not only are they early and authoritative examples of a closely controlled text of the Bible, which the discovery of the Bodmer papyri took back into the third century, but they also represent a revolution in the technology of the book, which has lasted until today.

The Creation of the Great Codices

NOTES

1 Note at the end of Ezra and Esther (Leipzig Universitätsbibliothek, MS gr. 1); *Codex Sinaiticus Petropolitanus. The Old Testament ... now reproduced in facsimile from photographs by Helen and Kirsopp Lake with a description and introduction to the history of the Codex by Kirsopp Lake* (Oxford: Clarendon Press, 1911), xi; New Testament (1922), viii.

2 The three ancient codices: Vaticanus, Vatican City, Bibliotheca Apostolica Vaticana, MS Vat. gr. 1209; Sinaiticus, London, British Library, Add. MS 43725; Alexandrinus, BL, Royal MSS, 1 D.v-viii.

3 T. C. Skeat, 'Irenaeus and the Four-Gospel Canon', *Novum Testamentum* xxxiv (Leiden: Brill, 1992), 194-9.

4 British Library, Papyrus 1532 verso; *Oxyrhynchus Papyri* iv. 657; *New Palaeographical Society* i. 47 (London, 1903-12); P^{13} in K. Aland, *Kurzgefasste Liste der griechischen Handschriften des Neuen Testaments* (Berlin: De Gruyter, 2nd edn, 1994), p. 4 and n. 6; R. Seider, *Paläographie der lateinischen Papyri* (Stuttgart: Hiersemann 1978) II, 1 nr. 14, Taf. X.

5 Fifteen more folios of ℵ were discovered at the Monastery of St Catherine in Sinai in 1975, and their publication is eagerly awaited.

6 E. G. Turner, *The Typology of the Early Codex* (Philadelphia: University of Pennsylvania Press, 1977) cf. nos 52, 279, 447, 459, 465, 466, 514.

7 *Typology*, nos 540, 47, 223a.

8 C. H. Roberts & T. C. Skeat, *The Birth of the Codex* (London: Oxford University Press for the British Academy, 1983, 2nd edn, 1987), 45-66.

9 N. Lewis, *Papyrus in Classical Antiquity* (London: Oxford University Press, 1974).

10 Hieronimus, De uiris inlustribus, ed. by E. Richardson, *Texte und Untersuchungen zur Geschichte der altchristlichen Literatur*, 14, 1a (Leipzig: J. C. Hinrichs, 1896) 51.

11 *Typology*, 55-71.

12 T. C. Skeat, 'Early Christian Book-Production: Papyri and Manuscripts', *The Cambridge History of the Bible. Vol. II: The West from the Fathers to the Reformation*, ed. by G. W. H. Lampe (Cambridge: University Press, 1969), 54-79.

13 Eusebius, Vita Constantini, iv.36 (J. P. Migne, *Patrologia Graeca* 20, 1185).

14 E. A. Lowe, *Codices Latini Antiquiores* (Oxford: Clarendon Press, 1934) i, nos 11, 13, 35.

15 *Typology* 36-7.

16 *Photographs of the Washington Manuscript of the Psalms in the Freer Collection*, by G. R. Swan (Ann Arbor: University of Michigan Press, 1919); *New Palaeographical Society* I.151; see also J. K. Elliot, *A Bibliography of Greek New Testament Manuscripts* (Cambridge: University Press, 1989), 48-9; Lowe, *CLA* i, no. 13.

17 C. R. Gregory, *Textkritik des neuen Testamentes* (Leipzig: J. C. Hinrichs, 1900-9), 32-40; photographic edn of Vatican, Bibliotheca Apostolica Vaticana, MS Vat. gr. 1209, ed. by J. Cozza-Luzi, 4 vols (Rome: Vatican Library, 1904-07), *Codices e Vaticanis Selecti* 4.

18 J. Leroy, *Les Types de réglures des manuscrits grecs* (Paris: Centre National de Recherches Scientifiques, 1976).

19 L. Gilissen, 'La composition des cahiers, le pliage du parchemin et l'imposition', *Scriptorium* 26 (1972), 3-33.

20 Janko Šagi, S.J., 'Problema historiae codicis B', *Divus Thomas* 75 (1972), 3-29; T. C. Skeat, 'The Codex Vaticanus in the Fifteenth Century', *Journal of Theological Studies*, 35 (1984), 454-65.

21 E. Gamillscheg & D. Harlfinger, *Repertorium der griechischen Kopisten 800-1600, 1. Teil Handschriften aus Bibliotheken Grossbritanniens* (Vienna: Österreichischen Akademie der Wissenschaft, 1981), no. 191.

22 H. J. M. Milne & T. C. Skeat, *Scribes and Correctors of the Codex Sinaiticus* (London: British Museum, 1938), App. 1 (pp. 87-90); G. Cavallo, *Ricerche sulla maiuscola biblica* (Florence: Le Monnier, 1967), 53.

23 H. J. M. Milne, *Catalogue of the Literary Papyri in the British Museum* (London: British Museum, 1927), 21-2.

24 H. von Soden, *Die Schriften des neuen Testaments in ihrer ältesten erreichbaren Textgestalt* (Berlin: Arthur Glaue, 1902) i, 402-11.

25 C. R. Gregory, *Canon and Text of the New Testament* (The International Theological Library; Edinburgh: T. & T. Clark, 1907), 344-5.

26 *Codex Sinaiticus Petropolitanus*, N.T. ix-xv, O.T. xii-xviii.

27 *Scribes and Correctors*, 66-9; *Catalogue of Additions to the Manuscripts 1931-1935* (London: British Museum, 1967), 207-12.

28 H. J. M. Milne & T. C. Skeat, *The Codex Sinaiticus and the Codex Alexandrinus* (London: British Museum, 1963 [1st edn 1938, 2nd edn 1955]), 8-9; F. H. A. Scrivener, *A Full Collation of the Codex Sinaiticus* (Cambridge and London, 1864), lx-lxxii.

29 Cavallo, *Richerche*, 57-8.

30 *Scribes and Correctors*, 60-5.

31 *Full Collation of the Codex Sinaiticus*, xvi, xviii.

32 *Scribes and Correctors*, 27-9.

33 *Scribes and Correctors*, 41.

34 *The Negotiations of Sir T. Roe in his embassy to the Ottoman Porte from the year 1621 to 1628 Inclusive*, ed. by Samuel Richardson (London: Society for the Encouragement of Learning, 1740), 335.

35 Report of the House of Commons Committee, 9 May 1732.

36 *Codex Sinaiticus and the Codex Alexandrinus*, 36-7; *Codex Alexandrinus, Reduced Photographic Facsimile, Old Testament*, IV (London: British Museum, 1957), Introduction.

37 T. D. Moschonas, Κατάλογοι τῆς πατριαρχικῆς βιβλιοθήκης, Τόμος Α. Χειρόγραφα (Alexandria, 1945; 2nd edn Salt Lake City: University of Utah Press, 1965, Studies and Documents 26).

38 E. Hatch & H. A. Redpath, *A Concordance to the Septuagint and the other Greek versions of the Old Testament* (Graz: Akademische Druck, 1954).

39 S. Jellicoe, *The Septuagint and Modern Study* (Oxford: Clarendon Press, 1968), 186.

40 Cavallo, *Ricerche*, 77-80.

GOSPEL HARMONY AND THE NAMES OF CHRIST
INSULAR IMAGES OF A PATRISTIC THEME

Jennifer O'Reilly

IMPERIAL POETS AND HISTORIANS mapping the horizon of the Roman world saw the western isles as its furthest limits. For Christian writers the Lord's final command to his disciples to teach and baptize all peoples (Matt. 28. 19-20) had a particular application to those islands whose conversion would complete the process of taking the Gospel to the ends of the earth. Accordingly, in the fifth-century pastoral epistles of St Patrick his mission to the Irish is presented as the fulfilment of scriptural prophecy: 'the Gospel has been preached to the limit beyond which no-one dwells'.[1] The theme is monumentally developed by Bede (c. 673-735) in his account of the conversion, by Irish as well as by Roman missionaries, of his Anglo-Saxon forefathers who had settled in post-Roman Britain and had become part of the Christian Roman world. Irish and Anglo-Saxon monks, conscious that living 'on the two uttermost islands of the Ocean' could be construed as coming from the back of beyond,[2] vigorously used the topos as a foil in asserting the orthodoxy and achievements of an insular monastic life and culture fully within the universal Church: 'For all we Irish, inhabitants of the world's edge, are disciples of Sts Peter and Paul … and we accept nothing outside the evangelical and apostolic teaching.'[3]

Incorporation into the Church meant embracing its learning. The Codex Amiatinus and the scholarship of Bede testify to the resources of the Northumbrian monastic community in which they were formed. Recent research on individual Irish scholars including Columbanus, Cummian, and Adomnán of Iona; on the production of works on grammar, computus, and exegesis in seventh-century Ireland; and on eighth-century Hiberno-Latin compendia and biblical commentaries has greatly increased awareness of the wide variety of sources from the Mediterranean world of Late Antiquity which were available to insular scholars, of the early reception date of some of those sources and of insular assimilation of patristic techniques.[4] At first glance, insular gospel-books do not seem to fit into this milieu. Unlike the Codex Amiatinus they could never be mistaken for sixth-century Mediterranean works. They are readily distinguished by their script and decorative intrusions on the text. Their adaptation of abstract motifs used in native metalwork in secular contexts and their highly stylized use of figural art, usually confined to the representation of the Evangelists and their symbolic beasts, have seemed to mark them out as magnificent but barbaric. Attempts to discern 'meaning' in some of these designs encounter obvious methodological problems. To some extent the Book of Kells bridges the two worlds by its combination of conventions and motifs peculiar to the insular gospel-book tradition with a wide range of figural images and

Mediterranean motifs.[5] Study of its most famous page has been fundamental in promoting the idea that certain features of the decorative highlighting of the text offer a visual exegesis.

GENEALOGY AND *CHI-RHO*

The name of Christ was conventionally rendered by its Greek initial letters *chi* and *rho*, depicted as Xp with Latin endings. A distinguishing characteristic of insular gospel-books is their enlargement and decoration of the *nomen sacrum*, often on the scale of a gospel incipit, where it occurs at Matt. 1. 18, *Christi autem generatio sic erat*. 'This magnifying is not found earlier and found later it can be taken as an insular symptom. One wonders why the Xpi section assumed such importance.'[6] Suzanne Lewis saw in the *chi-rho* in the Book of Kells fol. 34[r] a sacred riddle teeming with Christological and eucharistic allusions appropriate to the probable use of this text as a lection at the Vigil of the Nativity (Pl. 1). The letter *chi* announcing the sacred name could also denote the redeeming Cross; as depicted in Kells, the cosmological character of the *chi*-Cross helps identify the Christ revealed here in Matthew's account of the nativity with the Creator revealed in his creation. Lewis, following Otto Werckmeister, grounded this persuasive view in the exegesis of Irenaeus, noting that his 'exposition of salvation through the identity of the creating Logos with the incarnate and crucified Christ does not often occur in patristic writing' and that only Irenaeus explicates this relationship 'within the allegorical matrix of the sacred name'.[7]

Questions remain, however, concerning the nature of the connection between the patristic text and the insular image. Can this Christology be shown to have been familiar elsewhere in insular monastic culture and in contexts which might explain both its application to Matt. 1. 18 in insular gospel-books and their custom of showing the previous seventeen verses as a distinct unit?

Insular assimilation of relevant patristic themes is evident in the work of Bede. In a homily on Matt. 1. 18-25 for the Christmas Eve vigil, Bede ponders the etymology and Matthew's explanation of the significance of the three names and titles – Jesus, Emmanuel, Christ – and, like Irenaeus, also uses the opening of John's gospel to show that in the birth of the Saviour described by Matthew 'the Word was made flesh and dwelt among us'. The gospel passage on which Bede based the homily, however, does not begin with the opening words of Matt. 1. 18, *Christi autem generatio*, but, in the manner of known Roman lections, with the second part of that verse, *Cum esset desponsata mater eius Maria Ioseph*.[8]

Irenaeus (d. 202/3) had defended the divine authority of scripture by reconciling its apparently discordant elements. It was in this context that he used the acclamation of Christ's divinity in the opening lines of John's gospel to expound the account of Christ's human descent at the beginning of Matthew. He notes that Matthew does not say *Iesu*, but '*Christi* autem generatio sic erat' in order to show that Jesus born of Mary was the prophesied Messiah (Christ) whom Isaiah had called Emmanuel (God with us).[9]

Other patristic apologists were concerned to defend the four gospels as the complementary facets of a single gospel. Like Irenaeus, they cited scriptural texts which attest the divine order underlying the number four, particularly the heavenly theophanies of the four beasts described by the prophet Ezekiel (Ezek. 1) and the apostle John

(Rev. 4. 6-8), which were interpreted as figures of the revelation of Christ through the fourfold Gospel. The four beasts – the man, lion, ox and eagle – were read as symbols of the four Evangelists and of their gospels' distinctive but harmonious testimonies to the humanity, kingship, priesthood and divinity of Christ.

Unpromising though it may seem to modern readers, Matthew's enumeration of Christ's ancestors (Matt. 1. 1-17) was a crucial text in this apologetic task. The reconciliation of its inconsistencies and manifest differences from the genealogy listed in Luke 3. 23-38, and from the account of the Incarnation at the opening of John's gospel, became a standard means of demonstrating in miniature the harmony underlying the fourfold Gospel. Its most authoritative expression is in Augustine's *De consensu evangeliarum*.[10] The first book articulates the harmony of the distinctive testimonies of each of the four Evangelists symbolically embodied by their respective beasts. The second book illustrates this harmony through a textual and spiritual exposition of Matt. 1. 1-17 to reveal the complementary aspects of Christ's identity which lie concealed beneath the literal text of Christ's genealogy. Augustine stresses that Matthew's 'Book of the generation of Jesus Christ' shows the generation according to the flesh of the only-begotten Son of God, that 'the Word became flesh and dwelt among us' (Jn 1. 14). The text from John is reiterated in Augustine's detailed treatment of the Matthean genealogy in Sermon 51, alluding to the classic statement in Phil. 2. 6-11 that Christ emptied himself of his glory but not of his divinity at his incarnation and that, paradoxically, it was through his descent into humanity and the death on the Cross that his name, *Dominus Iesu Christus*, was exalted through all creation.

This rich exegetical tradition was part of the patristic inheritance of the West and illumines though does not, of itself, explain why insular gospel-books in particular should have highlighted and separated the Matthean genealogy (Matt. 1. 1-17) from the *chi-rho* marking v. 18. Gospel commentaries among the seventh- and eighth-century Hiberno-Latin exegetical works preserved in Carolingian manuscripts, however, provide a large body of contemporary evidence, not only of insular familiarity with the patristic tradition, but of a distinctive reading of Matt. 1. 1-18 which has some suggestive parallels with the visual structuring of the text in insular gospel-books.[11] Like St John, St Matthew was believed to have been an apostle and thus to have received his information directly from Christ. Matthew was regarded as the senior evangelist who wrote first and who was the only one of the four to write in Hebrew. Above all, Matthew's primacy in Jerome's ordering of the Vulgate gospel sequence and Jerome's own commentary on Matthew's gospel were influential in establishing his popularity with Hiberno-Latin gospel commentators. Such factors do not, however, explain the extraordinary emphasis which they place on the genealogy in Matthew; their exegesis freely incorporates material from Jerome's commentary, but often goes well beyond it.

Modern scripture scholars have shown how genealogies in the Old Testament are primarily used not to record biological descent but to establish identity, sometimes the collective identity of a tribe or group, or to authenticate the lineage of cultic office-holders such as priests and kings.[12] Genealogies were used also as a device to establish epochs and as a framework for historical writing. The clerical caste within insular barbarian society readily understood the importance of ancestry in establishing identity and in buttressing claims to office in the tribal society described in the Old Testament and would have shared many of the assumptions and techniques of biblical genealogists. Early Irish churchmen produced an unrivalled corpus of genealogical material, written with contemporary objectives, as Donnchadh Ó Corráin has shown; their view of themselves as 'the tribe of the Church' was in some respects, such as in the area of law and relationships with secular society, influenced by the Pentateuch model of the tribe of Levi and the hereditary priesthood of Aaron.[13] Patristic exegesis of the genealogy expounded not only Christ's priestly descent but the priestly nature of Christ's 'tribe', the Church, figured in Christ's Hebrew ancestors, even though, by definition, they lived before the Incarnation and the age of grace and many of them, notably Abraham, lived even before the age of the Law. Insular writers held a similar view of their own ancestors who had lived before the conversion of their people yet had a continuing contribution to make to the genealogy and therefore to the claims and identity of contemporary dynasts.[14]

The early Irish use of Jerome's *Liber interpretationis hebraicorum nominis* and Isidore's *Etymologiae* partly reflects the interest of non-Romans in Latin vocabulary and their appropriation of standard exegetical techniques, but they were drawn also to the more esoteric elements of the inheritance.[15] Their fascination with the potency of names, titles, epithets, numbers, lists, classifications, and instances of first occurrences in the biblical text became characteristic mannerisms, as did their regard for the Hebrew language, even though of necessity this was in practice largely focused on proper names in scripture. Such preoccupations help to explain the apparently disproportionate weight of commentary Hiberno-Latin writers placed on the opening verses of the first gospel and the visionary, incantatory quality with which they invested Matthew's enumeration of the epochs and generations of Christ's ancestors and his listing of their Hebrew names.

The Irish scholar Ailerán (d. 665) wrote two allegorical expositions of the names in the Matthean genealogy. Unlike Jerome in his commentary on Matthew, where he makes brief historical and technical comments on a select few of the names, Ailerán in the *Interpretatio mystica progenitorum Christi* assumes that every single name, irrespective of the historical significance of its original owner, is of importance because it contains some insight into the identity of Christ. Short scriptural extracts suggested by each etymology illumine the particular facet of Christ and his work of redemption mystically concealed within each ancestral Hebrew name. In the *Moralis explanatio eorumden nominum ab eodem compilata*, Ailerán shows how the believer should conform to each of the aspects of Christ which have already been elucidated through the exposition of each name's hidden meaning.[16]

The eighth-century Hiberno-Latin Matthew commentary in Orléans, Bibliothèque municipale, MS 65(62) gives Jerome's brief interpretation for every name in the genealogy but then applies to each name the same mystical interpretation and scriptural texts used by Ailerán in his first treatise. It selects a dozen particular ancestors and, either through interpretation of their names or through some word which particularly evokes their history, shows how they each prophesied Christ: how, in a sense, Christ was present in them, a pilgrim in Abraham, offered up in sacrifice in Isaac, reigning in David.[17] The Hiberno-Latin commentary on Matthew's gospel in Munich Clm 6233 devotes an astonishing 49 folios to the genealogy alone. It too gives a Latin interpretation for every single name, though often departing from those listed under Matthew's gospel in Jerome's *Liber Interpretationis*; it also draws on illustrative texts from the Old and New Testaments, occasionally coinciding with Aileráns's selection.[18] Detailed commentaries on the Matthean genealogy also appear in the great eighth-century Hiberno-Latin compilation known as the Irish Reference Bible and in various *collectanea*.[19]

Typically, these works give full weight to Matthew's opening phrase, 'The book of the generation of Jesus Christ, the son of David, the son of Abraham', which they see as containing the whole genealogy and even encapsulating the entire gospel. The individual words of the title are probed: *Liber*, simultaneously meaning a book, the freeing of souls, and the sonship revealed in Christ's divine and human descent. The genealogy itself is treated as a book. As the *Liber genesis* described the creation of heaven and earth and the beginning of corruptibility, Matthew's *Liber generationis* describes re-creation and the beginning of incorruptibility; it is compared with the *Liber generationis* of Adam (Gen. 5. 1) to show Christ as the Second Adam; it is likened to the book of the Law given to Moses, a memoria of the beginnings of salvation which is in Christ. Following both Jerome and Augustine, Matthew's *Liber generationis* is seen as the direct fulfilment of the prophecy of Isa. 53. 8, recalled in Acts 8. 33, 'Who shall declare his generation?'[20] The Matthew commentary in Orléans 65(62) asks why Matthew called his work 'the book of the generation' when in fact it records 42 generations and when the genealogy is only one small part of his gospel. The answer is that the genealogy describes only one generating and may properly be called the book of Jesus Christ; this is the sealed book which the prophets Isaiah and Ezekiel and John the Apostle in the Apocalypse commemorate.[21]

The second part of the title of the *Liber generationis* consists of the sacred names, Jesus Christ, which are given very great emphasis in Hiberno-Latin exegesis. They are related to Christ's divinity and humanity respectively; each name is given in Hebrew, Latin, and Greek, as in Isidore's *Etymologiae*. The scriptural exposition of the title *Christus* (the Anointed One) contains an entire Christology. Old Testament prophets, priests, and kings were anointed with oil (chrism) thereby prefiguring Christ's spiritual anointing at his incarnation, though only he combines all three orders. At his anointing he is revealed as man but remains never less than the Father in his divinity.[22] The third part of the genealogy's title describes Christ as 'the son of David, the son of Abraham'. A variety of scriptural texts is cited to show that Abraham and David had been divinely promised that Christ would come 'according to the flesh' (Ps. 131. 11; Gen. 22. 18; Gal. 3. 15). The commentaries then work through the list of Christ's ancestors and the spiritual significance of their Hebrew names, as already described, and often comment on the significance of the number of eras and generations they span. The epochs before, under, and after the Law, for example, are related to Abraham, David, and Christ yet shown to be all one period, just as there is one God, Father, Son, and Holy Spirit. Christ's royal descent, traced by Matthew through David's son Solomon, is perfectly reconciled with his descent traced by Luke through the priestly line of David's son Nathan.

The genealogy's long recapitulation of Christ's identity with his people Israel and the continuity of their history under divine providence reaches a dramatic climax in the disclosure that the last name in the list of ancestral names, Joseph, was not the father of Christ. Commentators emphasize that Mary assumed the lineage of her husband and that they were both from the same tribe, and note her blood relationship to the tribe of

Aaron, but the account of how the Son of God took his humanity from his virgin mother represents a radical dislocation in history. The account of the virginal conception and incarnation of Christ in Matt. 1. 18-25 is therefore the essential accompaniment to the genealogy in revealing the divine as well as the human identity of the prophesied Davidic Messiah, Christ. The Irish Reference Bible, like Irenaeus, draws attention to the fact that the opening of Matthew's account of the incarnation at 1. 18 does not use the name Jesus, a name yet to be supplied by the angel (v. 21), but 'Christi autem generatio sic erat'. Glossing the same line, the Matthew commentary in Munich, Staatsbibliothek, Clm 6233 quotes Jn 1. 14 to identify the Christ of the genealogy with the Word made flesh.[23]

In the light of this tradition, the layout of insular gospel books seems less arbitrary. Continental gospel-books which are marked for Roman lections treat the phrase *Christi autem generatio sic erat* as the conclusion of the genealogy and they begin the account of the incarnation with the next words of v. 18, *Cum esset desponsata mater eius Maria Ioseph*. In embellishing the name of Christ at precisely this moment in Matthew's text, however, and in separating the *chi-rho* from the foregoing account of the genealogy, insular gospel-books signify in a single word the Word incarnate and thereby mark the pivotal point of history and redemption.

In the St Gall Gospels an elaborate cross-carpet page faces the whole-page *chi-rho*, separating it from the genealogy.[24] The only cross-carpet page in the Book of Kells, now fol. 33ʳ, may also have been positioned originally to face the *chi-rho* on fol. 34ʳ in a glorious double opening. The insular development of the *chi-rho* at Matt. 1. 18 to rival and surpass the decoration of the gospel incipit and the treatment of the intervening text of the genealogy as a visual unit led to the formal separation of these two elements, to the treatment of the genealogy as an introductory book and Matt. 1. 18 as the second or proper opening of the gospel. In the Lindisfarne Gospels the rubric on the opening page of Matthew's gospel, fol. 27ʳ, reads *incipit evangelii genelogia mathei*. Only the opening words of the gospel, which also form the title-board of the genealogy, are displayed on the page, *Liber generationis Ihu Xpi filii David filii Abraham* (Pl. 2). The genealogy which immediately follows overleaf, laid out in columns, is entirely contained within the double opening fols 27ᵛ-28ʳ. Although fol. 28ᵛ is blank, the *chi-rho* and v. 18 is reserved for a whole-page display on fol. 29ʳ which bears the rubric, *Incipit evangelium secundum matheu* (Pl. 3).[25] The process of separation of genealogy and *chi-rho* is taken even further in the Cutbercht Gospels. The genealogy is followed, not preceded, by a portrait of Matthew who faces the decorated opening of the canon tables, and only after their completion (fols 18ᵛ-21ᵛ) does the text of Matthew's gospel resume at v. 18 with the *chi-rho* and panelled continuation lettering on fol. 22 which carries the superscription: *Incipit evangelium secdm mattheum*.[26] In the pocket-sized ninth-century MacDurnan Gospels the genealogy is decoratively set out and framed and then followed by a portrait of the evangelist facing the *chi-rho* at Matt. 1. 18 which is treated more lavishly than any gospel opening in the book.[27]

The opening gospel sequence in the Book of Kells (fols 28ᵛ-34ʳ) marks the culmination of the insular development of isolating ever fewer words more elaborately at Matt. 1. 1 and 18, distorting letter-forms and veiling them with clouds of ornament which render them illegible to those who do not know what they seek. In a double opening ornamented with the density of carpet pages (Pl. 4, 5) a portrait page faces the gospel incipit, which is reduced to the first two words, *Liber generationis* (fols 28^v-29^r). The ancestral names of the genealogy are enrolled in a continuous majuscule text which is arranged without spacing or punctuation in short lines filling two columns on each of the four following pages (fols 29^v-31^r). The centre margin of each page is formed by the shaft of a cross; rounded terminals meet with the rectangular frame at its four cardinal points (Pl. 6). After the emphatic pause of a blank opening, fols 31^v-32^r, there are two whole-page illustrations before the gospel text is resumed at v. 18. A scene of Christ enthroned is now positioned opposite a cross-carpet page (fols 32^v-33^r); following a blank verso the *chi-rho* appears at last on fol. 34^r sweeping across the entire page with a tiny abbreviated *autem generatio* at its foot (Pl. 1).[28] Several features which distinguish the sequence in Kells cannot be accounted for solely in terms of its decorative inventiveness in developing insular gospel-book conventions but may in part be explained as a more detailed and sustained visual exegesis of the text.

IMAGO HOMINIS

Following a prefatory four-symbols page, the theme of the Evangelist symbols is immediately resumed in the framed portrait of a magisterial figure which stands opposite the opening of Matthew's gospel, fols 28^v-29^r (Pl. 4, 5). There are miniature depictions of the heads of a calf and an eagle on the arms of the throne behind this figure and two lion heads symmetrically surmount the back of the throne. The omission of Matthew's own symbol, the man, from the group differentiates the image from the standing portrait of St Mark surrounded by tiny figures of all four evangelist symbols in the St Gall Gospels p. 78, which combines the function of a four-symbols page and an author portrait to show the individual gospel as part of a fourfold single gospel.[29] The figure in Kells, fol. 28^v, may allude both to the Evangelist Matthew and to his symbol. The iconography bears some comparison with the individual symbols of calf and eagle which preface the gospels of Luke and John respectively in the Book of Armagh: each has small roundel faces of the remaining *three* symbols on its wings (Pl. 7).[30] Fol. 28^v in the Book of Kells is not a conventional evangelist portrait but its association of the evangelist symbols and the Matthean genealogy is not unique in insular manuscripts. It may reflect the standard practice in Hiberno-Latin gospel commentaries of placing an introductory discussion of the harmony of the four evangelists before the detailed consideration of the harmony concealed within the Matthean genealogy, which is also treated as a prefatory text to Matthew's gospel. Augustine's work on Gospel harmony combines discussion of the four beasts and the Matthean genealogy, as already noted, and Jerome's influential commentary on Matthew's gospel is prefaced by an exposition of the four beasts as a figure of the harmony of the four gospels. This text, known by its opening words, *Plures fuisse*, serves as a preface in many gospel books. An idiosyncratic form of expression sometimes masks Hiberno-Latin continuity with patristic exegesis.[31] The same may perhaps be argued for certain features of insular iconography. In the MacDurnan Gospels, for example, three of the gospels are prefaced by author portraits but a four-symbols page faces the *Liber generationis* and the standing portrait of Matthew follows the genealogy. In the Book of Armagh three of the gospels are prefaced by drawings of their appropriate evangelist symbols but Matthew's gospel is instead preceded by a four-symbols page: all four symbols look right, towards the facing page on which the entire Matthean genealogy is set out in columns (fols 32ᵛ-33ʳ).[32]

In Ezekiel's vision, each of the four beasts has the aspect of a man, a lion, an ox and an eagle; in the Apocalyptic vision (Rev. 4. 7), four separate creatures attend the divine throne. In the Trier Gospels the bizarre image which faces the *Novum opus* (fols 5ᵛ-6ʳ) shows a standing human figure with the limbs of lion, calf, and eagle suspended from his waist, as though to visualise both the tetramorphic quality of each of the four living creatures of Ezekiel's vision and the prophet's obscure remark that 'there was the likeness (*similitudo*) of a man in them' (Ezek. 1. 5). The symbolic creature of Matthew is not shown in the same way as the other three but is implied in the central figure of the man. Whereas the four-symbols frontispiece in Trier is inscribed with the names of the four creatures who are displayed around the Cross, as though around the divine throne (*homo, leo, vitulus, aquila*), the tetramorph on fol. 5ᵛ is inscribed with the names of the four evangelists. The surviving pictures which preface the gospels of Mark and Luke in the Trier Gospels show author portraits accompanied by their symbolic beasts and the rubric, *incipit evangelium secundum marcum/lucam*, but the portrait page facing Matthew's gospel opening shows a figure holding a book and standing before a throne within an inscribed cruciform frame. The standing author portrait of Matthew in the Cadmug Gospels is inscribed *Imago Mathei*. The word 'imago' elsewhere accompanies the *symbols* of the evangelists, both in the tradition of the wingless 'terrestrial' type of symbol in the Echternach Gospels and the London-Cambridge Gospels and in the tradition of winged symbols with haloes and books which accompany the four evangelist portraits in the Lindisfarne Gospels. In both types Matthew's symbol is inscribed *imago hominis*. The figure of the man facing the opening of the genealogy in the Trier Gospels (fol. 19ᵛ) is inscribed *imago sci mathei euang* and may therefore suggest both the heavenly symbol and the earthly author of the gospel which particularly reveals the humanity of Christ in its opening text of the genealogy and Incarnation.[33] The Echternach Gospels depicts individual scenes of the lion, calf, and eagle before the gospels of Mark, Luke, and John respectively. Before the gospel of Matthew, however, the ambiguous symbol of the man is enthroned like an Evangelist at the centre of a quadripartite frame in which the Cross is strongly figured (Pl. 8). His open book shows seals (cf. Rev. 5. 1) and the title of the genealogy: *liber generationis ihu xpi*. The figure, inscribed *imago hominis*, is placed opposite the columned page containing the whole of Matthew's genealogy and may allude to the humanity of Christ about to be revealed in the text, as in the Incarnation.[34]

The Book of Kells is recognizably part of this insular tradition of iconographic experiment with images of the evangelists and their symbols, particularly at the opening of Matthew's gospel, which argues an interest in their meaning as well as in their value in decoratively marking the entrance to the sacred text. The additional details and greatly extended scale of illustration in Kells makes it possible to suggest more closely its parallels with a reading of the text widely attested in insular exegesis.

The central figure in the Kells portrait on fol. 28ᵛ (Pl. 4) holds a book but conceals his right hand within his robe. George Henderson regards this as a significant gesture indicating Christ 'in the bosom of the Father' (meaning the hidden counsels of God as revealed in Christ at the incarnation).[35] The Old Testament image of the hand or arm of the Lord is already applied to Christ in the gospels. St John describes the incarnate

Christ as the fulfilment of Isaiah's prophecy, 'To whom has the arm of the Lord been revealed?' (Jn 12. 38; Isa. 53. 1). In exegesis the image occurs in contexts relevant to Matthew's gospel opening and its traditional association with the harmony of the gospels figured in the visions of the four beasts. The detailed exposition of the names and titles of the Son of God in Isidore's *Etymologiae* includes the names Christ, Jesus, and Emmanuel but also describes him as *manus Dei*: 'He is the hand of God because all things were made through him [cf Jn 1. 3]. In this sense, and bearing in mind the result of his work of creation – for he formed all creatures – he is also called the right hand.' Immediately before this identification of the incarnate Christ with the Creator Logos, Isidore refers to the account of the incarnation in Phil. 2. 6-7, 'even when adopting the form of a slave, he demonstrated that he possessed in his person the image and immense greatness of the Father'.[36]

Gregory the Great had already used the combination of Jn 1. 3 and Phil. 2. 6-7 in describing the incarnation specifically in the context of expounding Ezekiel's vision of the four living creatures and its prefiguring of the fourfold gospel in which Christ's incarnation was to be revealed. Gregory interprets Ezekiel's enigmatic observation that the four creatures 'had the likeness of a man' (Ezek. 1. 5) as a revelation of Christ who 'took upon himself the form of a slave and was made in the likeness of men' (*in similitudinem hominum factus*) (Phil. 2. 7). This amplifies Gregory's gloss on Ezekiel's assertion that his vision was divinely inspired, that 'the Hand of the Lord was upon him' (Ezek. 1. 3). Gregory explains,

And the Hand or Arm of the Lord signifies the Son, for by him all things were made .... For the Hand of the Lord which through divine authority is begotten, not made, is [here] made from humanity, that it may cleanse the wounds of the human race. Therefore the prophet recognized the incarnation of the only-begotten when he saw the Hand of the Lord above him.[37]

Knowledge of this exegetical tradition confirms the initial impression that the figure on fol. 28ᵛ in the Book of Kells is not simply a portrait of Matthew or his symbol but a Christ-bearing image, a revelation of the incarnation and humanity of the Son of God prophesied in Ezekiel's vision and about to be announced in Matthew's gospel.

Bede's exposition of the vision of the four beasts as described in Rev. 4. 7 draws on yet another of Christ's traditional titles, 'the lion of Judah' (cf. Gen. 49. 9). Following Augustine, Bede, like several Hiberno-Latin commentators on Matthew's gospel, shows that Matthew revealed the kingly character of Christ in the account of Christ's human descent from the royal line of David and in the account of the Magi seeking 'the king of the Jews' (Matt. 2. 2).[38] In the mysterious visionary tableau described in Rev. 5. 17, 'the lion of the tribe of Judah, the root of David', is alone found worthy to take the sealed book from the right hand of the Almighty who is enthroned among the four beasts. Bede interprets the right hand as Christ in his divinity, the book as the mysteries of scripture, sealed until opened at his Incarnation: it is the sealed book prophesied by Isaiah and Ezekiel:

the Son of Man is said to have taken the book from the right hand of God, namely the economy of the Incarnation, appointed by the Father and by Himself, in that He is God; because both dwell with the Holy Spirit upon the throne. For Christ ... is also in His deity the right hand of the Father.[39]

The phrase 'Behold the lion of the tribe of Judah, the root of David, hath prevailed'

(Rev. 5. 5) is seen as Christ overcoming death at his Passion. Christ is the second person of the triune Godhead who ordains the incarnation and he is the incarnate Lord. Bede therefore sees Christ *simultaneously* in the figure enthroned among the four beasts and in the right hand of that figure. Christ at his Incarnation is figured in the book, Christ at his Passion is the lion that takes the book from the divine hand. The book, the right hand, the lion of Judah are among the traditional names of Christ: each reveals something of Christ's identity which cannot be circumscribed by any image.

The solemn vision in the Book of Kells (fol. 28ᵛ) does not directly illustrate the apocalyptic scene of the lion of Judah receiving the book as Carolingian Touronian bibles were to do. Instead, its details act as pictorial equivalents of rhetorical figures in exegesis to expound the uninscribed *imago hominis*. By its positioning in the manuscript the image might be expected to represent Matthew or his symbol, the man, but various accompanying features – the halo inset with three small triangles, the concealed right hand and the book, the throne and the beasts – also conceal clues to the identity of Christ as revealed in Matthew's gospel opening and traditionally expounded in exegesis of that text. The picture also draws on the ancient Mediterranean iconographic motif of two lions as the flanking attendants or guardians of images of divinity and majesty; the two confronted lions above the throne acclaim the central figure by touching him with their tongues.⁴⁰

Small depictions of peacocks, vines and fish, images of Mediterranean origin and Christological association, seed the gospel text and illustrations in the Book of Kells. Similarly, small lions and non-figural motifs – the equilateral, stepped cross, the *chi* and the lozenge – repeatedly embellish the sacred page but may also function as concealed allusions to Christ, just as the Hebrew names in the literal text of the genealogy render up their testimony to Christ's identity when interpreted spiritually. The role of such motifs in pages relevant to the present discussion may be briefly illustrated.

MAGNIFYING THE NAME

Nativitas Xpi, the opening words of the *breves causae* summarizing Matthew's gospel, are magnified and embellished on an unparalleled scale in the prefatory pages of the Book of Kells and face a figural image of the mystery of the incarnation which is without precedent in insular gospel books (fols 7ᵛ-8ʳ). The lion finial on the throne of Mary and the Christ child may allude to the throne of David and Christ's royal descent from the tribe of Judah, the jewelled Cross beneath the throne to his death and conquest of death. The Virgin holds the child in a tender human gesture but she is also depicted as a powerful icon of the Mother of God, the three crosses in her halo signifying the Incarnation as the work of the Trinity. The human and divine sonship of Christ are further suggested in the conspicuous double gesture of the unhaloed child who takes his human mother's right hand in his and points to the lozenge-shaped jewel on her breast. This rhomboid brooch with emphasised cardinal points recalls the tradition of cosmic schemata, which depicted the *tetragonus mundus*, and may here serve to show that the incarnate Christ, born of Mary, is the divine Creator.⁴¹ A tiny lozenge is also at the centre of the letter *chi* of Christ's title in the opening words of the facing text, *Nativitas Xpi*, and at the centre of each cross-framed page listing the names of his ancestors (Pl. 6). At the end of the genealogy which prepares for the aniconic rather than figural revelation of Christ's divine as well as human identity at his Incarnation, the enormously magnified *chi* of the name of Christ at 1.18 on fol. 34ʳ has the cosmological symbol of the lozenge as well as the Cross emblazoned at its centre (Pl. 1).

Facing the *imago hominis* flanked by two lions on fol. 28ᵛ, an image in which Christ is figured, is the opening of the genealogy (Pl. 5). A man extends a book towards the magnified words *Liber generationis*, probably articulating Isaiah's question, 'Who shall declare his generation?'[42] At first unnoticed among the rich ornament enshrining the title of the genealogy, is another pair of small confronted lions at the top of the initial letter. Their protruding tongues cross to form a perfect curved letter *chi*, declaring Christ's presence concealed in the book of generation. At the end of the genealogy the *chi* reappears on fol. 34 like an *inclusio* symbol on a gigantic scale, marking the moment when the long-prefigured Christ becomes incarnate: *Xpi (autem) generatio*. The device may be compared with the much more modest insertion of a tiny upright form of the *chi-rho* above the *Liber generationis* in the Augsburg Gospels, fol. 16, and of a small upright *chi-rho* and the sacred names *ihs xps* above the rubric *Incipit euangelii genelogia mathei* on the *Liber generationis* page of the Lindisfarne Gospels (Pl. 2).[43] The two pairs of confronted lion-heads at each of the cardinal points of the cross-carpet page, which probably once faced the *chi-rho* in the Book of Kells, again honour his royal title. The double-barred form of the cross refers to the title board and Pilate's inscription *Iesus Nazarenus Rex Iudeorum*. Irish exegetes insert the title *Christus* into the gospel text of the inscription which they interpret as showing his kingship of all believers. Similarly, in the Book of Kells fol. 124, the six words immediately following the description of the *titulus* in Matthew's account of the Crucifixion are dramatically framed and displayed within a large letter *chi* and the title *xpi* is inserted into the gospel text: *Tunc crucifixerant xpi cum eo duos latrones* (Matt. 27. 38). Hiberno-Latin interest in the etymology of Hebrew names in Latin and even Greek, and particularly in giving the names Jesus Christ in all three sacred languages 'which, as Jerome says, Christ consecrated in the inscription of the Cross' is nowhere more evident than in exegesis of the names of Christ and his Hebrew ancestors in the Matthean genealogy.[44]

In addition to the decoration of the opening sequence and related pages with motifs which may also function as a visual evocation of the names of Christ, the Matthean genealogy and the *chi-rho* are amplified by two other sequences in the Book of Kells, the Lucan genealogy and the opening of John's gospel. The magnificent five-page layout of the genealogy which follows Luke's account of Christ's baptism (fols 200ʳ-202ʳ) is utterly different from that in Matthew, as though to stress the differences in their literal texts. Small figural additions to Luke's list of ancestral names, however, point to a spiritual interpretation of the underlying meaning which is entirely complementary to that of Matthew's genealogy. In the Lucan genealogy and *breves causae* are small depictions of Luke's symbol, the sacrificial calf, and other allusions to the Old Covenant priesthood, an image which opens the text of Luke's gospel as a prelude to his account of the Incarnation of Christ as the new priesthood and Temple. The climax of the Lucan priestly genealogy in Kells is a whole-page visual exegesis of the new Temple. It is at once the incarnate body of 'Jesus, filled with the Holy Spirit', as the framed and ornamented text of Luke 4. 1 on the facing page proclaims (fols 202ᵛ-203ʳ), and it is his body the Church, built of the living stones of the faithful who are the spiritual descendants of Christ's human ancestors enumerated in the genealogy.[45] The first word in the gospel text immediately after the genealogy is crucial: in Matt. 1. 18 it is the title Christ, in Luke 4. 1 it is the name Jesus. The phrase *Iesus autem spiritu sancto*, with the abbreviated *Ihs* magnified and rendered as a mysterious cipher, occupies the entire page facing the image of the Temple. The layout and decoration of the Matthean and Lucan genealogies in Kells, which are by far the largest decorated sequences in the manuscript, highlight features found in contemporary insular exegesis of the texts. The two genealogical sequences demonstrate the harmony of the gospels. Together they reveal the incarnate Christ as king and priest, as the Davidic Messiah and Son of God. Together they expound the significance of his name and title, Jesus Christ.

The use of the *chi*-Cross and lozenge at Matt. 1. 18 in Kells has here been discussed in terms of an exegetical theme by no means confined to Irenaeus but present in Hiberno-Latin commentaries on Matthew, namely the application of the Christology of John's gospel opening to explain that the Christ descended from human ancestors and born of Mary is the Son of God, the Word made flesh. John's opening words, *In principio erat verbum*, recall the opening of the account of creation in Genesis; the famous vignettes of creatures from earth, air and water concealed within the decoration of the cosmic *chi* on fol. 34 reveal the Word made known not only in his incarnation but in his divine work of creation. While the *chi* is a recurring, and sometimes tiny or concealed, motif in the manuscript, the sign of the cosmological *chi*- Cross, dominates only one other whole page in the Book of Kells in a context which closely harmonizes with its use at Matt. 1. 18, namely fol. 290ᵛ which prefaces John's gospel. It is the only four-symbols page in insular art to be structured on a diagonal Cross (Pl. 9).

Hiberno-Latin commentaries on Matthew are customarily prefaced, like Jerome's commentary, by an exposition on the harmony of the four gospels in revealing Christ. Like Jerome they cite scriptural illustrations of the divine authority underlying the number four, particularly the four beasts in the visions of Ezekiel and St John. But they also develop another strand in the patristic tradition by referring, like Irenaeus, to the testimony of the fourfold nature of all creation in revealing the divine order and measure of its Creator. The four seasons, cardinal directions, elements, properties, and humours are listed and paired with the four gospels to expound, often very arcanely, characteristic features of each gospel and hence of Christ and redemption. The insistent listing of these cosmic quaternities finds some visual parallel in the distinctively insular development of the iconography of the four-symbols page which places the four heavenly creatures (rather than the four earthbound evangelists) in the four quarters of a quadripartite design.[46]

The four-symbols page acts as a frontispiece to some insular gospel-books, or occasionally substitutes for the symbol or evangelist picture prefacing Matthew. In the Lichfield Gospels the image of the four symbols around a Cross may have prefaced each gospel.[47] The theme of gospel harmony reaches a crescendo in the Book of Kells. Most obviously this is achieved through the repeated motif of the four evangelist symbols, depicted with prodigious variety, who animate the canon tables displaying the concordant passages of the four gospels and who are shown in three surviving four-symbols pages placed before individual gospels.

It has been argued here that gospel harmony in the Book of Kells, as in patristic and insular exegesis, is demonstrated also in the spiritual interpretation of paradoxes and apparent discrepancies of the gospel text itself, for which the Matthean genealogy acts as a synecdoche. All its mysteries point to Christ. The strong visual similarity between the *chi*-Cross at Matt. 1. 18 and that in the four-symbols page before John's gospel sustains that exegesis. On fol. 290ᵛ the extension of the four arms of the *chi*-cross to the four corners of the frame, the placing of the four evangelist symbols at its cardinal points, and the dominance of the lozenge-shaped symbol of the *tetragonus mundus* at its centre, present in abstract terms the idea of Christ the Creator-Logos revealed throughout his fourfold world as in his fourfold Gospel.

Like the picture facing the opening words of Matthew's gospel, the picture facing John's opening words (fols 291ᵛ-292ʳ) is not a conventional author portrait of the evangelist but evokes images of Christ embodied in the gospel. A figure in human form is partly concealed beneath the decorated area of the page, his youthful haloed head, hands, and feet projecting at the four cardinal points of the frame so that he is identified both with the cruciform structure undergirding all creation and with the sacred page itself, but is also partly hidden by both. Overlaying this is a majestically haloed and enthroned figure. In his right hand he holds a pen poised above an inkwell and raises a book inscribed with a *chi* within a lozenge.[48] The layered image evokes the Word as the creator of the universe and of the sacred text.

In the Book of Kells the image of the author on fol. 291ᵛ is in the middle of a three-page sequence, positioned between a stylized and symbolic rendering of John's apocalyptic vision of the four beasts, which conceals Christ's name in the *chi*-cross, and the opening words of John's gospel in which Christ's name, as the Word, *Verbum*, is magnified yet obscured by the ornament. The decorative veiling of the sacred text itself offers a metaphor of the art of spiritual reading to discern the meaning hidden within the literal letter of the fourfold Gospel. Exegetes had long compared the process to that of seeing the Creator hidden in his creation and apprehending his divinity clothed in human flesh. The strong visual connection between the *chi*-cross marking Matt. 1. 18 on fol. 34 and the *chi*-cross of the four-symbols page prefacing John's gospel on fol. 190ᵛ points to the harmony of the fourfold gospel, expounded in patristic and insular exegesis, which underlies the apparently divergent openings of Matthew and John. Spiritually interpreted, the *chi* denotes Christ's human generation and birth *and* the divine Logos by whom all things were made. The entire Gospel is subsumed in this sign. The Word imaged through a single word, indeed, a single letter, contains all other names of Christ.

NOTES

1 D. Conneely, *The letters of St Patrick* (Maynooth: An Sagart, 1993), Confessio, 41, 70.

2 *Cummian's letter De controversia paschali*, ed. by M. Walsh & D. Ó Cróinín (Toronto: Pontifical Institute of Medieval Studies, 1988), 73, 75. *Bede Ecclesiastical history of the English people*, ed. by B. Colgrave & R. Mynors (Oxford: Clarendon Press, 1969, repr. 1991), 301, 307.

3 Letter of Columbanus to Pope Boniface IV, 613: *Sancti Columbani opera*, ed. by G. S. M. Walker (Dublin: Institute for Advanced Studies, 1970), Ep. 5, 38-9.

4 D. Ó Corráin, 'The historical and cultural background of the Book of Kells', in *The Book of Kells*, ed. by F. O'Mahony (Aldershot: Scolar Press, 1994), 1-34; D. Ó Cróinín, *Early medieval Ireland 400-1200* (London & New York: Longman, 1995), 174-214.

5 *The Book of Kells, MS 58, Trinity College Library Dublin*, ed. by P. Fox (Lucerne: Faksimile

Verlag, 1990). Date and provenance are still debated: mid-late eighth-century, Iona or shortly after 800, Kells. Discussed by G. Henderson, *From Durrow to Kells: Insular Gospel-books 650-800* (London: Thames & Hudson, 1987), 179-98; B. Meehan, *The Book of Kells* (London: Thames & Hudson, 1994), 90-2.

6 P. McGurk, 'The Irish pocket Gospel Book' (*Sacris Erudiri*, 8, 1956), 249-70 (p. 258).

7 S. Lewis, 'Sacred calligraphy: the chi-rho page in the Book of Kells' (*Traditio*, 36, 1980), 139-59 (p. 143 and n. 13, referring to Irenaeus, *Adversus haereses* 4.17.6, 5.18.3). Werckmeister, *Irisch-northumbrische Buchmalerei des 8. Jahrhunderts und monastische Spiritualität* (Berlin: Walter de Gruyter, 1967), 147-70.

8 *Bede the Venerable: Homilies on the Gospels*, trans. by L. T. Martin & D. Hurst (2 vols. Kalamazoo: Cistercian Publications, 1991), 1, pp. 44-50, 73-83. C. Farr, 'Liturgical Influences on the Decoration of the Book of Kells', in *Studies in Insular Art and Archaeology*, ed. by C. Karkov & R. Farrell, American Early Medieval Studies I, 1991, 29.

9 Matt. 1. 18, 21-3; Isa. 7. 14. Irenaeus, *Adversus haereses* 3.16.2, ed. by F. Saguard (*Sources chrétiennes*, 34, Paris: 1952), 278.

10 H. Merkel, *Die Wiederspruche zwischen den Evangelien: Ihre polemische und apologetische Behandlung in der Alten Kirche bis zu Augustin* (Tübingen, 1971) reviewed by B. Metzer (*Journal of Biblical Literature* 92, 1973), 132-4. Augustine, *De consensu evangeliarum*: P. Schaf, *Augustine: Harmony of the Gospels* (New York: Library of Nicene and post-Nicene Fathers, 1888) 6, pp. 102-3.

11 'Hiberno-Latin' refers to works produced in Ireland and in Irish foundations and centres of influence on the continent. B. Bischoff, 'Turning-points in the history of Latin exegesis in the early Irish church AD 650-800', in *Biblical Studies: the medieval Irish Contribution*, ed. by M. McNamara (Dublin: Dominican Publications, 1976), 74-160, nos 16.1-26; C. D. Wright, 'Hiberno-Latin and Irish-influenced biblical commentaries, florilegia and homily collections', in *The Sources of Anglo-Saxon literary Culture: a trial Version*, ed. by F. M. Biggs, T. D. Hill, & P. E. Szarmach (Binghamton, New York, 1990), 87-123. Most of this material is unedited, much remains unpublished.

12 R. E. Brown, *The birth of the Messiah* (London: Geoffrey Chapman, 1977), 65-8.

13 D. Ó Corráin, 'Irish origin legends and genealogy: recurrent aetiologies', in *History and heroic tale*, ed. by T. Nybey, I. Pio, P. Sorensen, & A. Trommer (Odensee, 1985), 51-96; D. Ó Corráin, L. Breatnach, A. Breen, 'The laws of the Irish' (*Peritia* 3, 1984), 382-438 (394-412).

14 K. McCone, *Pagan Past and Christian Present in early Irish Literature* (Maynooth: An Sagart, 1991), 30-2, 71-2, 233-55.

15 The oldest extant ms. of the *Etymologiae* was written in Ireland, c. 650; the *Etymologiae* was used by at least ten Irish authors in the seventh century: J. N. Hillgarth, 'Ireland and Spain in the seventh century' (*Peritia* 3, 1984) 1-16 (8-10).

16 *Patrologia Latina* 80, 327-42. The Priscillian prologues to the gospels have an arcane interpretation of the Matthean genealogy; there is a good and probably early text preserved in a group of insular gospel-books, including the Book of Kells, see J. Chapman, *Notes on the early history of the Vulgate Gospels* (Oxford: Clarendon Press, 1908), 217-18, 225-6.

17 Unpublished. See Bischoff, 'Turning-points in the history of Latin exegesis', no. 16.1; also no. 17.1, 25 for Hiberno-Latin commentary on Matthew in Vienna 940 which uses Aileran's work.

18 Unpublished. Bischoff, 'Turning-points', no. 23. I am grateful to Dr Seán Connolly for generous permission to use his transcripts of the Matthean genealogy in Munich, Staatsbibliothek, Clm. 6233, fols 7^v-31^v, and the Irish Reference Bible New Testament, which he is editing. Clm. 6233, fols 15^v-16^v, develops the patristic chain Jn 1. 14; Jn 12. 32; Phil. 2. 6-11 (briefly used in Aileran and Orléans 65(62) under the entry for Booz) into an exposition on the incarnation as the work of the Trinity and on the humanity and divinity of Christ.

19 'Irish Reference Bible', unpublished, Paris, Bibl. Nat. lat. 11561, fols 137ᵛ-140. *Collectanea* probably written in centres of Irish influence on the continent: Angers 55 and Munich Clm. 14426 in *Scriptores Hiberniae minores 1*, ed. by R. McNally (*Corpus Christianorum* 108 B, Turnholt: Brepols, 1973), 146-9, 225-30.

20 Irish Reference Bible, fol. 137ᵛ, Munich Clm. 6233, fols 7ᵛ-8, Angers 55, fol. 10ᵛ; cf. R. McNally, 'Der irische *Liber de numeris*: eine Quellenanalyse des *ps-isidorischen Liber de numeris*' (Dissertation, Munich, 1957), 129, for multiple interpretations of *liber*.

21 Isa. 29. 11, Ezek. 2. 9, Rev. 5. 1.

22 Irish Reference Bible, fol. 138. Angers 55, like Irenaeus, relates the incarnation image of anointing to the Trinity: the Father anoints, the Holy Spirit is the ointment (chrism), the Son is the Anointed One (Christus): *Scriptores Hiberniae minores* (ed. by McNally), 1, 148.

23 Fols 31ʳ-32. Ps-Jerome, *Expositio in iv evangelia*, gives the etymology of Christus in glossing the line Matt. 1. 18 (*Patrologia Latina* 30), 535.

24 St Gall, Stiftsbibl., Cod. 51, ps. 6-7; J. J. G. Alexander, *Insular Manuscripts 6th to the 9th century* (London: Harvey Miller, 1978), cat. 44, pl. 200-1.

25 London, British Lib. Cotton MS Nero D.IV; Alexander, *Insular Manuscripts*, cat. 9, pl. 39, 44.

26 Vienna, Nationalbibl., Cod. 1224, fols 17ᵛ-18; Alexander, *Insular Manuscripts*, cat. 37, pl. 181-2. The Cadmug Gospels, Fulda, Landesbibl., Bonif. 3, also has *incipit evange. s. matheu.* above the *chi-rho*. McGurk, 'The Irish pocket Gospel Book', 257-8.

27 London, Lambeth Palace Lib., MS 1370, fols 4ᵛ-5; Alexander, *Insular Manuscripts*, cat. 70, pl. 321-2, 326. The Gospels of Mael Brigte, London, British Lib. Harley MS 1802 (Armagh, 1138) ends the genealogy with the word *finit* and inserts a Hebrew glossary and some ten folios of prefatory material between Matt. 1. 17 and the *chi-rho*.

28 The sequence is reproduced in colour in F. Henry, *The Book of Kells* (London; Thames & Hudson, 1974, repr. 1988), pl. 20-9.

29 Alexander, *Insular Manuscripts*, cat. 44, pl. 207.

30 Dublin, Trinity College Lib., MS 52, folios 68ᵛ, 90. Alexander, *Insular Manuscripts*, cat. 53, pl. 226. The creatures have four wings, as in Ezekiel's vision; Gregory the Great said of these creatures that each had the faces of all four because the four evangelists' knowledge of Christ is the same in one as simultaneously in the four: *Sancti Gregorii Magni. Homiliae in Hiezechihelem prophetam*, ed. by M. Adriaen (Corpus Christianorum 142, Turnholt: Brepols, 1971) Hom. 3.

31 Augustine, *De consensu evangeliarum* 1, 2; Jerome, *Commentariorum in Matheum* (Corpus Christianorum 77, Turnholt: Brepols, 1969), 1-4.

32 Alexander, *Insular Manuscripts*, cat. 70, pl. 321-2, 325-6 (MacDurnan Gospels, London, Lambeth Palace Lib., 1370, fols 1ᵛ-2, 4ᵛ-5); cat. 53, pl. 230.

33 Trier, Domschatz, Cod. 61: Alexander, *Insular Manuscripts*, cat. 26, pl. 110-14. N. Netzer, *Cultural interplay in the eighth century: the Trier Gospels and the making of a scriptorium at Echternach* (Cambridge: University Press, 1994), 90-111, pl. 1-4, 19-21 for pictures and facing texts.

34 Paris, Bibl. Nat., lat. 9389, fol. 18ᵛ: Alexander, *Insular Manuscripts*, cat. 11, pl. 54. Werckmeister, *Irisch-northumbrische Buchmalerei*, 7-53.

35 *From Durrow to Kells*, 155-9, referring particularly to Rev. 4 and 5.

36 *Etymologiae*, 7.2.

37 *The Homilies of St Gregory the Great on the Book of Ezekiel*, trans. by T. Gray (Etna, Calif.: Center for Traditionalist Orthodox Studies, 1990), Hom. 2, 24.

38 *De consensu evangeliarum* 2.6; repeated in Augustine's Tractates on John's gospel: *In Johannis evangelium*, ed. by R. Willems (Corpus Christianorum 36, Turnholt: Brepols, 1954), 36.5. Bede, *Explanatio Apocalypsis*, c. 710-16 (Patrologia Latina 93), 144 and *In Lucae*

evangelium expositio (ed. D. Hurst, Corpus Christianorum 120, Turnholt: Brepols 1960) 7-10.

39 *Explanatio Apocalypsis*, Patrologia Latina 93, 145. *The exposition of the Apocalypse by the Venerable Bede*, trans. by E. Marshall (Oxford and London, 1878) 5. 5-7 ps. 34-6; the explanation concerning the lion of Judah and the Passion is repeated in Bede's treatise on rhetorical figures, *De schematibus et tropis*. It was often used by Augustine, e.g. in *De doctrina christiana* 3. 35-6 (ed. by J. Martin, *Corpus Christianorum* 32, Turnhout: Brepols, 1962) 97-8.

40 Cf. Paris, Bibl. Nat., lat. 12168, f. Cb, c.770: P. Lasko, *The kingdom of the Franks* (London: Thames & Hudson, 1971), pl. 112. Two pairs of confronted lions flank and touch with their tongues the Tree of Life and the Cross which is symbolically portrayed beneath an arch with a lozenge at its centre and the *nomina sacra, Xpi Ihu*. Cf. Kells, fol. 114^r.

41 Literature on cosmic schemata and the lozenge motif discussed by J. O'Reilly, 'Patristic and insular traditions on the Evangelists: exegesis and iconography', in *Quadetui di Romano-Barbarica* 1, ed. by A. M. Fuiselli Fadda & E. Ó Carragáin, Rome, in press. For insular examples of the lozenge used in other media, see H. Richardson, 'Number and symbol in early Christian Irish art', *Journal of Royal Society of Antiquaries of Ireland* 114 (1984) 1-30.

42 Isa. 53. 8. The Anglo-Saxon Boulogne Gospels, Boulogne, Bibl. mun. MS 11, fol. 56, shows the figures of Isaiah and John the Baptist with prophetic scrolls alongside the opening words of Mark's gospel and pointing up to Christ whom they announced: E. Temple, *Anglo-Saxon Manuscripts* (London: Harvey Miller, 1976) cat. 44, pl. 150.

43 Now Augsburg, Universitätsbibl. Cod. 1.2.4°.2, fols 16-16^v: Alexander, *Insular Manuscripts*, cat. 24, pl. 123-4; cat. 44, pl. 39. The Barberini Gospels, Rome, Vatican, Bibl. Apostolica, Barberini Lat. 570, fol. 18 has a somewhat effete variant of the Kells lion-heads motif transposed to the decoration of the *chi-rho*: *Insular Manuscripts*, cat. 36, pl. 170.

44 *Cummian's letter De controversia paschale* (ed. by Walsh & Cronin) 57; R. McNally, 'The *Tres Lingua Sacrae* in early Irish Bible exegesis' (*Theological Studies* 19, 1958), 395-403 for examples of the *titulus* rendered *Hic est Iesus Christus Rex Iudeorum* and *Hic est Salvator unctus (Christus) Rex Confessorum*.

45 For the image of the Temple as related to the genealogy: J. O'Reilly, 'Exegesis and the Book of Kells: the Lucan genealogy', in *The Book of Kells* (ed. by O'Mahony), 344-97.

46 R. McNally, 'The Evangelists in the Hiberno-Latin tradition', in *Festschrift Bernhard Bischoff*, ed. by A. Hiergemann (Stuttgart, 1971) 111-22; additional Hiberno-Latin texts and four-symbols page iconography: J. O'Reilly, 'Patristic and Insular traditions on the Evangelists: exegesis and iconography'.

47 Four-symbols pages as frontispieces in Book of Durrow, Trier Gospels, MacDurnan Gospels; as preface to Matthew in the Book of Armagh, as preface to individual gospel in Lichfield Gospels: Alexander, *Insular Manuscripts*, pl. 13, 114, 325, 230, 81.

48 Werckmeister, *Irisch-northumbrische Buchmalerei*, 101-47.

THE PSALMS IN THE IRISH CHURCH

THE MOST RECENT RESEARCH ON TEXT, COMMENTARY, AND DECORATION – WITH EMPHASIS ON THE SO-CALLED PSALTER OF CHARLEMAGNE

Martin McNamara

IN EARLY IRISH HISTORY the psalter of David was very much at the centre of Christian life, indeed of the life of the literate community. In the schools children of seven learned reading itself from the Bible. In fact what appears to be the earliest specimen of writing we have from Ireland are the so-called Springmount Bog tablets from the early seventh century – wax tablets with Psalms 30-32 used, it would appear, to initiate the pupils into the arts of reading and writing. The psalter as a book in Ireland was loved and venerated. It was at the very centre of the monastic liturgy and Irish learning.

In 1973 I gave an account of the Irish psalter text and the study of the psalter in Ireland from the beginnings up to about the year AD 1200.[1] Since then a certain amount of work has been done in this field. In this paper I will not repeat what I have said there. Instead I propose to report what progress has been made in the field since then, and to indicate what I believe are areas deserving of further investigation.

I. TEXT

Only two Irish manuscripts with the *Gallicanum* text have been fully collated. These are the Cathach of St Columba (Dublin, Royal Irish Academy; MS with siglum *C*) and the *Gallicanum* of the Double Psalter of Rouen (Rouen, Bibl. mun., MS 24 (A. 41), with siglum *I*). These two manuscripts have good *Gallicanum* texts and are used in the Roman critical edition of the Vulgate. Seven other Irish *Gallicanum* texts await full collation, a collation necessary to determine the relation of later texts to the earlier Vulgate, and also the relationships of these later texts among themselves.

The only Irish text of the *Hebraicum* to be fully collated for the critical edition is that Rouen Double Psalter (to which we may add Karlsruhe Codex Aug. XXXVIII which has the typically Irish-form *Hebraicum* text (siglum *K*). Five other Irish *Hebraicum* texts await full collation.[2]

Martin McNamara

2. COMMENTARIES

We have a relatively rich commentary literature on the psalms from the early Irish Church, both in Latin from about AD 700 onwards and in vernacular Irish from about 800. In all these sources stress is laid on the importance of interpreting the psalms historically, within Jewish history, whether in the life of David and his contemporaries or as referring to later Jewish history, e.g. Hezekiah, the exile, return from Exile, the Maccabees. The basic commentary used was that of Theodore of Mopsuestia in the translation of Julian of Eclanum, and in an epitome of this. There is evidence that together with this Theodorean and Antiochene historical exegesis, there emerged early in Ireland (probably before 700) another form of historical exegesis which interpreted the psalms principally of David and his time. There is no evidence for such exegesis outside Ireland, and it may have originated within Ireland itself, or possibly in Iona-Northumbria.[3]

This historical exegesis has been transmitted in various ways. The Theodorean commentary and the epitome are found in the Milan Commentary, together with Irish glosses (Milan, MS Amb. C 301 inf.) Excerpts from it are found in the *Eclogae tractatorum in Psalterium* (c. 800; composed apparently in Ireland). The historical exegesis has also been transmitted in the *Tituli Psalmorum* attributed to Bede, in two manuscripts preserved and written on the Continent, i.e. Munich Clm 14387 (s. IX) and Paris, Bibl. Nat., lat. 12273 (s. XI). We may presume that these *Tituli* came to the Continent from Northumbria. A special commentary with Davidic interpretation has been partially preserved in Vatican Pal., MS lat. 68 (for Ps. 39. 11-151).[4] In the so-called Psalter of Charlemagne (Paris BN, lat. 13159) we have psalm headings which correspond to the Vatican commentary. We shall return to this manuscript further below. Professor Luc De Coninck is presently preparing for edition the glosses in the Double Psalter of St Ouen (Rouen, Bibl. mun. MS 24 [A. 41]). In the glosses on the *Hebraicum* he finds evidence of the use of four distinct historical commentaries on the psalms. One of those is Julian of Eclanum's translation of Theodore's commentary, and its epitome. Another is the psalter commentary of the kind found in Vatican Pal., MS lat. 68 (possibly dating from c. 700). The others are historical commentaries along the same lines, evidence it would appear of a developing historical psalm exegesis in Ireland.

Prof. De Coninck is also editing the gloss (mainly with the spiritual sense) on the *Gallicanum* of the Double Psalter of St Ouen, to be published in the *Corpus Christianorum* (Turnhout: Brepols) in a new 'Scriptores Celtigenae' sub-series. This draws on Cassiodorus, Augustine, Hilary, the *Glosa Psalmorum ex traditione seniorum*, and for Ps. 100 onwards on Prosper of Aquitaine (who commented only on Ps. 100-150). The gloss is also rather closely related to that of the Southampton Psalter (Cambridge, St John's College, MS C.9). One question arising from the evidence he produces will be the need to determine the date of the introduction of Prosper's work into Ireland, whether it was there at an early date or came only in the tenth century, when this double psalter seems to have been composed. P. O'Neill is completing an edition of the glosses of the Southampton Psalter, to be published in the *Corpus Christianorum* (Turnhout: Brepols) in a new 'Scriptores Celtigenae' sub-series.

The completion of these critical editions should help immensely in the study of the origins and development of psalm exegesis in Ireland. The evidence we have points to the involvement of the Irish schools in Northumbria and Ireland. From Northumbria the exegesis seems to have influenced southern England and West Saxon territory before 900 (the West Saxon prose translation of Ps. 1-50 by King Alfred). The introductory material in the Psalter of Charlemagne (795-800) and the Continental manuscripts of the *Tituli Psalmorum* of (Pseudo-?)Bede (MSS s. IX) indicate that at least the principles governing it were taken to the Continent, possibly from Northumbria. We know that the Irish-Northumbrian commentary of Vatican Pal., MS lat. 68 reached Rome from Germany (probably Lorsch). What, if any, impact this approach to the psalms made on the Continent is difficult to say. Apparently it was very little. There is evidence that texts of Julian's translation were known in Normandy, and also that the Theodorean-Julian commentary was known to Remigius of Auxerre (*c.* AD 841-908) or his circle and that parts of it found their way into an earlier edition of Remigius's commentary, but not in a later one.[5]

3. DECORATION

F. Henry has made a special study of the decoration of the three Irish psalters: BL, Cotton MSS, Vitellius F. XI, Cambridge, St John's College, MS C. 9 (the Southampton Psalter), and Rouen, Bibl. mun., MS 24 (A. 41).[6] The Cotton manuscript was damaged in the fire of 1731. It has two miniatures, David and Goliath and David playing the harp (or: *David Rex*), now bound at the beginning of the psalter. Henry has shown that they were once located at Psalms 51 and 101, at the beginning of the second and third fifties, where they framed initial pages as was the case in the Southampton Psalter.[7] The artist of the Southampton Psalter imitates the Vitellius, but is less original. The Southampton Psalter has three portraits: facing Ps. 1 David killing the lion; facing Ps. 51 the Crucifixion of Christ; facing Ps. 101 David and Goliath. Henry comments that as for the Crucifixion portrait heading the second section, it is not in itself a strange choice and it corresponds to the growing tendency to illustrate psalters with scenes from the life of Christ. Ps. 53 being one of the psalms closely connected with the Passion, a representation of the Crucifixion would come quite normally at the beginning of the section which contains it.[8] In the Rouen Double Psalter the decoration consists mainly of capitals at the beginning of each psalm. There are about three hundred of them, all of the knotted-wire type. They are finely drawn and the little animal heads are often of exquisite design. In addition there are designs in the margin and the text of a few pages, some of which are probably nothing more than 'doodles', while others may be intended to refer to the content of the biblical text.[9] In a later study on a century of Irish illumination (1070-1170) F. Henry & G. L. Marsh-Micheli[10] examine the illumination of four later Irish psalters or fragments of psalters: the so-called Psalter of Caimin (MS Franciscan House, Killiney, Co. Dublin); BL, Cotton MSS, Galba A. V; BL, Additional MSS, 36929 ('The Psalter of Cormac') and Vatican Pal., MS lat. 68. They note that the decoration of the Psalter of Cormac consists in three Introductory pages with framed pages opposite each of them. The frame of the first fifty is filled by a text headed '*absolutio bernarddi*' (*sic*); the two other frames are empty except for a *Dextra Dei* appearing in the corner of that facing '*Quid gloriaris*' (Ps. 51). It is likely, they continue, that they were meant to contain figure drawings which would then correspond with those in two other Irish psalters, BL, Cotton MSS, Vitellius F. XI and MS C. 9 in the library of St John's College, Cambridge.[11]

Martin McNamara

In an unpublished doctoral dissertation on the Tiberius Psalter for the University of Toronto, 'Images, texts and Contexts: the Iconography of the Tiberius Psalter, London, British Library, Cotton MSS, Tiberius C. vi,' K. M. Openshaw[12] has in ch. 5 made a special study of the illumination of the Southampton Psalter and its cultural background. In 1992 she published the substance of her work in an essay in the review *Arte medievale*.[13] Although she draws on the work of F. Henry, G. L. Marsh-Micheli, and the others who have written on the subject, she has done much personal research. The Psalter of Cormac she regards as an archaic Irish psalter of the early twelfth century, which appears to provide further evidence for the continuity of the Irish approach to the psalter decoration she has been studying, even though in some details of ornament it betrays the impact of new artistic influences. She says that the pages facing Ps. 51 and 101 were originally decorated with full-page figures. Regrettably the figures have been scraped off and we do not know their iconography for sure. However, an examination carried out by her under infra-red light suggests that at Ps. 101 there was a laterally-viewed image of David enthroned, much like the picture in the Vitellius Psalter. The Ps. 51 image is less easy to construe, though it seems possible that there were two upright figures, one of which was helmeted on the same style as David and Goliath in the Southampton Psalter. A strong vertical line divides the two figures, and this could well be David's staff that is so prominent in the Southampton and Vitellius David-and-Goliath pictures. On balance there is a fair likelihood that the Ps. 51 picture depicted David and Goliath, and that figural decoration of the Psalter followed in the tradition clearly seen in the Vitellius and Southampton Psalters.[14] She lays stress on David as the image of Christ in this tradition, using the evidence of the Durham Cassiodorus (Durham, Cathedral Library, MS. B II 30) with the figure of David as image of Christ as Ps. 51, and recalls the figure of David, albeit in different iconography, in the same position (Ps. 51) in the Vitellius Psalter. Three statements can be made, she writes, about the Durham Cassiodorus manuscript. First, the decoration of the manuscript is symbolic. These splendid full-page figures do not illustrate the text that they face in any specific way and they clearly do not represent a narrative sequence. Secondly, the decoration most emphatically emphasizes the typological relationship between the psalmist David and Christ, by unique and economical means. Finally, the triumph over evil is an important element of the decoration; and here, as in the Southampton Psalter, it is the triumph both of the psalmist and of Christ.[15] What is said of the Cassiodorus manuscript holds good for the Irish psalter tradition. Openshaw[16] does not agree with Henry's explanation of the choice of Crucifixion scene facing Ps. 51 in the Southampton Psalter, an explanation seeking, without success, relationships between the Irish psalter pictures and adjacent and nearby texts, and with regard to the positioning of this particular picture invoking a growing tendency to illustrate psalters with scenes from the life of Christ.

The final section of her essay[17] is devoted to some suggested ideological sources for the symbolic and typological psalter programmes of the Insular world. One must consider the thought-world, she notes,[18] within which this art was created, and examine the psalter exegesis that reflects it. Some of the early Irish exegesis of the psalms, she continues, displays a much more consistent view of the Davidic and Christological typology of the psalter than the standard patristic commentaries. For instance, in their prefaces Hilary and Cassiodorus make statements of the general Christological relevance of the psalter, but they tend not to see the book as relating to David in any broad sense. By contrast, in some eighth- and ninth-century Irish exegetical texts there is a more pronounced uniformity of approach in giving each psalm an historical interpretation first, and then a spiritual or Christological one, as part of unique Irish variants of the standard medieval fourfold exegesis. Knowledge of such psalter exegesis might very well have predisposed scribes to the use of unified typological programmes of decoration in their psalters.

Openshaw concludes by noting that, although it was a product of Irish scholarship, the tendency towards what is effectively a typological interpretation of the psalter was not reserved to Ireland. This particular facet of the Irish world view was absorbed and enhanced in Anglo-Saxon England. The enhancement is evident in the Anglo-Saxon prose translation of the first fifty psalms, now confidently ascribed to King Alfred, and executed in West Saxon territory just before 900. She also sees its influence in the Tiberius Psalter (BL, Cotton MSS, Tiberius C. vi). The kernel of the ambitious picture cycle of this psalter is clearly the symbolic and typological programme seen in the earlier Southampton Psalter; the cycle presents the psalmist David as a prefiguration of Christ, and his battles as forerunners of those of Christ. In the Tiberius Psalter, however, this earlier plan is expanded. Thus the Tiberius Psalter stands as a watershed in western psalter illustration, marking the transition from the symbolic and typological psalter schemes of earlier Insular Christianity to the elaborate historically oriented schemes of the Romanesque and Gothic, and marking also the assimilation of this particular Insular approach to psalter decoration into the European mainstream.[19]

4. MANUSCRIPT STUDIES: TWO BL COTTON PSALTERS (VITELLIUS F. XI; GALBA A. V) AND THE SO-CALLED PSALTER OF CHARLEMAGNE (PARIS BN, LAT. 13159)

4.1. *Introduction.* There are two Irish Psalters in the Cotton Collection of the British Library (Vitellius F. XI and Galba A. V). The Collection was brought together by Sir Robert Cotton (1570-1631), passed to his son John and later to public ownership. It was ravaged by a fire in 1731, and became part of the British Museum at its foundation in 1753. The collection was catalogued by Thomas Smith in 1696 and later by J. Planta in 1802. The collection comprises 25,000 distinct articles in Planta's catalogue.

James Ussher (1581-1656) was on friendly terms with Robert Cotton and made regular use of the library, beginning, it would appear, around 1606. Ussher's biographer Richard Parr[20] tells us that after 1609 'he [Ussher] constantly came over to England once in three years, spending one month of the summer at Oxford, another at Cambridge, and the rest of the time in London, spending his time chiefly in the Cottonian Library, the noble and learned Master of which affording him free access, not only to that but his own conversation.' Barr[21] prints a letter of Cotton to Ussher, then Bishop of Meath, dated 26 March 1622, in which he mentions the return of eight manuscripts of his which Ussher had.

Possibly it is to this early period of his career that we should date the manuscript of Ussher now in the Bodleian Library Oxford, with the shelfmark Add. A. 91 (S. C. 27719). This text is a study by Ussher of certain Latin psalters. Two of these, to which he gives the sigla F and G, are the two Irish psalters from the Cotton library. He describes F (=Vitellius F. XI) as follows (Add. A. 91 [S. C. 27719], fol. 72ᵛ):

Psalterium admodum antiquum in Hibernicis literis quadratis (Hibernicis seu Saxonicis) descriptum. habetur in eadem Bibliotheca. In fine additur: **Bendacht dé formúiretach/comall glé robsen sutin sunn insúi niropdutham sunn/ haré intapthanth[é] ha**[superscript 'o']**bthaid/ flatha de**[written over a crossed-out 'il'.²²

Immediately afterwards Ussher describes the manuscript with the siglum G, which is clearly Galba A. V:

G Psalterium charactere [following word unclear but apparently *uetustissimo*] *Hibernico descriptum in eadem Bibliotheca. Cui praefixa fuerunt haec verba is liber oswini deirorum regis.*

Thomas Smith (Smith, 1696, p. 103) describes F. XI as follows:

Vitellius F. XI. 1. *Psalterium vetustum cum canticis Mosis ad filios Israel characteribus Hibernicis exaratum.*
2. *Quaedam Hibernica, charactere Hibernico.*
3. *Oratio in benedictione panis novi.*

He thus describes the other psalter:

Galba A. V. *Psalterium Davidis, characteribus Hibernicis vetustissimis, cum cantico Mosis, Hannae & trium puerorum. Additur in fine folium, Hibernice. Dicitur fuisse liber Oswini regis.*

Smith apparently wrote after personal examination of the manuscripts. There is no indication that he knew of Ussher's work. The *Quaedam Hibernica* in the description of Vitellius F. XI probably indicates the Irish text at the end noted by Ussher. A new element in his description of Galba A. V is the mention of a page in Irish at the end of the manuscript.

Planta did not have access to Vitellius F. XI, damaged in the 1731 fire. Under this heading he simply entered 'Desideratur'. He thus describes Galba A. V:²³

Galba A. V. *Codex membran. in 8vo minori, constans hodie foliis 35 igne et madore nimium corruptus.*
Psalterium Davidis characteribus Hibernicis vetustissimis; dicitur fuisse liber Oswini regis.

As we shall see, Planta's description bears little resemblance to the Galba manuscript, yet it has influenced later descriptions.

4.2. *Cotton Vitellius F. XI.* In modern times the first serious study of Vitellius F. XI was made by J. O. Westwood.²⁴ Westwood notes how it had only been recently discovered in the British Museum after the disastrous fire of 1731, and was carefully mounted under the direction of Sir F. Madden. Westwood compares the illumination (David's combat with the lion; David's combat with Goliath) with the psalter of St John's College, Cambridge (MS C.9, the Southampton Psalter). He regarded the script and the illumination of both to be the same and believed that Vitellius F. XI was by the same scribe as that of the Southampton Psalter. With regard to date, he considered that the drawing of Vitellius F. XI may be referred to the ninth or first half of the tenth century.

F. Henry published a study of the illumination of the psalter in 1960.²⁵ The illuminations, she notes, have a violence of style which connects them closely with the carvings on the tenth-century high crosses. There is a particularly close connection between the painting of David killing Goliath at the beginning of the third fifty and the same scene on the cross of Muiredach at Monasterboice. The Muiredach whose name is on this cross was probably the person who became abbot about 887 and died in 923. Taking the two works as contemporary, Henry dates the psalter to the early tenth century, as Westwood had earlier done. In the same study Henry examines the illumination of the Southampton Psalter which, with others, she dates to the beginning of the eleventh century. She believes that the illuminator was inspired by Vitellius F. XI. His style, however, she remarks, is more formal and less natural: in the representations of David and Goliath, for instance, he hardly understands what he is copying.

Later A. O'Sullivan[26] drew attention to the Irish text at the end of the psalter, given by Ussher. It confirms Henry's connection of the work with Muiredach. O'Sullivan translates the Irish text as follows:

> The blessing of God on Muiredach, bright fulfilment!
> May the scholar be successful and long-lived there,
> May his time here not be short;
> may the outstanding(?) abbot without falsehood
> be a dweller in the kingdom of God.

A closer examination of this psalter is called for since this is one of the few Irish manuscripts from the tenth century.[27]

There are two interlinear glosses in the text. The first is to *multiplicasti filios hominum* of Ps. 11. 9 and reads: *id est in Adam corporaliter in Christo spiritualiter* (fol. 3ᵛ). The same gloss is found to these same words on the *Gallicanum* in the Double Psalter of St Ouen. The orthography *spiritualiter* (clearly with a *u*) indicates a post-900 date for the entry of the gloss in Vitellius F. XI. The other gloss is in fol. 42ʳ, over *Beel Phegor* of Ps. 105. 28. The gloss (read by fibre-optic reader) over *Beel* reads *id est idulum*, and that over *Phegor id est ciuit(as) ut* (read: est) *terrae Moab et Ammon et Midian*. This is identical with the gloss of the commentary in Vatican Pal., MS lat. 68 on these words.[28] The Double Psalter of St Ouen has the gloss *idulum* to *Beel*, but not the other gloss.

This manuscript merits palaeographical consideration (abbreviations system, etc.). A partial collation of the biblical text shows agreements with I (*Gallicanum* of Rouen Psalter) and sometimes with specific readings of the Southampton Psalter. A full collation is called for, to determine its agreements with, and deviations from, the Irish *Gallicanum* text, and also with that of the Southampton Psalter, with which it is very close in the illumination.

4.3. *Cotton Galba A. V.* Planta's description of this manuscript is very misleading. It is not badly damaged by fire and damp (*igne et madore nimium corruptus*); in fact it is in an excellent state of preservation, apparently in no way affected by the 1731 fire. It has 62 folios (in present foliation), not the 35 of Planta's catalogue, with an additional unnumbered folio Irish at the end.

F. Henry & G. L. Marsh-Micheli published a study of the illumination of the codex in 1962. Their opening description of the codex seems dependent on Planta:[29] 'It is no more than the ruin of a book, its pages having been turned brown, shrunk and split by the 1731 fire which ravaged the Cotton Library. It consists now of thirty-five folios,

5 in. by about 3 in., but it probably shrank considerably in the fire.' This description seems to have been written before a personal inspection of the codex. The essay goes on to give the results of the authors' personal inspection of the work, including reference to the illuminated initial of Ps. 101 in fol. 48^r. They consider the work to be of artistically inferior quality, and believe that the painter was copying indiscriminately from several manuscripts. This psalter, they say, is likely to be a fairly late imitation (twelfth century?), impossible to localize.

I had the opportunity to examine the codex rapidly in August 1994 and January 1995. As already said, the psalter text is in an excellent state of preservation. The present manuscript Galba A. V has a continuous foliation from 1 to 63. The psalter text ends at fol. 62^v, at Ps. 148. 14. Fol. 63^{rv} contains an Irish text. There is evidence for an earlier foliation, or foliations, for most folios. The contents of the present codex are as follows:

Fol. 1^r. Outside. In three colours, blue, brown and yellow, with some writing, not legible to naked eye. Not in Irish script.

Fol. 1^v. Small page with writing; 17 lines to page. Latin. Illuminated initials. Not in Irish script.

Fol. 2^r. The same Latin text. Not in Irish script.

Fol. 2^v. Writing. 17 lines to page. Some rubrics, with words *quomodo psal ...*, preceded in black ink by words: *te populo tuo* and followed by what seems to be a prayer.

Fol. 3^r. This seems to have been the outer cover of a book.

Fol. 3^v. Inside cover apparently; faded; whitish grey colour. Has some writing, hard to decipher. Above (apparently): *Catalogus. In isto (?) volumine.* Below this, but in page partly torn: *charactere Hibernico/uetustissimo (/) olim erat/ haec uerba Liber oswim (=oswini) regis.*

Fol. 4^r (older foliation fol. 1). Psalter text in Irish script begins: *Beatus uir.*

This Irish psalter is divided according to the three fifties. Some of the original folios are now lost, as is the last folio with Ps. 148. 15-150 (or 151). A page in Irish has been added at the end (as fol. 63).

It would appear that the present fols 1-2 and the final fol. 63 are additions to the codex known to James Ussher, who makes no mention of a folio in Irish at the end. This final page would seem to have been there when T. Smith examined it (1696). The Irish text of fol. 63 has been identified by Aoibheann Nic Dhonnchaidh of the School of Celtic Studies, Dublin, as a computus text, and part (of folio 4) of the Cotton manuscript Cotton Appendix LI (written AD 1589). It would appear to have been added as a kind of end cover.[30]

4.4. The so-called Psalter of Charlemagne (Paris BN, lat. 13159).

The work referred to as the 'Psalter of Charlemagne' was written AD 795-800 in some centre in northern or north-eastern France.[31] It contains the Gallican psalter preceded by headings and introductory material. On the outer margins of the manuscript, at the beginning of each psalm, a triangular cartouche contains the Series III of psalm headings. Each psalm has an illuminated capital. At the end of each psalm there is a psalter collect, from the African Series. The manuscript also contains Litanies.

The date of transcription is assured by the prayer for Pope Leo (III) (795-816) and *pro rege Carolo* (not yet emperor, AD 800). The place of transcription is not agreed on by all. F. Masai[32] believed it was transcribed for the abbey of St Riquier, probably at Corbie. M. Huglo[33] maintained it was written at St Riquier. E. A. Lowe[34] describes as follows: 'Written in a centre with insular connections situated somewhere on the Rhine or in Belgium or East France, to judge by the local saints mentioned in the litanies.' B. Bischoff[35] says that details in the Psalter's litany point in particular to the border region between north-east France and north-west Austrasia,[36] noting (against Masai's view) that this codex is utterly different from everything that we know of Corbie's script and book decoration. It belongs to the same group (and presumably is from the same scriptorium) as the Essen Münsterschatz Gospels in minuscule, the ornamentation of which is dominated by the same wild inventiveness, tamed only be the draughtsman's skill. B. Fischer[37] explicitly rejects St Riquier or Corbie origin, and opts for one in the Rhein-Maas-Gebiet region, without possibility of more precise localization.

What is granted by all is that, whatever the precise place of composition, the work depends on an Insular original. Lowe[38] notes the misuse of *s* typical of Insular scribes: *hierussalem, abysus, dissolauerunt (desolauerunt)*. The extent of this dependence must be determined for each of the elements. An attempt should also be made to determine as precisely as possible the nature of the 'Insular' influence, for instance, whether it came from Ireland or Northumbria. (The 'Insular' influence is clearest in the decoration and we shall return to this point. However, the litanies represent, in the main, Continental devotion, pointing to north-east France or north-west Austrasia in M. Coens's opinion.[39])

The **psalter text** is *Gallicanum*. It is Q of the Roman Benedictine edition.[40] Its text is of an inferior quality, replete with errors, probably due to pressure of time for completion.[41] This psalter text seems to represent influences from various text forms, for instance the Palace School model, represented by W of the Benedictine edition (Vienna, Österreichische Nationalbibliothek, MS 1861). This psalter by the scribe Dagulf (and known as Dagulf's Psalter) was written AD 783-93.[42] It was presented by Charlemagne to Pope Hadrian I,[43] is of the Stuttgart-Alcuin Type and shows Irish influence.[44]

It is difficult to say whether the **psalm headings**, Series III, in cartouches in the margins, derive from an Irish original. This Series has been edited by P. Salmon[45] according to a Spanish tradition of *Iuxta Hebraeos (Hebraicum)* psalters. The Series, however, was not originally composed for the *Hebraicum* text, nor inspired by the *Hebraicum*. It is a well-constructed text, rich in ideas, directing the mind to the New Testament, but without attributing the greater part of the psalms to Christ himself. Outside of Spanish texts it is found in two Swiss psalters (Zürich, Stadtbibl. Rh. 34, and Stadtbibl. C. 12) as well as in the Psalter of Charlemagne. H. J. Lawlor[46] made a collation of the psalter in BL, MS Egerton 1139, a Gallican psalter written in England about 1140. The headings in this are inspired, often somewhat freely, by Series III. Salmon notes that the Series III headings of Paris 13159 often agree with Zürich, Stadtbibl. Rh. 34 (assigned the siglum D) against the Spanish tradition. In Series III, then, the Psalter of Charlemagne may represent Continental (French) rather than Irish or Insular tradition.

With regard to the **psalm collects** (of which there are three series), the Psalter of Charlemagne is the only manuscript that has the African Series (Series I). Each of these three series has its own particular orientation. In comparison with the other two it has been noted that the African Series has a more pronounced theological character and that it issues from a doctrine influenced by Augustinian thought. In the domain of Christology it stresses the historical redemptive work of Christ and its great stages, leaving in the shadow the dogmatic reflections on his human-divine being.[47] The African Series, the oldest and most original of the three, has been transmitted by this single manuscript. It is called the African Series because the African psalter text, represented principally by the *Veronensis*, is the principal text used. Brou[48] thinks that this Series I was composed in Africa in a time of persecution, probably by the Vandals, during the century after the death of Augustine of Hippo. There may have been a variant form of this text intended for times of peace. Brou[49] believes that the text in the Psalter of Charlemagne derives from an Insular original. 'All that remains now is to find the Insular manuscript that serves as a model for the scribe of St-Riquier' (where he believes Paris BN, lat. 13159 was written). Since these psalm collects, for the greater part at least, are collective prayers of petition under the inspiration of the individual psalm, it seems difficult to detect in them an influence of any particular exegetical approach, historical or Christological. With regard to the place of composition, one may, I believe, query the need for an African origin. The *Veronensis*, after all, is a north-Italian manuscript (s. VI-VII), and Series I might conceivably have originated there. From there the Series could have come to Ireland and Northumbria with the Julian commentary and the epitome of this, works which stand behind the psalm headings in the psalter of Charlemagne.

With regard to the **psalm headings**, the composite introduction prefaced to each psalm contains first of all the opening words of the psalm, which is then often described as *Psalmus Dauid*. One or more historical heading is then given, after which there generally comes the mystical heading. Occasionally certain important words of the psalm are then explained. In practically every one of these elements the introductory material of the so-called Psalter of Charlemagne is very closely related to the corresponding material in the Hiberno-Latin psalm commentary of the Vatican Pal., MS lat. 68. This holds for peculiarities of the historical references and a peculiar form of the Series I mystical headings.[50] This introductory material, or psalm headings, of the psalter of Charlemagne presupposes a certain unified approach to the understanding of the psalms, an entire commentary on the psalter. This commentary has come down to us in the psalm gloss of Vatican Pal. lat. 68 and in the glosses on the *Hebraicum* of the Double Psalter of St Ouen (Rouen, Bibl. mun., MS 24 [A. 41]).

The **psalm grouping**, or the division of the Psalter of Charlemagne, merits special consideration, because it might yield valuable evidence on the traditions lying behind it. In Irish literary texts from the eighth century onwards the psalter is commonly referred to as 'The Three Fifties', which might lead one to believe that psalters known to Irish writers were so divided. This is the case for the second-oldest Irish psalter we know, BL, Codex Vitellius F. XI, from the early tenth century, and for all later Irish psalters, where each of the divisions (at Ps. 1; 51; 101) was preceded by a special illuminated page. However, our oldest Irish psalter, the *Cathach* (c. AD 650) has no tripartite division, and perhaps had no division at all (the text has not been completely preserved). Another division of the psalter known from the eighth century onwards (found in both Gallican and *Romanum* psalters) is an eightfold division, again noted by special illuminated initials.[51] This division would appear to have corresponded to the psalms assigned to the Night Hours of the office according to the Roman usage.[52]

In this the psalms for the Night Hours were to be drawn from Ps. 1-108, with twelve psalms for each of the days of the week and (in some traditions at least) twice twelve psalms for the Sunday Night Hours during the winter period. This eightfold division is clearest in the Vespasian Psalter (BL, Cotton MSS Vespasian A.I; England, probably Canterbury, St Augustine's Abbey, c. 720-30).[53] In this an elaborately decorated incipit marks the beginning of certain psalms: thus for Ps. 17, 26, 38, 52, 68, 80, 97, 109, and 118. The last of these is clearly intended to be less elaborate than the others; the first lacks the pointed background of the others, but its size is the same as that of the following incipits.[54] Of these, Ps. 26-97 inclusive are the opening psalms for the Night Hours of Monday through Saturday in the Roman Office. The special illumination of Ps. 109 indicates the Psalm for Sunday Vespers. Verses of Ps. 118 were used during the hours of Terce, Sext and None. Ps. 17 was the beginning of the second group of psalms for the Night Office on Sunday. Two other English psalters have both a threefold and eightfold division, namely Berlin, Deutsches Staatsbibliothek, Hamilton 553 (the Salaberga Psalter, Psalterium Romanum et Cantica),[55] Northumbria, first half of eighth century; and New York, Pierpont Morgan Library, MS M. 776 (*Psalterium Romanum*), England, and probably southern England, middle of the eighth century. In the Psalter of Charlemagne there is no trace of any threefold division (with special initials for Ps. 51 and 101). It does, however, have special illumination for Ps. 1, no particularly large initial for Ps. 17, but very specially decorated large initials for Ps. 26, 38, 52, 68, 80, and 97. There are also large initials for Ps. 109 and 118. The Psalter of Charlemagne thus belongs to the tradition of the eightfold division represented by the English psalters, and that of Northumbria as represented by the Salaberga Psalter. It goes with the Roman Office usage for the Night Hours, and our available evidence indicates that this usage was not followed in Ireland.[56]

It would appear, then, that in eightfold division of the psalter Paris BN, lat. 13159 does not represent Irish tradition. The Roman tradition it represents would seem to have been mediated through a Northumbrian, or possibly even directly from a Roman model, since Charlemagne in his *Admonitio generalis* of 789 says his father Pepin had ordained that the Night Hours and the Gradual Office be celebrated in accord with Roman usage and the will of the apostolic See.[57] Unfortunately, we have no early Roman or French examples of psalters with an eightfold division. On balance, the model used by the Psalter of Charlemagne for this division would seem to have been Northumbrian or English.

All that remains to be studied of this Paris manuscript is the **illumination**, the decorated initials. That the decoration of the psalter is Insular, or at least of Insular inspiration, is admitted by all who have examined it. F. Masai speaks of 'sa décoration d'inspiration insulaire (une lettrine au début de chaque psaume) ...';[58] 'L'atelier qui l'a decoré témoigne ... d'une forte influence insulaire'.[59] Masai (arguing for an origin at Corbie) remarks that the Psalter of Amiens (Amiens, Bibl. mun. 18), from the renowned Abbey of Picardie, is the closest known relation of our codex from the point of view of decoration.

G. L. Marsh-Micheli examined the illumination of the manuscript in some detail in 1939,[60] in a study in which she considers in particular the cross-channel influences on the three manuscripts: the Essen Gospels, the Psalter of Charlemagne, and the Amiens Psalter. In these three works she sees the presence of strong cross-channel influences.

She notes the giant initials of the Psalter of Charlemagne, arranged with a sense of articulated composition transmitted by Insular works. Some are isolated and alone; more often they are double, with intertwining. This she compares with the cross-channel gospel-books, in those of Lindisfarne or Durham. She considers the abundance of illuminated letters surprising, although interlace predominates. The initials with birds are of the traditional type of Corbie.[61]

In his treatment of the manuscript, E. A. Lowe writes with regard to the illumination:[62] 'Numerous initials of curious design, skilfully drawn in pen and ink, showing the plait motif, imaginary dog-like beasts, birds (fols 52[v], 74[v], 79[r], 156[v]), serpents and a mermaid (fol. 13[v]) here and there with a dart of red, yellow or green; the form of many initials is manifestly copied from Insular models. ... A pen-and-ink drawing of Christ and two angels at the end of fol. 118[v] seems a slightly later addition.' J. Porcher[63] notes the 'initiales grandes et petites, certaines rehaussées de rouge, de style insulaire'. U. Kuder[64] has devoted a doctoral dissertation to the initials of the Amiens Psalter, which he considers quite different from Paris BN, lat. 13159.[65] Apart from this observation and a summary of the discussion of its place of origin[66] he has very little to say on the psalter, although he does note the mermaid in fol. 13[v].[67]

The illumination of these initials of the Psalter of Charlemagne merits detailed examination, to determine if possible the predominant tradition behind it, whether this is Continental (Merovingian France) or Insular, and if Insular, whether this is Northumbrian or Irish. The two differing forms of illumination for Ps. 109 on fol. 119[r] and the facing fol. 118[v] may indicate a clash of cultures – the animal initial D of *Dixit* representing the 'Insular' tradition, the pen-and-ink drawing of Christ (added later, but contemporaneously) indicating local interests. For a study of the psalter's illumination we have rich variety in the initials, since the same initial opening letters or words are differently treated in the different occurrences.[68] As already noted, each of the eight divisions of the psalter is introduced by a specially large illuminated letter, occupying from a half page (the *DNS* of Ps. 26; fol. 28[v]) to almost an entire page (the S of Ps. 68, fol. 70[r]).

With such a study of the psalter's illumination we should have advanced a step further towards determining the traditions behind the Psalter of Charlemagne, the relationships between Merovingian France and Britain, and the interrelationships of Ireland with both.

NOTES

1 See M. McNamara, 'Psalter Text and Psalter Study in the Early Irish Church (AD 600-1200)', *Proceedings of the Royal Irish Academy* 73C (1973), 201-76, with appendix by M. Sheehy, 277-98.
2 On both text-forms see McNamara, 'Psalter Text', 263-4.
3 See McNamara, 'Psalter Text'; also McNamara, 'Tradition and Creativity in Early Irish Psalter Study', in *Ireland and Europe*, ed. by P. Ní Chatháin & M. Richter (Stuttgart: Klett Cotta, 1984), 364-6; *Glossa in Psalmos: the Hiberno-Latin Gloss on the Psalms of Codex Palatinus Latinus 68 (Psalms 39. 11-151. 7)* (Studi e Testi 310, Vatican City: Biblioteca Apostolica Vaticana, 1986).
4 *Glossa in psalmos* (ed. McNamara) (n. 3 above).

5 See A. Vaccari, 'Il genuino commento ea salmi di Remigio di Auxerre', *Biblica* 26 (1952), 52-99 (98-99) (=A. Vaccari, *Scritti di erudizione e di filologia*, vol. 1 (Rome: Edizioni di storia e litteratura 18, 1952), 283-329 (327-8).

6 F. Henry, 'Remarks on the Decoration of Three Irish Psalters', *Proceedings of the Royal Irish Academy* 61C (1960-1; published 1960), 23-40.

7 Henry, 'Remarks', 31.

8 ibid., 35-6.

9 ibid., 38.

10 F. Henry & G. L. Marsh-Micheli, 'A Century of Irish Illumination', *Proceedings of the Royal Irish Academy* 62C (1961-2; published 1962), 101-65 (161-3 for the Psalter of Cormac).

11 Henry & Marsh-Micheli, 'A Century', 163.

12 K. M. Openshaw, 'Images, Texts and Contexts: the Iconography of the Tiberius Psalter, London, British Library, Cotton MSS, Tiberius C.iv' (unpublished doctoral dissertation; University of Toronto [1990]).

13 K. M. Openshaw, 'The Symbolic Illustration of the Psalter: an Insular Tradition', in *Arte Medievale* 2 ser. 6 (n. 1, 1992), 41-60.

14 ibid., 47-8.

15 ibid., 48.

16 ibid., 46.

17 ibid., 53-7.

18 ibid., 54.

19 ibid., 57.

20 R. Parr, *The Life and Times of the Most Reverend James Usher late Lord Arch-Bishop of Armagh Primate and Metropolitan of All Ireland* (London, 1686), 11.

21 Parr, *The Life*, 79.

22 A. O'Sullivan, 'The Colophon of the Cotton Psalter (Vitellius F. XI)', *Journal of the Royal Society of Antiquaries of Ireland* 96 (1966), 179-80.

23 J. Planta, *A Catalogue of the Manuscripts in the Cottonian Library deposited in the British Museum* (London, 1802), 42.

24 J. O. Westwood, 'On the Peculiarities exhibited by the Miniatures and Ornamentation of Ancient Irish Illuminated Manuscripts', *Archaeological Journal* 7 (1850), 16-25.

25 Henry, 'Remarks', n. 6 above.

26 O'Sullivan, 'The Colophon' (n. 22 above).

27 The others are 'The Lambeth Commentary', London, Lambeth Palace, MS 119); the Double Psalter of St Ouen (Rouen, Bibl. mun., MS 24 [A. 41]); fragments of the sister codex of this in Dublin, Trinity College, MS 1337 (H.3.18), fols 2*-3*; Vatican Pal., lat. 49 (if written in Ireland), in Continental script. Professor Denis Brearley was kind enough to examine the text in June 1994, noting that about 60 per cent of the text seemed legible. In August of that year and again in January 1995 I had an opportunity to examine the text.

28 *Glossa in Psalmos* (ed. McNamara) (n. 3 above).

29 Henry & Marsh-Micheli, 'A Century', n. 10 above, 141-2; see also 102.

30 On this manuscript see S. H. O'Grady, *Catalogue of Irish Manuscripts in the British Museum* (vol. 1. London: British Museum, 1926); (reprint under title *Catalogue of Irish Manuscripts in the British Library (formerly British Museum)* (Dublin: Institute for Advanced Studies, 1992), 285-237. This fine Irish psalter still awaits proper palaeographical examination. It also merits full collation to situate it within the history of the psalter text in Ireland.

31 E. A. Lowe, *Codices latini antiquiores* (12 parts; Oxford: University Press, 1934-71), V, 652. On this psalter, together with the works cited below, see V. Leroquais, *Les psautiers manuscrits latins des bibliothèques publiques de France*, tome II (Macon: Protat Frères, 1940-1), no. 338 (pp. 112-15).

32 F. Masai, 'Observations sur le psautier dit de Charlemagne (Paris lat. 13159)', *Scriptorium* 6 (1952), 299-303.

33 M. Huglo, 'Un Tonaire du Graduel de la fin du VIIIe siècle, Paris, B. N. lat. 13159', *Revue Grégorienne* 31 (1952), 176-86; 224-33.

34 Lowe, *Codices latini antiquiores* V, 652.

35 B. Bischoff, *Manuscripts and Libraries in the Age of Charlemagne*, trans. & ed. by M. Gorman (Cambridge studies in Palaeography and Codicology 1, Cambridge: University Press, 1994), 29, with reference to M. Coens, 'Litanies *carolines* de Soissons et du Psautier de Charlemagne', in *Receuil d'études bollandiennes, Subsidia Hagiographica* (Brussels, 1963), 296-98 (297).

36 Bischoff refers to Coens, 'Litanies', 297.

37 B. Fischer, 'Bibeltext und Bibelreform unter Karl dem Grossem', in *Karl der Grosse, Lebenswerk und Nachleben*, hg. von. Wolfgang Braunfels, Band II: *Das geistige Leben*, hg. von B. Bischoff (Pädagogischer Verlag Schwamm-Bagel GmbH, Am Wehrhahn 100: Düsseldorf, 1965), 156-216; reproduced in B. Fisher, *Lateinische Bibelhandschriften im Frühen Mittelalter* (Aus der Geschichte der lateinischen Bibel 11, Freiburg: Herder, 1985), 101-202, at 167.

38 Lowe, *Codices latini antiquiores* V, 652.

39 See Coens, 'Litanies', n. 35 above.

40 *Liber Psalmorum ex recensione Sancti Hieronimi*, 1953 (Biblia Sacra iuxta Latinam Vulgatam Versionem ad codicum fidem 10, Rome: Vatican Polyglot Press), 1953, pp. ix-x.

41 P. Salmon, *Les 'Tituli Psalmorum' des manuscrits latins* (Collectanea Biblica Latins 12: Rome & Vatican City, 1959), 31-2.

42 Lowe, *Codices latini antiquiores* X, 1504.

43 *Liber Psalmorum* (n. 40 above), x; Fisher, 'Bibeltext', 166-7.

44 Fischer, 'Bibeltext', 167.

45 Salmon, *Les 'Tituli'*, 97-113.

46 H. J. Lawlor, 'The Cathach of St. Columba', *Proceedings of the Royal Irish Academy* (23C, 1916), 413-36.

47 Salmon, *Les 'Tituli'*, 55.

48 L. Brou in A. Wilmart & L. Brou, *The Psalter Collects from V-VIth century Sources*, ed. with introduction, apparatus criticus and indexes by Dom Louis Brou (Henry Bradshaw Society 83: London, 1949); 'Études sur les Collectes du Psautier', *Sacris Erudiri* (6, 1954), 73-95.

49 Brou, 'Etudes', 94, note.

50 See *Glossa in Psalmos* (ed. McNamara) (n. 3 above), 43-5.

51 On this point see U. Kuder, 'Die Initialen des Amienspsalters (Amiens, Bibliothèque municipale MS 18)' (unpublished Ph.D. dissertation, Ludwig-Maximilians-Universität, München, 1977), 67-83 (67-74).

52 See M. Righetti, *Storia liturgica*, ed. 2 (Rome, 1950); Spanish trans. by C. Urtasan Irisarri, *Historia de la liturgia*, vol. I (Madrid: Biblioteca de Autores Cristianos, 1955), part I, ch. 4, §329-39 (pp. 1107-27 in the Spanish translation). Curiously, in his chart on the distribution of psalms in the Roman Office (facing §330; Spanish trans. p. 1109), Righetti gives the following as the first psalm: Sunday Noct. 1 Ps. 1; Noct. 2, Ps. 15; Monday Ps. 27; Tuesday Ps. 39; Wednesday Ps. 53; Thursday Ps. 68; Friday Ps. 80; Saturday Ps. 96.

53 On this psalter and its divisions see D. H. Wright & A. Campbell, *The Vespasian Psalter* (Early English Manuscripts in Facsimile 14: Kopenhagen, 1967); p. 47 for the psalter decoration.

54 Wright & Campbell, *Vespasian Psalter*, 47.

55 On the Salaberga Psalter see D. Ó Cróinín, *Psalterium Salabergae. Staatsbibliothek zu Berlin – Preussischer Kulturbesitz Ms. Hamilt. 555* (Codices illuminati medii aevi 30. Colour

Microfiche Edition. Introduction and Codicological Description by Dáibhí Ó Cróinín: München: Edition Helga Lengenfelder, 1994); on the special initials, p. 17 (for Ps. 17, 118, 26, 38, 52, 68, 80, 97, and 109).

56 For the divine office in Ireland see M. Curran, *The Antiphonary of Bangor* (Dublin: Irish Academic Press, 1984), 159-91; for the Iona tradition see A. O. & M. O. Anderson, *Adomnan's Life of Columba* (London: Nelson, 1961), 121-2.

57 '... *ut cantum romanum pleniter discant et ordinabiliter per nocturnale uel graduale officium peragatur ... ob unanimitatem apostolicae Sedis'* (*Monumenta German. Legum*, sect. 2, tom. 1, 61. Cited in Righetti (n. 52 above), Spanish trans, p. 1123).

58 F. Masai, 'Observations sur le psautier dit de Charlemagne (Paris lat. 13159)', *Scriptorium* (6, 1952), 299-303 (299).

59 Masai, 'Observations', 303.

60 G. L. Micheli, *L'Enluminature du haut Moyen Age et les influences irlandaises: Histoire d'une influence* (Brussels, 1939), 84-7, 132-3.

61 Masai, 'Observations', 84-5.

62 Lowe, *Codices latini antiquiores* V, 652.

63 J. Porcher, J., *Bibliothèque Nationale. Les manuscrits à peinture en France du VIIe au XIIe siècle* (Paris: Bibliothèque Nationale, 1954), no. 18.

64 Kuder, 'Die Initialen' (n. 51 above).

65 Kuder, 'Die Initialen', 35, n. 2.

66 ibid., 35, n. 2.

67 ibid., 249.

68 The following is the frequency of occurrence of the Psalm Initials: the letter D with 43 occurrences; C with 15; B with 11; I with 11; L with 10; Q with 10; A with 7; M with 7; N with 5; S with 5; V with 4; U with 3; P with 2; O with 1; T with 1.

A NORTHUMBRIAN TEXT FAMILY

Christopher Verey

WHILE I WAS PREPARING THIS PAPER I found myself halfway up a mountain in southern Tuscany and I was struck by the following phrase in the local guidebook (which I translate), 'Jerome's version [of the Latin Bible] was copied early, above all in Italy and in Spain, and subsequently in Ireland ...'. Notable in that potted summary of the early history of the Vulgate was the absence of any reference to England. There was an irony in this: the place was the Abbazia del San Salvatore – the mountain, Monte Amiata. This was the very home for upwards of a thousand years of the celebrated Codex Amiatinus, the great early-eighth-century copy of the Latin Bible produced at the Anglo-Saxon twin foundation of Wearmouth-Jarrow in northern England, and in-tended as the gift of its abbot Ceolfrith to the Pope.[1]

To be fair to the guidebook's author, he was quoting a work written in the 1920s.[2] Even long after it was recognized that 'Peter the Lombard' on the dedication page of the Codex Amiatinus was in fact a falsification of the original 'Ceolfrith of the English', the book, in its splendid, uncompromising uncial, was thought to be the work of Italian scribes imported into England.[3] The scholarly preconception at the time was that the inspiration behind book production in the early Anglo-Saxon church would have owed far more to Ireland than to Italy.

Fortunately, the demonstrably Insular, late-seventh-century Lindisfarne Gospels[4] contained the same excellent gospel text as the Codex Amiatinus. This ensured that in Wordsworth & White's great critical edition of the Vulgate gospels, which a hundred years later still remains the basis for the way we understand the groupings of texts of the Latin gospels, there was at least some express acknowledgement of an Anglo-Saxon contribution – in the family of texts designated 'Italo-*Northumbrian*'.[5]

The general perception was that the gospel texts copied in the British Isles from the seventh and eighth centuries could be loosely grouped as 'Celtic' or 'Irish'.[6] The scholar quoted in the guidebook was doing little more than reflecting received wisdom: for the most part the Anglo-Saxons could be disregarded as a distinct force in the transmission of the Latin gospels.

Few now doubt that Codex Amiatinus was produced by local scribes in a North-umbrian scriptorium. But the competition of scholarly nationalisms across the Irish Sea continues to dispute the inspiration behind such Insular products as the Lindisfarne, the Durham, and the Echternach Gospels, and the Books of Durrow and Kells.[7] And any discussion of that most portable of features, namely the text, all too often becomes a side-show or is ignored. In many respects our understanding of the textual transmission is little advanced since the end of the last century. Then, and for some time thereafter, all inspiration behind script and ornament in these books was seen as essentially 'Irish'. We can hardly blame text scholars for following suit.

Particularly from the middle of the present century the scholarly pendulum on script and ornament swung towards Northumbria.[8] The key work of François Masai[9] was built upon by Julian Brown and Rupert Bruce-Mitford, who argued a Lindisfarne origin for the three great luxury gospel-books, the Durham and the Echternach as well as the Lindisfarne Gospels.[10] For these scholars the synthesis of the various traditions reflected in these books – Celtic, Saxon, Italian and even Pictish – was primarily Northumbrian, and more specifically the work of the Lindisfarne scriptorium around the turn of the seventh and eighth centuries. Furthermore the Durham and Echternach Gospels were attributed to one great original calligrapher, who was seen as the source of the major evolution in Insular book-hands, the development of phase II half-uncial.[11]

The argument was further developed that the Lindisfarne scriptorium was the source of scribal practice at Echternach, the great centre (in modern Luxembourg) founded at the end of the seventh century by the Northumbrian Willibrord.[12] Finally, and as if to pour salt on the wounds, it was claimed that those great treasures fundamentally associated with early Irish monasticism, the Books of Durrow and Kells, if not of Northumbrian origin, certainly owed their main inspiration to Northumbria.[13] Such a Northumbrian stranglehold was not going to be taken lying down across the Irish Sea.

Many felt the role of Lindisfarne overstated; there is a tendency to focus on the known, paying insufficient regard to the implications of the fragmentary nature of the surviving evidence.[14] The most considered counter-argument has come from Dr Dáibhí Ó Cróinín. He has espoused the claims of the monastery at Rath Maelsigi in Ireland, probably in Co. Carlow. Rath Maelsigi was the home of the exiled Northumbrian Willibrord for twelve years before his mission to Frisia in 690 and the founding of Echternach in 697 or 698. For Ó Cróinín Ireland, and specifically Rath Maelsigi, is seen as the key to the development of the Echternach scriptorium – and, indeed, the key to phase II half-uncial. He does not contest the conclusion that the Echternach Gospels and the Durham Gospels share a close common heritage, but for him the link between the Echternach Gospels, whose Northumbrian origin he will not accept, and the Durham Gospels, whose early Northumbrian provenance he cannot deny, is Rath Maelsigi. The influence of Rath Maelsigi is thought to have extended variously to the Echternach scriptorium on the continent, which he regards as the likely origin of the Echternach Gospels, and to the origin of the Durham Gospels, for which the options are various – from Ireland or from Echternach and subsequently imported early into Northumbria, or from an Irish outpost in Northumbria, owing its skill directly to Rath Maelsigi. The permutations seem endless.[15]

Ó Cróinín has made two important contributions. First, in recounting the Northumbrian Willibrord's lengthy stay in Ireland at Rath Maelsigi, he reminds us of the close ties between the Irish and Anglo-Saxon churches at this time. By the same token we need to be careful not to confuse the geographical location of Rath Maelsigi with any particular cultural bias, since Rath Maelsigi was a Northumbrian community in exile.[16] Second, he has rightly drawn attention to a probable Irish influence in early scribal practice at Echternach – the work of the scribe Virgilius and the Augsburg Gospels, for example. But Irish influence on the first generation of Echternach manuscripts does not lead necessarily to undermining the idea of a Northumbrian, and specifically Lindisfarne, origin for the phase II half-uncial seen in later Echternach books – for example in the work of the scribe Thomas in the Trier Gospels.[17]

I should like to turn to another book to move the debate forward. The 'Cambridge-

London Gospels' comprise fragments from an original gospel-book now preserved in Cambridge, Corpus Christi College Library, MS 197B, and in the British Library, Cotton MS, Otho C.V – together probably with the bifolium of canon tables in BL, Royal MS 7.C.xii.[18] The Cambridge-London Gospels exhibit various close similarities with both the Durham and the Echternach Gospels. If the former conclusions about the sources of these two books are questioned, to what extent do the Cambridge-London Gospels provide new clues? Does the evidence from this book support, or undermine the relative claims of Rath Maelsigi and Lindisfarne?

The earliest evidence for the provenance of the Cambridge-London Gospels is from the sixteenth and early seventeenth centuries, when Archbishop Matthew Parker and Sir Robert Cotton first appear as the owners of the Cambridge and London portions respectively. The Royal fragments of the Canon Tables previously belonged to Cardinal Wolsey. There is no evidence for medieval provenance, though the fact that both Parker and Cotton identify their separate portions as once belonging to St Augustine himself may just suggest a Canterbury provenance.[19]

The Cotton portion was damaged in the Ashburnham House fire in 1731, as a result of which some leaves were lost, and those surviving were severely damaged. There survive about half the original leaves of Matthew and all but one of Mark, with a set of prefaces before Mark, comprising a chapter list, a set of Hebrew names, and a prologue. Further understanding of the prefaces is helped by a reliable facsimile of one page made before the fire.[20] Most of the Cotton leaves remaining have suffered water shrinkage and loss through burning of part of the original page area.[21] In Corpus 197B the surviving leaves have been severely trimmed, but for the most part the written area is intact. These leaves preserve about a third of Luke and one-sixth of John. The surviving decorative scheme is represented by major initials to the openings of Mark and John, facing full-page evangelist symbols.[22] There is a profusion of text initials, generally marking the opening of Eusebian sections.

The most immediately obvious parallels with other Insular books appear in the decorative schemes and in detail of some of the ornamental repertoire.[23] The striking full-page evangelist symbols in their fretwork frames on plain vellum fields are very like those in the Echternach Gospels.[24] The effect is different, but the evidence suggests a common model handled differently: the symbols in the Cambridge-London Gospels are more naturalistic (note the differentiation between the legs of the eagle and the forelegs of the lion to give depth), whereas those in the Echternach Gospels emphasize two-dimensional pattern. If the original model of the eagle was akin to that on the Knowe of Burrian stone in Orkney, then we can speak of the Cambridge-London symbols being closer to the originals.[25] Other decorative features find closest parallel with both the Durham and the Echternach Gospels. Two initial pages survive in the Cambridge-London Gospels: to Mark (much damaged) and to John. They reflect different models. The opening initials to Mark dominate only the top and left-hand quarter of the page.[26] The scheme harks back to earlier Insular practice, such as in the Book of Durrow. More significantly it matches closely the layout in the Echternach Gospels.[27] In contrast, the opening *In principio* to John dominates the page in a scheme close to that of the Lindisfarne Gospels, but particularly to that of the Durham Gospels.[28] Again there is the sense of the Cambridge-London Gospels sharing common models with the Durham and Echternach Gospels. There are other close similarities with the Durham Gospels. So, for example, the pre-fire facsimile of the opening *marcus* of the Mark prologue shows a decorated *M* with many features identical to the exactly corresponding initial in the Durham Gospels.[29] Another example would be *F* with the split stem now much damaged on the initial page to Mark in the Cotton leaves, which corresponds closely to a similar form of decorative initial in the Durham Gospels.[30]

There are three distinct hands in the Cambridge-London Gospels. They reflect a centre closely influenced by the scriptorium which evolved phase II half-uncial, as found in the Lindisfarne and Durham Gospels; but there are also indications of the influence of older Insular practice.[31]

The parallels in decoration and script between the Cambridge-London Gospels and the Echternach and Durham Gospels are matched by parallels between the texts of these books. The texts of the prefaces are close to those in the Echternach Gospels, and the texts of the gospels of Mark and Luke are particularly close to those in the Durham Gospels.

The one surviving set of prefaces, to Mark, comprises a list of chapters, the set of glosses on Hebrew names and the gospel prologue – in that order. Precisely the same three items in that order occur in the Durham and Echternach Gospels.[32] With the exception of the Hebrew names, the textual tradition of the prefatory matter in the Durham Gospels is different (see below). The only other early occurrence of this order is in John in the Vatican Barberini Gospels.[33] (There appear to be few other parallels between the Cambridge-London Gospels and Barberini.) Otherwise the arrangement in these three gospel-books is matched nowhere elsewhere in the surviving early tradition.[34] If the common source behind the arrangement in the Durham and the Echternach Gospels was Rath Maelsigi, it found no wider following in Ireland or otherwise in the early gospel-books associated with Echternach.[35]

The inclusion of a set of glosses on Hebrew names is an Insular 'trade mark'. These glosses occur in only eleven early gospel-books, ten of them of Insular origin or with distinct Insular associations, with the earliest surviving occurrence in the seventh-century *Usserianus Primus* of almost certain Irish origin. The only exception with no obvious Insular connection is a late-eleventh-century volume in Stuttgart.[36] The text of the list in the Cambridge-London Gospels is close to those in the Durham and the Echternach Gospels, the Book of Durrow, and the Book of Armagh. There is a confused, conflate John-Mark version in the Book of Durrow (omitted in Kells, which otherwise matches the peculiar arrangements of prefaces in Durrow), and the Book of Armagh gathers all four lists of names into one list before Matthew.[37] The Cambridge-London Gospels shares none of the peculiarities of arrangement in Durrow and Armagh. Otherwise the textual relationship within this group generally is close, and there is little to point to any significant alternative recensions. In one interesting respect the Cambridge-London Gospels may show affinity with the Echternach Gospels, namely in the rubric *cata marcum*, which in the former is elevated to a row of grand initials as a decorative opening to the list of Hebrew names. The scribe cannot have understood what he was copying since these words form no part of the Hebrew names. They do, however, reflect the form of rubric in the Echternach Gospels at this point (fo. 74ʳ in Echternach), which reads at the close of the chapter list, *explicit breuis disputatio cata marcum*, leading into the opening rubric of the Hebrew names, *incipit interpraetatio nominum eiusdem* – did a common exemplar have *cata marcum* in both, or did the two rubrics become confused, by the scribe of the Cambridge-London Gospels, or previously?

No comparable set of Hebrew names occurs in the gospel-books associated with Echternach (other than in the Echternach Gospels themselves). Indeed, in contrast to the tradition described above, the Trier Gospels contain a wholly different, unique survival of a much fuller set. Certainly, the earliest, the Augsburg Gospels, closest to the Irish sources, contains no list of Hebrew names.[38]

The prefaces before Mark contain a set of chapter lists. This was a list of brief summaries of the contents of the various 'chapters' into which the gospel was sub-divided, cross-referred to identifying numbers in the margins of the gospel text. There were various families of chapters, and Mark could be divided into as few as 13 and as many as 50 chapters depending on the family; the corresponding lists of summaries were equally distinct.[39] The list found in the Cambridge-London Gospels belongs to family 'I'. This is the family common to the early Irish tradition – indeed no other family is found in books generally assigned an Irish origin. It is the family found in three of the four early gospel-books associated with Echternach.[40] But it is far more widespread – it is the family associated with the Old Latin gospel text. The presence of the 'I' family of chapter lists in the Cambridge-London Gospels does not point necessarily to any one source, but, particularly taking account of the details of its readings, the text is likely to derive from an Irish tradition.

The details of the text of the chapter list in the Cambridge-London Gospels find their closest parallels with the lists in the Echternach Gospels and in the Book of Kells and Durrow. (The chapter lists in Kells and Durrow reflect a common recension.) The relationship between the Cambridge-London Gospels and the Echternach Gospels and Durrow/Kells is fairly close. Allowing for the fragmentary nature of the surviving text, of the seventeen substantial (excluding common orthographical) variations between the Cambridge-London Gospels and the other three books, in four Cambridge-London is unique, in five the Echternach Gospels and/or Durrow/Kells make simple errors or omissions (usually promptly rectified). Of the remaining eight, in three cases Cambridge-London agrees with Echternach against Kells (Durrow is missing in part), and in five with Kells against Echternach.[41] The balance of agreement/disagreement between the four books is fine. In their division and layout the summaries in the Cambridge-London Gospels appear marginally closer to those in the Echternach Gospels; so they avoid the running together of the summaries for ch. 19 and 20, and for ch. 25 and 26, as found in Kells. Moreover, as noted above, in its arrangement of the chapter lists before each gospel, the Cambridge-London Gospels match the Echternach Gospels more than the Books of Durrow and Kells.

There are two distinct traditions of the so-called Monarchian gospel prologues – one of which is closely associated with the Irish.[42] It is to this 'Irish' tradition that the form of the prologue to Mark in the Cambridge-London Gospels belongs. The surviving text is very fragmentary, but it does contain six key readings indicative of the 'Irish' version.[43] The form of text found in the Cambridge-London Gospels finds closest parallel with the Echternach Gospels and with the Books of Durrow and Kells, and, while the surviving evidence is too patchy to draw firm conclusions, the matching of particular readings as between the Cambridge-London Gospels and, on the one hand, the Echternach Gospels, and, on the other, Durrow/Kells is, again, fairly finely balanced. The influence of the 'Irish' version of the prologues was widespread: for example, its readings are found in the gospel prologues in that otherwise decidedly un-Insular edition of the gospels in Codex Amiatinus.

Particularly when the ordering of the material and the version of the Hebrew names (in not reflecting the conflate John/Mark version in the Books of Durrow and Kells) are taken into account, the closest surviving parallel with the prefatory matter in the Cambridge-London Gospels is found in the Echternach Gospels. The textual differences would appear to preclude a direct dependence one on the other. But the two books do reflect a fairly close common textual family.

How does the incidence of this family contribute to the debate on the relative claims of Rath Maelsigi and Lindisfarne for the honours of the Echternach and the Durham Gospels? With the exception of the Hebrew names, the texts of the prefatory matter in the Durham Gospels derive from a fundamentally different tradition, not shared with that of the Echternach Gospels, or indeed with any early Irish books.[44] Similarly, discounting the disputed Echternach Gospels themselves, none of the gospel-books associated with Echternach has a comparable list of Hebrew names (that in the Trier Gospels[45] is fundamentally different); only the Trier Gospels has all three elements of the prefatory matter, but orders the material differently; the other books follow the customary order of prologue followed by chapter list (which is the reversal of that in the family of the Cambridge-London Gospels and associated books); and though all reflect variously family 'I' chapter lists, these are widely found also outside the Insular tradition and could have come from a range of sources.[46] To sustain the argument that Rath Maelsigi formed the key to the Echternach scriptorium and the Echternach Gospels, and to the Durham Gospels and phase II half-uncial in Northumbria, one would need to discount the prefaces as part of any shared tradition. On the other hand, the close links between the texts of the prefaces in the Cambridge-London and the Echternach Gospels, on the one hand, and those in the Books of Durrow and Kells, on the other, would seem more obviously to point to the influence of the Columban *paruchia*; Iona-Lindisfarne seems a more obvious axis than Rath Maelsigi-Echternach.

When we turn to the evidence of the gospel text itself, the close textual relationship with the Durham Gospels and with another book of almost certain Northumbrian origin, the idea of the Rath Maelsigi link becomes even less convincing.

An interesting feature of some early gospel-books is the way in which the texts of the gospels themselves can come from a tradition different from those of their prefaces. This can be seen in the mismatch between the division of the chapter list before the gospel and the chapter numbers in the margins of the gospel itself (unless these coincide the list is useless). In the Cambridge-London Gospels the list prefacing Mark and the surviving marginal numbers in the gospel text belong to different families. Four fragments of chapter numbers survive in the margins of the gospel text.[47] All belong to family 'B'. The evidence fits no other family; the marginal numbers do not match family 'I' as found in the one surviving chapter list. Even allowing for the severe damage to margins of the Cotton leaves, and the trimming of the Corpus leaves, there is sufficient surviving material to show that there was no comprehensive marking of chapter numbers in the margins of the gospel text. It follows that the random survival of a few marginal numbers is likely to indicate that they were an intrinsic part of the tradition of the exemplar of the gospel text, not an addition from another source.

No chapter numbers survive in the margins of Mark itself, and since no chapter list other than that for Mark has survived in the Cambridge-London Gospels, we cannot compare marginal numbers and lists for the same gospel. But the type of gospel text in Mark when found elsewhere (such as in the Durham Gospels, see below) has family 'B' chapters. There are no examples of family 'B' in Irish gospel-books, or in the early books from Echternach. Accordingly it seems unlikely that the inclusion of family 'B' chapters in the Durham as well as the Cambridge-London Gospels (but not in the Echternach Gospels) could have been influenced by practices at Rath Maelsigi. The family 'B' chapters are common in later gospel-books from southern England.[48]

The gospel of Matthew (with the exception of a very few of the opening, very fragmentary surviving folios) and that of John in the Cambridge-London Gospels are written in the same hand. His style is more old-fashioned than that of the scribes of Mark and Luke; he is a careless copyist making numerous errors. In Matthew the most frequent agreement of variations from the text of Wordsworth & White is with the eighth-century Insular gospel book in Durham, Cathedral Library, A.II.16[49] – but the evidence is insufficient to draw firm conclusions. The evidence of John, while showing the type of admixture of Old Latin and other corruption of the Vulgate in ways akin to that found in the so-called Irish family, shows no close relationship with any one member of that family.[50] (John now bound in Durham, Cathedral Library, A.II.16 may come from a different book; it contains the distinct Italo-Northumbrian text.) As noted above, in both Matthew and John there are random survivals of marginal chapter numbers of family 'B' which are likely to have been transmitted with the gospel text. This would tend to point away from the Irish tradition, and very possibly towards direct Italian import – the four early, non-Insular occurrences of this chapter family are all in uncial books of probable Italian origin from the sixth and seventh centuries.[51] It is possible that the scribe of John himself contributed to the admixture of Old Latin and like corruption in the 'Irish' manner.[52]

Mark and Luke are in different hands. Sufficient text survives to allow worthwhile comparisons with other gospel-books. Here the picture is of a text overwhelmingly close to that found in the Durham Gospels. For the purposes of the following analysis I have compared the Cambridge-London and the Durham Gospels directly against each other to define the totality of disagreement between the two, as well as against the control of Wordsworth & White so as to characterize their agreement, by reference to shared significant alternatives which can be related to other witnesses.

In the passages of Mark where the Cambridge-London and the Durham Gospels both survive, excluding *common* orthographical alternatives there are some 240 places where one or the other or both differ from the control. In 60 per cent of these the two books agree between themselves. The comparable figures for Luke are some 170 places and just over 60 per cent. Straight percentages can be misleading. The nature of the agreement is striking. The detail of agreement embraces errors and some peculiar readings, to say nothing of a high degree of coincidence in frequently random factors such as orthography of proper nouns and the choice of common pronoun (such as *is/hic/ille*). Virtually all the differences between the two reflect common alternatives, mistakes (often promptly corrected) or that embellishment of the text, often to aid comprehension, of a type I have described elsewhere as a 'textual overlay', prevalent in the so-called Irish gospel text, and common to Insular gospel texts more generally.[53] Discounting such features there is only a relatively small number of substantive variations between the two gospel-books. Of these, in only one or two places might the differences conceivably be attributed to admixture from an alternative textual tradition. I list at the Appendix here these substantive textual variations between the Cambridge-London and the Durham Gospels.

This suggests a remarkably close relationship. Where the two books diverge, they appear to do so not because of any alternative textual influence, but by corruption and *sui generis* emendation of a common archetype through a seemingly very limited intermediate tradition.

In Mark the same text type as in the Cambridge-London and the Durham Gospels is found also in the eighth-century gospel-book in Durham Cathedral Library, A.II.16.[54] Discounting orthographical variants, of those readings shared by the Cambridge-London and the Durham Gospels against the control of Wordsworth & White (i.e. significant alternative readings), over 65 per cent are found also in Durham A.II.16. Once again a high proportion of the 35 per cent disagreements are errors or otherwise of seemingly little textual significance.

If we look at the total 97 readings in Mark where the Cambridge-London and the Durham Gospels disagree, in 44 cases A.II.16 agrees with Cambridge-London against Durham, and in 40 places with Durham against Cambridge-London. This would suggest that the common text type shared by these books was transmitted to the Cambridge-London and to the Durham Gospels in parallel, and not in sequence, via one or the other. Once again, the closeness of the texts would suggest that there were few intervening stages between the three and their common source. It is significant that this closely common text type was transmitted in parallel to the Durham Gospels and to two other books, and that for one at least of these other two (Durham A.II.16 – see below) there is a sound (or as yet not disputed) case for a Northumbrian origin. If the Durham Gospels derived from Rath Maelsigi (or even Echternach), as Ó Cróinín suggests is possible, and as O'Sullivan asserts,[55] it cannot have been the agency for the import of the text type into Northumbria – it was already there.

In my published study of the Durham Gospels I pointed out that there were strong links between the text type found there and that in two uncial gospel-books from Italy, known to have been in England at an early date. These are Oxford, Bodleian Library, Auct. D.2.14, and Cambridge, Corpus Christi College, MS 286 (the latter conceivably amongst the treasures brought to England by St Augustine himself).[56] Wordsworth & White assigned these two the *sigla* 'O' and 'X' respectively, and recognized the relationship between their texts.[57] These two gospel-books represent a version of Jerome's revision with some admixture of Old Latin found in central Italy from at least the sixth century. They also contain family 'B' chapters. The relationship between the Durham Gospels and O is the stronger.

In my earlier work I identified for Mark 42 places where I believed that the Durham Gospels shared with O significant and occasionally distinct readings.[58] The Cambridge-London Gospels survive for 24 of these, and in every one of these 24 places agrees with the Durham Gospels, and thus with O. For Luke I concluded that the relationship between the Durham Gospels and the text found in O did not appear so pronounced. Nonetheless I observed 21 readings in the Durham Gospels which I saw as significant to a relationship with the text in O.[59] The Cambridge-London Gospels survives for 9 of these, and in all 9 places follows the Durham Gospels, and thus O. Further analysis shows that for less distinct readings there is wider agreement between the Cambridge-London and the Durham Gospels on the one hand and with Bodleian Auct. D.2.14, O, on the other.

Notwithstanding the early arrival of the Bodleian book in England, it need not be regarded as the source of the text type found in these three Insular gospel-books. But it seems probable that the text type behind the Durham and the Cambridge-London Gospels and Durham A.II.16 stemmed from an imported Italian book of a closely similar type. Italian pedigree does not of necessity point more to Northumbria than to Ireland. Italy was the great source of texts in this period – doubtless for the Irish as well as for the Anglo-Saxons. But the various strands of evidence, when taken together, point to Northumbria as the probable home of the archetype of the text behind the three books, and as the place of their production. Other interpretations are possible, but they seem to strain the evidence unnecessarily.[60]

Two of the three witnesses to the text type have an early Northumbrian provenance. The earliest explicit evidence for A.II.16's links with Durham belongs to the twelfth century.[61] By the ninth century the gospel of John, with its distinct Italo-Northumbrian text (not necessarily exclusively, but in the main an essentially Northumbrian product), was associated with Matthew, Mark, and Luke.[62] Matthew, Mark, and Luke in A.II.16 were written in a centre which used both Insular half-uncial and uncial, both reflecting Northumbrian influences.[63] The presence of the uncial hand would seem to rule out an Irish origin, and suggest that the early Northumbrian provenance also reflects a Northumbrian origin.[64]

The Durham Gospels were almost certainly at Lindisfarne around the turn of the seventh and eighth centuries. This is the most natural interpretation of the work of its main corrector. He punctuated the text *per cola et commata* in an arrangement very close to that in the Lindisfarne Gospels, and incorporated readings from its Italo-Northumbrian text.[65] Moreover, the hand of the corrector is identical with a correcting hand in the Lindisfarne Gospels.[66] In arguing that the book was imported into Northumbria from Ireland, or from even further afield on the Continent, and that it was subsequently corrected, both Ó Cróinín and O'Sullivan overlook the evidence that Julian Brown and I adduced in the study of the Durham Gospels to the effect that the main corrector was not undertaking a separate, later activity. His work appears to overlap with the work of the first hand, and he takes some of its detail, notably the marginal chapter numbers, from the *original* exemplar of the Durham Gospels.[67]

The evidence of a close common archetype behind the texts of Mark in the Durham Gospels and in Durham A.II.16 reinforces me in my conclusion that the Durham Gospels are a Northumbrian (quite possibly Lindisfarne) book. The close relationship between the texts of Mark and Luke in, and the stylistic connections between, the Cambridge-London Gospels and the Durham Gospels suggests to me a Northumbrian origin also for the former. The common text behind these three gospel-books is indicative of a Northumbrian text family. The same family and its associated chapter division is not found in extant books from Ireland or Echternach. I can see little reason to explain the sources of the Durham Gospels by reference to Rath Maelsigi.

Is Rath Maelsigi necessary to understand the origins of the Echternach Gospels? If the Durham and the Cambridge-London Gospels are Northumbrian, then the script, the ornament, and the text of the prefaces of the Echternach Gospels can be understood by reference to Northumbrian models. In contrast, if the Echternach Gospels were produced at Echternach itself under the distinct influence of Rath Maelsigi, then it must be observed that such an influence finds little following in the texts of the gospel-books otherwise associated with Echternach. Such an omission, while not excluding, does nothing to enhance the claims of Rath Maelsigi. While the first phase of book production at Echternach may well reflect the influence of Willibrord's spiritual exile at Rath Maelsigi, there seems every reason to continue to uphold Julian Brown's argument that phase II half uncial was a Northumbrian development and that it reached Echternach from there. The idea of a wandering scribe from Rath Maelsigi to Northumbria may not fit the case of the Durham Gospels, but the scribe of the Durham Gospels might have wandered from Lindisfarne to Echternach (there is recorded contact between the two centres).[68] The fact that the gospel text of the Echternach Gospels does not fit into the otherwise surviving picture in Northumbria does not refute the possibility of Northumbrian sources for its other features – prefatory matter, script, and ornament. The original gospel text of the Echternach Gospels (as opposed to the extensive work of emendation by the main corrector) does not fit into any obvious Irish (or indeed Echternach) context either – the intervention of a Rath Maelsigi no more explains it.[69]

Returning to the San Salvatore guidebook, whatever the Irish achieved, there is also a significant and distinct Anglo-Saxon role in the transmission of the Latin gospels. The evidence of the Durham Gospels, the Cambridge-London Gospels and of Durham A.II.16 points to a gospel text family in Northumbria deriving from an archetype closely akin to the text found in the seventh-century Italian uncial gospel-book, Bodleian Auct. D.2.14. This sits alongside that other Northumbrian gospel family – the Italo-Northumbrian – as witness to the impact of texts imported directly from Italy, distinct from the influence of the Irish tradition. The text of the prefaces of the Cambridge-London Gospels, in contrast, shows that other key influence on Northumbria, Ireland. As in Northumbria, so in Echternach it is mistaken to seek singleton lines of influence.

APPENDIX

Textual Comparison Between the Cambridge-London and the Durham Gospels

Excluding common orthographical variants (such as *ae/e, e/i, i/ii, b/u, s/ss*) there are approximately a hundred places in Mark and some seventy in Luke where the Cambridge-London and the Durham Gospels disagree. Many of these are mistakes in copying, which are often promptly corrected – such as *turba* for *turba a*, *quianibus* for *quia in manibus*, *eis eis* for *eis*. There are also omissions with no textual significance and probably due to mistaken copying, again frequently promptly corrected. Another category of limited significance is the alternative use of *is, hic* or *ille*, which tend to be loosely interchangeable – even so there is a remarkable measure of agreement in use between the two books. There are also features designed to aid comprehension, such as changes in word order or the addition of clarifying nouns or adjectives – a process common in Insular books, and one of the defining features of the so-called Irish gospel text; few examples find obvious, or consistent parallels in Irish witnesses – most of such examples can just as likely be *sui generis*. When such features are discounted, the substantive variation between the surviving texts of Mark and Luke in these two books is as follows (letters in [] are missing through damage to the Cambridge-London Gospels):

	Cambridge-London	*Durham*
Mark		
1:21	in sinagoga	in synagogam
1:24	scio quia sis sanctus dei	scio quis es sanctus dei
1:30	discumbebat	decumbebat
1:31	leuauit	eleuauit
1:32	uaris langoribus et demonia (assimilated to v. 34)	et daemonia
1:41	misertus est	misertus
2:12	mirare[ntur]	admirarentur
2:21	[uestimen]to ueri	ueteri
3:28	blasfemauerint	blasfemauerunt
6:6	et mirabatur	admirabatur
6:22	simul	simulque
6:25	statim et	statim
7:19	quoniam	quia
7:32	depraecabuntu[r]	depraecabantur
7:37	facit	fecit
8:1	conuocatis discipulis	conuocans discipulis
8:33	post	retro
8:38	confitetur	confundet
8:38	suis	sanctis
	(probable misreading of *nomina sacra* in Cambridge-London)	
9:24	credo	credo domine
9:25	non	ne
12:14	tu uerax es	uerax es
13:3	[seder]et	sederent (assimilated to *interrogabant*)
13:7	nondum est finis	nondum finis
14:41	peccatorum	hominum peccatorum
14:49	inplea[ntur]	adinpleantur
16:2	prima una	prima
16:5	[in monume]nto	in monumentum
Luke		
4:9	pinnam	pinnaculum
5:13	lepra	lepra eius
6:44	cognoscitur	agnoscitur
6:47	omnis	omnis enim
8:25	uentis imperat et mare	et uentis imperat et mare
12:58	mittat	tradat
19:28	ascendens hierusolyma	ascendens in hierusolima
19:31	soluitis	soluistis eum
19:32	misi erant	misi erunt

Few of the above appear to have any particular significance for the tradition of the text. Common alternatives and alternative tenses feature. Where words are added, these could have featured in the common tradition and, thus, could equally be regarded as careless omission in the other book. Only the following appear to have any significance (all in Mark):

1:24 – the Cambridge-London Gospels shares the reading with Durham A.II.16 and some of the 'Irish' family; the Durham Gospels with the Italo-Northumbrian and mixed Italian (OX) families;

1:32 – while found also in one or two witnesses to the 'Irish' text, such assimilation to verse 34 could occur independently;

2:21 – *ueri* is a mistake for *ueteri*, otherwise such expansion to clarify by the addition of *uestimento* is a common 'Irish' feature, though there are no ready parallels at this particular point;

8:38 – the odd reading in the Cambridge-London Gospels occurs also in Durham A.II.16 and the Lindisfarne Gospels.

NOTES

1 Florence, Biblioteca Medicea-Laurenziana Amiatino 1; E. A. Lowe, *Codices Latini Antiquiores* (12 parts; Oxford: University Press, 1934-71; 2nd edn of part II, 1972) (cited here as *CLA*) III, n. 299, and J. J. G. Alexander, *Insular Manuscripts from the 6th to the 9th Century* (A Survey of Manuscripts Illuminated in the British Isles, Volume I; London: Harvey Miller, 1978) (cited here as Alexander, *Insular Manuscripts*), n. 7. Codex Amiatinus is the oldest extant complete Latin Bible, one of three such Bibles, or 'pandects', produced at Wearmouth-Jarrow on the orders of Ceolfrith – one each to be placed in the churches at Wearmouth and at Jarrow, and the third intended as a gift to Rome (from the foundation of St Peter at Wearmouth to the successor to St Peter in Rome, as witness to the capability of the (upstart) Northumbrian monastery to match the achievements of even Rome). The texts of its individual books derive from varying exemplars (the 'edition' was a local creation), several of which are among the best early witnesses to the Vg revision.

2 *Guida e Storia Abbazia del SS. Salvatore al Monte Amiata* (Abbazia SS. Salvatore, 1991), 51. The work quoted is Angelo Mercati, 'Per la storia del codice amiatino' (*Biblica* iii, 1922), 324-8, which does go on to acknowledge the English origins of Codex Amiatinus.

3 For a convenient summary of the discovery of, first, the English origins, and, subsequently, the English manufacture of Codex Amiatinus see E. A. Lowe, *English Uncial* (Oxford: University Press, 1960), 8-13.

4 London, British Library, Cotton MS, Nero D.IV (*CLA* II, n. 187; Alexander, *Insular Manuscripts*, n. 9).

5 *Nouum Testamentum Domini Nostri Iesu Christi Latine secundum editionem Sancti Hieronymi: pars prior, Quattuor Euangelia*, ed. by J. Wordsworth & H. J. White (Oxford: University Press, 1889-98) (cited as Wordsworth & White). Many early gospel texts have been examined since Wordsworth & White's great work, and some re-examined where their work was inadequate, so notably in the Insular world the Book of Kells, Dublin, Trinity College 58 (*CLA* II, n. 274; Alexander, *Insular Manuscripts*, n. 52). But by far the major portion of their analysis of the families of early Latin gospel texts still conditions our way of thinking. In some cases this is sound, so the Italo-Northumbrian text, where there is evident close correlation between a series of witnesses; whereas it is less sound in other areas, notably the so-called Irish family, where their analysis has in many respects confused rather than clarified the relationships between the texts of Insular gospel-books (see C. D. Verey, T. J. Brown and E. Coatsworth, *The Durham Gospels* (Early English Manuscripts in Facsimile, 20; Copenhagen: Rosenkilde & Bagger, 1980) (cited as *Durham Gospels*), 70-1. A recent and most valuable summary of the state of play on the Irish text of the Latin gospels is that of M. McNamara, 'The Celtic-Irish Mixed Gospel Text: some recent contributions and centennial reflections' (*Filologia mediolatina*, II; Spoleto: Centro Italiano di Studi sull'Alto

Medioevo, 1995), 69-108. Bonifatius Fischer's great work of collating a sample of passages from all pre-900 gospel texts has added much material, but Fischer has not (as yet) drawn conclusions therefrom on the transmission of the text (B. Fischer, *Die lateinischen Evangelien bis zum 10. Jahrhundert* (Aus der Geschichte der lateinischen Bibel 13, 15, 17, 18; Freiburg im Breisgau: Herder, 1988, 1989, 1990, 1991)) – for the most part his groupings are on the basis of broad codicological, not text grounds. I share McNamara's opinion that the understanding of the families must come from the study of individual complete texts: so often text types change, and Fischer's selected passages offer only limited coverage, particularly since so many surviving gospel texts are often fragmentary.

6 Indeed Samuel Berger went as far as to argue 'Irish' readings in the two Italian uncial gospelbooks we know to have been imported early into England, the production of one of which may well predate the mission of Augustine in 597, Cambridge, Corpus Christi College 286 (*CLA* II, n. 126) and, of later production, Oxford, Bodleian Library, Auct. D.2.14 (*CLA* II, n. 230) – S. Berger, *Histoire de la Vulgate pendant les premiers siècles du Moyen Age* (Paris, 1893; reprinted New York, 1956), 35-6. Seemingly any Old Latin admixture was to be laid at Irish doors! Berger influenced Wordsworth & White's analysis (n. 5 above).

7 Durham Gospels: Durham, Cathedral Library, MS A.II.17, fols 2-102 (*CLA* II, n. 149; Alexander, *Insular Manuscripts*, n. 10); Echternach Gospels: Paris, Bibliothèque Nationale, lat. 9389 (*CLA* V, n. 578; Alexander, *Insular Manuscripts*, n. 11); Book of Durrow: Dublin, Trinity College MS 57 (*CLA* II, n. 273; Alexander, *Insular Manuscripts*, n. 6).

8 Perceptions have moved around over the centuries since scholars started to study these books. In the seventeenth and eighteenth centuries the illustrious likes of Mabillon and Wanley claimed such work for the Saxons, in the nineteenth century the balance shifted towards the Irish. The changes of scholarly judgements on the sources of inspiration behind early Insular book production are conveniently summarised in T. J. Brown, 'Northumbria and the Book of Kells' (*Anglo-Saxon England*, I; Cambridge: University Press, 1972), 220-4.

9 François Masai, *Essai sur les Origines de la Miniature dite irlandaise* (Publications de Scriptorium, I; Brussels & Antwerp, 1947). It is important to stress (since it is a charge laid by the counter-arguments of Ó Cróinín and O'Sullivan – see below) that Julian Brown ('Northumbria and the Book of Kells', 219) was not uncritical of Masai's work (see also R. Bruce-Mitford, 'The Durham-Echternach Calligrapher' in *St Cuthbert, his Cult and his Community*, ed. by G. Bonner, D. Rollason & C. Stancliffe; Woodbridge: Boydell Press, 1989 (cited as Bonner, *St Cuthbert*), 178).

10 *Euangeliorum quattuor Codex Lindisfarnensis*, ed. by T. D. Kendrick, T. J. Brown, R. L. S. Bruce-Mitford, and others (2 vols; Olten & Lausanne: Urs Graf-Verlag, 1956-60) (cited as *Codex Lindisfarnensis*), vol. II, 95-102 and elsewhere.

11 See T. J. Brown in *Durham Gospels*, 46-8, and Brown. 'The Irish Element in the Insular System of Scripts' in *Die Iren und Europa im früheren Mittelalter*, ed. by H. Lowe; 2 vols; Stuttgart, 1982, I, particularly 108-10 (reprinted in *A Palaeographer's View: the Selected Writings of Julian Brown* (ed. J. Bately, M. P. Brown, & J. Roberts (London: Harvey Miller, 1993), 208-11.

12 *Codex Lindisfarnensis* II, 90-1, 103-4.

13 So, notably, Brown, 'Northumbria and the Book of Kells', *passim*, and *Codex Lindisfarnensis* II, 255-7. Various questionable arguments have been advanced for the Northumbrian origins of the Book of Durrow, among the more spurious being that which effectively argues that since its gospel text is relatively pure it cannot be Irish – so F. C. Burkitt, 'Kells, Durrow and Lindisfarne' (*Antiquity* IX, 1935), 33-7.

14 On the dangers of taking surviving manuscript evidence as typical, see, for example, R. Gameson, 'The Royal 1.B.vii Gospels and English book production in the seventh and eighth centuries' in *The Early Medieval Bible*, ed. by R. Gameson (Cambridge: University

Press, 1994), 24-52. I believe he overplays the 'low grade' status of the Royal book; it 'feels' like an attempt to recreate a local version of a plain, earlier Italian uncial gospel-book, many of which type would have been imported into England. The evidence from the 1989-91 excavations at Flixborough, South Humberside, is a timely reminder of a hitherto unknown, seemingly important literary centre in early Anglo-Saxon England (*The Making of England: Anglo-Saxon Art and Culture AD 600-900*, ed. by L. Webster & J. Backhouse (London: British Museum Press, 1991), 94-101).

15 D. Ó Cróinín, 'Pride and Prejudice' (*Peritia* 1, 1982), 352-62; 'Rath Melsigi, Willibrord, and the Earliest Echternach Manuscripts' (*Peritia* 3, 1984), 17-49; and 'Is the Augsberg Gospel Codex a Northumbrian Manuscript?', in Bonner, *St Cuthbert*, 189-201. W. O'Sullivan developed some of Ó Cróinín's thinking in 'The Lindisfarne Scriptorium: For and Against' (*Peritia* 8, 1994), 80-94. Much of what I have to say in this paper is an attempt to take the debate forward in response to Ó Cróinín.

16 N. Netzer, *Cultural Interplay in the Eighth Century, the Trier Gospels and the making of the scriptorium at Echternach* (Cambridge: University Press, 1994), 4.

17 Julian Brown acknowledged the possibility that the earliest scribes at Echternach may have been Irish ('The Irish Element in the Insular System of Scripts', 112). For the best post-Ó Cróinín analysis of the development of the Echternach scriptorium see N. Netzer, 'Willibrord's Scriptorium at Echternach and its Relationship to Ireland and Lindisfarne' in Bonner, *St Cuthbert*, 203-12, and her *Cultural Interplay*, particularly ch. 1 and 4.

18 *CLA* II, n. 125; Alexander, *Insular Manuscripts*, n. 12. My work primarily on the text of the Cambridge-London Gospels has been part of a study of all aspects by a group of scholars including Dr Michelle Brown, Dr Nancy Netzer, and Dr Mildred Budny. It is hoped that this work may be published in a monograph, the textual aspects of which would expand on my arguments in this paper. I am indebted in particular to Patrick McGurk (for a continuing source of wise counsel on Insular gospel-books, and for the very practical contribution of the loan of material), to Nancy Netzer (for the sharing of ideas), and especially to Michelle Brown (for the stimulus of discourse on these matters and for much practical assistance, not least in arranging for slides to support this paper when given at the Hampton Court symposium). I am grateful to The Scriptorium: Center for Christian Antiquities for inviting me to participate in the symposium on *The Bible as Book*, and for the invitation to publish this paper. It would be remiss not to thank Dáibhí Ó Cróinín – without his tenacious search for the alternative perspective on these gospel-books, I may not have felt so moved to argue back!

19 Matthew Parker, Master of Corpus Christi College, Cambridge, from 1544 to 1553, Archbishop of Canterbury from 1559 to his death in 1575. Sir Robert Cotton, 1571-1631, statesman and antiquarian, whose collection of books was one of the foundations of what is now the British Library. In the 1621 catalogue of his collection (London, British Library, Harley MS 6018) Cotton has added in his own hand that the book once belonged to Augustine, Apostle of the English. Parker also believed that his fragments belonged to Augustine. The date of the book would preclude this. But the seemingly independent opinions of both Cotton and Parker may well suggest that there was an association with Canterbury. The various studies of my colleagues into the physical condition and other aspects of the book (including later medieval additions) have failed to establish any provenance earlier than ownership by these two antiquarians. Thomas Wolsey (1475-1530, Archbishop of York from 1514 and Cardinal from 1515) records his ownership of the bifolium on fol. 2ʳ of the Royal canon table fragments.

20 Contained in London, British Library, Stowe 1061 (36). Reproduced in part in T. Astle, *The Origins and Progress of Writing* (London, 1784), pl. XV.1; for a full reproduction see J. Backhouse, 'Birds, Beasts and Initials in Lindisfarne's Gospel Books' in Bonner, *St Cuthbert*, pl. 13.

21 Only two fols (59 and 60) retain at least parts of all original 19 lines per page (as also in the Corpus leaves), whereas some folios have only two or three part lines surviving.

22 In a publication such as this it is not possible to illustrate all the details. The most convenient source of illustration is G. Henderson, *From Durrow to Kells: the Insular Gospel-books 650-800* (London: Thames & Hudson, 1987), particularly ch. 3 – pl. 91, 92, 94-96, 109, and 112 reproduce the main decorative elements of the Cambridge-London Gospels.

23 The arguments here about the ornamental parallels can be followed, for the most part, by reference to the plates in ch. 3 of Henderson, *From Durrow to Kells.*

24 ibid., pl. 105 and 112 (for comparison of the lion symbol pages in both) and 108 and 109 (the eagle symbol pages).

25 ibid., pl. 107 to 109.

26 ibid., pl. 94.

27 ibid., pl. 98. While the decorative detail is different (e.g. the absence of zoomorphic decoration in panels of the 'INI' in Echternach), the layout and structure of the major 'INI' in both books is similar, and the run of decorative initials thereafter contains common elements, so the 'TIUM' with its C-shaped 'T' embracing the 'I', and the bar of the 'M' crossing the 'U' (note how seemingly much of the same model is found in the detail of the opening initial to Mark in the Lindisfarne Gospels – *From Durrow to Kells*, pl. 152).

28 ibid., pl. 78 (Durham), 92 (Cambridge-London), and 160 (Lindisfarne part – for the full page see J. Backhouse, *The Lindisfarne Gospels* (Oxford: Phaidon Press, 1981), pl. 35). In all three the 'P' (of *principio*) forms part of the major ensemble, and in all three has a double bow; the scheme of lesser decorative initials has an almost identical layout up to *uerbum* (the exception being the odd syllabification *cipi/o* in lines 3 and 4 of Cambridge-London); both the Durham and the Cambridge-London Gospels have the first two decorative lines split *ri/n* (Lindisfarne has *rin* on the one line); in all three books the space to the right of the major 'P' is filled with the same letters (discounting for the peculiar syllabification noted above); the allocation of the words of the rubric either side of the top of the 'NP' is identical in Durham and Cambridge-London (but different in Lindisfarne).

29 *From Durrow to Kells*, pl. 75; or Backhouse, *Lindisfarne Gospels*, pl. 13 (Durham) compare with Backhouse in Bonner, *St Cuthbert*, pl. 13 (facsimile of Cotton leaf).

30 *From Durrow to Kells*, pl. 94 (Cambridge-London: the split 'f' of *fuit* though much damaged is clearly visible at the bottom of the plate) and pl. 77 (Durham); in both there are hair-line spirals at the finials, of a type which are one of the hallmarks of the Durham-Echternach calligrapher.

31 One scribe wrote most of Matthew, the prefatory matter to Mark, and John – his hand displays pre-phase II features. A second scribe wrote Mark. A third scribe wrote a few of the opening surviving leaves of Matthew, and Luke.

32 The so-called 'architecture' of these early Latin gospel-books is set out in P. McGurk, *Latin Gospel Books from A.D. 400 to A.D. 800* (Les Publications de Scriptorium V; Paris & Brussels, 1961) – see, in particular, appendix III, 112-13.

33 Vatican, Biblioteca Apostolica Vaticana, Barberini MS lat. 570 (*CLA* I, n. 60; Alexander, *Insular Manuscripts*, n. 36). The book is probably from southern England from the late eighth century.

34 For a comment on the possible origins of this ordering see *Durham Gospels*, 24-5.

35 The Irish books display some distinctly irregular architecture – McGurk, *Latin Gospel Books*, App. III, section 7. Other than the Echternach Gospels, gospel-books early associated with Echternach are: the Trier Gospels (Trier, Cathedral Treasury MS 61), the Augsburg Gospels (Augsburg, Universitätsbibliothek Cod. 1.2.4° 2), and the Maeseyck Gospels (Maeseyck, church of St Catherine s.n.) – see Netzer, *Cultural Interplay*, 4-11 and 21-3.

36 For the most recent and most comprehensive survey of the evidence of these somewhat

esoteric word lists see O. Szerwiniack, 'Des Recueils d'Interprétations de Noms Hébreux chez les Irlandais et le Wisigoth Théodulf' (*Scriptorium* XLVIII, 1994, 2), 187-258. Szerwiniack builds on Patrick McGurk's and my own earlier analysis. In *Durham Gospels*, 23-4, I had shown the close textual relationship between these lists in the early Insular books, and suggested that they might represent a cut-down version of Jerome's *Liber Interpretationis Hebraicorum Nominum*. Szerwiniack widens the debate on sources. I am grateful to Patrick McGurk for lending me a copy of this article.

37 For a discussion of the version in these books and for an analysis of the family of texts see P. McGurk, 'An edition of the abbreviated and selective set of Hebrew names found in the Book of Kells', *The Book of Kells: Proceedings of a conference at Trinity College Dublin 6-9 September 1992*, ed. by F. O'Mahony (Aldershot: Scolar Press, 1994), 102-32.

38 See n. 35 above. Netzer, *Cultural Interplay*, 22-3; Ó Cróinín, 'Is the Augsberg Gospel Codex a Northumbrian Manuscript?', 195.

39 For a convenient summary of the occurrence of the various families in the early gospel-books see McGurk, *Latin Gospel Books*, 113-17. The classification derives from D. DeBruyne, *Sommaires, Divisions et Rubriques de la Bible latine* (Namur: Auguste Godenne imprimeur-editeur, 1914).

40 The Maeseyck and Augsburg Gospels (see n. 35 above), and the Echternach Gospels themselves.

41 Of the eight readings, with Echternach against Kells as follows ([] indicates letters lost in Cambridge-London, the number is that of the chapter): 11. *ecce/et ecce*, 15. *[s]anat/saluat*, 36. *[baptism]um/baptisma*; with Durrow/Kells against Echternach as follows: rubric *[bre]ues cau[sae]/breuis disputatio*, 18. *discipuli/discipuli eius*, 21. *edere/manducare*, 46. *sequebatur/sequebatur eum*.

42 See J. Regul, *Die antimarcionitischen Evangelienprologe* (Aus der Geschichte der lateinischen Bibel, 6; Freiburg im Breisgau: Herder, 1969).

43 These are 14, 15, 17-20 in Regul's list.

44 *Durham Gospels*, 18-23.

45 See n. 38 above.

46 McGurk, *Latin Gospel Books*, 113-17; over 40 per cent of the surviving chapter lists for Mark in the pre-800 gospel-books belong to this family.

47 The surviving evidence is as follows ([] indicates missing text, the line number is given after the folio):

BL Otho C.V 16r7	[]XUII	Matthew 26:30
Corpus 197b 3r18	II	John 2:1
Corpus 197b 6r8	UII	John 7:1
Corpus 197b 22r4	UIIII	John 9:18

48 So, for example, Stockholm, Royal Library A.135 (Stockholm 'Codex Aureus') (*CLA* XI, n. 1642; Alexander, *Insular Manuscripts*, n. 30) and London, British Library, Royal I.E. VI (*CLA* II, n. 214; Alexander, *Insular Manuscripts*, n. 32).

49 Durham A.II.16 is a composite volume (there is also a fragment from this book in the Pepysian Library in Magdalene College Library, Cambridge, MS 2981(18)) (*CLA* II, n. 148a, 148b, 148c; Alexander, *Insular Manuscripts*, n. 16). Three distinct scripts are found, and at least two very distinct text traditions. Fols 103-34 contain much of John in Insular half-uncial with a text belonging closely to the distinct Italo-Northumbrian family (found in, for example, Codex Amiatinus and the other products of the Wearmouth-Jarrow scriptorium, and in the Lindisfarne Gospels). Matthew, Mark, and Luke are in a mixture of hands, Insular half-uncial and a fairly low-grade uncial (there are two uncial hands), with a text at least part of which is closely related to both the Durham and the Cambridge-London Gospels – see below. Both parts (John and the rest) may possibly come from the same eclectic scriptorium

(the fundamentally different textual traditions do not rule this out), and either jointly or severally from Northumbria, and are generally dated to the eighth century, possibly the first half.

50 See *Durham Gospels*, 70-1. The so-called Irish text of the gospels represents more a way of handling the text than a set of readings indicative of a common archetype.

51 Cividale, Museo Archeologico s.n. (*CLA* III, n. 285), London, University College, Fragm. Lat. 1 (*CLA* II, n. 221), Cambridge, Corpus Christi College 286 (St Augustine's Gospels) (*CLA* II, n. 126), and Oxford, Bodleian Library, Auct. D.2.14 (*CLA* II, n. 230). The last two were in England from an early date – see below.

52 See n. 50 above.

53 *Durham Gospels*, 71.

54 See n. 49 above. It is interesting to observe that in the view of Dr Michelle Brown (see n. 18 above) there are parallels in the details of the various hands as between this book and Durham A.II.16, both of which reflect a scriptorium where there was the toleration of different scribal traditions. The option of a common scriptorium, or very closely related scriptoria, is not ruled out.

55 See n. 15 above. O'Sullivan ('The Lindisfarne Scriptorium: For and Against', 89): 'from there [Rath Maelsigi via Iona] the Durham Gospels would have been carried to Wearmouth-Jarrow and so ended up at Chester-le-Street with the other remants of that library' (Chester-le-Street was the resting place of the exile Lindisfarne community from 883 to 995, following which it transferred to Durham). By proposing that the Durham Gospels were amended at Wearmouth-Jarrow, O'Sullivan is determined to write Lindisfarne out of the equation, but he keeps the detail of his argument very much to himself.

56 See n. 51 above. The Corpus book is probably of the sixth century; it contains numerous corrections in an eighth-century English uncial hand (Lowe, *English Uncial*, 17). The Bodleian book is of the seventh century and was in England by the end of the eighth, when an inscription was added in an Anglo-Saxon hand referring to St Chad (of Lichfield) (Lowe, *English Uncial*, 17).

57 Wordsworth & White, 710.

58 *Durham Gospels*, 72.

59 ibid.

60 The evidence that the texts of John in the Durham Gospels and in the Book of Kells are related and may well reflect the influence of the OX test on the latter also (*Durham Gospels*, 72-3) could be used to argue that the OX text type was imported into Northumbria via Ireland – and, indeed, possibly even supportive of the argument of Berger (see n. 6 above) that the Irish text and that found in OX are essentially the same – McNamara suggests that the relationship needs to be studied ('The Celtic-Irish Mixed Gospel Text', 107). But the text type of John in Kells is different from that of the other Kells gospels (P. McGurk, *The Book of Kells*, Commentary volume, ed. Peter Fox (Lucerne: Faksimile Verlag Luzern, 1990), 68). All things are possible; but the balance of probabilities, not least taking account of the weight of evidence of the influence of the OX type on the English side of the Irish Sea and the lack (discounting the limited evidence of the Book of Kells) of any clear evidence from Irish material, points to the text type being imported into Northumbria directly from Italy or via southern England, and not via Ireland.

61 A.II.16 contains three twelfth-century entries relating to Durham.

62 The same, probably ninth-century hand has marked the Passion narrative in Luke and the Resurrection narrative in John *c* and *l* (*cantor* and *lector*). It is not easy to detrmine how and when the two parts of A.II.16 came together. The assumption that they originated apart stems from the different dimensions and better quality vellum of the John leaves, coupled with the distinct text of John. It is possible that John was written to complete an incomplete book, not to replace a lost section of a previously complete one.

63 There is no obvious distinction between the uncial and half-uncial portions of A.II.16 Matthew, Mark, and Luke: the text by each hand complements the other in that there are no gaps, excepting folios since lost; (see C. D. Verey, 'A Collation of the Gospel Texts contained in Durham Cathedral MSS. A.II.10, A.II.16 and A.II.17' (unpublished M.A. thesis, University of Durham, 1969), part IIIC). Matthew and Luke are in a mixture of both hands, whereas Mark (the text with which the present comparison is most concerned) is in uncial. The uncial is described by Lowe as 'Northumbrian uncial distinctly on the decline' (*English Uncial*, 20).

64 'One cannot speak of Irish uncial, since not a single manuscript or fragment in uncial characters has reached us from Ireland – a curious fact, but hardly due to accident' (*CLA* II (1972 revision), xx). Given the early history of what was to become Durham Cathedral Library (the dislocation of Northumbrian culture following the Viking raids on Lindisfarne and elsewhere), it is reasonable to conclude that all the earliest books in the present collection were in the region of Northumbria from the eighth century or earlier, and that they were either made there or were early imports. Later gifts (such as those of Athelstan in the tenth century) would not have included books from the earliest period. In the later medieval period it is difficult to see how Durham would have acquired books from the earliest period (indeed, at the dissolution it lost them, for example the Lindisfarne Gospels, to name but one of the treasures removed).

65 *Durham Gospels*, 17-18, 38 and 74-75.

66 My own judgement of 1972 (appendix to T. J. Brown, 'Northumbria and the Book of Kells', 243-5) was supported by Julian Brown at the time, and subsequently in our joint work on the Durham Gospels (*Durham Gospels*, 44-7). William O'Sullivan asserted at the Durham St Cuthbert conference in 1987, and later in print in 1994 ('The Lindisfarne Scriptorium: For and Against', 86), that Brown had come to reject the identity of hand. Sadly, Julian Brown's untimely death in 1987 prevents him from speaking for himself; but if he did change his mind then he seems to have expressed such an opinion to no one else. The two books were together in Durham in 1987 and direct comparison was possible. The conclusion of this comparison was recorded by J. Backhouse in Bonner, *St Cuthbert*, 172, n. 31: 'No clear-cut conclusion was reached. The additions in Lindisfarne seem less decisively written than those in Durham and the ink is weaker. This may account for some of the variations noted. I am myself prepared to accept that the two are by the same hand.' Whether these two sets of corrections are by the very same hand must remain in dispute, but at the very least they represent two scribes with near identical training.

67 *Durham Gospels*, 18-21 and 38.

68 This would make the Durham Gospels the earlier of the two, unless the scribe returned to Northumbria. For various reasons, notably the process of textual emendation in the Durham Gospels, I do not accept the sequence, argued on primarily art-historical grounds, of: the Echternach Gospels, the Lindisfarne Gospels, with the Durham Gospels last (*Durham Gospels*, 107-8).

69 Since writing this paper I have established a close Northumbrian connection for the gospel text in the Echternach Gospels, namely with Durham Cathedral A.II.16, in the first 22 chapters of Matthew. This is the subject of a paper to be published as part of the proceedings of The Golden Age of Northumbria conference, held in Newcastle, England, in July 1996.

CULTURAL TRANSMISSION:
ILLUSTRATED BIBLICAL MANUSCRIPTS FROM THE MEDIEVAL EASTERN CHRISTIAN AND ARAB WORLDS

Lucy-Anne Hunt

PORTABLE, AND PRECIOUS IN CONTENT AND FORM, biblical manuscripts played a key role in the interaction between societies in the Middle Ages, as well as within the religious, cultural and intellectual life of the individual Christian communities that produced them. But how did this take place? This paper aims to explore this question through a selection of manuscripts of biblical texts or complete Bibles produced by Christian communities in the Middle East before the rise of Islam through to the fifteenth century. Three major themes present themselves. The first, parallelism, emerges from the problem of early Coptic-Insular manuscript connections; that is to say, the links suggested between the monastic communities of early Christian Egypt and the British Isles from the fourth to the early eighth centuries. The second, continuity, can be viewed through the ongoing production of biblical manuscripts in the indigenous Christian communities, especially of Syria and Mesopotamia, between the sixth and the thirteenth centuries. Finally, the development of biblical, especially New Testament, books in Arabic is viewed as a response to Christian-Muslim coexistence, attesting to a Christian response to the religious, cultural, and political domination by Islam. These are considered in the light of the communities that produced them and the cross-cultural connections they propose between different Christian communities, and between Christian and Muslim communities. All three cases offer instances of the place of manuscripts within the processes by which interaction takes place between medieval societies, comprising exchanges and networks of individuals and institutions.

The emphasis here is on manuscripts produced in Egypt, Syria, and Palestine, loci of cultural contact between different Christian communities during the Middle Ages, with reference to other western and Mediterranean societies. All three areas were retained in Muslim hands after the Arab invasions of the early seventh century, except during the return to Byzantine rule in Syria between the later tenth and eleventh centuries and the Crusader period between the later eleventh and thirteenth centuries, when the Holy Land and much of Syria were in Latin hands.

It is often assumed that the eastern Christian churches in these areas became isolated from the mainstream theological developments of the Latin and Greek churches. However, the manuscripts themselves tell a different story, one which reaffirms that while differences were acknowledged, textual and artistic traditions and developments were shared between the different churches through networks of individuals and institutions. This remained the case, despite the theological divisions over the nature of Christ, crystalized at the Council of Chalcedon in 451, after which the churches of Egypt, Syria, and Armenia (often referred to as the 'Monophysite' or 'separated' churches) broke ranks with the Byzantine Orthodox church over theological definition of the nature of Christ. The predominant Christian community in Egypt was – and is – the Coptic church; that in Syria was the Orthodox (Jacobite) church, in addition to the (Nestorian) Church of the East. The Melkite communities in both areas, as well as Palestine, remained affiliated to the Byzantine, Chalcedonian, Church.

I. PARALLELISM: MANUSCRIPTS FROM THE PRE-ISLAMIC MIDDLE EAST AND THE PROBLEM OF THE TRANSFERENCE OF STYLE[1]

The earliest preserved illustrated biblical book from Coptic Egypt is the Glazier Codex, a complete book of the first half of the Acts of the Apostles in the Middle Egyptian Oxyrhynchite dialect dating to *c.* 400.[2] An interlace ankh cross serves as the finispiece to the book (Pl. 10). Derived from pharaonic funerary imagery and symbolizing eternal life, the cross is rooted in early Christian imagery with the addition of leaved fronds linking the base to the arms, with affronted peacocks and other birds, one encircled at the top. The rediscovery of this manuscript in 1961 stimulated a revival of debate concerning the possible influence of early Christian Egypt, the home of monasticism, on Insular manuscript production. It was suggested that the miniature represented the 'missing link' in the potential Coptic sources contributing to the development of seventh-century Insular manuscript art.[3] The argument was that the Glazier codex miniature exemplified the departure in the late fourth century from 'classical' plaitwork forms in two ways. These are (1) discordant plaiting, whereby the passage of the individual ribbons through the design is interrupted, and (2) discontinuous colouring, in which the same ribbon changes colour as it passes through the interlace. These two features were traced into Insular manuscript art of the second half of the seventh century, in the Durham Gospels (Durham, Cathedral Library, MS A.II.10) and the Book of Durrow (Dublin, Trinity College, MS A.4.5[57], fol. 85ᵛ) respectively.[4] These changes were posited as a form of subversion of the logic of Graeco-Roman interlace as preserved in Egyptian textiles of the third to fourth centuries.[5]

Study of the Glazier Codex reaffirmed a link between the Mediterranean and Insular worlds through the common use of interlace. The exclusive origin of such interlace in Coptic Egypt has, however, subsequently been questioned, since interlace appears elsewhere, including Byzantium and Italy.[6] So how direct was the link? The likely answer is that manuscripts from Coptic Egypt were prominent among those from the Mediterranean at the disposal of Insular artists up to and during the seventh century, but thereafter parallelism took over from direct influence. The fact that interlace was not exclusive to Egypt does not of itself discount contact with Egypt, especially up to the seventh century. The early development of monasticism in Egypt and the stimulus to literacy and religious life would endorse such contact. Complementary bookbinding techniques further suggest the introduction of such books from Egypt to the west. The technique of moulded leather over boards of the gospel-book buried with St Cuthbert in 687 (owned by Stonyhurst College, Lancashire and on loan to the British Library), as well as its method of sewing, is of a type used in Coptic Egypt.[7] This is a technique common to other Coptic leatherwork, with the earliest preserved Coptic example itself also dating to the late seventh century.[8]

Transmission took place through the travels of individuals, including monks and pilgrims, as well as other processes of mutual exchange. The career of the monk John Cassian, who founded monasteries in southern Gaul after immersing himself in eastern Christianity in Egypt between 385 and 399 or 400, is a case in point.[9] Trade networks between east and west account for the introduction of eastern Mediterranean pottery and goods excavated at British sites.[10] Jars stamped with crosses containing wine and oil were imported, probably to serve the liturgical requirements of Christian communities in the British Isles.[11] Books would have formed part of such exchanges, forging links between communities. But by c. 600 a common east-west repertory of motifs and figural imagery was shared between east and west, and the search for exact prototypes in one area or another becomes increasingly fruitless.[12] Direct trading was disrupted by the rise of Islam during the seventh century and this would have undermined the ongoing import of contemporary books from the Mediterranean world.[13] As far as trading contacts are concerned, therefore, the emphasis must now be placed on the sixth century, with Gaul as a likely intermediary.[14]

Coptic manuscripts illustrated with figural imagery attest to this parallelism, or common fund of imagery, between east and west after the seventh century. Rich as they are, they can no longer be seen, as they were in the 1960s, as the primary source of such imagery in Insular manuscripts, not least since they largely post-date their counterparts in the British Isles.[15] By the time of the production of the Book of Kells in the later eighth to early ninth century the claim of a uniquely Coptic contribution is even more difficult to justify. The argument has been put forward that the full-page miniatures in the Book of Kells (Dublin, Trinity College, MS A.1.6 [58]) were dependent on Coptic book illumination, with the focus on the Enthroned Virgin and Child.[16] This Virgin and Child surrounded by angels (fol. 7ʳ, Pl. 11), is characterized by the display of affection given by the child to his mother through touch.[17] This has prompted the suggestion that a Nursing Mother image was seen by the artist. Certainly this was a motif common in Coptic Egypt, as the frontispiece to a Sahidic Coptic manuscript of Pseudo-John Chrysostom's *Eulogy of the Four Incorporeal Animals* (New York Morgan Library MS 612, fol. 1ʳ) of 893, makes clear.[18] A highly developed interest in Virgin and Child, as well as apocalyptic, theophanic imagery is, it is true, apparent in Coptic monastic apse painting at Bawit and Saqqara during the seventh to eighth centuries in particular, prior to the major survivals of Coptic manuscript illumination from the ninth and tenth centuries onward. But the fact that the earliest preserved Christian image of the Nursing Mother (Galaktotrophousa) image was produced in late fourth-century Constantinople discounts any unique claim to maternal sentiment on the part of Coptic Egypt.[19] Thus, although an eastern-Mediterranean image of the Virgin and Child imported to the west can be seen as the direct or indirect model for the Kells Virgin and Child, this was not necessarily a Coptic one. Images of the Virgin and Child must have been in circulation prior to the production of the Book of Kells. Neither is the Kells Virgin and Child unique. The 'complementary profiles' of the Kells Virgin and Child, in which the lower part of the Virgin's body is turned to the side, mirroring the pose of the Child, has a precedent in the Virgin and Child carved on St Cuthbert's coffin at the end of the seventh century.[20] An image of the Virgin and Child could have been acquired by Benedict Biscop during his travels in the eastern Mediterranean referred to by Bede, or by the monastery at Lindisfarne through monastic networks.[21] In this way, influences from the eastern Mediterranean, of which Coptic Egypt formed a part, can be seen to have contributed to a store of imagery developed by the end of the seventh century which was drawn on and adapted in parallel in subsequent manuscript illumination.

The assertion of the ongoing primacy of Coptic Egypt over the Insular world has deflected attention from the more interesting question, that of the common context or framework in which similar works of manuscript illumination were produced between east and west after the seventh century. With the focus more firmly on the function and liturgical use of manuscripts, the choice of comparable images in different but parallel areas of the Christian world appears less surprising. This takes account of cross-cultural exchange between east and west, and the book as cultural object within its monastic environment. This shifts the emphasis from competing prototypes to parallels between imagery of significance and relevance to monastic communities in both east and west.

2. CONTINUITY: BIBLICAL MANUSCRIPT PRODUCTION IN SYRIA AND MESOPOTAMIA, SIXTH TO THIRTEENTH CENTURIES

If Coptic and Insular manuscripts show how parallelism can develop, so manuscripts produced by Syriac-speaking communities illustrate continuity in indigenous Christian book production in the Middle East itself. The Syriac Rabbula Gospels in Florence were written by a group of scribes supervised by the monk of that name at the monastery of St John at Beth Zagba on the Euphrates in Mesopotamia in 586.[22] Its vivid illustration is grouped at the beginning of the manuscript. This comprises full-page frontispieces and canon tables, most of them flanked by figures of prophets, and two by the Evangelists. Narrative Gospel illustration from the Annunciation to Zacharias to Christ before Pilate is fitted into the margins below. Pl. 12 shows Canon 1, with Moses receiving the Law, opposite Aaron, with Zacharias below initiating this Old/New Testament sequence. The illustration synthesizes the concerns of eastern-Mediterranean sixth-century art, linking the correspondence between the Old and New Testaments with a topography and narrative of Christ's life and passion. The eastern Christian devotion to the Virgin is epitomized in the full-page scene of the Virgin and Child enthroned (fol. 1ᵛ), the only full-page representation of the Virgin and Child to predate that in the Book of Kells.[23] It is the educated monastic milieu in which the Rabbula Gospels themselves were produced that is portrayed on fol. 14ʳ with a monk among the ecclesiastics with Christ enthroned, two of whom offer books.[24] The Rabbula Gospels, preserved in its Syrian monastic environment under Islamic rule throughout the destructive period of Iconoclasm in Byzantium during the eighth and early ninth century, attests to the richness of early Christian manuscript production in the eastern Mediterranean. Inscriptions in the manuscript tell of its retention in monastic libraries until its move to Florence in the fifteenth century.[25]

In common with the Rabbula Gospels, the later-sixth/early-seventh-century Syriac Peshiṭta Bible in Paris (Bibl. Nat. Syr. 341) is stylistically akin to other manuscript and monumental art of its time. It follows a different format, however, in that its illustrations act as headpieces to the particular books of the Old and New Testament to which they refer.[26] In this way, the illustrations served to break up the text, acting as a guide to the reader to identify the respective texts during its liturgical use.[27] The illustrations that are preserved are of three types. Some are narrative, historical scenes, such as Moses before Pharaoh opening the Book of Exodus (fol. 8^r). Others are symbolical, such as the title-piece to Proverbs (fol. 118^r) which shows the Virgin holding Christ in front of her in a womb-like aureole as the embodiment of the source of Wisdom.[28] Wisdom enshrined in a codex is held by Solomon, author and king, on the Virgin's right. On the Virgin's left a richly-bound volume is held by a figure personifying the wisdom of the New Testament Church. The third group, of author portraits, shows single standing prophets before their texts.[29] While now lacking its colophon, the manuscript is known to have been in Upper Mesopotamia, north-east of Mardin, before it was acquired by the Bibliothèque Nationale in Paris at the beginning of the twentieth century. Having fallen under Muslim rule shortly before the mid-seventh century, this area was one of those taken back into Byzantine hands by the early eleventh century. By the time of the death of the Emperor Basil II in 1025, this applied to northern and southern Mesopotamia, Melitene, and Cilicia, as well as the north Syrian province of Antioch.[30] By the end of the eleventh century the latter province had fallen under Latin, Crusader rule, ushering in a new cultural dimension to the region.

The Syriac Peshitta Bible tradition continued, represented in the twelfth century by the Buchanan Bible in Cambridge (Cambridge, University Library, MS Oo. 1. 1.2) undertaken for Orthodox (Jacobite) church usage.[31] Scenes and figures again precede the texts to which they refer, with historical scenes and standing prophets predominating. Now the overall programme is adapted to take account of the contemporary political situation of Christian-Muslim conflict in the area. Datable to the 1190s, the Bible is attributable to the monastery of the Mother of God near Edessa, one of the monasteries at the southern end of the Amanus range to the west of Antioch, then under Latin rule. Its illustration shows the interweaving of the different indigenous Christian communities in the area. The portraits of John (fol. 265^v) and James (fol. 306^r) in the New Testament section are inscribed in Greek and Armenian as well as Syriac. The iconography confirms that books in all three languages would have been consulted by the artists in monastic libraries locally, and across the region. This is not surprising: the Black Mountain was a multicultural area populated by Greeks, Armenians, and Georgians and both Syrian Orthodox and Melkite, as well as Latin, monasteries during the time of Latin rule. Several Syriac manuscripts from the region state in their colophons that they were copied directly from Greek manuscripts, dating to the Byzantinization of the region in the tenth to eleventh centuries, which contributed to the Constantinopolitanization of the Melkite Church in Syria.[32] Important in regard to the Buchanan Bible, manuscripts would also have been exchanged through the Syrian Orthodox (Jacobite) church network functioning at this time, during the patriarchate of Michael, Syrian Orthodox Patriarch of Antioch and historian and statesman (1166-99). Monks and others travelled from one monastery to another across political boundaries taking books with them.

The cultural contact proposed by the illustration of the Buchanan Bible is also highly political. The Old Testament imagery is harnessed in support and justification of the Latin presence in the region. Judith beheading the tyrant Holofernes (fol. 191^r) and the

Maccabees with their mother and Eleazar (the priest who was martyred with them for upholding Judaic law), frontispiece to Maccabees IV (fol. 226ᵛ), are Old Testament types for the opposition of tyranny. The scenes represent Syrian Orthodox (Jacobite) justification for the Latin Christian cause against Islam.[33]

This interaction between Syrian and other indigenous Christians with Latin Christians occurs elsewhere in the twelfth-century Mediterranean, including Palestine and Sicily. Here, again, manuscripts overlap with other art forms. Mosaics at the Church of the Nativity in Bethlehem dated 1169 are inscribed in Greek, Latin, and Syriac. The name of one of the mosaicists, Basil, appears in Latin and Syriac accompanying an angel, above one of the rows of church councils in the nave of the church, and is repeated in Greek in abbreviated form opposite.[34] The Syriac, which specifies that he was a deacon, is framed like the signature in a colophon which suggests he was also a scribe: the star prefacing the Syriac inscription is like that preceding a sentence in a Syriac manuscript.[35] As an ecclesiastic as well as an artist, it is probable that he was from one of the local monasteries of the area.[36] The work of this Basil in the multilingual environment of the Latin kingdom of Jerusalem shows how works of art and books cross over and serve more than one community simultaneously. Service books and biblical manuscripts in all three languages would have been produced for the liturgies of the various Christian communities worshipping in the Church of the Nativity.

Alongside the primarily liturgical languages, including Syriac, Arabic as the spoken language of indigenous Christian communities in the Mediterranean played an increasingly important role by this time. This manifested itself in religious as well as secular literary traditions. The Melkite Admiral George of Antioch, principal minister to the Norman Roger, king of Sicily, evidently prayed, at least in part, in his mother tongue of Arabic. Wooden beams at the base of the dome of his church of the Martorana bear the text of a liturgical hymn in Arabic, accompanying the mosaics of a liturgical procession of angels around Christ.[37] But the dominant language of power in the twelfth century was Latin. George's use of his mother tongue for prayer is consistent with the recognized generic functioning of bilingualism for such private activities.[38]

By the thirteenth century biblical illustration can be seen to be arabized, even secularized. The Syriac Lectionary in London (British Library, Add. MS 7170) probably produced at the monastery of Mar Mattaï near Mosul in c. 1220 demonstrates this.[39] The dual portrait of Luke and John (fol. 6ʳ), which displays arabized ornament as well as everyday items of furniture, retains the informal tone of Arab secular manuscripts of the day and an awareness of popular culture. The western *fleur de lys* design below Luke also shows an inclusion of western motifs. Christianity is arabized here and thus is reinforced by a new ethnic consciousness. In the Prayer of the Centurion (fol. 82ʳ), the kneeling centurion who pleads with Christ to heal his son, and his two companions, are ethnically differentiated as Arabs by their facial features, dress, and turbans.

Thus the illustration of biblical books by indigenous communities in Syria and elsewhere in the eastern Mediterranean shows continuity in production while adapting to the changing circumstances. These are apparent in the interrelations between the Christian communities themselves and the response to (Islamic) Arab and Latin infiltration. The manuscripts epitomize the resulting linguistic, political, and social shifts.

3. CO-EXISTENCE: THE PRODUCTION OF NEW TESTAMENT MANUSCRIPTS IN ARABIC UNDER ISLAMIC RULE

Contemporaneous with this ongoing indigenous production of biblical manuscripts was the development of biblical books, particularly the Gospels, in Arabic. The need for Arabic books intensified when the indigenous religion and culture of the particular minority group under Islam was in danger of being overwhelmed. An initial reason for their production, then, was pragmatic and due to the decline of the indigenous Christian languages of the Christians. There was also need to uphold Christianity in primarily Muslim environments, but this also raised the issue of employing the language of Arabic, the language of Islam. We see the indigenous Christian Arabs readjusting and realigning; transferring, hence preserving, their own heritage in Greek, Syriac, and Coptic by translating texts into Arabic. The process is both a linguistic and cultural one in which books played a special role.

There is little evidence for the systematic development of the Gospels in Arabic before the ninth century. Sidney Griffith has argued that it is in the Melkite monasteries of Palestine in the ninth century that the major impetus in the development of Christian Arabic texts took place, with the earliest surviving manuscripts or manuscript fragments preserved at the monastery of St Catherine's, Mount Sinai.[40] Texts were translated from Greek and Syriac into Arabic, with the illustration sometimes also being transmitted. Thus Greek inscriptions on the Evangelist portraits of one of the Arabic manuscripts found at the monastery in 1975, a ninth-century Gospel Lectionary, betray the manuscript's origins.[41] These Gospels were very often accompanied by Christian apologetic texts, or written by the same scribes as apologetic texts. This showed the interest in the Gospels from the liturgical point of view of an emergent Christian Arabic monastic culture, as the representation of a church and an altar with ciborium, in a gospel-book dated 859, suggests.[42] Although the Gospel manuscripts have a continuous text, not in Lectionary form, they are marked off with liturgical divisions.[43] But they also provided the focus of the formulation by Christians of their faith in the vernacular in the face of Islam. It was in the interests of Muslims also to have access to an Arabic version of the Gospels, both in order to refute them and to interpret the Gospels from their own, Qur'ānic viewpoint, with the Gospels as the sayings transmitted from God to Jesus. Thus Sinai, with other Palestinian monasteries – Mar Sabas, for example – and Syrian monasteries, was a focus for translation from Greek and Syriac into Arabic, with accompanying illustrations transmitted as well.

In Egypt in the later twelfth to early thirteenth century, the Coptic Church resigned itself to the rising encroachment of the vernacular language of Arabic at the expense of Coptic. Arabic Gospels were produced, collated from Coptic, Greek, and Syriac, as colophons indicate. Books produced for the Coptic church in upper Egypt during this period are invariably bilingual, with the scribes increasingly more at home in their better-written everyday Arabic than the liturgical language of Bohairic Coptic. A gospel-book dated 1173 has the Evangelist Mark struggling with the Coptic text, with the by now more fluent Arabic text in front of him on the book stand (Oxford, Bodleian Library, Huntingdon MS 17, fol. 120ᵛ, Pl. 13).[44] Manuscript illumination, while strongly based on Byzantine models, was itself becoming increasingly arabized. The visual vocabulary, formerly the primary preserve of Qu'rān manuscript illumination, becomes appropriated for Christian use in the illustration of Biblical manuscripts. The frontispiece added to a gospel-book dated 1203-4 (Vatican, Copto, fol. 1^v) makes this plain.[45] The aniconic representation of the cross appropriates ornament in a Christian cause: here is the creation of a Christian Arab manuscript art forged in an increasingly monolingual society. The carpet page is an example of comparability in which primarily or wholly aniconic art is a stimulus to contemplation in the common monotheistic frameworks of both Christianity and Islam. The oriental Christian churches had long acted as an intermediary between Byzantine and Islamic art. But here is an assimilation of cultural traditions, the culmination of the process of cultural transmission.

This takes place in private rather than exclusively monastic circles. An equilibrium is achieved in a meticulously written and illustrated New Testament produced in Cairo in 1249-50 (Paris, Institut Copte-Arabe 1/Cairo, Coptic Museum, Bibl. 94).[46] Gabriel the scribe – the future Coptic Patriarch Gabriel III – took pains in writing both the Coptic and the Arabic text columns, as he described in recording his method of collation in the colophon of a different manuscript. There he records that he has 'striven with the utmost exertion in Coptic and Arabic with all possible diligence'.[47] Since he wrote this latter manuscript a few years earlier in the house of his patron, Sheikh al-Amjad, one of the four scholar sons of al-'Assāl, he would have had access to his patron's library to produce the New Testament. It is no coincidence that the New Testament was commissioned by a private patron, the intellectual and deacon al-Rahib, the teacher of the al-'Assāl brothers.[48] One of these brothers himself produced a new version of the Arabic Gospels in the mid-thirteenth century.[49] Books such as these that were produced in the houses of private patrons point to the increasing importance of the private library and the interests of an intellectual élite. As in the medieval west at this time, the commissioning and production of manuscripts was becoming secularized, with scribes and artists producing secular as well as religious texts.

Private patrons continued to commission books for their own libraries in the fourteenth century that have a similarly luxurious quality and illumination and bear similarities to Qu'rān manuscripts. An example in the British Library is an Arabic manuscript of the four Gospels (Add. MS 11856) of 1337 written by a named scribe and decorated with frontispieces and brightly coloured Evangelist portraits.[50] The dual frontispieces preceding Matthew's Gospel (fols 1^v-2^r, Pl. 14) display a similar geometric 'trellis' design emanating from a central star with foliage as the frontispiece of volume VII (fols 1^v-2^r, Pl. 15) of the Qu'rān of Baybars al-Jāshnagīr, painted by the illuminator Ṣandal in 704-5 AH/1304-6 AD (BL, Add. MSS 22406-13).[51] The portrait of Mark (Pl. 13) has the saint seated under a cusped arch similar to that of Luke's portrait mentioned above, with birds replacing the griffons. This luxuriousness argues for the manuscript's production in Cairo, in an élite Christian milieu similar to that of the New Testament. Behind him is a gold interlocking arch, attached to the throne, with a cross to the left and a vessel to the right. Like his bishop's garb, this gives Mark prominence as the founder of the Church of Alexandria. He holds his gospel-book, which has a decorated binding, stamped with a central gilded interlace knot. Although Old Testament books were produced, the emphasis was on the New Testament, especially gospel-books.[52]

A fourteenth-century gospel-book with Syrian connections, now in the Topkapi Sarayi Müzesi Library (Ahmet III 3519), can, I would argue, be associated with Coptic patronage.[53] Made for the library of the late Faḫr al-Dīn Abu l'Alā,[54] the book opens with the intercessionary Deisis image opposite a title-page reminiscent of Qu'rān illumination (Pl. 16). The juxtaposition nicely links the aniconic 'carpet' page with prayer and contemplation. The role of calligraphy in enshrining the sacred is apparent in the title-page. Islamic calligraphers were highly respected: writing the Qu'rān was moral responsibility and regarded as the highest art form in Islamic art.[55] The carpet page is an example of comparability in which aniconic art is a stimulus to contemplation in the common monotheistic frameworks of both Christianity and Islam.

To close by going full circle back to the western interest in the east, the text of this last mentioned manuscript was annotated in Latin in the margin in a few places in the text, including the geneaology of Christ at the beginning of Matthew's Gospel (fol. 11ᵛ). These annotations were written in an Italian humanist hand, in the first half, possibly even the first quarter, of the fifteenth century.[56] This westerner must have studied the manuscript, stamped later as belonging to the imperial Ottoman library of Sultan Beyazit (1481-1512) in Istanbul.[57] Italian interest in the Greek world is fundamental at this time, but this attests to the study by westerners of Arab Christian manuscripts as well.[58]

CONCLUSION

Channels by which cultural contact was made between Christian communities and between Christians and Muslims in the Middle Ages, and the role of illustrated Biblical manuscripts in that process, have been explored here. The identifiable loci of inter-action include monasteries and trading networks, as well as individuals and libraries, including those of private patrons. The three case studies alluded to here demonstrate ways in which manuscripts linked medieval societies. Parallelism is suggested as the way to view the trans-cultural associations between Mediterranean and Insular manuscripts after the seventh century, replacing more direct contacts, including the import of Coptic manuscripts. Continuity is evident in the production of eastern Christian biblical manuscripts in Syria and Mesopotamia, drawn into the Mediterranean orbit during the Crusader period of the twelfth/thirteenth centuries, and exemplifying the secularization of biblical themes at the end of the period. Finally, assimilation is exemplified in the development of Arabic Christian Biblical manuscripts, with the emphasis on cultural transmission. All three case studies demonstrate ways in which Biblical manuscripts were central to the processes of cultural transmission between medieval societies.

NOTES

1 N. Åberg, *The Occident and the Orient in the Art of the Seventh Century* (3 parts; Stockholm: Wahlström & Widstrand, 1943-1947), III, 41-2 referred to the 'transference of style' in the merger of barbarian and Roman artistic traditions in the seventh century.

2 New York, Pierpont Morgan Library, William S. Glazier Collection, MS G. 67: Leo Depuydt, *Catalogue of Coptic Manuscripts in the Pierpont Morgan Library* (Corpus of Illuminated Manuscripts, 4: Leuven: Peeters, 1993), no. 278, pp. 480-3; *Age of Spirituality: Late Antique and Early Christian Art, Third to Seventh Century Catalogue of the exhibition at The Metropolitan Museum of Art*, ed. by K. Weitzmann (New York: The Metropolitan Museum

of Art with Princeton University Press, 1977), 494-5. The cover is studied by J. S. Kebabian, 'The Binding of the Glazier Manuscript of the Acts of the Apostles (IVth or Vth Century)', *Homage to a Bookman: Essays on Manuscripts, Books and Printing written for Hans P. Kraus on his 6oth Birthday*, ed. by H. Lehmann-Haupt (Berlin: Mann, 1967), 25-9.

3 H. Bober, 'On the Illumination of the Glazier Codex: a Contribution to Early Coptic Art and its relation to Hiberno-Saxon Interlace', in *Homage to a Bookman*, 31-49, esp. 42, 46.

4 Bober, 'Glazier Codex', 46-7 and 47-9 respectively, with figs 1, 16-18. See also for the latter *Evangeliorum Quattuor Codex Durmachensis* (2 vols; Olten, Lausanne, & Freiburg i. Br.: Urs Graf Verlag, 1960), I, fol. 85ᵛ in colour; II, 121-2. Prefatory pages with crosses and carpet pages, with interlace, are seen as the main elements derived from the eastern Mediterranean: J. J. G. Alexander, *Insular Manuscripts: 6th to 9th Century: a Survey of Manuscripts in the British Isles* (London: Harvey Miller, 1978), 30-2.

5 Bober, 'Glazier Codex', 42, 44. Elsewhere (45) he refers, somewhat over-emphatically, to the 'anti-classicism of the Coptic centers in Egypt'. This tallies with Åberg's view, from the western perspective, that art of the seventh century represented a synthesis of Germanic and classical, the one zoomorphic, the other ornamental interlace: Åberg, *Occident and Orient*, III, 36-9.

6 See the remarks by C. Nordenfalk, 'Corbie and Cassiodorus: a pattern page bearing on the early history of bookbinding', *Pantheon XXXII* (1974), 225-31, esp. 230-1 where he cites interlace as appearing 'all over the Mediterranean world' as well as the mosaics, textiles and wallpaintings of Egypt. C. Nordenfalk, *Celtic and Anglo-Saxon Painting: Book Illumination in the British Isles, 600-800* (London: Chatto & Windus, 1977), 14.

7 R. Powell, 'The Binding of the Stonyhurst Gospel' in *The Relics of St Cuthbert*, ed. by C. F. Battiscombe (Oxford: University Press, 1956), 362-74, notes (367) that 'the sewing is unfamiliar except in terms of Coptic, or at least Mediterranean, binding ... the thread alone joins the boards to the text and the sections to each other.' R. Ettinghausen, 'Foundation-moulded Leatherwork – a Rare Egyptian Technique also used in Britain', *Studies in Islamic Art and Architecture in Honour of Professor K. A. C. Cresswell*, with contributions by C. L. Geddes et al. (Cairo: The American University in Cairo, 1965), 70, with pl. 11.

8 This is a pouch rather than a book cover: T. C. Petersen, 'Early Islamic Bookbindings and their Coptic Relations', *Ars Orientalis* I (1954), 51, n. 10; R. Ettinghausen, 'Near Eastern Covers and their Influence on European Bindings', *Ars Orientalis* III (1959), 119 with pl. 4; Ettinghausen, 'Foundation-moulded Leatherwork', 68, with pl. 12. The other examples cited by Ettinghausen (63-71) date from the tenth century. Nordenfalk, 'Corbie', 229-30, with colour pl. p. 227, suggested the fourth-century folio added to Paris, B.N. MS Lat. 12190, to have been a pattern sheet from a model-book for bookbinders which he attributes to Cassiodorus' library at the monastery of Vivarium. Again, if true, this argument could be turned on its head in favour of that of the dissemination of the influence of east Mediterranean, including or even especially, Coptic books.

9 F. Henry, *The Book of Kells* (London: Thames & Hudson, 1977), 214; O. Chadwick, *John Cassian: a Study in Primitive Monasticism* (Cambridge: University Press, 2nd edn, 1968).

10 Ettinghausen, 'Foundation-moulded Leatherwork', 70 with n. 3 assessed the evidence for Coptic and Coptic-style bronze vessels buried in Anglo-Saxon graves until shortly after the mid-seventh century. For comment on trading links in relation to manuscripts see Henry, *Book of Kells*, 213-14.

11 Henry, *Book of Kells*, 13-14.

12 See, in general, the remarks of E. Rosenthal, 'Some Observations on Coptic Influence in Western Early Medieval Manuscripts', *Homage to a Bookman*, 74. Traditional knitting offers a similar phenomenon, with similar patterns evolved in different places and times.

13 Henry, *Book of Kells*, 214.

14 This is the view of C. Thomas, 'The Eastern Mediterranean and the Western Provinces: A British Perspective', in *Churches Built in Ancient Times' Recent Studies in Early Christian Archaeology*, ed. by K. Painter (Vol. 16 of Occasional Papers from The Society of Antiquaries/The Acordia Research Centre, University of London, 1994), especially 255-77. But, as he points out (277): 'The paradox is that the more we find out, the less apparent any such influence seems to be.'

15 Martin Werner suggested in 1969 that the animal-headed Evangelist symbols employed in the Book of Durrow and elsewhere in Insular manuscripts were dependent on Coptic models: M. Werner, 'The Four Evangelist Symbols Page in the Book of Durrow', *Gesta* VIII (1969), 3-17. However, in proposing their origin in depictions of Christ in Majesty surrounded by the four beasts, he cited much later examples, attracting justifiable criticism on grounds of method: ibid., esp. 8-13 for later examples, including tenth-century Coptic manuscript illumination and the thirteenth-century wallpainting at the monastery of St Anthony's at the Red Sea. For a critique of Werner's approach see L. Nees, 'A Fifth-Century Book Cover and the Origin of the Four Evangelist Symbols Page in the Book of Durrow', *Gesta* XVII/1 (1978), 3-8, who also questioned Werner's assumption of the anthropomorphic qualities of the animal symbols and proposed an Italian model instead. Nees (6, n. 2) summed up the Coptic origins problem thus: 'The general validity of this oft-repeated theory is not at issue here, but in my opinion it is necessary to underscore the general methodological point that in examining the parallels between Insular and certain Eastern Mediterranean works of art one must also be extremely scrupulous in noting the existence of the same forms and motifs where they occur in other and less remote areas as well.' Countering Nees, Werner, 'The Durrow Four Evangelist Symbols Page Once Again', *Gesta* XX/1 (1981), 23-41, reassessed the arguments.

16 The miniature reinforces the opening word 'nativitas' of the chapter list in Matthew which it precedes: Alexander, *Insular Manuscripts*, 71-6, esp. 74. Martin Werner, 'The Madonna and Child Miniature in the Book of Kells', Part I *Art Bulletin* LIV/1 (March 1972), 1-23 and II *Art Bulletin* LIV/2 (June, 1972), 129-39. For previous discussion of the connections between the Book of Kells Virgin and Child and eastern models see Rosenthal, 'Some Observations on Coptic Influence', 51, 55-62.

17 Henry, *Book of Kells*, 186-8, with pl. 10 in colour.

18 Werner, 'Madonna and Child', 8, pl. 10; J. Leroy, *Les Manuscrits Coptes et Coptes-Arabes Illustrés* ('Institut Français d'Archéologie de Beyrouth, Bibliothèque archéologique et historique', XCVI; Paris: Paul Geuthner, 1974), 94-5 with pl. 31; *Beyond the Pharoahs: Egypt and the Copts in the 2nd to 7th Centuries A.D.*, ed. by F. Friedman (Exhibition Catalogue, Museum of Art, Rhode Island School of Design, 1989), 221 no. 134.

19 Werner, 'Madonna and Child', I, esp. 4, 8, proposed Egypt as the place of origin of the Virgo Lactans on these grounds. For the Theodosian sculpture, as part of the Adoration of the Magi scene on a sculpted marble vessel in the Museu Nazionale in Rome, see H. G. Severin, 'Oströmische Plastik unter Valens und Theodosius I', *Jahrbuch der Berliner Museen* XII (1970), 216, 218, 238-9, with Abb. 5.

20 E. Kitzinger, 'The Coffin Reliquary', in *The Relics of St Cuthbert* (cited above, n. 7), 248-64 with pls IV and X suggested they were both copies of the same model, displaying elements of Hellenistic, Roman and early Byzantine, including secular, art. Henry, *Book of Kells*, 186-7, proposed an icon as the direct model.

21 Kitzinger, 'Coffin Reliquary', 263.

22 Florence, Laur. Plut. I, 56: C. Cecchelli, G. Furlani & M. Salmi, *The Rabbula Gospels: Facsimile Edition of the Miniatures of the Syriac Manuscript Plut. I. 56 in the Medicaean-Laurentian Library* (Olten & Lausanne: Urs Graf Verlag, 1959), with colour reproductions; J. Leroy, *Les manuscrits syriaques à peintures conservés dans les bibliothèques d'Europe et d'Orient* (Paris: Geuthner, 1964), 139-53, pls 20-34; K. Weitzmann, *Late Antique and Early*

Christian Book Illumination (London: Chatto & Windus, 1977), 18, 21-2, 29, pls 34-8. The exact location of Zagba is disputed: see Leroy, *Manuscrits syriaques*, 155-6.

23 Cecchelli et al., *Rabbula Gospels*, 48-9 with plate; Leroy, *Manuscrits syriaques*, 140 with pl. 20; Henry, *Book of Kells*, 186.

24 Cecchelli et al., *Rabbula Gospels*, 72; Leroy, *Manuscrits syriaques*, 153 with pl. 31,2; pl. 37.

25 From present-day Lebanon: Leroy, *Manuscrits syriaques*, 157; Weitzmann, *Late Antique and Early Christian Book Illumination*, 29.

26 Leroy, *Manuscrits syriaques*, 208-19, pls 43-8, admits (214) that without a colophon it cannot categorically be stated to have been made for the usage of the Orthodox (Jacobite) or the (Nestorian) Church of the East; Weitzmann, *Late Antique and Early Christian Book Illumination*, 22, 29, pls 39-40, figs XII-XIII; R. Sörries, *Die Syrische Bibel von Paris: Paris Bibliothèque Nationale, syr. 341: Eine frühchristliche Bilderhandschrift aus dem 6. Jahrhundert* (Wiesbaden: Reichert Verlag, 1991), passim, with colour reproductions.

27 Sörries, *Syrische Bibel*, 20.

28 The Virgin 'Platytera'. Leroy, *Manuscrits syriaques*, 210 with pl. 43 (1); Sörries, *Syrische Bibel*, 33-6 with Abb. 8.

29 Sörries, *Syrische Bibel*, 36-47, Abb. 9-22.

30 See G. Ostrogorsky, *History of the Byzantine State* (Oxford: Blackwell, 1968), Map 3, facing 204.

31 For the Buchanan Bible: W. Wright, *A Catalogue of the Syriac Manuscripts preserved in the Library of the University of Cambridge* II (Cambridge: University Press, 1901); *List of Old Testament Peshitta Manuscripts*, ed. by the Peshitta Institute, Leiden (Leiden: 1961), 4, no. 12a1; Leroy, *Manuscrits syriaques*, 241-53, 438, pls 61(3)-64; L.-A., Hunt, 'The Syriac Buchanan Bible in Cambridge: Book Illumination in Syria, Cilicia and Jerusalem of the later Twelfth Century', *Orientalia Christiana Periodica* LVII, fasc. 2 (1991), 331-69, with plates and map. The Rabbula Gospels was still in use as a second list of readings was added in the twelfth century: Leroy, *Manuscits syriaques*, 154, n. 2.

32 S. Brock, 'Syriac Manuscripts on the Black Mountain, near Antioch', *Lingua Restituta Orientalis. Festgabe für Julius Assfalg, Aegypten und Altes Testament* XX, ed. by R. Schulz & M. Görg (Wiesbaden: Harrassowitz, 1990), 59-67.

33 Hunt, 'Buchanan Bible', 361 with figs 8, 12.

34 L.-A. Hunt, 'Art and Colonialism: the Mosaics of the Church of the Nativity in Bethlehem (1169) and the Problem of "Crusader" Art', *Dumbarton Oaks Papers* XLV (1991), 69-85, esp. 74, with pl. 2; G. Kühnel, 'The Twelfth-Century Decoration of the Church of the Nativity: Eastern and Western Accord', in *Yoram Tsafrir* (ed.), *Ancient Churches Revealed* (Jerusalem: Israel Exploration Society, 1993), 197-203, esp. 203 with pl. XIId.

35 Hunt, 'Art and Colonialism', 75 with n. 44, incorporating the observations of S. Brock.

36 One Basil the Notary signed a Greek manuscript now at Sinai, MS 220, the following year, 1167, at the *kellion* at Bethlehem: A. W. Carr, *Byzantine Illumination 1150-1250: The Study of a Provincial Tradition* (Chicago & London: The University of Chicago Press), 20 with n. 8.

37 The Epinikios hymn for the anaphora and the Great Doxology: E. Kitzinger, *The Mosaics of St Mary's of the Admiral in Palermo* (Washington: Dumbarton Oaks, 1990), 131 with n. 35. The dome mosaics are reproduced, pls 3, 4-15. The trilingual Arabic, Greek and Latin Psalter in the British Library (Harley MS 5786), produced within Roger II's court circle in Palermo between 1130 and 1153, may have served a different purpose. It has been viewed rather in the context of multilingual Catholic rite services at the Cappella Palatina for palace converts from Islam: see J. J. Johns, 'The Greek Church and the Conversion of Muslims in Norman Sicily?', *Byzantinische Forschungen* 21 (1995), 139, 141-3.

38 S. Romaine, *Bilingualism* (Oxford UK and Cambridge USA: Blackwell), 31, includes praying

amongst the 'inner functions' of bilingualism, alongside counting, reckoning, cursing, dreaming, diary-writing, and note-taking, and speech to oneself or thinking aloud.

39 Leroy, *Manuscrits syriaques*, 302-413 with pls 70-8, 80-99; *The Glory of Byzantium: Art and Culture of the Middle Byzantine Era A.D. 843-1261*, ed. by H. C. Evans and W. D. Wixom (Exhibition Catalogue, Metropolitan Museum of Art, New York, 1997), 385 no. 254, with colour plate. It can be dated through its relationship to MS Vatican, Syr. 559: ibid., 280-302 with pls 70-99 and G. de Jerphanion, *Les miniatures du manuscrit syriaque no. 559 de la Bibl. Vat.* (Città del Vaticano, 1940). See the remarks of H. Buchthal, 'The Painting of the Syrian Jacobites in its Relation to Byzantine and Islamic Art', *Syria* XX (1939), 136-50, and R. Ettinghausen, *Arab Painting* (repr. London & Basingstoke: Skira, 1977), 96, and L.-A. Hunt, 'Christian-Muslim Relations in Egypt of the Twelfth to mid-Thirteenth Centuries: Sources of Wallpainting at Deir es-Suriani and the Illustration of the New Testament MS Paris, Copte-Arabe 1/Cairo, Bibl. 94', *Cahiers Archéologiques* XXXIII (1985), 111-55, esp. 130.

40 S. H. Griffith, 'The Gospel in Arabic: an enquiry into its appearance in the first Abbasid century', *Oriens Christianus* 69 (1985), 126-67, repr. in Griffith, *Arabic Christianity in the Monasteries of Ninth-Century Palestine* (Aldershot: Variorum, 1992), no. II.

41 Sinai New Finds, no. 14, with portraits of Mark, Luke and John preserved: I. E. Meïmarê, *Katalogos tôn neôn arabikôn cheirographôn tes hieras monês hagias aikaterinês tou orous sina* (Athens: Epitalophos A.B.E.E., 1985), 27, with pls 16, 17, where it is described as a gospel-book of the tenth or early eleventh century. This is corrected in Y. Meimaris, 'The Arabic Manuscripts', in *Sinai Treasures of the Monastery of Saint Catherine*, gen. ed. K. A. Manafis (Athens: Ekdotike Athenon S.A., 1990), 357-8 with pl. 12.

42 Meimaris, *Katalogos* 27 no. 16 with pl. 20.

43 Griffith, 'The Gospel in Arabic', 163.

44 Leroy, *Manuscrits Coptes et Coptes-Arabes* 110 with pl. 39 (1); Hunt, 'Christian-Muslim Relations', 111-55, esp. 115.

45 Leroy, *Manuscrits Coptes et Coptes-Arabes*, 152 with pl. A in colour; Hunt, 'Christian-Muslim Relations', esp. 115.

46 Leroy, *Manuscrits Coptes et Coptes-Arabes*, 174-7 with pls 10 (2), 20 (1-2), 93-5; Hunt, 'Christian-Muslim Relations', 125-41.

47 Cairo, Coptic Museum, Bibl. 93: G. Horner, *The Coptic Version of the New Testament in the Northern Dialect* (4 vols; Oxford: University Press, 1898-1905), I, xci-xcii; Thesis p. 26.

48 A. Y. Sidarus, 'Ibn ar-Râhibs Leben und Werke: ein koptisch-arabischer Encyclopädist des 7/13 Jahrhunderts', *Islamkundliche Untersuchen*, 36 (Freiburg: Klaus Schwarz, 1975), 8-10, 23 n. 82; W. Abullif, 'Vita e Opera del Pensatore Copto al-Safi Ibn al-'Assâl (sec. XIII)', *Studia Orientalia Christiana Collectanea* XX (1987), 134-5.

49 Abullif, 'Al-Safî Ibn Al-'Assâl', 135 with notes 23-4; S. K. Samir, 'La version arabe des évangiles d'Al-As'ad/bn Al-'Assâl', *Parole de l'Orient* XIX (1994) 441-551.

50 *Catalogus Codicum Manuscriptorum Orientalium qui in Museo Britannico asservantur. Pars Secunda: Codices Arabicos Amplectens* I (London, 1846), 11-13; H. Buchthal & O. Kurz, *A Hand List of Illuminated Oriental Christian Manuscripts* (repr. Nendeln: Kraus, 1968), 26 no. 82. The miniatures are hitherto unpublished.

51 D. James, *Qu'râns of the Mamlûks* (London: Alexandria Press/Thames & Hudson, 1988), 34-72, 220, esp. 47-8 with pl. 25.

52 Berlin, Staatsbibliothek ar. 10173/Diez A. Fol. 41 is a Prophet Book produced in Cairo in 1325, with illustrations of standing prophets: K. Weitzmann, 'An Early Copto-Arabic Miniature in Leningrad', *Ars Islamica* IX (1942), 132-3; J. Lowden, *Illuminated Prophet Books: a Study of Byzantine Manuscripts of the Major and Minor Prophets* (University Park & London: Pennsylvania University Press, 1988), 74, 89; Hunt, 'Syriac Buchanan Bible', 352.

53 J. Leroy, 'Un Évangélaire arabe de la Bibliothèque de Topkapi Sarayi à décor Byzantin et Islamique', *Syria* XLIV (1967), 119-30, with pls IX-XII; R. S. Nelson, 'An Icon at Mt Sinai and Christian Painting in Muslim Egypt during the Thirteenth and Fourteenth Centuries', *Art Bulletin* LXV/2 (June 1983), 214-18, with pls 25-6, 29-30. I am grateful to Drs. Filiz Çağman and Banu Mahir for facilitating my recent study of this manuscript, made possible by a British Academy Research grant in the Humanities and to be included in my study in progress of painting in Egypt between the twelfth and fourteenth centuries.

54 Leroy, 'Évangélaire', 123.

55 Y. Safadi, *Islamic Calligraphy* (London: Thames & Hudson, 1978), 31.

56 Identification kindly made by Professor Albinia de la Mare from my photograph (personal communication), pointing out some resemblance with the hand of the Florentine humanist and lawyer Guglielmino Tanaglia, although doubting that the latter knew Arabic.

57 Leroy, 'Évangélaire arabe', 121. The manuscript may have come into the possession of the imperial Ottoman library under Mehmet I, the Conqueror: see Yildiz Demiriz, 'Topkapi Sarayi III. Ahmed Kütüphanesinde bir Arapça Incil', *Sanat Tarihi Yilliği* (1966-8), 94. I am grateful to Dr. Rhoads Murphey for assistance in translating this article.

58 See J. Raby, 'Mehmed the Conqueror's Greek Scriptorium', *Dumbarton Oaks Papers* XXVII (1983) 15-34, esp. 26-7, who points to the continuing use of Greek in diplomatic relations with Italy after the Ottoman Conquest.

BOOKS OF HOURS
'IMAGING' THE WORD

Christopher de Hamel

I OUGHT AT THE OUTSET TO ADMIT that I did not myself choose the topic for the present paper and that it was originally presented to me on the conference programme already titled as 'Books of Hours: Imaging the Word'. On the face of it, the subject of Books of Hours seems an odd choice for a conference on the Bible, for these were books of private devotion to the Virgin Mary and a host of medieval saints, and in religious terms they are about as far removed as is possible from the study of the apostolic scriptures. Nevertheless, Books of Hours are the most common surviving medieval manuscripts containing biblical text: tens of thousands of them must exist. The British Library and the Fitzwilliam Museum have over 300 copies each. I see Books of Hours now nearly every day of my working life. In the last twenty years I have had to describe or list hundreds and hundreds of Books of Hours. The two Sotheby's medieval manuscript sales of 1995, for example, included no fewer than 37 manuscript Books of Hours, and fragments of a good many more. In the late Middle Ages such books would have been very common indeed. There was probably a Book of Hours in almost every substantial fifteenth-century household, especially in France, the Netherlands (north and south), and England. For many medieval families it was the only book they ever owned, and for countless of our ancestors it was probably the only book they had ever even seen.[1]

A Book of Hours was a book for a lay person, not a priest or a monk. It was not a liturgical book, in the sense that it was not for use in church or as part of a public service, but was a text for private contemplation.[2] When one comes to look, however, it is in fact almost entirely biblical. After the Calendar (which is a detachable and infinitely variable preliminary found in many classes of medieval book), a Book of Hours actually begins 'In principio erat verbum ...', 'In the beginning was the Word', the Word of God being the actual theme of the four Gospel Sequences which generally open a Book of Hours. They are biblical readings comprising John 1. 1-14, Luke 1. 26-38, Matthew 2. 1-12 and Mark 16. 14-20, in that order, with John the Baptist crying in the wilderness, and then Gabriel announcing the Incarnation to the Virgin, the coming of the Magi in fulfilment of the prophesies, and, finally, at the end of Christ's life on earth, his command to the apostles to preach the Word throughout all nations. These are, in fact, the lections from the Mass of the four great feasts (Christmas, Epiphany, Ladyday, and the Ascension) and they form a kind of condensed précis of the Gospels on the coming and the propagation of the Word of God. That is how a Book of Hours opens.

The Office of the Virgin follows. It comprises texts to be recited daily at each of the eight canonical 'hours' of the day, that is, Matins, Lauds, Prime, Terce, Sext, None,

Vespers, and Compline. This is the principal component and absolute central text of a Book of Hours, and for a manuscript to be defined as a Book of Hours at all it must include this Office or Hours of the Virgin. The hour of Matins in a Book of Hours begins, as still used in Morning Prayer in the Church of England, 'O Lord open thou my lips, And my mouth shall show forth thy praise' (Ps. 50. 17). The Hours comprise 35 complete psalms (two of them repeated), four biblical canticles (plus the *Te Deum*), together with short responses and lections which vary from one Use to another but which are extracted almost entirely from Ecclesiasticus and the Song of Songs.[3] The choice of psalms recited at each hour is largely fixed by a tradition which goes back at least to the beginning of monasticism, and they include some echo of the time of day that each hour was used. Matins was to be read in private in the dark before dawn. Ps. 8 refers to the shining of the moon and the stars, but, by Ps. 96 in the third nocturn of Matins, light rises to the just in verse 11. By Lauds it is nearly dawn: Ps. 62 opens 'O God, my God, to thee do I watch at break of day', and later 'If I have remembered thee upon my bed, I will mediate on thee in the morning' (Ps. 62. 7). By Terce at mid-morning Ps. 120 predicts 'the sun shall not burn thee by day' (Ps. 120. 6). By Vespers Ps. 112 refers to the rising of the sun and the going down of the same (Ps. 112. 3). Compline is the last office at day: 'even until night, let Israel hope in the Lord', says Ps. 129. 6. The thirty-five psalms of the Office of the Virgin are thus divided among the eight hours of the medieval day.

The two other principal components of Books of Hours are the Penitential Psalms and the Office of the Dead. The seven Penitential Psalms are said to have been recited by King David for each of the Seven Deadly Sins which he had committed in the course of his life of sin and repentance. They are Ps. 6, 31, 37, 50, 101, 129, and 142, only one of which overlaps with a psalm used in the Hours of the Virgin. The Office of the Dead has another twenty-one psalms (and one repeat), nine of them duplicating psalms already appearing earlier in the Book of Hours, with three biblical canticles and nine variable readings from the book of Job, ch. 7 to 19.[4] These are themselves interspersed with short antiphons and responses which are almost entirely made up from biblical sentences.

These sections occur in almost every Book of Hours and are the core texts. Around them are an infinitely variable choice of other separate and usually even detachable components, such as the short Hours of the Cross and of the Holy Ghost, prayers to the Virgin and to saints (often very lengthy), and sections which are completely biblical, such as the Passion Sequence, the fifteen Psalms of Degree, the ten Psalms of the Passion, the Psalter of St Jerome, the Verses of St Bernard, and the Commendation of Souls, all entirely from the Scriptures. We will return to some of these in a moment. In the three essential texts alone – the Hours of the Virgin, the Penitential Psalms with Litany, and the Office of the Dead – there are fifty-three different psalms (eleven of them more than once), five biblical canticles (two of them more than once), and nineteen biblical readings (from Song of Songs, Ecclesiasticus, and Job). Even adding in dox-ologies, hymns, prayers, and so forth, and if I have done my sums right, line by line, just over 77 per cent of these three central texts of a regular Book of Hours are taken word-for-word from the Bible.

This has two very important implications for the theme of a symposium on the medieval Bible. The first is that the text was known by heart by nearly every person of any education whatsoever in late medieval Europe. It was the text from which children first learned to read (a 'Primer' is the Middle English for a Book of Hours) and then recited every subsequent day of their lives. It is easy to say that relatively few Bible manuscripts were made in the fifteenth century, but here is a good body of scriptural text brought into almost every medieval household and into extreme daily familiarity. I have not investigated the question, but I am willing to lay bets that when, for example, a late medieval secular writer quotes the psalms (and they do), they will be quoting not from a complete Bible or Psalter but from a Book of Hours.

The second very striking observation about this considerable wealth of biblical text in the three main components of a Book of Hours is that almost all of it is from the Old Testament. The Psalms, the Canticles, the lections from Ecclesiasticus, the Song of Songs, and Job are all from Old Testament books. This is actually very odd if you think of a Book of Hours as an entirely medieval Christian devotional text. It is even more odd when you look through its pictures which are famous for showing scenes from the Gospels: the annunciation, the birth in the stable in Bethlehem, the shepherds in the field, the flight into Egypt, and so forth. I think that when I was asked to speak on 'Imaging the Word', what the conference organizers had in mind is that I would speak on the pictures in Books of Hours and how these present in visual form the biblical text they illustrate. But here is another odd observation. The miniatures is a Book of Hours do not illustrate the text at all. This is probably the single most important point of this paper. The Office of the Virgin does not describe the Annunciation, or even mention the Visitation, or Bethlehem, or the shepherds or the kings, or Herod and the flight into Egypt, or the coronation of the Virgin. Miniatures of all these subjects are almost universal in Books of Hours, and they do not, on the face of it, illustrate the text.

The opening miniature for Matins in a Book of Hours generally shows the moment of the Annunciation when the Virgin looked up from her own devotions to see the archangel Gabriel entering or descending to greet her as full of grace and blessed among women and to say that she has found favour with the Lord and will conceive and bring forth a son whose name shall be Jesus. The scene takes place in settings with which the medieval owner of a Book of Hours could identify from daily life – often in an open-air loggia in Italian manuscripts, in a private chapel with stained glass windows in French Books of Hours, or set in a corner of the Virgin's homely bedroom in Netherlandish manuscripts. The image of Mary herself mirrors that of donor or owner portraits in Books of Hours, kneeling at devotions before an open manuscript on a prayer-desk. An owner of a medieval Book of Hours knelt exactly like this to look at the miniature of the Virgin doing the same. Just as meditation on the Passion is facilitated by imagining the wounds of the crucifixion in one's own hands and feet, so the adoration of the Virgin required one to identify oneself with the Virgin at that moment. Mary was said to have been reading her devotions from the Old Testament at the instant Gabriel surprised her. So medieval readers of a Book of Hours might have before them the very same Old Testament text. This is, I am sure, a conscious device to help the reader of a Book of Hours to identify more closely with the Virgin who, quite unexpectedly and in the midst of daily devotion, found favour with God.

Not all users of Books of Hours were young girls, like the Virgin Mary. An older woman could perhaps empathize more easily with St Elizabeth shown outside her manor house at Lauds, suddenly filled with the Holy Ghost. A prince or noble owner would certainly see himself parallelled in the scene of the adoration of the Magi, who in royal manuscripts are sometimes actually given identifiable characteristics, like the personal badge of Louis d'Orléans worn by the youngest of the Magi in the Boucicaut Hours.⁵ Farmers might identify with the shepherds in the fields at Terce, clerics with the high priest Simeon at None who finally recognizes the saviour of the world, and older men perhaps with Joseph at Vespers who casts off his buffoon image of medieval theatre and becomes the wise traveller and guardian of Christ on the flight into Egypt. All these types of people and levels of society used Books of Hours in the Middle Ages, and all had parallels in the figures who played active roles in the infancy of Christ and the life of the Virgin. All the New Testament prototypes for these roles could have prayed from the very same psalms and lections as in a Book of Hours – 'seven times a day I have given praise to thee' (Ps. 118. 164) still a prime injunction in Judaism – and in the hope of recapturing the moment of supreme spiritual enlightenment a medieval owner of a Book of Hours used what were hoped to be the same Old Testament devotions.

The Hours of the Virgin, as its name implies, honours events in the life of the Virgin Mary. These are shown in the illustrations. The pictures show biblical scenes which are believed to have taken place at the very same hour of day as the medieval user of the manuscript would recite the devotions. The Annunciation took place before dawn. Thus in Books of Hours the Virgin is often beside her bed, having just risen; in Dutch manuscripts there is sometimes a clock on the wall, which may be a double or even treble pun on the Virgin's Hours and the Clock of Wisdom. The Visitation took place at dawn. In Lauds we often see the scene at first light in a landscape fresh with dew. The birth of Christ occurred in the early morning on Christmas Day and it therefore figures at Prime. The annunciation to the Shepherds may historically have taken place at night, but in a Book of Hours it is set at Terce in the full sun of mid-morning, sometimes with the shepherds breaking for an early lunch. The Magi arrived in Bethlehem around mid-day on 6th January, when the sun and the star from the East were simultaneously overhead. The kings' arrival is illustrated at Sext, in miniatures flooded with midday light and colour. The Christ Child was brought to Simeon in the afternoon, around the hour of None. The flight into Egypt occurred at dusk, and after a long day the Holy Family is sometimes shown resting at Vespers beneath a tree which bends down miraculously to offer them fruit. Sometimes, especially in Parisian manuscripts, the background is formed of an amazing sunset. Compline at night is often illustrated by the coronation of the Virgin in the heavens, the culmination of a life of devotion and her establishment as Queen of Heaven to watch over the world throughout the night.

These eight miniatures in the Hours of the Virgin, therefore, do not image the Word, if I understand that verb 'to image'; they do not illustrate the text as such, but they do form a focus for devotional meditation on the Virgin's life, they offer a historical context for the use of the psalms and Old Testament readings, and they act as a kind of indexing system for finding one's place in a Book of Hours, a text with few headings and no numbered chapters or pages. The constant repetition of the same pictures from one manuscript to another makes it very easy indeed to locate a particular office in a Book of Hours, just by flipping through the pages. There is slightly more variation in the illustrations for the Penitential Psalms and for the Office of the Dead.

The Penitential Psalms in some of the earliest Books of Hours (and in Flemish copies through to the mid-fifteenth century) are illustrated with a miniature of God in majesty or judgement. Most others from around 1400 show the author of the psalms, King David, kneeling in prayer, with his harp, like a Beatus initial from a gothic Psalter. This image gradually becomes more complicated as the fifteenth century unfolds, with David moving to a setting outside his palace in Jerusalem, sometimes reprimanded by Nathan. By about 1460 the depiction incorporates other scenes from his life (like his battle with Goliath) and by around 1480 David's sins are illustrated – his sending of Uriah into battle to be killed and especially (and in increasingly lascivious detail) Bathsheba idling naked in the fountain as David watches – or even blatantly leers – from a window of his renaissance palace. Thus the pictorial evolution over 150 years is from the Last Judgement to the personification of personal sin, an interesting enough comment on the Penitential Psalms on the eve of the Reformation.

Likewise the illustrations for the Office of the Dead evolve considerably.[6] Until about 1420 we see a funeral Mass taking place in a church, which transforms into a burial scene in a medieval churchyard with hooded mourners in black. Around 1470 the theme for the Office of the Dead changes quite quickly to the imminence of death itself, with pictures of Death as a skeleton with a scythe, or the three Living and the three Dead, or Death on a tombstone. There is a unique miniature in the Hours of Mary of Burgundy showing the duchess herself on horseback galloping through the countryside and suddenly three figures of Death spring up behind and knock her unexpectedly from her horse.[7] The manuscript dates from the late 1470s, and certainly belonged to Mary of Burgundy, and the extraordinarily haunting fact is that Mary herself, in her late 20s, died suddenly in 1482 by falling from her horse. By about 1500 the image for the Office of the Dead has changed again, and (for the first time) becomes illustrative. It shows a choice of scenes from the life of Job, feasting with his family, on the dung-heap outside the ruins of his castle, or taunted by his friends. This illustrates the readings for the Office of the Dead, which are taken from the narrative of the Book of Job, and these in the early sixteenth century are the first true biblical illustrations of text which we have encountered in the present paper.

I began by recounting how a Book of Hours often opens with the Gospel sequences. In early Books of Hours these are often unillustrated. If they have miniatures at all – and this happens especially after about 1450 – the Gospel Sequences do not show the narratives described but have instead author portraits of the Evangelists in the very act of writing (curiously like the early Irish and Carolingian Gospel Books) emphasizing the fact that this is the Word of God put into written form. St John is often shown on the island of Patmos writing on a scroll as a little devil creeps up behind him with a grappling hook to try to steal the evangelist's ink-pot and pen-case, with the vain hope of preventing the Gospel's being written. It is not the story told by St John which is foremost in the artist's mind but that fact that his Gospel is a sacred text.

By the late fifteenth century it is clear that the Book of Hours, at least in France, has become a holy text in everything but name and was the most sacred object in the house. Bindings of Books of Hours were increasingly elaborate, as we learn both from extant manuscripts and from inventory descriptions, 'clasped with silver and gilte', for example.[8] Ownership inscriptions begin to include complicated curses against theft or promises of reward (often wine, not money) to anyone who should return the book if lost. Pilgrim badges were kept safe in Books of Hours. All manuscript Books of Hours were on vellum, and practically every Book of Hours was illuminated. Books of Hours became heirlooms, like the Victorian family Bibles, and were used for recording family dates of deaths and christenings, not often earlier than about 1450 and very often after 1500. From these inscriptions we can glimpse Books of Hours being given as sixteenth-century wedding presents and being prepared or refurbished for great occasions.

I have said a good deal about the central texts of Book of Hours being mostly made up from long or short quotations from the Bible. This was not primarily how fifteenth-century people learnt the Bible stories, which must have come through the *Speculum Humanae Salvationis* and the *Biblia Pauperum* and the many versions of the *Bible Historiale*, quite apart from sermons. Yet the Book of Hours had an efficacious value because it used the very words of the Scriptures. It included all the little pieces of the Bible needed for salvation. We find the assertion on the title-pages of early printed Books of Hours that the text is '*tout au long sans riens requerir*', in full, with everything you could need. Two of the optional texts of a Book of Hours give a good idea of this, and these are my two final examples. One is the so-called Psalter of St Jerome, especially common in England and the southern Netherlands. The rubrics explain that people who are ill or too busy or on a journey may not have time to recite the entire psalter for salvation and so an angel dictated to St Jerome a list of 190 verses from the Psalms which contain all that is absolutely crucial, a sort of Reader's Digest psalter.[9] But if you are really pressed for time, turn to the Verses of St Bernard. The rubrics in Books of Hours often explain.[10] One day the Devil appeared to St Bernard and boasted that he knew of eight magical verses of the Psalms, so holy that whoever used even these eight daily would know in advance the day and hour of his or her death and would be certain of salvation. 'What are they?' cried Bernard, understandably. 'Shan't tell you,' said the Devil (all this we find recounted in the manuscripts). 'In that case,' St Bernard replied, 'I shall have to recite the entire Psalms every day in order to be sure of chancing upon the magic verses' and the Devil, so horrified at this excessive devotion, quickly revealed these eight efficacious verses from the Bible.

Even the most passionate advocate of Books of Hours must admit that there is a good deal of preposterous mumbo-jumbo in the supplementary texts grafted on the core Hours of the Virgin, Penitential Psalms, and Office of the Dead. But the essential components of a Book of Hours are biblical, word for word, even if very carefully selected and edited. This was the first time in the history of Christianity that books truly reached a mass audience. Bibles were rare in the fifteenth century but Books of Hours were exceedingly common, and they carried with them parts of the Bible to the widest audience it had ever received.

NOTES

1 There is no definitive edition of the Book of Hours or full study of the text. The essential textbooks are the large catalogue by V. Leroquais, *Les Livres d'Heures Manuscrits de la Bibliothèque Nationale*, 3 vols. (Paris, 1927, with supplement, 1943), and the catalogue of an exhibition at the Walters Art Gallery, R. S. Wieck, *Time Sanctified: the Book of Hours in Medieval Art and Life* (Baltimore & London, 1988). There are wise observations by L. M. J. Delaissé, 'The Importance of Books of Hours for the History of the Medieval Book' in *Gatherings in Honor of Dorothy Miner*, ed. by U. E. McCracken, L. M. C. Randall, & R. H.

Randall, Jr. (Baltimore, 1974), pp. 203-25. Other accounts include J. Harthan, *Books of Hours and their Owners* (London, 1977), and J. Backhouse, *Books of Hours* (London: The British Library, 1985).

2 Perhaps it is this private aspect of Books of Hours which has historically attracted Protestant interest. The collection on which I wrote my first naive book in Dunedin was assembled by a practising Baptist and biblical fundamentalist, A. H. Reed (1875-1975), who collected Bibles as the Word of God and Books of Hours as representing the trusting piety of the medieval laity; he actively admired and modelled himself on those free-church Baptist and Quaker bibliophiles like Andrew Gifford (1700-84), Francis Fry (1803-86) and Alexander Peckover (1830-1919), who all owned Books of Hours.

3 In the Use of Rome the Hours of the Virgin include: Matins, Ps. 94, 8, 18, 23, 44, 45, 86, 95, 96, and 97, with the *Te Deum* and lections from Eccl. 24. 11-13, 15-16 and 17-20; Lauds, Ps. 92, 99, 62, 66, 148, 149, and 150, with the canticles *Benedicite* (Dan. 3. 57-88) and *Benedictus Dominus* (Lk. 1. 68-79) and capitulum from Song of Songs 6. 8; Prime, Ps. 53, 84, and 116, with capitulum from Song of Songs 6. 9; Terce, Ps. 119, 120, and 121, with capitulum from Eccl. 24. 15; Sext, Ps. 122, 123, and 124, with capitulum from Eccl. 24. 16; None, Ps. 125, 126, and 127, with capitulum from Eccl. 24. 19-20; Vespers, Ps. 109, 112, 121, 126, and 147, with the *Magnificat* (Lk. 1. 46-55) and capitulum from Eccl. 24. 14; and Compline, Ps. 128, 129, and 130, with the *Nunc Dimittis* (Lk. 2. 29-32) and capitulum from Eccl. 24. 24.

4 In the Use of Rome the Office of the Dead includes: Vespers, Ps. 114, 119, 120, 129, 137, and 145, and the *Magnificat* (Lk. 1. 46-55); Matins, Ps. 5, 6, 7, 22, 24, 26, 29, 39, and 41, with nine lections (1), Job 7. 16-21, (2), Job 10. 1-7, (3), Job 10. 8-12, (4) Job 13. 22-28, (5) Job 14. 1-6, (6) Job 14. 13-16, (7) Job 17. 1-3 and 11-15, (8) Job 19. 20-27, and (9), Job 10. 18-22; Lauds, Ps. 50, 64, 62, 148, 149, 150, and 129, and the canticles *Ego Dixi* (Is. 38. 10-20) and *Benedictus Dominus* (Lk. 1. 68-79).

5 M. Meiss, *French Painting in the Time of Jean de Berry, The Boucicaut Master* (London, 1968), pp. 10-11.

6 The iconography of the Office of the Dead has received separate treatment in G. Bartz & E. König, 'Die Illustration des Totenoffiziums in Stundenbüchern' in *Liturgie als Sterbe- und Trauerhilfe, Ein interdisziplinäres Kompendium*, ed. by H. Becker, B. Einig, & P. O. Ullrich, 1987 (*Pietas Liturgica*, III-IV), I, pp. 487-528.

7 Berlin, Kupferstichkabinett MS. 78.B.12, fol. 220ᵛ.

8 C. Wordsworth & H. Littlehales, *The Old Service-Books of the English Church* (London, 1904), p. 250, citing a will of 1498.

9 Leroquais, *Livres d'Heures*, pp. xxviii-xxix.

10 ibid, pp. xxx-xxxi.

'ASK WHAT I AM CALLED'
THE ANGLO-SAXONS AND THEIR BIBLES

Richard Marsden

THE ANGLO-SAXONS LOVED RIDDLES and the riddling way of thought. It was a means of exploring and celebrating their world and the particularity of the things of that world, a way of understanding those things by, paradoxically, mystifying them.[1] Bibles were not exempt from the riddler's scrutiny and I start with an example, one of the longer Old English riddle-poems:[2]

Mec feonda sum   feore besnyþede,
woruldstrenga binom,   wætte siþþan,
dyfde on wætre,   dyde eft þonan,
sette on sunnan,   þær ic swiþe beleas
herum þam þe ic hæfde.   Heard mec siþþan
snað seaxses ecg,   sindrum begrunden.
Fingras feoldan   ond mec fugles wyn
geond speddropum   spyrede geneahhe,
ofer brunne brerd   beamtelge swealg,
streames dæle,   stop eft on mec,
siþade sweartlast.   Mec siþþan wrah
hæleð hleobordum,   hyde beþenede,
gierede mec mid golde.   Forþon me gliwedon
wrætlic weorc smiþa,   wire bifongen.
Nu þa gereno   ond se reada telg
ond þa wuldorgesteald   wide mære
dryhtfolca helm,   nales dol wite.
Gif min bearn wera   brucan willað,
hy beoð þy gesundran   ond þy sigefæstran,
heortum þy hwætran   ond þy hyge bliþran,
ferþe þy frodran,   habbaþ freonda þy ma,
swæsra ond gesibbra,   soþra ond godra,
tilra ond getreowra,   þa hyra tyr ond ead
estum ycað   ond hy arstafum
lissum bilecgað   ond hi lufan fæþmum
fæste clyppað.   Frige hwæt ic hatte,
niþum to nytte.   Nama min is mære,
hæleþum gifre   ond halig sylf.[3]

In the following prose translation, I have made no attempt to reproduce the effect of the Old English alliterating half-lines, which are an essential part of the poet's art:

An enemy robbed me of life, took away my mortal strength, wet me, dipped me in water, took me out again, and put me in the sun, where I quickly lost the hairs I had. A hard knife-blade then cut me, once smoothed of blemishes. Fingers folded me, and the bird's delight repeatedly make tracks across me with lucky droppings; it swallowed tree-dye, a portion of fluid, and advanced across me again, travelled its black trail. Then a man covered me with defensive boards, stretched hide over me, adorned me with gold, and further embellished me with the fine work of smiths, enveloped with wire. Now let the decoration and red dye and wondrous settings proclaim far and wide protection for people, and let the foolish man not find fault. If the sons of men will make use of me, they shall be the sounder, the more sure of victory, bolder in mind, blither in spirit, wiser in heart, and shall have more friends, dear ones and close, true and noble, good and faithful, who will surround them with grace and clasp them in the firm embraces of love. Ask what I am called, useful to men: my name is famous, bringing grace to men, and itself holy.

Some Old English riddle-poems still puzzle scholars, but this is not one of them. Our ready recognition of the identify of the 'thing' of the riddle – a Bible, or perhaps more specifically a gospel-book – is essential to its effect on us, and the process of exploration of it is the whole point of the exercise.[4] That process involves the accumulation of both stark detail (beginning with the brutal transformation of animal skin into parchment page) and allusion (to baptism, to the church militant, to salvation), and enacts persuasively, through an affective association of the material and the spiritual, a demonstration of the authority and ineffable power of Scripture. The first image brings to mind another Old English prosopopoeic poem, known as *The Dream of the Rood*, in which the sentient object is not an animal but the tree which was cruelly wrenched from its woodland home to become the cross of Christ and thus, ultimately, the instrument of salvation for mankind. In our Bible riddle, the sombre opening is soon forgotten in a series of exhilarating images, including the instrument used for writing on the parchment as 'the bird's delight': how dull a mere 'quill pen' would have sounded. The poem is suffused with an almost provocative spiritual assurance, which encourages the riddler to use the bold metaphor of 'lucky droppings' (*speddropum*) for the written words of Scripture. The element *sped* in fact encompasses a wide range of meaning, including 'prosperity' and 'wealth' as well as 'luck' or 'success', and a *dropa* may be simply a 'drop' of liquid in the modern sense, but 'lucky droppings' (the inspired translation of S. A. J. Bradley) seems to me entirely appropriate in the context of delight in the physicality of natural experience.[5] The production of written pages is only the beginning, however. Next come the contributions of the binder and the craftsmen in fine metals, who between them adorn and embellish the volume and render it materially precious, and then that of the artists who 'rubricate' and decorate its pages. The long peroration of the riddle (lines 15-28) is a claim for the power of the Gospel among men, predicated on the simple premise, 'If men are willing to use me ...', with the verb *brucan* offering a sense of 'enjoy' as well as 'use'. Understatement invests the closing lines with special power: 'Ask (or discover) what I am called, of advantage to men ...'. The synonym for these men in the last line, *haleþ*, hints at the idea of the Christian warrior and is used also in *The Dream of the Rood* for the heroic Christ who willingly climbs Calvary. The detailed knowledge shown by the riddler of the elaborate ritual involved in the production of books, from the preparation of parchment through the supplying of ink to the making and embellishing of exquisite bindings, is not of course surprising in a period when literacy and Christianity were still synonymous and the monastic scriptorium was the hub of manuscript transmission. Yet it still seems to me of great significance that the riddle should have been composed at all: you write and tell such riddles only about things with which you are intimately familiar and which are unavoidably present in your life. The Bible riddle proselytizes, of course (and very effectively), but it celebrates, too, the dramatic presence and active life of a particular 'thing': it is a compunction-inducing drama, in which an animal skin enacts its own story of violence, death, and triumphant rebirth.

In the survey of Anglo-Saxon Bibles which follows, I shall draw attention where I can not only to the physical evidence which survives but also to what we may deduce about the Anglo-Saxon people's own perception of the 'Bible as book'. The manuscripts are almost exclusively of the Latin Vulgate, the staple scriptural fare of England throughout the Anglo-Saxon age and beyond, but in a final section I shall allude briefly also to the first attempts to put Scripture into English.

I. THE EARLY PERIOD: c. 600-900

The Bible riddle alerts us to what is a distinctive feature of Bible production and use in the earlier period of Anglo-Saxon England, as far as the ninth century, when Insular Christianity was still comparatively young: the Bible or part-Bible as dramatic hero. One of the earliest references to a biblical manuscript in England comes in a Latin life of Wilfrid, Bishop of Hexham (c. 633-709). Wilfrid was a powerful, proud, and energetic ecclesiastic who had been a prime instigator in ensuring that the practices and ethos of the Roman church, rather than the Celtic, should prevail in Anglo-Saxon England.[6] That matter had been settled at the synod of Whitby in 664, at which such practical problems as the method of dating Easter had been resolved in Rome's favour and after which the simpler ascetic Christianity of the Irish tradition lost its influence on mainstream English, or at least Northumbrian, devotional life. Wilfrid built a great stone church at Ripon, on a site formerly occupied by Irish monks, and his hagiographer, Stephen, tells of a book which the bishop caused to be made for the new foundation. It was, says Stephen, 'a marvel unheard of before our times. He ordered the four Gospels to be written in purest gold on purpled parchment, and illustrated.'[7] The stir made by the arrival and ceremonial presentation of this magnificent book is confirmed by the fact that it was mentioned in the epitaph on Wilfrid's tomb, which was carefully recorded by Bede in his *Ecclesiastical History of the English People*: 'Here also [sc. in the church of St Peter at Ripon] he set on high the trophy of the cross, wrought in gleaming ore, and likewise commanded the four books of the Gospels to be written in gold in due order, and made for them a worthy casing of red gold.'[8]

Was Wilfred's treasure, presented at Ripon about 678, an English-made gospel-book? We are not told, and the volume itself does not survive. Although (as we shall see) books were indeed being made in Northumbria itself by the mid-seventh century, it is likely that Wilfrid commissioned his on the Continent, which he visited frequently, and more specifically Italy, where there is evidence of early gospel-books with purpled pages.[9] The first Bibles of the Anglo-Saxons were inevitably imports. Christianity had been fairly well established in Britain during the latter part of the Roman occupation (with biblical manuscripts in use, without a doubt, though none survives), but the Germanic tribes who were the ancestors of the Anglo-Saxons and who settled from the mid-fifth century onwards – pushing the native Britons (the Celts) to the fringes – were pagans. The Christian religion had subsequently to be reintroduced in the area which would become England. It came famously in two ways: first, direct from Rome with the mission of St Augustine to Kent in 597, which led to the founding of the archepiscopal see at Canterbury and whose effect reached as far as Northumbria, though only temporarily; and secondly from Ireland, via Iona, with the setting up of a monastery on Lindisfarne by Aidan in 635 and his re-conversion of the Northumbrians, this time for good.[10] Both the Celtic and the Roman missions must have been equipped with gospel-books, psalters and perhaps lectionaries of Old Testament and other readings. An attractive little uncial gospel-book now in the Parker Library in Cambridge (Corpus Christi College, MS 286) is traditionally supposed to have arrived with St Augustine in Kent in 597, although there is no proof.[11] Measuring only 245×180 mm, it had been copied in Italy in the sixth century and originally carried a number of illustrations, but only the evangelist page for Luke survives; it shows Luke in the tympanum and scenes from the life of Christ surrounding it.[12] In addition to such books as arrived in England with Augustine, we know from Bede that when Pope Gregory subsequently sent Augustine more 'colleagues and ministers of the word' from Rome, they brought with them a variety of further devotional requisites 'and very many manuscripts', though we are not told what they were.[13]

On the other hand, the fledgeling church and monasteries in Northumbria, with their strongly Celtic Christianity, seem to have been supplied initially with Irish biblical manuscripts which transmitted their own characteristic textual traditions.[14] Our earliest surviving remains of a Bible made in England, dating from the middle of the seventh century, have a text which was copied from an exemplar predominantly Irish in origin, and by an Irish scribe or one trained in the Irish tradition. These are a dozen leaves from a gospel-book, preserved piecemeal in three codices in Durham Cathedral Library (A. II. 10 + C. III. 13 and 20).[15] The text is characterized above all by readings in an Old Latin textual tradition, pre-dating the revisions made at the end of the fourth century by Jerome, which became part of what would eventually be known as the Vulgate.[16] In its decoration, executed in several colours, it shows Irish influence also. Produced a little after the gospel-book, perhaps about 675, was the Book of Durrow (Dublin, Trinity College, MS A. 4. 5 (57)), named after the Irish monastery in County Meath where, by the twelfth century, it had been located. The book was in Ireland even earlier than this but it is still disputed whether it was written there or in Northumbria, or even at the Irish foundation on the Isle of Iona.[17] It has a Vulgate text.

However, the years following the synod of Whitby, with the Celtic-Roman argument settled in Rome's favour, were a watershed in English Bible history. Within a short time a massive import initiative seems to have been under way in Northumbria, drawing largely on Italy and dwarfing anything that had gone before. Men like Wilfrid of Hexham may have been involved in a small way but the greatest entrepreneur without a doubt was Benedict Biscop, a wealthy Northumbrian nobleman who had turned his back on the temporal world at the age of 25.[18] Benedict founded the twin monasteries of Wearmouth (673-4) and Jarrow (681), both richly endowed by the Northumbrian king, Ecgfrith (670-85), and both veritable showhouses of Roman influence. Their activities are well documented by two chroniclers, one of whom was Bede, who spent all his long life at Jarrow from the age of seven.[19] Benedict made numerous trips to the Continent, nearly always including Italy, and each time he returned laden with treasures. These included church paintings and devotional artifacts of many kinds but above all there were books, with which Benedict built an unprecedentedly large and comprehensive library at Wearmouth-Jarrow.[20] They included many works of history, commentary, and exegesis but among them also were volumes of Scripture, including a pandect of the 'Old Latin' Bible, as we know from Bede, and also without a doubt a series of part-Bibles: gospel-books and other books of the Old and New Testaments in small collections.[21] A fragment of Maccabees of sixth-century Italian origin now in Durham comes very probably from one of these part-Bibles and was used in turn for subsequent copying (Cathedral Library, MS B. IV. 6, fol. 169*).[22] For the time being Italy seems to have supplied the Anglo-Saxons with their biblical exemplar texts, and for a while also the quintessential Italian script, uncial, predominated.

It is inconceivable that Bibles did not continue to be imported also into the south of England after the time of Augustine and his immediate followers. Indeed, even those books which ended up in Northumbria will have entered England through southern or south-eastern ports. Furthermore, during the last quarter of the seventh century, Canterbury became the site of a remarkable educational enterprise run by the newly appointed archibishop, the Greek expatriate Theodore, and his assistant Hadrian, an African.[23] Only recently have the range and level of erudition associated with the Canterbury school, which was highly praised by Bede, been fully appreciated; both secular and sacred learning were taught and the curriculum included computation, astronomy, and the art of metre. Evidence of the biblical exegesis taught at the school comes from surviving commentaries derived directly from notes taken in the Canterbury classroom, and the textual evidence of the Vulgate citations in these notes, sparse though it be, suggests that manuscripts independent of those used in the north were in use at Canterbury.[24] There can be little doubt that Hadrian and Theodore brought books with them from Rome, and these probably included biblical volumes. None survives, however, nor is there any reliable report of their arrival or distribution, though a gospel-book mentioned by Bede in connection with Theodore's duties at the synod of Hatfield in 679 may have been one.[25]

There is in fact another 'sighting' of a Bible manuscript in the south at about this time, reported by the early-twelfth-century historian of the English church, William of Malmesbury.[26] Without corroboration his report is probably apocryphal and yet some solid tradition, now irrecoverable, may lie behind it. William's tale concerns Aldhelm, a nobly-born cleric who had been a pupil at Theodore's school at Canterbury and became one of the eighth century's most renowned scholars.[27] In 706 Aldhelm was made bishop of Sherborne and shortly after his consecration was walking by the shore near Dover, according to William, when he encountered some sailors who had apparently arrived from Gaul with a complete copy of the Old and New Testaments (presumably a pandect) for sale. Their price, however, was as high as their manners were insolent and they would not lower it for Aldhelm. Instead they put out to sea again with the Bible. However, retribution came at once in the form of a violent storm, putting them in great peril. They shouted to Aldhelm to help them, and he did so by making the sign of the cross, at which the storm died away and the ship was blown safely back to the shore. The sailors were now only too willing to sell Aldhelm the Bible at a fair price. According to William (who died about 1143), it was still to be seen at Malmesbury in his own day, but no trace of it now remains.

Whatever the antics of inept nautical entrepreneurs, the flow of books into England from the Continent by Aldhelm's time, the early eighth century, had probably lessened to a trickle. Indeed, the traffic was now in the reverse direction. Using her comprehensive base of imported exemplar manuscripts and her rapidly developed calligraphic expertise, England became a net producer of books and was soon renowned as Europe's major book supplier. Many of the books were biblical, and most of these were gospel-books. More than half of all 138 Latin gospel-books surviving in whole or part from before 800 have been identified as Insular – that is, originating within the area now comprising Britain and Ireland; the majority of them are English.[28] Undoubtedly the main focus of copying was Northumbria, whence the earliest clear evidence of the large-scale English production of biblical manuscripts all derives, predating that of the south by several generations. Indeed, for a time Northumbria seems to have been the intellectual centre of western Christendom. The conditions which had stimulated the founding of churches and monasteries and a consequent renaissance of learning – relative political stability and generous royal patronage, coupled with the embracing of the example of Rome in matters artistic as well as devotional – ensured that manuscripts of many sorts were being copied in Northumbria by the end of the seventh century. A magnificent series of decorated gospel-books, along with a complete Bible, constitute the most celebrated of Northumbria's manuscripts, though the uncertainty which persists about which side of the Irish Sea specific works were in fact copied reminds us of the early and still vital debt of Northumbria to Ireland, which I have noted above. Some of the decorative features, especially the large initials so characteristic of these gospel-books, were subsequently exported to the Continent, where they influenced the production of Carolingian books.[29]

The most widely studied of the English gospel-books has long been the Lindisfarne Gospels (London, BL, Cotton MSS, Nero B.iv) made at the monastery on Lindisfarne (or Holy Island, off the Northumbrian coast), which had been founded in 635 by the Irish monk Aidan. He had been brought from Iona at King Edwin's request. No expense seems to have been spared in producing this magnificent gospel-book, which measures 340×240 mm and has 258 folios.[30] Among its features are evangelist miniatures and carpet pages for each Gospel and there are sixteen pages of canon table arcades; some forty pigments were used in the decoration. The magnificence was deliberate, for the gospel-book was created specially to adorn the shrine of St Cuthbert, the greatest of the northern saints (c. 635-87), who had been bishop of Lindisfarne and was buried there. It is likely that it was made for the occasion of his exhumation and elevation about 698, and its symbolic presence must have played a substantial part in the subsequent success and prosperity of his cult during the next two hundred years. In its character, the Lindisfarne Gospels presents a record of the meeting of Celtic and Roman Christianity to which I have alluded already. In its conception and its decoration the book was thoroughly and triumphantly Insular (and specifically Celtic) but in some of its illustrations (the evangelist portraits), and above all in its text, it was Roman, copied from Italian exemplars. When, as we shall see, the book reached Chester-le-Street in the ninth century, a complete Old English interlinear gloss was added above the Latin text, and the glossator supplied a colophon also, which identified first the scribe, then the binder, and then the man responsible for applying gems and precious metals to the cover.

The Lindisfarne Gospels' own story became a creative force in the cult of Cuthbert, whose fame lasted into the later Middle Ages. When the threat of the Vikings caused the monks of Lindisfarne to abandon their island in 875, the gospel-book appears to have gone with them, along with the body of Cuthbert and other relics, on an epic seven years of wandering before they found a resting place at Chester-le-Street, where they stayed until their removal to Durham, their final home, in 995. At one point, according to the account of Symeon, the twelfth-century historian of Durham, the harassed monks decided to set sail for Ireland from Whithorn on the Solway Firth.[31] But the saint had no intention of accepting exile, and hardly had the party put to sea when a terrible storm blew up. Three huge waves swamped the boat and the water turned to blood. The terrified monks turned back, but not before the treasured copy of the Gospels had slipped overboard and sunk. However, some time later, following guidance given to one of the monks by Cuthbert in a dream, the volume was found lying about three miles out on the strand during an unusually low tide. Needless to say, the magnificent memorial of the saint and symbol of his intercessory power was quite undamaged by its immersion in salt water.

Three other gospel-books which survive fragmentarily have been attributed to the Lindisfarne scriptorium also: the 'Durham Gospels' (Durham, Cathedral Library, MS A. II. 17 + Cambridge, Magdalene College, Pepys MS 2981 (19));[32] the 'Otho-Corpus Gospels' (London, BL, Cotton MSS, Otho C. v + Cambridge, Corpus Christi College, MS 197B) which, though now badly damaged, were probably once as fine as the Lindisfarne Gospels and were written also in formal half-uncials;[33] and the 'Echternach Gospels' (Paris, Bibliothèque Nationale, lat. 9389), a somewhat less distinguished volume, executed in a cursive minuscule script.[34] The Lindisfarne attributions remain circumstantial, however, and our knowledge of the scriptorium there is limited.[35] A further book, a beautiful little copy of the Gospel of John, is associated with St Cuthbert, too (London, BL, Loan MS 74). Measuring only 135 × 90 mm and still bound in its original cover of red goatskin over boards of birch, it was found in the saint's coffin when his relics were transferred to the sanctuary of the newly built Durham Cathedral early in the eleventh century.[36] This book was made not at Lindisfarne, however, but at Wearmouth-Jarrow. It had perhaps been presented by that community to Lindisfarne on the occasion of the raising of Cuthbert's body in 698. It is to Wearmouth-Jarrow, undoubtedly the most important centre of manuscript production in early Northumbria, that I now turn my attention. Luckily we know a great deal about the house, owing largely to the survival of the two chronicles which I have already noted and the writing of which in itself testifies to its importance.[37]

It was at Wearmouth-Jarrow that another great English Bible was made. Now known as the 'Codex Amiatinus' and housed in the Biblioteca Medicea Laurenziana in Florence (Amiatino I), it was completed in the early years of the eighth century, before 716, under the direction of Abbot Ceolfrith, who had become head of the twin house after Benedict's death in 688. Amiatinus is the earliest surviving complete Vulgate Bible, not only from England but from anywhere.[38] We know from the chroniclers that it was only one of three such pandects copied there; the first two were made for the two home churches, of St Peter at Wearmouth and St Paul at Jarrow, and Amiatinus was the third, probably planned from the start as a presentation volume.[39] It is a massive book, with dimensions of 505 × 340 mm and a thickness of 250 mm, and it weighs some 75 pounds. It had arrived at the Laurenziana in a state of disrepair towards the end of the eighteenth century and the present fine binding of chestnut leather with brass fittings dates from the middle of the last century.[40] There are 1030 leaves, the last of them blank, and the complete Vulgate text of both testaments is written in a consistently excellent uncial, the carefully developed product of the native scribes of Northumbria, using Italian models. The Bible as a whole is undecorated, apart from coloured initials and rubrics, and devices such as the *hedera* alongside some page headings, but there are three magnificent and well-preserved painted miniatures. One, on fol. 796[v], preceding the New Testament, shows Christ in Majesty; the other two, the so-called 'Ezra miniature' on the present fol. 5[r] and a two-page depiction of the tabernacle on fols 2[v] and 3[r], are part of the first quire, the original page order of which is now uncertain.[41] The quire contains also dedicatory verses, a prologue, a list of contents, diagrams of various ways of dividing the books of Scripture, and comments on the Pentateuch.

The Ezra miniature is one of the most famous of early medieval paintings.[42] It shows in the foreground a scholar at work with his pen in an open volume, presumably of Scripture. On the shelves of the large cupboard behind him is a Bible in nine volumes: we know this from the titles on the spines, though they are no longer easy to read. Ostensibly the scholar is the prophet Ezra, famed for the part he played in the survival of the Jewish nation during the Babylonian captivity by preserving the Scriptures, for a Latin epigraph above the miniature states: 'The sacred books having been consumed by fire through enemy aggression, Ezra, zealous for God, restored this work.'[43] It is highly likely that the miniature was copied into Amiatinus at Wearmouth-Jarrow from a version in the Old Latin pandect which, as I noted above, Benedict Biscop had brought from Italy and which has been identified convincingly with the so-called *Codex grandior*, one of the Bibles used by the civil servant turned scholar Cassiodorus at Vivarium, in Italy, in the late sixth century.[44] The 'Ezra' figure probably represented Cassiodorus in its original version.[45] Certainly, in the context of the monastic scriptorium, the painting makes an open self-referential statement: the image of a scholar producing a Bible prefaces a Bible produced by scholars (among whom, in the case of Amiatinus, will have been Bede), and the work of the scriptorium in the propagation of the divine word is endorsed and celebrated.

The Codex Amiatinus thus promoted the story of its own creation and it does not seem unjust to assume that the volume was, in part at least, launched as an advertisement for a monastery proud of its achievements at the remote edge of the civilized (that is, Christian) world.[46] The dedication written on the verso of the present first folio, before the book was sent from England in 716, along with other treasures, as a gift for St Peter's at Rome, read originally: 'To the body of the illustrious Peter, justly to be honoured, whom lofty faith consecrates head of the church, I, Ceolfrith, abbot from the farthest ends of England [*Anglorum in extremis finibus abbas*], send tokens of my devoted feeling, desiring for me and mine that we may have for ever a remembered place in the heavens, among the joys of so great a father.' It is significant that almost everything about the Codex Amiatinus – except its place of making and its makers – is deliberately Italian, including the text.[47] It was not that Italy needed Bibles but that Wearmouth-Jarrow wanted to boast of its credentials as a creator of the finest examples of such Bibles.

The elderly Ceolfrith himself did not reach Rome. He died on the way at Langres in Burgundy, but some of the monks continued their journey and, according to the anonymous chronicler's account, the Bible reached St Peter's, though there is no incontrovertible evidence of this.[48] Whatever the case, by the end of the ninth century it was at the monastery of San Salvatore at Monte Amiata in the Appennines, some seventy miles north of Rome. Ceolfrith who, as I have noted, died in France during the journey, would perhaps have been gratified to know that the Italians received the codex as one of their own, though he would have been less happy to know of the downside of such recognition, the obliteration of his name. This took place when the codex reached San Salvatore. Peter the Lombard was then the abbot of this Cistercian house, and hence the altered form of the dedication which we see today: first, *cenobium* replaced *corpus* and *saluatoris* replaced *Petri*, so the reference to St Peters's became 'the monastery of the illustrious saviour' (i.e. San Salvatore); then *Petrus* replaced original *Ceolfridus* and *Langobardorum* replaced *Anglorum*, so the subject of the declaration became 'I, Peter of the Lombards'. The 'Italian' identity of Amiatinus remained unchallenged for more than nine centuries: only in the 1880s was its English origin rediscovered.[49] By this time it had reached its present home in Florence through the agency of the emperor Leopold (1765-90), who rescued San Salvatore's books when the monastery was abandoned towards the end of the eighteenth century.

The other two pandects which Ceolfrith had ordered to be made, older sisters to Amiatinus, stayed in Northumbria, one each being placed in the churches at Wearmouth and Jarrow for the edification of the brothers.[50] One subsequently disappeared without trace, perhaps destroyed in the Viking attacks in the 790s. But we know that the other found its way to Worcester towards the end of the eighth century, where it can be identified with the Bible known as 'Offa's Bible', which the celebrated eighth-century king of Mercia of that name gave to the cathedral priory at Worcester. As to how Offa came by it, one very plausible theory is that the Bible was a diplomatic gift to him on the occasion of his marriage to the daughter of the king of Northumbria in 792. A rival theory is that the Vikings had stolen the book and that Offa ransomed it back from them. This, too, is plausible; as we shall see shortly, the commercial enterprise of our aggressive Scandinavian cousins, in respect of books which they knew to be desirable to moneyed Anglo-Saxons, is well attested in respect of the Codex Aureus. Offa's Bible seems to have survived intact at Worcester until the time of the Reformation, when it was broken up and some of the leaves used as document binders in the estate office of an English man of property. By great good fortune a dozen of these leaves survive in the British Library, having turned up in three separate locations over a period of some eighty years.[51]

Thus Northumbria earned its dominant place in the history of the Anglo-Saxon Bible. Assessments of southern production are more difficult. We do not know how soon after Augustine's arrival at Canterbury in 597 books were being copied there or elsewhere in the south or south-east. Certainly before the end of the seventh century charters, at least, were being written (in uncial) in Kent, Mercia, and Essex.[52] Then, in the early part of the eighth century, the Vespasian Psalter, whose Latin text was later glossed in Old English, was made at St Augustine's, Canterbury.[53] The earliest surviving southern biblical manuscript, however, was not written until the middle part of that century, probably also in Kent. Aptly named the 'Codex Aureus' (Stockholm, Kungliga Biblioteket, A. 135), it turns out to be one of the most sumptuous of all Anglo-Saxon gospel-books, sporting purple pages with gold, silver, and white script, and showing unmistakable Roman influence.[54] The codex had an eventful life. Where it was written and spent its early years is not clear but we do know that it was at one point plundered by a Viking army, for an inscription written on fol. 11 tells us it was ransomed back from such an army for gold. The money was paid by Ælfred, who was probably ealdorman of Surrey and whose will was drawn up at some time between 871 and 889, and his wife Werburh. The couple presented this most desirable gospel-book to Christ Church, Canterbury, where it will have earned them regular and deserved prayers for their souls.[55] By the end of the seventeenth century, however, it was back in Scandinavian hands, in the Royal Library in Stockholm, where it remains to this day.

One further important source of indirect evidence of manuscript production and use in the south is the correspondence of the Anglo-Saxon missionary and martyr, Boniface, a man of Wessex born in about 675.[56] He spent most of his life from 716 until his death at the hands of heathens, nearly forty years later, working among the tribes of Germany, and he regularly asked his friends in England to send him books of Scripture and commentary to help him in his mission. In 735, for instance, he wrote to Eadburh, abbess of Minster-in-Thanet, Kent, thanking her for the books and other gifts which she had already sent him and begging her 'to continue the good work you have begun by copying out for me in letters of gold the Epistles of my lord, St Peter, that a reverence and love of the Holy Scriptures may be impressed on the minds of the heathens to whom I preach.'[57] Later, writing at some time between 742 and 746 to Daniel, bishop of Winchester, he asked for the *liber prophetarum* which he said had belonged to his late master, Abbot Winbert of Nursling, Hampshire. It was the one, he explained, 'in which six prophets are to be found together in a single volume, written out in full with clear letters'.[58] In this case, we gather, the form of presentation requested was not primarily related to enhancing the force of the scriptural message but was a practical necessity, because of the missionary's failing eyesight. We do not know whether this book of the Prophets was an import (perhaps therefore written in uncials) or a native product (in which case half-uncial is more likely to have been used), but the missionary's requests together indicate that among the monasteries of southern England there were books of Scripture to spare and that the copying of others in quality form was quite usual – and, we may note, by a woman. However, the northern scriptoria drew Boniface's attention, too. By the 740s he had become aware of the renown of the works of Bede, who had died in 735, and in 746 or 747 he wrote directly to the then abbot of Wearmouth-Jarrow, Hwætbert, to ask for copies of Bede's commentaries on Scripture to be made and sent to him; and twice he wrote to Egbert, archbishop of York (735-66), for more of the same.[59]

The story I have told thus far of the Bible in Anglo-Saxon England, as far as the ninth century, has been a dramatic and often glorious one. Its heroes have been books with special and specific purposes: to adorn the altar at Ripon, to act as a worthy focus for the cult of St Cuthbert and his intercessory powers, to cross the world to Rome as an advertisement of the achievements of English Bible-makers. It has been the story, in the main, of luxury books in which, whether in ways Celtic or Italian, no expense had been spared to emphasize the status of the individuals or institutions involved in their production or reception and to dazzle the ignorant with the ineffable power of the Word in them.

However, this story is incomplete and therefore misleading. The superb artifacts which I have briefly described, and the dramas associated with them which I have related, represent only one dimension, the most visible one, of Bible history. The most treasured manuscripts, the most valuable in terms both of their material structure and of their symbolic status or associations with particular people or places, were the most likely to be preserved both in substance and in memory. It has been estimated that by the beginning of the ninth century over two hundred ecclesiastical foundations of one sort or another must have been in existence in England.[60] Although there were a number of very prominent centres of learning and devotion, such as Canterbury, Malmesbury, and Wimborne in Southumbria, and Wearmouth-Jarrow, Lindisfarne, Whitby, and York in Northumbria, the majority will have been small. Yet it is inconceivable that each of them did not have the basic literary necessities of a devotional life: the psalter, a gospel-book, service books, and sources of Old Testament readings – either lectionaries or part-Bibles. Richard Gameson has suggested that to meet the obvious demand at least three hundred gospel-books alone must have been required to be produced in England during the two centuries following St Augustine's arrival.[61] It is clear that all cannot have been on a par in calligraphic quality and cost of adornment with the Codex Aureus or the Lindisfarne Gospels. Gameson has made an illuminating comparison between the latter and a distinctly unimposing gospel-book probably copied in Northumbria in the eighth century, London, BL, MS Royal 1. B. VII.[62] This may have spent time on the Continent but, if so, was certainly back in England during the later Anglo-Saxon period, for there is a manumission by King Athelstan (924-39) recorded about 925 in a blank space on fol. 15ᵛ. For Gameson, the significance of Royal 1. B. VII and of other manuscripts similar in conception, such as the Hereford Gospels (Hereford, Cathedral Library, MS P. 1. 2) or the gospel-book from which a single leaf survives in London (BL, Cotton MSS, Tiberius B. v), is precisely that they are not *de luxe* volumes, although they might still be written clearly and competently.[63] The splendid books which attract our attention today are not representative. The great demand for gospel-books and other scriptural manuscripts will have meant that much of the work will have been done, of necessity, quickly and by scribes of the second rank, probably in scriptoria far from the few important centres of which we know. Even at Wearmouth-Jarrow, a continuing demand for books from other parts of England and abroad (to which the success of Bede's works contributed enormously) caused problems which were partly solved by a change of house script from stately uncial to a speedier form of Insular minuscule.[64]

A total of twenty-nine more or less complete gospel-books and a further fifteen fragments have been identified as having been written or at least owned in Anglo-Saxon England through the eighth century.[65] This would indicate a survival rate of roughly 15 per cent for this early period, if we use the figure of an original three hundred gospel-books as a guide; as that percentage looks somewhat high, the figure of three hundred may in fact be an underestimate. To this considerable number of gospel-books, most of them functional and calligraphically undistinguished, we must certainly add a large number of other part-Bibles, containing either New or Old Testament books. What survives indicates that these, too, were workaday productions; some of them, at least among the Old Testament manuscripts, were neither attractively nor competently copied. I have noted only four surviving manuscripts from New Testament part-Bibles other than gospel-books: the earliest is an imported bilingual copy of Acts (Latin and Greek) used by Bede at Jarrow and originating in Italy in the sixth or seventh century;[66] and the others, all English and originating in the first half of the eighth century, are a copy of the Pauline Epistles and a fragment of Corinthians (both probably Northumbrian) and a copy of Acts from St Augustine's, Canterbury.[67] The latter may have been copied by St Boniface's correspondent, Abbess Eadburh, at Minster-in-Thanet, though in this instance she did not use letters of gold.[68] The tally of Old Testament part-Bibles is only six, though it would not be surprising if originally it approached or even exceeded that of the gospel-books, in view of the large range of Old Testament material available. Five of the witnesses are fragmentary: the Italian leaf of Maccabees which I noted earlier, copied in the sixth century;[69] a leaf of Leviticus (probably Northumbrian);[70] a leaf of Daniel and a leaf of Minor Prophets, both of which, separately, may have been part of volumes mixing the Minor Prophets with one or two Major Prophets;[71] and one leaf of Numbers and three of Deuteronomy, now scattered in three different libraries but probably all from a part-Bible which may have been a Heptateuch, made at Salisbury perhaps as late as the early years of the ninth century.[72] The sixth Old Testament witness is substantial, the 48-folio 'Egerton Codex' of five wisdom books, Proverbs, Ecclesiastes, Song of Songs, Wisdom, and Ecclesiasticus (London, BL, MS Egerton 1046). The text is not complete in Proverbs and Ecclesiastes and the codex seems to be a compilation of sections of two originally separate Northumbrian part-Bibles, one of fairly high presentational, though not textual, quality, the other quite the opposite.[73] I have classified all the above as the remains of part-Bibles (rather than complete Bibles) from a consideration of page size, which can be established quite accurately even when only fragments remain. Wherever comparisons can be made (and they are backed up by Continental analogies), it is clear that complete Bibles, in which a huge amount of material must be gathered in one, or sometimes two, volumes, have larger pages than part-Bibles, in which space is not at such a premium. A page of the Egerton Codex, for example, measures 310×225 mm, that of the Codex Amiatinus 505×340 mm.[74] According to this criterion, there is manuscript evidence for only one other complete Bible from the earlier period of Anglo-Saxon England after the three Wearmouth-Jarrow pandects made at the turn of the seventh century. It survives but fragmentarily, as a set of the Gospels and a portion of Acts – a total of seventy-nine leaves – distributed now between three different English libraries.[75] Quire signatures in the extant portions indicate that they once formed part of a complete Bible, though whether a pandect or a two-volume work cannot be ascertained. It was a sumptuous book, written in half-uncial and hybrid minuscule with splendidly decorated pages, and dates from the end of the early period, in the first half of the ninth century. It originated south of the Humber, probably at St Augustine's, Canterbury. Without doubt it was made for a special purpose – its being both a complete Bible and a luxurious volume was highly unusual by this time. Overall, the business of the propagation of Scripture was conducted by means of part-Bibles (including gospel-books) throughout the earlier part of the Anglo-Saxon period. These small-format, modestly (and sometimes poorly) produced volumes were relatively quick to make and within the means of centres with limited or overstretched resources, and, most importantly, easy to distribute and to use.

2. THE LATER PERIOD: *c.* 850-1080

A natural break in the cultural history of England occurred in (and comprised much of) the ninth century. It was a period of monastic decline, in a context of Viking threat and political instability. By the second half of the century the standards of literacy even within the rich metropolitan see of Canterbury were abysmal and the 'golden age' of Bede's Northumbria was little more than a memory.[76] It was, however, an influential memory and it stirred King Alfred (871-99) to make a fresh start and instigate a new era of education, for which of necessity he had to use learned monks imported from the Continent.[77] Alfred reintroduced the habits of learning and the skills of literacy on which the great monastic reformers of the mid-tenth century, and the scholars who followed them, would build.

The Bible-history of this later Anglo-Saxon period is unfortunately far less well documented than that of the earlier; no chronicler seems to have thought fit to discuss Bible transmission or Bible making.[78] In outline, history seems to have repeated itself in the later period: renewed contacts with the Continent, begun in Alfred's reign and accelerated during those of his successors, prompted a new import initiative – though now the biblical manuscripts were likely to be Carolingian in origin, rather than Italian, for Italy had long ceased to be the fount of Vulgate transmission – and this was eventually followed by the renewed production of manuscripts in home scriptoria, using the new Continental imports as exemplars.[79]

Most of our specific information about biblical manuscripts at the start of this later period, nearly all of them gospel-books, involves King Athelstan (924-39). His reign was crucial in encouraging a continuation of the revival of religion and learning begun by Alfred, his grandfather, and laid a firm foundation for the great monastic reforms and expansion which were to be carried out mainly under his nephew, Edgar (958-75).[80] We know from inscriptions that Athelstan made gifts of gospel-books to religious houses throughout England and most of them seem to have been of recent Continental origin. One, perhaps written at Lobbes, Belgium, at around the turn of the century, was given to St Augustine's, Canterbury (London, BL, Cotton MSS, Tiberius A. ii).[81] Neighbouring Christ Church received one which may have originated in Brittany at about the same time (BL, MS Royal 1. A. XVIII) and another of Irish origin, a 'pocket' gospel-book known now as the 'MacDurnan Gospels' and copied probably at Armagh in the second half of the ninth century (London, Lambeth Palace, MS 1370).[82] Athelstan gave yet another gospel-book to the community of St Cuthbert at Chester-le-Street (where the saint still rested before his final journey to Durham), and again this seems to have originated in Brittany (London, BL, Cotton MSS, Otho B. ix).[83] The king's many gifts, designed to secure the prayers and goodwill of the churches, were not confined to gospel-books, however; they probably included, for instance, a psalter of ninth-century Continental origin presented to the Old Minster at Winchester.[84] He was also an inveterate collector of relics and these, too, he distributed generously.[85]

Most of Athelstan's gifts, as I have noted, were imports, and biblical (and other) manuscripts would continue to be imported throughout the tenth and eleventh centuries; among these, Patrick McGurk has listed nine further gospel-books from either Brittany or the Loire region, two more from Ireland and one from western Britain.[86] However, another book given by Athelstan to the community of St Cuthbert at Chester-le-Street, this time not a gospel-book but a collection of texts celebrating the life of the saint, proves that high-quality manuscripts were in fact already being written in England again during the king's reign. This one originated probably in the south-west between 934 and 939.[87] However, the earliest surviving 'native' biblical manuscript of the late Anglo-Saxon period is a gospel-book copied around the middle of the century at an unidentified English centre, perhaps in the south or south-west (now Boulogne, Bibliothèque Municipale, 10).[88] Its decoration, which includes elaborately made canon tables and initial letters but only one sketched evangelist portrait (of John), is reminiscent of earlier Insular work. Now in two volumes, its first recorded provenance, early in the seventeenth century, was Continental, at St Vaast, Arras.

Nothing else as early survives, but production in home scriptoria was in full swing at least by the last decade of the tenth century. Five surviving gospel-books from these years include the magnificent Arenberg Gospels, made probably at Christ Church, Canterbury (New York, Pierpont Morgan Library, MS 869),[89] and the York Gospels, also probably a Canterbury book but in York by 1020-3 and still used there today at the installation of senior clergy (York Minster, Chapter Library, MS Add. 1).[90] Nine more gospel-books are extant from those produced in the opening decades of the eleventh century, including the so-called Royal Gospels (London, BL, MS Royal 1. D. IX), the mutilated Kederminster Gospels (BL, Loan 11), the Trinity Gospels (Cambridge, Trinity College, B. 10. 4), the outstanding Eadui Gospels, which were in Germany by the eleventh century (Hanover, Kestner Museum, WM XXI[a]36), and the fine Grimbald Gospels, apparently made for the New Minster at Winchester, whose founder in the Alfredan period had been Grimbald, one of Alfred's Continental helpers (London, BL, Add. MS 34890).[91] Most of the surviving late Anglo-Saxons gospel-books can be grouped together under shared scribes or patrons.[92] One group is associated with the celebrated scribe of Christ Church, Canterbury, Eadui Basan; he wrote the Eadui Gospels and the Grimbald Gospels, and made additions to the Royal Gospels and the York Gospels. It would seem that Christ Church had become a particular centre for the production of Gospel manuscripts, though it is just as plausible, as McGurk points out, to suggest that the Canterbury scribe had been borrowed on behalf of first King Æthelred (978-1016) and then Cnut (1016-35) by some *ad hoc* centre for the preparation of what are mostly presentational copies.[93] Four later gospel-books with a similar purpose, all written in the mid-eleventh century, constitute a further group, united by their sharing of a scribe and by their having apparently been written for Countess Judith of Flanders, widow of Tostig, ill-fated earl of Northumbria, and wife of Welf IV, Duke of Bavaria.[94]

Meanwhile, as I have noted above, gospel-books had continued to be imported from outside England – the larger number probably from Brittany – during the tenth and eleventh centuries. It is worthy of note that some of the imports are obviously less luxurious than the twenty 'native' survivors and show signs of being more frequently used. It would be interesting to know for how long, and to what extent, the supply of other biblical manuscripts for practical use (part-Bibles of the Old Testament or other parts of the New) was met from the Continent or elsewhere, but sadly we have no manuscript evidence whatsoever. Notably absent in our late evidence are biblical manuscripts of low quality, calligraphically or textually inept, of the sort represented by one or two of the earlier part-Bibles (notably the Egerton Codex); thus it seems, from the available evidence, that standards were uniformly good. The fact that most of the native gospel-books seem to have been commissioned by patrons for specific religious foundations highlights the close relationship evolving in England between church or monastery and the state, encouraged by monastic reformers who were keen to promote their interests and acquire security for their foundations.

This link between the use of biblical manuscripts (above all, gospel-books) and affairs of state is vividly illustrated by the York Gospels. About 1020, the blank verso of fol. 157 at the end of the book was used for the writing, in Old English, of texts relating to three estates in the West Riding owned by the archbishops of York. About the same time a new gathering of four leaves (fols. 158-61) was added and was used for three tracts by Archbishop Wulfstan, a letter from King Cnut to his people, and miscellaneous further items, including an inventory of church treasures and some bidding prayers.[95] The king's letter appears to have been written from abroad during a visit to Denmark about 1019-20, with the purpose of keeping the English people informed about his activities on their behalf and asserting his royal authority. He promises security (declaring that the Danes will pose no more danger), promises punishment for evil-doers, and instructs his officials to enforce both divine and secular law. Archbishop Wulfstan appears to have adapted and amplified Cnut's letter, for the closing sentences on the keeping of pledges, honouring God and shunning evil are in his style. One of the three tracts noted above is Wulfstan's celebrated *Sermo Lupi* (sermon of the wolf). This harrangue to the English people was composed in 1014, at a time of worsening national decline in the face of Danish persecution, in an attempt to correlate England's suffering directly with her people's moral backsliding. The habit of using Bibles, and other sacred books, to record texts of special significance is a characteristic of the later Anglo-Saxon period; no instance of this use is known before the tenth century.[96] It is no surprise, perhaps, to find another general difference between the biblical manuscripts of the earlier and later periods. The almost numinous aura which attended so many Bibles of the seventh and eighth centuries – a consequence in part of the natural wonder which such precious artifacts still provoked, in part of the awed devotion which seems to have accompanied a still vigorously evangelizing Christianity – has become barely detectable in the tenth; it has been replaced by the politics of patronage. Politics and Bibles had not been total strangers to each other before, of course, as is demonstrated by the apparent use of one of the great Wearmouth-Jarrow pandects as part of a royal marriage settlement; but what impresses in the later period is the extent of the association. Even Athelstan's gift of gospel-books to St Cuthbert's shrine was presumably an astute political act, for the north of England was still uncertain territory for the king and the cult of the saint was a pervasive and cohesive force.

Architectural and textual features of the later gospel-books suggest that they were copied from a variety of exemplars and that those which survive are probably a small proportion of those made.[97] Thirty complete gospel-books, and another four fragments, written or owned in England between the end of the ninth century and the end of the eleventh, have been identified.[98] However, as far as other part-Bibles are concerned, not a single manuscript witness appears to survive. This picture is almost certainly an abberation. Most of the gospel-books, as we have seen, were presentational volumes, precisely the sort of book which would be treasured and preserved, whereas collections of Old Testament books or New Testament epistles, even if produced to the same consistently competent calligraphic and textual standards enjoyed by most of the gospel-books, are likely to have been largely functional. Yet from the purely practical point of view, just as gospel-books remained a cornerstone of monastic devotions, so other part-Bibles must have continued to be useful for study and private reading. Remaining old copies (if there were any) can scarcely have supplied in full the needs of the late period of monastic expansion. Two booklists give us some insight into the content of later Anglo-Saxon libraries, though both in fact date from just after the Conquest. On the first list, among about fifty books apparently procured for the church of Exeter by Bishop Leofric after his arrival there in 1050, are two large ornamented gospel-books, a volume of four Prophets and separate volumes of Isaiah, Ezekiel, Song of Songs, and Maccabees, as well as epistolaries, psalters and other devotional and exegetical works.[99] The second list, detailing thirty-three volumes which may represent the personal library of Sæwold, abbot of Bath, includes a gospel-book decorated in silver and a Hepta-teuch.[100]

As for complete Bibles in the later period, we have evidence of four, produced between the end of the tenth century and the middle of the eleventh. With one important exception, however, the evidence has reached us precariously, in the form of single fragmentary leaves. The exception is London, BL, MS Royal 1. E. VII + VIII, a Bible which survives intact, although a few leaves were supplied after the Norman Conquest.[101] It is the only complete Anglo-Saxon Bible which we possess, apart from the Codex Amiatinus, and was probably written, to judge from the character of the Caroline minuscule script, shortly before the end of the tenth century. It is a large work (with pages of *c.* 560×340 mm) and has been in two volumes (of 208 and 203 folios) at least since the thirteenth century, if we are right to identify it with the 'Biblia bipartita ... in duo uoluminibus' noted in a catalogue of the books at Christ Church, Canterbury, between 1284 and 1331.[102] We know that it was at Christ Church at the latest shortly after the Conquest, for a recognized scribe of that house undertook a thorough revision of the text throughout.[103] There is no evidence, however, for the long-held view that the Bible was originally written at Christ Church. Now in modern bindings, it is an imposing work by virtue of its size and consistently good calligraphic and textual quality, but it is not opulent. Although it has a most interesting painted miniature, now fol. 1ᵛ, which shows diagrammatically God's act of creation as told in Genesis 1. 6-10, it is otherwise without decoration.[104] No aura of heroism or superhuman endeavour attaches to this solid and worthy book, and it is hard to imagine there being any adventure involved in its transmission to Canterbury, from a scriptorium perhaps somewhere in the south or south-west. What it advertises is not virtuosity but the confidence which comes from established scribal and codicological competence in the context of a well-organized and thriving monasticism. Such were the practical qualities of this late-tenth-century Bible that, as we have seen, it continued to be used after the Conquest, albeit with some modifications by an assiduous scribe, which brought it into line, presumably, with Continental ways.[105]

My assumption is that Royal 1. E. VII + VIII was a characteristic product of the period when the monastic reforms had been consolidated and the concomitant intellectual achievements, epitomized by the voluminous works of Abbot Ælfric, were at their most evident. The fragments noted above, which appear to be from three other Bibles of similar format and quality, support this view. Each had been used as a binding strip in later books. All three happen to come from the Old Testament: parts of three Minor Prophets (Micah, Nahum, and Habbakuk), copied probably a little before the Royal Bible (Columbia, University of Missouri-Columbia, Fragmenta Manuscripta 4); the end of Song of Songs with the beginning of the *capitula* for Wisdom, from the first half of the eleventh century (London, BL, Add. MS 34652, fol. 6); and part of Numbers 1-2 from the same period (London, BL, MS Sloane 1086, no. 109).[106] From the purely practical point of view, as I have noted, part-Bibles must have continued to be useful for study and private reading, and the two booklists noted above seem to prove the case. Yet the evidence of these four manuscripts, and especially the fact that they seem to be of a reliable 'standard' grade without any special decorative features, suggests to me that such complete Bibles had become common by the end of the Anglo-Saxon period.

3. THE VERNACULAR BIBLE

This cursory account of the Bible as it was known in Anglo-Saxon England has been concerned entirely with the Latin Bible, the Vulgate, for that is how Scripture was transmitted almost exclusively at this time (and indeed until the fourteenth century), but the vernacular Scriptures, such as they were, deserve a mention before I conclude. Certainly the Anglo-Saxons never knew a complete vernacular Bible, yet the first bold steps in this direction had already been taken long before the Norman Conquest of 1066 compelled the English language to take third place as a literary medium for the next two hundred years, behind both Latin and French.[107] On a small scale, mostly for teaching purposes, passages of Scripture had been put into English at least since the time of Bede, and poetical versions of parts of some Old Testament books (Genesis, Exodus, Daniel, and Judith) had been composed, probably during the eighth or ninth centuries. Then King Alfred set in motion the development of Old English prose with his own or commissioned translations from the Latin, most of them works of exegesis or history but including also his own prose version of the first fifty psalms. But only in the second half of the tenth century, during that last great phase of Anglo-Saxon intellectual history associated with the reform of monasticism and characterized by a veritable explosion of vernacular translation and original composition, did the first substantial Old English versions of parts of Scripture appear. A full and accurate translation of the four Gospels was made perhaps about 970 or 980, though we do not know where or by whom, and was widely copied, to judge by the fact that six complete manuscripts plus other fragments have survived.[108] Around the turn of the century a compilation of Old Testament translations was made to produce a vernacular Hexateuch in one of its manuscript versions and a Heptateuch in another.[109] Again the date, place, and compiler are unknown, although we know the identity of the translator of the first half of Genesis. This was Abbot Ælfric of Eynsham, the most prolific prose writer of the period, composer of two volumes of homilies and sermons and a volume of saints' lives. Sufficient numbers of manuscripts or fragments again remain to prove that this vernacular part-Bible was much copied and, interestingly, that it was being read and annotated well after the Norman Conquest, even as late as the thirteenth century. Apart from Genesis, none of the books is fully translated, but these versions, along with those of the Gospels, represent the first sustained effort by the English to produce vernacular Scripture and this is the moment, during the later Anglo-Saxon period, when the history of the Bible in English began.

The part-Bibles in Old English were not, however, the products of the sort of movement for direct access to Scripture for the general population associated with later translators of the Bible into English (the Wycliffites, for instance) and they never became popular icons. Everything about the manuscripts which survive, including the corrections and annotations, suggests that their use was more or less confined to the monastery. In one manuscript of the Gospels, rubrics are present relating particular passages to the feast-days on which they are to be read, but there is no reason to think that Old English was used in the actual mass. More likely, Old English translations were used as adjuncts to the Latin, which remained sacrosanct. They may have had a role in the education of young monks learning Latin, particularly at a time when the monastic system in England was being reformed and expanded. In addition, their use by noble and pious laymen is probable, for we know from his own preface that Ælfric's translation of the first half of Genesis was made at the request of his patron, the ealdorman Æthelmær, who founded with his son both the monasteries associated with Ælfric (Cerne Abbas and Eynsham).[110]

4. CONCLUSION

This account began with an Old English riddle, in the vernacular, which seems to give to the (Latin) Bible a sort of heroic status, linking this sense of creative viability with the great *de luxe* manuscripts of the earlier Anglo-Saxon period. I have suggested further (at the risk of over-simplification) that most of the drama, and much of the sparkle, had disappeared by the time that Bible production got under way again in the later period, when the status of the biblical manuscript no longer derived primarily from ostensible devotional role but at least as much from a political one, as a dynamic function of the politico-ecclesiastical world of the unified English state.

I end, however, with one last Bible story from the earlier period, a drama which pleasingly marries the miraculous and the mundane. It is from the description of the death of our English missionary, Boniface, given in the account of his life written in 769 by a fellow English monk, Willibald.[111] Boniface, who spent most of his adult life evangelizing in Germany, was eventually murdered by a pagan rabble. After squabbling among themselves, with much further bloodshed, the rabble proceded to break open some of the missionary's boxes, hoping for gold. Instead they found only books of Scripture, whose value was not apparent to them. 'Thus deprived,' wrote Willibald, 'they scattered some of the volumes over the field and threw away others, some into the reed-beds of the marshes, and others they hid. But by the grace of God and by the prayers of St Boniface himself, they were found unharmed and unstained after the passage of a great space of time, and were sent back by all the various finders to the monastery at Fulda [the monastery founded by Boniface], in which they advance the salvation of souls to this day.'[112] Most of these volumes, it is likely, were Anglo-Saxon manuscripts, copied in England by monks and sent abroad as part of the missionary effort. It is among such English monks, including the self-exiled Willibald and Boniface, that the riddle of the book with its 'lucky droppings' would have been most clearly understood and most loved. No doubt it was one such as they who composed it.

NOTES

1 For a useful treatment, with translations, see C. Williamson, *A Feast of Creatures: Anglo-Saxon Riddle-Songs* (Philadelphia: University of Pennyslvania Press, 1982), and for text and commentary his *The Old English Riddles of the Exeter Book* (Chapel Hill: University of North Carolina Press, 1977).

2 This riddle is usually identified as no. 26 of ninety-five surviving (from probably one hundred) in the 'Exeter Book' of Old English poetry, but Williamson, *Old English Riddles*, designates it no. 24.

3 Cited from *The Exeter Book*, ed. by G. P. Krapp & E. V. K. Dobbie, Anglo-Saxon Poetic Records 3 (New York: Columbia University Press, 1936), 193-4. On some problematical readings, see Williamson, *Old English Riddles*, 211-15.

4 A strong Latin tradition influenced the Anglo-Saxon riddlers, though only in a few cases are the Old English riddles direct translations of Latin versions. The imagery here appears to be entirely original. Latin analogues relevant to the Bible riddle will be found in translation in D. G. Calder & M. J. B. Allen, *Sources and Analogues of Old English Poetry: the Major Latin Texts in Translation* (Cambridge: Brewer, 1976), 166. On the several Old English riddles specifically associated with the making of manuscripts, see L. K. Shook, 'Riddles Relating to the Anglo-Saxon Scriptorium', in *Essays in Honour of Anton Charles Pegis*, ed. by J. R. O'Donnell (Toronto: Pontifical Institute of Mediaeval Studies, 1974), 215-36.

5 Bradley, S. A. J., trans., *Anglo-Saxon Poetry* (Everyman: London, 2nd edn, 1995), 374.

6 On Wilfrid, see P. Hunter Blair, *The World of Bede* (Cambridge: University Press, 2nd edn, 1990), 151-3, and H. Mayr-Harting, *The Coming of Christianity to Anglo-Saxon England* (University Park, PA: Pennsylvania State University Press, 3rd edn, 1991), 129-47.

7 *The Life of Bishop Wilfrid by Eddius Stephanus*, ed. by B. Colgrave [with parallel translation] (Cambridge: University Press, 1927), ch. 17: '[Addens] ... inauditum ante seculis nostris quoddam miraculum. Nam quattuor euangelia de auro purissimo in membranis depurpuratis coloratis ... scribere iussit' (p. 36).

8 *Historia Ecclesiastica* V.19: 'Quin etiam sublime crucis radiante metallo/ Hic posuit tropeum, necnon et quattuor auro/ Scribi euangelii praecepit in ordine libros,/ Ac thecam e rutilo his condignam condidit auro'; *Bede's Ecclesiastical History of the English People*, ed. by B. Colgrave & R. A. B. Mynors (Oxford: Clarendon Press, 1969), p. 528.

9 Blair, *The World of Bede*, 227-8.

10 C. J. Godfrey, *The Church in Anglo-Saxon England* (Cambridge: University Press, 1962), 1-126; F. Stenton, *Anglo-Saxon England* (Oxford: Clarendon Press, 3rd edn, 1971), 96-129; and Mayr-Harting, *The Coming of Christianity*, 51-68 and 94-102. One of the reasons why the king of Kent, Ethelbert, was so amenable to Augustine's mission was the fact that his Frankish wife Bertha was already a Christian, and Hunter Blair points out that the queen and her Frankish chaplain must have had copies of the Gospels and certain service books; *The World of Bede*, 216. On Christianity in Britain during the Roman occupation, see P. Salway, *Roman Britain* (Oxford: Clarendon Press, 1981), 717-39.

11 E. A. Lowe, *Codices Latini Antiquiores: a Palaeographical Guide to Latin Manuscripts prior to the Nineth Century*, 11 vols. and suppl. (Oxford: Clarendon Press, 1934-71; 2nd edn of vol. II, 1972) [hereafter CLA], II, 126. P. McGurk, *Latin Gospel Books from A.D. 400 to A.D. 800*, Les publications de Scriptorium 5 (Paris & Brussels: Editions Erasme, 1961), no. 3 (25-6); *The Making of England: Anglo-Saxon Art and Culture AD 600-900*, ed. L. Webster & J. Backhouse (London: British Museum Press, 1991), no. 1 (17-19, with excellent reproduction of the Luke page at 18).

12 See F. Wormald, 'The Miniatures in the Gospels of St Augustine, Corpus Christi College,

Cambridge, MS 286', in *Francis Wormald: Collected Writings, I, Studies in Medieval Art from the Sixth to the Twelfth Centuries*, ed. by J. J. G. Alexander, T. J. Brown & J. Gibbs (London: Harvey Miller, 1984), 13-35.

13 *Historia Ecclesiastica* I.29: 'et codices plurimos' (ed. Colgrave & Mynors, 104).

14 See P. Doyle, 'The Latin Bible in Ireland: its Origins and Growth', in *Biblical Studies: the Medieval Irish Contribution*, ed. by M. McNamara, Proceedings of the Irish Biblical Association 1 (Dublin: Dominican Publications, 1976), 30-45 (37-9), and M. McNamara, 'The Text of the Latin Bible in the Early Irish Church. Some Data and Desiderata', in *Irland und die Christenheit: Bibelstudien und Mission*, ed. by P. Ní Chatháin & M. Richter (Stuttgart: Klett-Cotta, 1987), 7-55.

15 *CLA* II, 147; *The Making of England*, ed. Webster & Backhouse, no. 79 (111 and 112); J. J. G. Alexander, *Insular Manuscripts 6th to the 9th Century*, A Survey of Manuscripts Illuminated in the British Isles 1 (London, 1978), no. 5; McGurk, *Latin Gospel Books*, no. 9; G. Henderson, *From Durrow to Kells: the Insular Gospel Books 650-800* (London: Thames & Hudson, 1987), 27-9 and 58-9. On the text, see C. D. Verey, 'The Gospel Texts at Lindisfarne at the Time of St Cuthbert', in *St Cuthbert, his Cult and his Community to AD 1200*, ed. by G. Bonner, D. Rollason, & C. Stancliffe (Woodbridge: Boydell, 1989), 143-50 (145-6).

16 On the Old Latin tradition in Ireland, see J. F. Kenney, *The Sources for the Early History of Ireland: Ecclesiastical. An Introduction and Guide*, with addenda by L. Bieler (New York: Octagon Books, 1966), 625, and A. Cordoliani, 'Le texte de la Bible en Irlande du Ve and IXe siècle', *Revue Biblique* 57 (1950), 5-39 (13-15). Also R. Marsden, *The Text of the Old Testament in Anglo-Saxon England*, Cambridge Studies in Anglo-Saxon England 15 (Cambridge: University Press, 1995), 5-18 (on the Vulgate) and 49-54 (on the persistence of Old Latin).

17 *CLA* II, 273; and J. Backhouse, *The Lindisfarne Gospels* (Oxford: Phaidon, 1981), 36 and *passim*. For a list of some sixty biblical manuscripts written, or allegedly written, in Ireland or abroad under Irish influence, see Kenney, *Sources for the Early History of Ireland*, 627-58.

18 Blair, *The World of Bede*, 155-64.

19 See Bede's *Historia abbatum* ('History of the abbots') and the anonymous *Vita Ceolfridi* ('Life of Ceolfrith', who was the abbot of the twin house between 688 and 716); the former is translated in D. H. Farmer & J. F. Webb, *The Age of Bede*, rev edn (Harmondsworth: Penguin, 1983), 185-208, the latter in *English Historical Documents c. 500-1042*, ed. by D. Whitelock (London: Oxford University Press, 2nd edn, 1979), no. 155. On the foundation of Wearmouth-Jarrow, see Blair, *The World of Bede*, 165-83.

20 See especially P. Meyvaert, 'Bede and the Church Paintings at Wearmouth-Jarrow', *Anglo-Saxon England* 8 (1979), 63-77. According to *Historia abbatum*, ch. 11, during his final illness Benedict 'gave orders that the fine and extensive collection of books that he had brought back from Rome ... should be carefully preserved intact and not allowed to decay through neglect or be split up' ('Bibliothecam quam de Roma nobilissimam copiosissimamque aduexerat ... sollicite seruari integram, nec per incuriam fedari, aut passim dissipari praecepit'; C. Plummer, *Venerabilis Baedae Opera Historica*, 2 vols [Oxford: Clarendon Press, 1896] I, 375).

21 On the pandect, see Bede's *Historia abbatum*, ch. 15.

22 *CLA* II, 153; Marsden, *The Text*, 83-5.

23 M. Lapidge, The School of Theodore and Hadrian', *Anglo-Saxon England* 15 (1986), 45-72; and *Biblical Commentaries from the Canterbury School of Theodore and Hadrian*, ed. by B. Bischoff & M. Lapidge, Cambridge Studies in Anglo-Saxon England 10 (Cambridge: University Press, 1994), 172-9. See also Bede, *Historia Ecclesiastica*, IV.2.

24 R. Marsden, 'Theodore's Bible: the Pentateuch', in *Archbishop Theodore: Commemorative Studies on his Life and Influence*, ed. by M. Lapidge, Cambridge Studies in Anglo-Saxon England 11 (Cambridge: University Press, 1995), 236-54.

25 *Historia Ecclesiastica* IV.17; Marsden, *The Text*, 62.

26 The tale is told in *Willelmi Malmesbiriensis monachi de gestis pontificum anglorum*, ed. by N. E. S. A. Hamilton, Rolls Series 52 (London: Longman/Trübner, 1870) V, 377-8.

27 On Aldhelm's life and writings, see M. Lapidge & M. Herren, *Aldhelm: the Prose Works* (Ipswich: Brewer, 1979), 1-19.

28 McGurk, *Latin Gospel Books*, 11.

29 ibid., 11-12.

30 CLA II, 187; McGurk, *Latin Gospel Books*, no. 22; Alexander, *Insular Manuscripts*, no. 9; *The Making of England*, ed. Webster & Backhouse, no. 80 (111-14); Backhouse, *The Lindisfarne Gospels*; and, for a facsimile and extensive volume of commentary, *Evangeliorum quattuor codex lindisfarnensis. Musei britannici codex cottonianus Nero D. iv*, ed. by T. D. Kendrick *et al.*, 2 vols (Olten/Lausanne: Urs Graf, 1956-60).

31 *Historia Dunelmensis ecclesiae* II, chs. 11-12, ed. by T. Arnold in *Symeonis monachi Opera omnia*, Rolls Series, 75, 2 vols (London: Longman/Trübner, 1882-5), I, 63-8, and *The Church Historians of England*, vol. III, ii, *containing the Historical Works of Symeon of Durham*, trans. by J. Stevenson (London: Seeleys, 1855), 660-3.

32 CLA II, 149; McGurk, *Latin Gospel Books*, no. 13; Alexander, *Insular Manuscripts*, no. 10; *The Making of England*, ed. Webster & Backhouse, no. 81 (114-15). For a facsimile, see *The Durham Gospels Together with Fragments of a Gospel Book in Uncial (Durham Cathedral Library, MS. A. II. 17)*, ed. by C. D. Verey, T. J. Brown, & E. Coatsworth, Early English Manuscripts in Facsimile 20 (Copenhagen: Rosenkilde & Bagger, 1980).

33 CLA II, 125; McGurk, *Latin Gospel Books*, no. 2; Alexander, *Insular Manuscripts*, no. 12; and *The Making of England*, ed. Webster & Backhouse, no. 83 (117-19).

34 CLA V, 578; McGurk, *Latin Gospel Books*, no. 59; Alexander, *Insular Manuscripts*, no. 11; and *The Making of England*, ed. Webster & Backhouse, no. 82 (114, 116).

35 See M. P. Brown, 'The Lindisfarne Scriptorium from the Late Seventh to the Early Ninth Century', in *St Cuthbert*, ed Bonner *et al.*, 151-63. Brown notes (153) that, had the Lindisfarne Gospels not 'jumped ship', their provenance might have become Ireland and academic debate about their origins might have been very different.

36 CLA II, 260; McGurk, *Latin Gospel Books*, no. 37; *The Making of England*, ed. Webster & Backhouse, no. 86 (121); *The Stonyhurst Gospel of St John*, ed. by T. J. Brown (Oxford: University Press for the Roxburghe Club, 1969).

37 On the chronicles, one by Bede, see above, n. 19. On Wearmouth-Jarrow see R. Cramp, 'Monkwearmouth-Jarrow: the Archaeological Evidence', in *Famulus Christi: Essays in Commemoration of the Thirteenth Centenary of the Birth of the Venerable Bede*, ed. by G. Bonner (London: S.P.C.K., 1976), 5-18; Hunter Blair, *The World of Bede*, chs. 15-18; and Marsden, *The Text*, 76-83. Four gospel-books, or their remains, have been ascribed also to Wearmouth-Jarrow, though none appears to have matched the quality of the Lindisfarne book.

38 CLA III, 299; Alexander, *Insular Manuscripts*, no. 7 and illus. 23-7; Marsden, *The Text*, 67-90, 98-123 and *passim*; and R. L. S. Bruce-Mitford, *The Art of the Codex Amiatinus*, Jarrow Lecture 1967 (Jarrow: Parish of Jarrow, [1968]), repr. *Journal of the British Archaeological Association*, 3rd ser. 32 (1969), 1-25 and pl. I-XX.

39 The first two, Bede tells us in the *Vita Ceolfridi*, ch. 20, were put in the two churches for the convenience of the brothers. On the relative dating and use of all three pandects, see Marsden, *The Text*, 98-106.

40 ibid., 108 and n. 4.

41 I preserve the form of folio numbering, which varies between Arabic and Roman, found in the manuscript.

42 See esp. Bruce-Mitford, *The Art of Amiatinus*, 9-14. There is a colour reproduction in my 'Job is his Place: the Ezra Miniature in the Codex Amiatinus', *Scriptorium* 49 (1995), 3-15, pl. 6.

43 'Codicibus sacris hostili clade perustis/ Esdra Deo feruens hoc reparauit opus.'

44 *The Text*, 116-23.

45 On Bede's probable part in identifying the figure as Ezra, see Paul Meyvaert's important reassessment of the issue in his 'Bede, Cassiodorus, and the Codex Amiatinus', *Speculum* 71 (1996), 827-83.

46 The remains of one of the two sister pandects indicate that it, and probably the third, were rather inferior to Amiatinus in their calligraphic presentation. We do not know whether they shared any of the paintings.

47 There are interesting exceptions in the case of one or two books, including Psalms, whose text appears to be of Irish origin, proving that, even at this new outpost of Rome, the Celtic influence had not quite faded; see Marsden, *The Text*, 141.

48 *Vita Ceolfridi*, ch. 37. A letter brought back from the Pope, cited by the chronicler (ch. 39), appears to acknowledge the gift, though the reference is not specific. I shall examine this matter further in a forthcoming article.

49 Marsden, *The Text*, 88-90.

50 As Bede tells us in the *Vita Ceolfridi*, ch. 20.

51 The leaves are Additional 37777 (known as the 'Greenwell leaf', with III Kings 11. 29-12. 18), Additional 45025 (the 'Middleton leaves', ten complete leaves and fragments of another, with parts of III-IV Kings), and Loan 81 (the 'Bankes leaf', with Sirach 35. 10-37. 2); see *CLA* II, 177; *The Making of England*, Webster & Backhouse, 122-3; and Marsden, *The Text*, 90-8 and pl. II.

52 An uncial charter of Hlothhere of Kent is dated 679 (London, BL, Cotton MSS, Augustus ii. 2); see P. H. Sawyer, *Anglo-Saxon Charters: an Annotated List and Bibliography* (London: Royal Historical Society, 1968), no. 8, and *The Making of England*, ed. Webster & Backhouse, 43-4 (no. 27, with reproduction).

53 BL, Cotton MSS, Vespasian A. i. For descriptions, see *CLA* II 193, and N. R. Ker, *Catalogue of Manuscripts Containing Anglo-Saxon* (Oxford: Clarendon Press, 1957; re-issued with suppl., 1990), 266-7 (no. 203). For a facsimile, see *The Vespasian Psalter*, ed. by D. H. Wright & A. Campbell, Early English Manuscripts in Facsimile 14 (Copenhagen: Rosenkilde & Bagger, 1967); and for an edition, S. M. Kuhn, *The Vespasian Psalter* (Ann Arbor: University of Michigan Press, 1965).

54 *CLA* XI, 1642; McGurk, *Latin Gospel Books*, no. 111; Alexander 1978, no. 30; Hunter Blair, *The World of Bede*, 226 and 229; and *The Making of England*, ed. Webster & Backhouse, no. 154 (199-201; with colour reproduction of the miniature of St Matthew, fol. 9ᵛ).

55 N. Brooks, *The Early History of the Church of Canterbury: Christ Church from 597 to 1066* (Leicester: University Press, 1984), 151-2, 164, and 201-2, and *The Making of England*, ed. Webster & Backhouse, no. 239 (263-4). On the inscription, see Ker, *Catalogue of Manuscripts*, 456 (no. 385). Although Canterbury has usually been promoted as the origin of the manuscript, Richard Gameson finds Minster-in-Thanet, also in Kent, a more likely candidate. See his *The Early Medieval Bible: its Production, Decoration and Use*, Cambridge Studies in Palaeography and Codicology 2 (Cambridge: University Press, 1994), 46, n. 103.

56 The *Vita Bonifatii* by Willibald, written soon after Boniface's death, is ed. by W. Levison in *Vitae Sancti Bonifatii archiepiscopi Moguntini*, Monumenta Germaniae Historica,

Scriptores rerum Germanicarum 57 (Hanover & Leipzig: Hahn, 1905), 1-57, and trans. by C. H. Talbot in *The Anglo-Saxon Missionaries in Germany* (New York: Sheed & Ward, 1954), 25-62. See also Stenton, *Anglo-Saxon England*, 167-74; and *The Greatest Englishman: Essays on St Boniface and the Church at Crediton*, ed. by T. Reuter (Exeter: Paternoster Press, 1980). Boniface's letters are ed. by M. Tangl in *Die Briefe des Heiligen Bonifatius und Lullus*, Monumenta Germaniae Historica, Epistulae selectae I (Berlin: Weidmannsche Buchhandlung, 1916), and many are translated in Talbot, *The Anglo-Saxon Missionaries*.

57 '... ut augeas quod cepisti, id est, ut mihi cum auro coinscribas epistolas domini mei sancti Petri apostoli ad honorem et reuerentiam sanctarum scripturarum ante oculos carnalium in predicando ...'; *Die Briefe des Heiligen Bonifatius*, ed. by Tangl, no. 35 (60); trans by Talbot, *The Anglo-Saxon Missionaries*, 91; and see the comments of P. Hunter Blair, *Northumbria in the Days of Bede* (London: Gollancz, 1976), 150. One manuscript copied by the abbess may have survived; see below, 12, and n. 68.

58 'ubi sex prophete in uno corpore claris et absolutis litteris scripti repperientur'; *Die Briefe des Heiligen Bonifatius*, ed. Tangl, no. 63 (131); trans. Talbot, *The Anglo-Saxon Missionaries*, 118.

59 *Die Briefe des Heiligen Bonifatius*, ed. Tangl, nos 76, 75, 91; trans. Talbot, *The Anglo-Saxon Missionaries*, 128, 127, and 138, respectively.

60 R. Gameson, 'The Royal 1. B. vii Gospels and English Book Production in the Seventh and Eighth Centuries', in his *Early Medieval Bible*, 24-52 and pls 2.1-4, at 43-4.

61 Gameson, ibid., 45.

62 Gameson, ibid.; *CLA* II, 213; and S. Keynes, 'King Athelstan's Books', in *Learning and Literature in Anglo-Saxon England: Studies Presented to Peter Clemoes on the Occasion of his Sixty-fifth Birthday*, ed. by M. Lapidge & H. Gneuss (Cambridge: University Press, 1985), 185-9 and pl. XI.

63 On the Hereford Gospels, see *CLA* II, 157, Alexander, no. 38, *The Making of England*, ed. Webster & Backhouse, no. 91; on the Tiberius leaf, *CLA* II, 190.

64 Gameson, *Early Medieval Bible*, 47.

65 H. Gneuss, 'Liturgical Books in Anglo-Saxon England and their Old English Terminology', in *Learning and Literature*, ed. Lapidge & Gneuss, 91-141, at 106. The majority were copied in England.

66 Oxford, Bodleian Library, MS Laud Gr. 35 (1119); *CLA* II, 251; see M. L. W. Laistner, *The Intellectual Heritage of the Early Middle Ages*, ed. by C. G. Starr (Ithaca, NY: Cornell University Press, 1957), 157-9.

67 Respectively, Cambridge, Trinity College, MS B. 10. 5 (216) + BL, Cotton MSS, Vitellius C. viii, fols 85-90 (*CLA* II, 133); Paris, Bibliothèque Nationale, MS lat. 9377, fol. 3 (*CLA* Suppl., 1746); and Oxford, Bodleian Library, MS Selden supra 30 (3418) (*CLA* II, 257).

68 Gameson, *Early Medieval Bible*, 46, n. 103; Brooks, *The Early History*, 201; and cf. above, p. 154.

69 Durham, Cathedral Library, MS B. IV. 6, fol. 169* (*CLA* II, 153).

70 Durham, Cathedral Library, MS C. IV. 7, flyleaves, s. viii (*CLA* II, 154).

71 Respectively, Cambridge, Gonville and Caius College, 820 (h), s. viii^{ex} (*CLA* II, 129) and Cambridge, Magdalene College, Pepys 2981 (4), (s. viii/ix).

72 Bodleian Library, Lat. bib. c. 8 (P) + Salisbury, Cathedral Library, MS 117, fols 163-4 + Tokyo, T. Takamiya private collection, Takamiya 21 (formerly Phillipps MS 36183; Geneva, M. Bodmer private collection) (s. viii-ix). On these manuscripts, see Marsden, *The Text*, 40-9 and *passim*.

73 ibid., 262-306. Many of the mysteries of this intriguing manuscript remain to be unravelled.

74 See the tables and discussion in my *The Text*, 43-4.

75 London, BL, MS Royal 1. E. VI + Canterbury, Cathedral Library, MS Add. 16 + Bodleian Library, MS Lat. bib. b. 2 (P) (*CLA* II, 214 and 244).

76 On Canterbury, see Brooks, *The Early History*, 164-74, esp. 171-4.

77 On Alfred, see A. J. Frantzen, *King Alfred* (Boston, MA: Twayne Publishers, 1986) and S. Keynes & M. Lapidge, *Alfred the Great* (Harmondsworth: Penguin, 1983), 9-58.

78 Modern surveys include, for gospel-books, P. McGurk, 'Text', in *The York Gospels: a facsimile with introductory essays by Jonathan Alexander ... [et al.]*, ed. by N. T. Barker (London: Printed for presentation to the members of the Roxburghe Club, 1986), 43-63, with an invaluable list at 43-4, and, for the Old Testament, Marsden, *The Text*, 321-94. Useful catalogues are E. Temple, *Anglo-Saxon Manuscripts 900-1066*, A Survey of Manuscripts Illuminated in the British Isles 2 (London: Harvey Miller, 1976) and *The Golden Age of Anglo-Saxon Art: 966-1066*, ed. by J. Backhouse, D. H. Turner, L. Webster, *et al.* (London: British Museum Publications, 1984).

79 According to F. A. Rella, 'Continental Manuscripts acquired for English Centers in the Tenth and Early Eleventh Centuries: a Preliminary Checklist', *Anglia* 98 (1980), 107-16, thirty-four books, most of them ecclesiastical or exegetical in character, are known to have reached England from the Continent during the tenth and the early eleventh centuries.

80 See especially S. Keynes, 'King Athelstan's Books', in *Learning and Literature*, ed. Lapidge & Gneuss, 143-201.

81 Keynes, 'King Athelstan's Books', 147-53 and pl. IV, and Temple, *Anglo-Saxon Manuscripts*, 12, 41 (see no. 12) and 25 (fig. 30).

82 Keynes, 'King Athelstan's Books', 165-70 and pl. VII, and 153-9 and pl. V, respectively.

83 ibid., 170-9 and pl. VIII.

84 London, BL, Cotton MSS, Galba A. xviii.

85 See J. A. Robinson, *The Times of Dunstan* (Oxford: Clarendon Press, 1923), 71-80.

86 McGurk, 'Text', p. 45 and n. 4.

87 Cambridge, Corpus Christi College 183; see Keynes, 'Athelstan's Books', 180-5 and pl. IX, and Temple, *Anglo-Saxon Manuscripts*, 37-8 (no. 6). Keynes find no evidence for the oft-cited identification of Winchester as the location of the scriptorium receiving this royal patronage ('Athelstan's Books', 184-5).

88 McGurk, 'Text', no. 1; Temple, *Anglo-Saxon Manuscripts*, 40-1 (no. 10) and illus. 38.

89 McGurk, 'Text', no. 4; *Golden Age*, ed. Backhouse *et al.*, no. 47 (68 and pl. XI).

90 McGurk, 'Text', no. 5; facs. *The York Gospels*, ed. Barker; *Golden Age*, ed. Backhouse *et al.*, no. 54; Temple, *Anglo-Saxon Manuscripts*, no. 61.

91 McGurk, 'Text', nos 7-11; Temple, *Anglo-Saxon Manuscripts*, nos 70, 71, 65, 67, and 68; and *Golden Age*, ed. Backhouse *et al.*, nos 52, 51, 49, 56, and 55.

92 McGurk, 'Text', 54, after T. A. M. Bishop; and see T. A. Heslop, 'The Production of *de luxe* Manuscripts and the Patronage of King Cnut and Queen Emma', *Anglo-Saxon England* 19 (1990), 151-95.

93 'Text', 54. The other main group in this earlier period is associated with Bishop's 'scribe B' (see n. 92), who appears to have written the Kederminster, Royal, and Trinity Gospels.

94 McGurk, 'Text', nos 16-19, all of Continental provenance but written in England (or perhaps by an English scribe abroad): New York, Pierpont Morgan Library, MSS 708 and 709; Fulda, Landesbibliothek Aa. 21; and Monte Cassino, Archivio della Badia, BB. 437, 439. See P. McGurk and J. Rosenthal, 'The Anglo-Saxon Gospelbooks of Judith, Countess of Flanders: their Text, Make-up and Function', *Anglo-Saxon England* 24 (1995), 251-308.

95 For full description and discussion, see S. Keynes, 'The Additions in Old English', in *The York Gospels*, ed. Barker, 81-99.

96 Ibid. 81. The habit may have begun under Celtic influence.

97 McGurk, 'Text', 52.

98 Gneuss, 'Liturgical Books', 106.

99 M. Lapidge, 'Surviving Booklists from Anglo-Saxon England', in *Learning and Literature*, ed. Lapidge & Gneuss, 33-89 (64-9).

100 ibid., 58-62.

101 Marsden, *The Text*, 321-78.

102 M. R. James, *The Ancient Libraries of Canterbury and Dover: the Catalogues of the Libraries of Christ Church Priory and St Augustine's Abbey at Canterbury and of St Martin's Priory at Dover* (Cambridge: University Press, 1903), 51 (no. 321).

103 See T. Webber, 'Script and Manuscript Production at Christ Church, after the Norman Conquest', in *Canterbury and the Norman Conquest: Churches, Saints and Scholars, 1066-1109*, ed. by R. Eales & R. Sharpe (London: Hambledon Press, 1995), 145-58 (155-6).

104 On the painting, which is not well preserved, see Wormald, *English Drawings*, 71 (no. 37), with 63 (no. 15), 68 (no. 32) and 79 (no. 56) and pls 20, 30, and 31; Heimann, 'Three Illustrations', 53-4; and Temple, *Anglo-Saxon Manuscripts*, 119-20 (no. 102) and 100, and pl. 319.

105 These emendations included not only a number of textual changes, where the example of specific current Continental traditions seems to have been followed, but also the imposition of Norman orthographical proprieties. An extraordinary number of minor spelling changes were effected with a thoroughness bordering on fanaticism, though none was necessary for an accurate reading of the text. For a more thorough description see Marsden, *The Text*, 333-4.

106 On these fragments, see ibid., 379-94.

107 For accounts of the earliest English translations of Scripture, see H. Hargreaves, 'From Bede to Wyclif: Medieval English Bible Translations', *Bulletin of the John Rylands Library* 48 (1965), 118-40; G. Shepherd, 'English Versions of the Scriptures before Wyclif', in his *Poets and Prophets: Essays on Medieval Studies*, ed. by T. A. Shippey & J. Pickles (Woodbridge: D. S. Brewer, 1990), 59-83; and R. Marsden, 'Cain's Face, and Other Problems: the Legacy of the Earliest English Translations', *Reformation* 1 (1996), 29-51.

108 See the edition by R. M. Liuzza, *The Old English Version of the Gospels. Volume I. Text and Introduction*, Early English Text Society 304 (Oxford: University Press, 1994).

109 See the edition by S. J. Crawford, *The Old English Version of the Heptateuch, Ælfric's Treatise on the Old and New Testament and his Preface to Genesis*, Early English Text Society 160 (London: Oxford University Press, 1922; repr. 1969, with the text of two additional manuscripts transcribed by N. R. Ker) and the facsimile of one of the manuscripts, with commentary, in C. R. Dodwell & P. Clemoes, *The Old English Illustrated Hexateuch. British Museum Cotton Claudius B. IV*, Early English Manuscripts in Facsimile 18 (Copenhagen: Rosenkilde & Bagger, 1974).

110 Marsden, 'Cain's Face'.

111 *Vita Sancti Bonifatii*, ed. Levison, 45-51, ch. 8.

112 I use the translation of Whitelock in her *English Historical Documents c. 500-1042*, no. 158, 781-2.

APPENDIX

Manuscripts of the Bible in Anglo-Saxon England

In this catalogue of the manuscript evidence for Bibles, gospel-books and other part-Bibles written or owned in England during the Anglo-Saxon period, I have included all manuscripts copied up to about the end of the eleventh century. Within the main divisions, of Latin manuscripts copied in the earlier Anglo-Saxon period and of Latin and vernacular manuscripts copied in the later period, items are sub-divided according to their original identity as complete Bibles, gospel-books, or other part-Bibles, as far as this can be ascertained in the case of fragments. I have followed McGurk ('Text', 45 and no. 4) in excluding what are clearly gospel lectionaries (such as 'St Margaret's Gospels', Oxford, Bodleian Library, Lt. liturg. f. 5, and the 'Hereford Gospels', Cambridge, Pembroke College, 302) but including several manuscripts, such as those associated with Countess Judith (my nos 70, 82, 83, and 84), which are to some extent selective also but are nevertheless substantial. The precise codicological origins of some of the listed Gospel fragments cannot be known for certain. Within the sub-divisions, manuscripts are listed alphabetically by the location of the libraries which hold them today. Except where otherwise indicated, the manuscripts are complete, or substantially complete. Origins, when they are known or suspected, are given immediately following the known or estimated date of copying; later medieval provenance, when known and when different from origin, is indicated after a slash. It is not always possible to be certain whether a manuscript was copied in England itself or by English scribes on the Continent. Abbreviated reference is made after each entry to the published sources on which this catalogue is based; the numerals following the abbreviations identify item numbers, not page numbers, in the works concerned, unless otherwise indicated. The results of recently scholarship have led to the omission of a few of the manuscripts which are identified as English in origin or provenance in these sources. The sources are abbreviated as follows:

G: H. Gneuss, 'A Preliminary List of Manuscripts written or owned in England up to 1100', *Anglo-Saxon England* 9 (1981), 1-60.

CLA: E. A. Lowe, *Codices Latini Antiquiores. A Palaeographical Guide to Latin Manuscripts prior to the Ninth Century*, 11 vols. and suppl. (Oxford, 1934-71; 2nd edn of vol. II, 1972).

M1:   P. McGurk, *Latin Gospel Books from A.D. 400 to A.D. 800*, Les Publications de Scriptorium 5 (1961).

M2:   P. McGurk, 'Text', in *The York Gospels*, ed. by N. T. Barker (London, 1986), 43-63.

A: J. J. G. Alexander, *Insular Manuscripts: 6th to the 9th Century*, A Survey of Manuscripts Illuminated in the British Isles 1 (London: Harvey Miller, 1978).

T: E. Temple, *Anglo-Saxon Manuscripts 900-1066*, A Survey of Manuscripts Illuminated in the British Isles 2 (London: Harvey Miller, 1976).

ME: L. Webster & J. Backhouse, *The Making of England: Anglo-Saxon Art and Culture AD 600-900* (London: British Museum Press, 1991).

GA: J. Backhouse, D. H. Turner, & L. Webster, *The Golden Age of Anglo-Saxon Art 966-1066* (London: British Museum Press, 1984).

K: N. R. Ker, *Catalogue of Manuscripts Containing Anglo-Saxon* (Oxford: Clarendon Press, 1957; re-issued with suppl., 1990).

On Old Testament manuscripts see further R. Marsden, *The Text of the Old Testament in Anglo-Saxon England*, Cambridge Studies in Anglo-Saxon England 15 (Cambridge: University Press, 1995), 39-49; on illustrated gospel-books, see T. A. Heslop, 'The Production of *de luxe* Manuscripts and the Patronage of King Cnut and Queen Emma', *Anglo-Saxon England* 19 (1990), 151-95; and on the vernacular manuscripts, see S. J. Crawford, *The Old English Version of the Heptateuch, Ælfric's Treatise on the Old and New Testament and his Preface to Genesis*, Early English Text Society 160 (London, 1922; repr. 1969, with the text of two additional manuscripts transcribed by N. R. Ker), 1-9, 443-4 and 456-7, and R. M. Liuzza, *The Old English Version of the Gospels. Volume I. Text and Introduction*, Early English Text Society 304 (Oxford: 1994), xvi-lxxiii.

    Other abbreviations:

B: Bible

BL: British Library

BN: Bibliothèque Nationale
Britt: Brittany
Bury: Bury St Edmunds, Sussex
CantA: St Augustine's, Canterbury
CantCC: Christ Church, Canterbury
cap.: *capitula*
Ch-le-St: Chester-le-Street, County Durham
Durh: Durham
Eng: England
frag(s): fragment(s)
G: Gospels
Germ: Germany
lvs: leaves
M'sbury: Malmesbury, Wiltshire
N'h: Northumbria
P'boro: Peterborough
SEng: southern England
W-J: the twin monastery of Wearmouth and Jarrow, Northumbria
WinchNM: New Minster, Winchester
WinchOM: Old Minster, Winchester

Latin manuscripts *c.* 600–*c.* 850

Bibles

1	Florence, Biblioteca Medicea Laurenziana, Amiatino 1 [Cdx Amiatinus]	before 716	W-J	G.825; *CLA* III, 299; A.7
2	London, BL, Add. 37777 + Add. 45025 + Loan 81 [12 lvs, frags; III-IV Kgs, Sir]	s. vii^ex	W-J	G.293; *CLA* II, 177
3	London, BL, Royal 1. E. VI + Canterbury, Cathedral Library, Add. 16 + Oxford, Bodleian Library, Lat. bib. b. 2 (P) (2202) [4 G; frag. Acts]	s. ix^1	?CantA	G.448; *CLA* II, 214, 244, Suppl. 214, p. 5; A.32; T.55; *ME* 171

Old Testament Part-Bibles

4	Cambridge, Gonville and Caius College, 820 (h) [frag. Min. Proph.]	s. viii^ex	Eng	G.121; *CLA* II, 129
5	Cambridge, Magdalene College, Pepys 2981 (4) [frag. Dan]	s. viii/ix	?N'h	G.126
6	Durham, Cathedral Library, B. IV. 6, fol. 169* [frag. Macc]	s. vi	Italy/?W-J	G.245; *CLA* II, 153
7	Durham, Cathedral Library, C. IV. 7 [frag. Lev]	s. viii^1	N'h	G.249; *CLA* II, 154
8	London, BL, Egerton 1046 [Prov, Eccl, Song, Sir, Wisd]	s. viii	N'h	G.410; *CLA* II, 194a-b
9	Oxford, Bodleian Library, Lat. bib. c. 8 (P) + Salisbury, Cathedral Library, 117, fols 163-4 + Tokyo, T. Takamiya private collection, Takamiya 21 [4 lvs Num, Deut]	s. viii-ix	Mercia or SEng/ Salisbury	G.646; *CLA* II, 259

Gospel-Books

10	Brussels, Bibliothèque Royale, II.436 [lf Lk]	s. viii	?Eng	CLA X, 1549
11	Cambridge, Corpus Christi College 286 ['G of St Augustine']	s. vi	Italy/ CantCC	G.83; CLA II, 126; M1.3; ME 1
12	Cambridge, Magdalene College, Pepys 2981 (2) + London, BL, Sloane 1086, fol. 119 [frags Lk]	s. viii	Eng	G.124; CLA II, 132; M1.4 and 30a
13	Cambridge, University Library, Kk. 1. 24 + London, BL, Cotton Tiberius B. v, fols 74, 76 + Sloane 1044, fol. 2 [111 lvs Lk, Jn]	s. viii	?N'h/Ely	G.21; CLA II, 138; M1.5, 25 and 30
14	Dublin, Trinity College, A. 1. 6 (58) [Book of Kells]	s. viii^2	?N'h/Kells	G.214; CLA II, 274; A. 52
15	Dublin, Trinity College, A. 4. 5 (57) [Book of Durrow]	c. 675	?N'h/ Ireland	G.213; CLA II, 273; M1.86; A.6
16	Durham, Cathedral Library, A. II. 10, fols 2-5, 338-9 + C. III. 13, fols 192-5 + C. III. 20, fols 1-2 [frags]	s. vii^{med}	N'h/Durh	G.218; CLA II, 147; M1.9; A.5; ME 79
17	Durham, Cathedral Library, A. II. 16 + Cambridge, Magdalene College, Pepys 2981 (18) [59 lvs Mk, Mt, Lk]	s. viii	N'h/Durh	G.219; CLA II, 148abc; M1.10-12; A.16
18	Durham, Cathedral Library, A. II. 17, fols 2-102 + Cambridge, Magdalene College, Pepys 2981 (19) [Durham G]	s. viii	?N'h/ Ch-le-St	G.220; CLA II, 149; M1.13; A.10; ME 81
19	Durham, Cathedral Library, A. II. 17, fols 103-111 [frag. Lk]	s. vii-viii	W-J/ Ch-le-St	G.221; CLA II, 150; M1.14
20	Hereford, Cathedral Library, P. 1. 2 [Hereford G]	s. viii/ix	WMidlands or Wales	G.266; CLA II, 157; M1.15; A.38; ME 91
21	Leipzig, Universitätsbibliothek, Rep. I. 58a + Rep. II. 35a [5 fols Mt]	s. viii^1	?N'h/Germ	G.840; CLA VIII, 1229 + Suppl., p. 11; A.15
22	Lichfield, Cathedral Library, Lich 1 [Mt-Lk 3.9; Lichfield G/G of St Chad]	s. viii^1	?Wales/ Lichfield	G.269; CLA II, 159; M1.16; A.21; ME 90
23	Lincoln, Cathedral Library, 298 (1) [frag. Jn]	s. viii^2	?N'h	G.275; CLA II, 160; M1.17
24	London, BL, Add. 21213, fols 2-25 [palimpsest]	s. viii^{ex}	?Eng	CLA II, 169; M1.19
25	London, BL, Add. 40618 [66 lvs 4 G]	s. viii^2	Ireland/ ?CantA	G.299; CLA II, 179; M1.20; A.46; T.15
26	London, BL, Cotton Nero D. iv [Lindisfarne G]	s. vii^{ex}	Lindisfarne/ Ch-le-St	G.343; CLA II, 187; M1.22; A.9; ME 80

27	London, BL, Cotton Otho C. v + Cambridge, Corpus Christi College 197B, fols 1-36 [frags 4 G; Cambridge-London G]	s. vii/viii	?N'h	G.63; *CLA* II, 125; M1.2; A.12; *ME* 83ab
28	London, BL, Cotton Tiberius B. v, fol. 75 [Mt]	s. viii	?N'h/ ?Exeter	G.374; *CLA* II, 190
29	London, BL, Loan 74 [90 lvs; Stonyhurst Gospel of John]	s. vii^ex	W-J/ Durh	G.756; *CLA* II, 260; M1.37; *ME* 86
30	London, BL, Royal 1. B. VII	s. viii^1	N'h/ CantCC	G.445; *CLA* II, 213; M1.28; A.20; *ME* 84
31	London, BL, Royal 7. C. XII, fols 2-3 [frag. canon tables]	s. vii/viii	?N'h	G.471; *CLA* II, 217; M1.29
32	Munich, Bayerische Staatsbibliothek, Clm 29155d [frag. Jn]	s. viii^in	?N'h	G.853; *CLA* IX, 1335
33	Munich, Bayerische Staatsbibliothek, Clm 29155e [frag. Lk]	s. vii^ex	Eng	G.854; *CLA* IX, 1336
34	Oxford, Bodleian Library, Auct. D. 2. 14 (2698) ['G of St Augustine']	s. vii	Italy/ ?Lichfield	G.529; *CLA* II, 230; M1.32
35	Oxford, Bodleian Library, Auct. D. 2. 19 (3946) [McRegol/Rushworth G]	s. ix^in	Ireland/ Harewood	G.531; *CLA* II, 231; M1.33; A.54; K.292
36	Oxford, Bodleian Library, Lat. bib. d. 1 (P) (31089) [frag. Jn]	s. viii^2	Eng	G.647; *CLA* II, 245; M1.34
37	Oxford, Lincoln College 92, fols 165, 166 [Lk]	s. viii^1	?N'h	G.677; *CLA* II, 258; M1.36
38	Paris, BN, lat. 281 + 298 [Cdx Bigotianus]	s. viii^ex	?Eng/ ?Normandy	G.878; *CLA* V, 526; M1.58; A.34; *ME* 155
39	Paris, BN, lat. 9389 [Echternach G]	s. vii/viii	?N'h/ Echternach	G.893; *CLA* V, 578; M1.59; A.11; *ME* 82
40	Prague, Universitní Knihovna, Roudnice VI. Fe. 50 [2 lvs Mk]	s. viii^med	SEng/Germ	G.904; *CLA* X, 1567
41	St Omer, Bibliothèque Municipale, 257, fols 1-7 [cap.; Mk]	s. viii^1	?N'h	G.931; *CLA* VI, 826; M1.65
42	St Petersburg, Public Library, F. v. 1. 8	s. viii^ex	?N'h or Kent/ France	G.841; *CLA* XI, 1605; M1.126; A.39
43	St Petersburg, Public Library, O. v. I. 1 + Avranches, Bibliothèque Municipale, 48, fols i, ii; 66, fols i, ii; 71, fols A, B [frags Mk, Lk, Jn]	s. viii^1	?CantA	G. 842; *CLA* VI, 730; M1.49, 127
44	Stockholm, Kungliga Biblioteket, A. 135 [Cdx Aureus]	s. viii^med	?CantA/ CantCC	G.937; *CLA* XI, 1642; A.30; *ME* 154
45	Utrecht, Universiteitsbibliotheek, 32 (Script. eccl. 484), fols 94-105 [frags. Mt, Jn]	s. viii^in	W-J	G.940; *CLA* X, 1587; A.8

46	Vatican City, Biblioteca Apostolica, Barb. lat. 570 [Barberini G]	s. viii²	Mercia or N'h	G.907; *CLA* I, 63; M1.137; A.36; *ME* 160
47	Worcester, Cathedral Library, Add. 1 [3 lvs Mt, Mk]	s. viii²	Eng	G.770; *CLA* II, 262; M1.38
48	Würzburg, Universitätsbibliothek, M. p. th. f. 68 [Burchard G]	s. vi s. vii-viii	Italy ?W-J/Germ	G.945; *CLA* IX, 1423ab; M1.80

Other New Testament Part-Bibles

49	Cambridge, Trinity College B. 10. 5 (216) + London, BL, Cotton Vitellius C. viii, fols 85-90 [Pauline Epistles]	s. viii¹	?N'h	G.173; *CLA* II, 133
50	Oxford, Bodleian Library, Laud Gr. 35 (1119) [Acts (Gk and Lat)]	s. vi/vii	Italy/?W-J	G.654; *CLA* II, 251
51	Oxford, Bodleian Library, Selden supra 30 (3418) [Acts]	s. viii¹	Kent/ CantA	G.665; *CLA* II, 257
52	Paris, BN, lat. 9377, fol. 3 [II Cor]	s. viii¹	?N'h/ France	G.892; *CLA* Suppl. 1746

Latin manuscripts c. 850-c. 1100

Bibles

53	Cambridge, Trinity College, B. 5. 2 (148)	s. xi^ex	Lincoln	G.169
54	Columbia, Missouri, University of Missouri Library, Fragmenta Manuscripta 4 [frag. Min. Proph.]	s. x²	SEng	G.811
55	Durham, Cathedral Library, A. II. 4 [Carlief Bible]	s. xi^ex	Durh	G.217
56	Lincoln, Cathedral Library, 1 (A. 1. 2)	s. xi^ex	Lincoln	G.270
57	London, BL, Add. 34652, fol. 6 [frag. Song, cap. Wisd]	s. xi^med	SEng	G.289
58	London, BL, Royal 1. E. VII + VIII [2vols]	s. x^ex	SEng/ CantCC	G.449; T.102
59	London, BL, Sloane 1086, no. 109 [frag. Num]	s. xi^med	SEng	Marsden, *Text*, 390-4
60	San Marino, California, Henry E. Huntington Library, HM 62 [Gundulf B]	s. xi^ex	Rochester	G.934

Gospel-Books

61	Besançon, Bibliothèque Municipale, 14	s. x/xi	?WinchNM/ France	G.796; T.76
62	Boulogne, Bibliothèque Municipale, 10	s. x^med	Eng/ St Vaast, Arras	G.798; M2.1; T.10
63	Cambridge, Fitzwilliam Museum, 45-1980 [Bradfer-Lawrence G]	s. ix^ex	Britt	G.119; K.7*
64	Cambridge, Pembroke College 301	c. 1020	?P'boro	G.138; M2.12; T.73
65	Cambridge, St John's College 73 (C. 23)	s. xi/xii	Bury	G.149
66	Cambridge, Trinity College B. 10. 4 (215) [Trinity G]	s. xi¹	?CantCC	G.172; M2.9; T.65; *GA* 49

67	Coburg, Landesbibliothek 1 [Gandersheim G]	c. 860	?Metz	G.809
68	Copenhagen, Kongelige Bibliotek, G. K. S. 10 (2°) [Copenhagen G]	s. x/xi	?P'boro/ Scandinavia	G.812; M2.3; T.47; GA 48
69	Fulda, Landesbibliothek Aa. 21	s. xi^{med}	?Eng/ Weingarten	M2.18
70	Hannover, Kestner-Museum, W.M. XXIa, 36 [Eadui G]	s. xi^{in}	CantCC/ Germ	G.831; M2.10; T.67; GA 56
71	London, BL, Add. 9381 [Bodmin G]	s. ix/x	?Britt/ Bodmin	G.279; M2. p.45, nn. 3, 4
72	London, BL, Add. 34890 [Grimbald G]	s. xi^1	CantCC/ WinchNM	G.290; T.68; GA 55
73	London, BL, Add. 40000 [Thorney G]	s. xi^{in}	?Britt/ Thorney	G.295
74	London, BL, Cotton Otho B. ix	s. ix^2	Britt or Loire area/ Ch-le-St	G.354
75	London, BL, Cotton Tiberius A. ii	s. ix	?Lobbes, Belgium/ CantA	G.362
76	London, BL, Harley 76 [Bury G]	s. xi^{in}	?CantCC/ Bury	G.413; M2.13; T.75; GA 58
77	London, BL, Loan 11 [Kederminster G]	c. 1020	?P'boro/ Windsor	G501; M2.8; T.71; GA 51
78	London, BL, Royal 1. A. XVIII	s. ix/x	?Britt/ CantA	G.444
79	London, BL, Royal 1 D. III	s. xi^{med}	Rochester	G.446; M2.15
80	London, BL, Royal 1 D. IX [Royal G]	s. xi^1	?P'boro/ CantCC	G.447; M2.7; T.70; GA 52
81	London, Lambeth Palace Library, 1370 [MacDurnan G]	s. ix^2	?Armagh/ CantCC	G.521; A.70
82	Monte Cassino, Archivio della Badia, BB. 437, 439	s. xi^{med}	?Eng/ Monte Cassino	G.851; T.95
83	New York, Pierpont Morgan Library, 708 [Judith G]	s. xi^{med}	?Eng/ Weingarten	G.860; T.94
84	New York, Pierpont Morgan Library, 709 [Judith G]	s. xi^{med}	?Eng/ Weingarten	G.861; T.93
85	New York, Pierpont Morgan Library, 869 [Arenberg G]	s. x^{ex}	CantCC/ Cologne	G.864; M2.4; T.56; GA 47
86	Oxford, Bodleian Library, Auct. D. 2. 16 (2719) [Leofric G]	s. x	?Britt/ Exeter	G.530; K.291
87	Oxford, Bodleian Library, Auct. D. 5. 3 (27688)	s. ix/x	Britt or Loire area	G.532; K.293
88	Oxford, Bodleian Library, Bodley 155 (1974)	s. xi^{in}	Barking	G.554; M2.14; T.59; GA 35
89	Oxford, St John's College 194	s. ix/x	?Britt/ CantCC	G.688; T.12
90	Paris, BN, lat. 272	s. x^2	Winch/Fr	G.877
91	Paris, BN, lat. 14782	s. xi^2	Exeter	G.900

92	Rheims, Bibliothèque Municipale 9	s. xi^med	Eng/ Rheims	G.906; M2.20; T.105
93	St Lô, Archives de la Manche, 1	s. xi²	SEng	G.930; T. p. 16, fig. 25
94	York, Minster Library, Add. 1 [York G]	c. 1000	?CantCC/ York	G.774; M2.6; T.61; GA 54

Part-Bibles in Old English

Old Testament

95	Cambridge, Corpus Christi College 201, pp. 151-60 [Gen 37-47]	s. xi^med	WinchNM	G.65; K.49, art. 56
96	Lincoln, Cathedral Library, 298, no. 2 [2 lvs Num]	s. xi²		G.276; K.125
97	London, BL, Cotton Claudius B. iv [Hexateuch]	s. xi¹	CantA	G.315; K.142; T.86
98	London, BL, Cotton Otho B. x [Gen 37-end]	s. xi¹		G.355; K.177, art.A19
99	New York, Pierpont Morgan Library, G. 63 (P) [frags Ex]	s. xi²		G.866; K.418
100	Oxford, Bodleian Library, Hatton 115 (5135) [excerpts Jdg]	s. xi²	Worcester	G.639; K.332
101	Oxford, Bodleian Library, Laud. Misc. 509 (1042) [Heptateuch]	s. xi²		G.657; K.344

Gospel-Books

102	Cambridge, Corpus Christi College 140	s. xi¹	Bath	G.44; K.35
103	Cambridge, University Library, Ii. 2. 11 + Exeter, Cathedral Library, 3501 (fols 0, 1-7)	s. xi²	Exeter	G.15; K.20
104	London, BL, Cotton Otho C. i, vol. 1	s. xi^med	?M'sbury	G.358; K.181
105	New Haven, Beinecke Library, Beinecke 578 [frags Mk]	s. x/xi		G.859; K.1
106	Oxford, Bodleian Library, Bodley 441 (2382)	s. xi¹		G.577; K.312
107	Oxford, Bodleian Library, Eng. bib. C. 2 (31345) [4 lvs Jn]	s. xi		G.621; K.322

Manuscripts not listed separately above

LAY LITERACY,
THE DEMOCRATIZATION
OF GOD'S LAW,
AND THE LOLLARDS*

Christina von Nolcken

THIS ESSAY WILL CONSIDER some of the historical circumstances surrounding six English manuscripts in the Van Kampen collection (VK MSS 637-42). The manuscripts, which probably date to the first half of the fifteenth century, contain parts of what was almost certainly the first translation of the whole Bible into English.[1] Five (VK MSS 637-40, 642) contain the New Testament or parts of it.[2] The sixth (VK MS 641), now a two-quire fragment, contains part of a text that often accompanies the translation, a table of readings for the ecclesiastical year.[3] Because this table is here in a version – also not uncommon – in which Old Testament readings are given in full, we can assume that it too originally accompanied a complete New Testament.[4]

Manuscripts like these are now extremely valuable and seldom on the market.[5] Yet more than 250 have reached us, more than for any other medieval English text.[6] That we have so many partly testifies to the high value late medieval English society placed on the biblical text. But these manuscripts also come when increasingly streamlined methods of book production had been bringing down the price of books. Books were not yet exactly cheap: according to one estimate even unpretentious examples like our six would have set their original purchasers back by roughly the price of a horse.[7] But largely thanks to the growth of a commercial book trade, books were reaching a far wider segment of society than ever before.[8] For the first time in English history persons or groups of persons even fairly low on the social scale could at least contemplate owning them.

Cheaper books would have meant little if more people had not been able to read them. But book-learning was also rapidly spreading beyond the old clerical elite.[9] Again, it does not seem that more than about 15 per cent of the lay population was able to read in the fifteenth century (though estimates have also been as high as 50 per cent).[10] As Jo Ann Hoeppner Moran has shown, however, laymen were increasingly manoeuvring in Latin, long the prerogative of the clergy.[11] And more importantly, texts were increasingly making their way out of Latin into the vernacular languages then current in England. At first they made their way primarily into the more prestigious French or Anglo-Norman still spoken by the upper echelons of society, but by the end of the fourteenth century they were making their way almost exclusively into English. Lay people in all walks of life were gaining direct access to all sorts of information, including the information they believed they needed to achieve salvation.[12]

With these developments came a good deal of social unrest. In theory at least, late medieval society still subscribed to the notion that it consisted of three grades or estates, those whose duty it was to protect it physically (the secular lords), those whose duty it was to maintain its spiritual health (the clergy), and those whose duty it was to provide for it materially (the vast majority of the lay population).[13] To persons committed to this notion – in effect to all those committed to maintaining the status quo – social stability depended on these grades maintaining their traditional relations of deference and service one with another.[14] For such persons the blurring of social distinctions that came with spreading literacy could not but constitute a threat. The threat remained submerged as long as the clergy still controlled the rate at which book-learning reached the other grades. It began to surface, however, as soon as these other grades began taking over this control for themselves.

Where this threat surfaced particularly noticeably in late medieval England was in relation to the Bible. During the whole of the fourteenth century this had been cautiously reaching beyond the clerical elite, though hardly in ways that would have much affected most of the population.[15] Copies in Latin remained rare, their content accessible only to the specially trained.[16] And although copies became available in French from the end of the thirteenth century and in Anglo-Norman from the mid-fourteenth, these also remained rare, the almost exclusive possession of a privileged minority.[17] To be sure, even monolingual English speakers learned something of the Bible's content from preachers and artists.[18] But what they learned would have been much affected by layers of interpretative commentary. Like John the carpenter in Chaucer's *Miller's Tale*, they would surely have known that Noah (or Nowel perhaps) survived the flood. But they would probably have known rather more about that creation of commentary, Noah's uppity and obstreperous wife.[19] For most of the century it is unlikely that many were informed enough to care, but towards the end of the century increasing numbers of laymen began wanting to investigate the Bible for themselves.

The translation that enabled them to do this was from the start almost certainly the great achievement of John Wyclif (d. 1384) and those he inspired, the Wycliffites or Lollards (terms their contemporaries used interchangeably).[20] Both Wyclif and his early followers were learned men, trained within the church and universities, and often priests themselves – Wyclif would eventually die at his parish at Lutterworth in Leicestershire.[21] But politically and on the subject of religious education they aligned themselves with lay rather than ecclesiastical interests. They proved pivotal in the spread of literacy in England.

Wyclif probably did not translate any of the Bible himself. But he was already being associated with such activity in the later 1380s by Henry Knighton, an Augustinian canon at the abbey of St Mary's, Leicestershire:

The Gospel, which Christ gave to the clergy and the doctors of the church, that they might administer it to the laity and to weaker brethren, according to the demands of the time and the needs of the individual, as a sweet food for the mind, that Master John Wyclif translated from Latin into the language not of angels but of Englishmen. (Hic magister Iohannes Wyclif euangelium quod Cristus contulit clericis et ecclesie doctoribus, ut ipsi laycis et infirmioribus personis secundum temporis exigenciam et personarum indigenciam cum mentis eorum esurie dulciter ministrarent, transtulit de latino in Anglicam linguam non angelicam.)[22]

And even if Wyclif did not do any of the actual translating, his inspiration surely lies behind its every turn. He was a theorist par excellence, an Oxford don who, as Knighton himself put it, was 'the most eminent theologian of that time. He was reckoned second to none in philosophy, and incomparable in scholastic learning' ('doctor in theologia eminentissimus in diebus illis, in philosophia nulli reputabatur secundus, in scholasticis disciplinis incomparabilis').[23] He was also a fervent advocate of the Bible as ultimate authority (that is, as coming from God and therefore as transcending any purely human authority, including the accumulated authority of the church).[24] For much of his career he had little to say on the subject of translation, but certainly towards the end of this career he wanted the laity to be able to study the gospel for themselves.[25] He inspired a group of able students and colleagues with his views, and they in turn inspired others. The Wycliffite message began making its way to ever wider circles in England and beyond.[26]

Among those Wyclif initially inspired must have been most if not all the actual Bible translators. As the Wycliffites were well aware (for they were no mean historians and they made it their business to know such things), they were far from the first to turn parts of the Bible into English prose.[27] They regularly refer to translations they thought were by Bede and King Alfred, ones 'of so oolde Englische that vnnethe can any man rede hem'.[28] They refer also to translations made closer to their own time. They found their best precedent in a work some of their colleagues would in fact take over, a Psalter translation with commentary by the mystical writer Richard Rolle (d. c. 1349), which Rolle seems to have primarily addressed to Margaret Kirkby, a nun and later a recluse.[29] They also looked to a now mysterious Bible 'in Englische of northern speche'.[30] But the Wycliffites were almost certainly the first to translate the whole Bible into English. They were also certainly the first to make such a translation available on a relatively wide scale.[31]

Scholars continue to argue about how the translators set about their task.[32] What seems to have happened is something like the following. At some time in the 1380s (maybe a bit earlier) a group located probably in Oxford began turning the Latin Bible word for word into English.[33] They may have worked like this because they believed this was the only way to preserve the sacred quality of the biblical text (the general view was that Jerome had been inspired when he translated the Bible from Greek and Hebrew into Latin); they may also have been uneasy about preparing a translation that did not finally redirect its users towards the Latin.[34] But they may also have worked like this because it was a recognized method of translating to start with a construe and then revise towards something more readable.[35] We don't have their literal translation in its earliest form, but a relatively finished version did go into circulation, one modern commentators refer to as the Early Version of the Wycliffite Bible (EV).[36] It may have been in place by 1390; it was almost certainly in place by 1407, when the Archbishop of Canterbury, Thomas Arundel, drafted legislation against the further translation of biblical texts as well as the reading of such texts in any book, booklet, or tract made in or after the time of Wyclif.[37]

Most modern readers would probably agree with Anne Hudson when she refers to EV as 'very literal, stilted, and at times unintelligible'.[38] But EV is not the version of the Wycliffite Bible represented by most manuscripts. Either while it was still being prepared or shortly after it went into circulation the translators, perhaps now located somewhere outside Oxford, began work on a more readable as well as a more scholarly version partly based on this literal version. The last chapter of a *General Prologue* they designed to accompany their translation of the Old Testament gives us the details; we have to be impressed by the scholarly way in which they set about their task.[39] First they tried to establish a good original by comparing old Latin Bibles and biblical texts preserved in various commentaries.[40] Then they consulted 'elde gramariens, and elde dyuynis' over particular interpretative difficulties, including ones that arose in the course of translating.[41] The last were various and had to be decided on a case-by-case basis; the writer of the *General Prologue* notes, for example, that a Latin participial construction whose literal rendering would be 'the maistir redinge, I stonde' could be interpreted *because the master reads I stand, if the master reads I stand*, or *while the master reads I stand*.[42] Once the translators had made all their decisions about matters like this, 'manie gode felawis' helped check the translation.[43] And for several years following a good deal of energy must have gone into copying and distributing the text they had reached.

This text is traditionally known as the Later Version of the Wycliffite Bible (LV); it is represented by some 85 per cent of extant manuscripts, including all the New Testaments in the Van Kampen collection as well as the Old Testament readings in its table.[44] It may have been in place by 1395; it was certainly in place before 1408, the date of one of its manuscripts.[45] Stylistically it may not have achieved the elegance of certain other translations of the period.[46] Even so, as the following passage (Matt. 7. 6-11) can indicate, it has achieved a fluency not unlike that of many later English biblical translations;

Nile ʒe ʒyue hooli thing to houndis, nethir caste ʒe ʒoure margaritis bifore swyne, lest perauenture thei defoulen hem with her feet, and *the houndis* be turned, and al to-tere ʒou. Axe ʒe, and it schal be ʒouun to ʒou; seke ʒe, and ʒe schulen fynde; knocke ʒe, and it schal be openyd to ʒou. For ech that axith, takith; and he that sekith, fyndith; and it schal be openyd to hym, that knockith. What man of ʒou is, that if his sone axe hym breed, whethir he wole take hym a stoon? Or if he axe fische, whether he wole take hym an edder? Therfor if ʒe, whanne ʒe ben yuele men, kunnen ʒyue good ʒiftis to ʒoure sones, hou myche more ʒoure fadir that is in heuenes schal ʒyue good thingis to men that axen hym?[47]

It fittingly anticipates such later achievements as Tyndale's New Testament and the Authorized Version.

The institutional church was not particularly opposed to biblical translation until after the Wycliffites had brought such activity into disrepute.[48] Given that book-learning of all sorts was making its way out of Latin into English, therefore, had the Wycliffites not produced their translation when they did, someone else almost assuredly would.[49] Had this person produced it as part of the church's own teaching programme, however, it would almost certainly have looked and read very differently from that of the Wycliffites, and it would not have been prepared in as many copies, at least initially. It would also almost certainly have been addressed only to persons the church considered safe, religious women like Rolle's nun, for example, or lay persons firmly ensconced in the upper echelons of society.[50] And it would very probably have been hedged about with interpretative commentary, or what were then termed glosses. These might have been arranged around the biblical text, as they are in Rolle's Psalter translation.[51] Or they might have been actually interwoven with the text, as they are in another fourteenth-century Psalter translation, the Midland Psalter.[52] In either case they would have been intended to protect the biblical text from solipsistic readings uncontrolled by the accumulated authority of the church. And even then they might have been further mediated by an officer of this church, as occurred in the fifteenth century when a priest read 'þe Bybyl wyth doctowrys þer-up-on' to the illiterate housewife Margery Kempe.[53]

The Wycliffites, by contrast, directed their translation not at any safe audience but at 'alle men in oure rewme, whiche God wole haue sauid'.[54] This was not because they necessarily believed that God wanted very many in the kingdom to be saved (the comma after *rewme*, which could make the relative clause non-restrictive, is editorial). But they were determinedly of the opinion that among those God did want saved were very likely some from the very lowest echelons of society.[55] They accordingly spread their nets as widely as possible, by having their scribes work in a dialect that seems calculated to reach the maximum possible number of people, for example, and by making their translation available in what Hargreaves has termed 'more workaday volumes' as well as more elaborate ones.[56] And far from protecting the Biblical text, they wanted its meaning to radiate forth in as unimpeded a way as possible. They hated the kind of interpretative glossing they associated in particular with the friars.[57]

When the Wycliffite translators started work they may have thought they could entirely avoid inserting themselves between their readers and the biblical text's meaning, that their job was merely to turn the Bible's words from Latin into English. If so, they must soon have adjusted their ideas. For, as the General Prologue makes clear, when trying to make the Bible's sense 'as opin, either openere, in English as in Latyn'[58] they also found themselves having to act as interpreters – when they had to decide what to do with those Latin participial constructions, for example. But they did not let this faze them, for unlike their contemporaries they did not accept that English was too crude an instrument to convey the nuances of the Latin.[59] And they firmly believed that provided they worked with the right disposition they would finally be able to solve their interpretative problems once and for all:

(A) translatour hath greet nede to studie wel the sentence [...], and he hath nede to lyue a clene lif, and be ful deuout in preiers, and haue not his wit ocupied about worldli thingis, that the Holi Spiryt, autour of wisdom, and kunnyng, and truthe, dresse him in his werk, and suffre him not for to erre. [...] Bi this maner, with good lyuyng and greet trauel, men moun come to trewe and cleer translating, and trewe vndurstonding of holi writ, seme it neuere so hard at the bigynnyng.[60]

Given the Wycliffites' interest in making the biblical text available in so unimpeded a form, it may seem surprising that especially in LV the books of the Bible are frequently accompanied by prologues, usually translations of those by Jerome.[61] In several manuscripts the Wycliffite translation is also accompanied by explanatory glosses, some of which seem to go back to the translators: the author of the General Prologue tells us, indeed, that he has been glossing Job, the Psalms and the major prophets, and that he hopes soon to finish the minor prophets.[62] But the Wycliffites were by no means against such glossing, provided it remained strictly subordinate to the biblical text itself. While apparently resembling their contemporaries in their liking for explanatory or interpretative material, therefore, they took greater care than their contemporaries usually did to keep this material distinct, by underlining any words they added (as illustrated by the Old Testament passage in Pl. 17), for example,[63] by clearly identifying their prologues (as illustrated by Pl. 18), and by relegating all explanatory glosses to the margins. They also seem to have wanted what they added to be mainly historical and factual – it is here, indeed, that they importantly reveal their interest in the historical sense of the Bible.[64] And they did finally diverge significantly from their contemporaries. For, as attested by all six of the Van Kampen manuscripts, they were quite prepared to let their translation go out into the world entirely unaccompanied by any such added material. This was partly because they did not want to compromise the biblical text: '[L]oke eche man, that he wryte the text hool bi itself, and the glose in the margyn, ethir leve it al out,' observes a scribe in a rubric to Isaiah.[65] But it is also surely because they wanted to keep some of their manuscripts relatively inexpensive. For those who could afford it the Wycliffites provided the biblical text together with some of the human learning that had helped them reach their own interpretations.[66] But for those of more slender means they let the 'naked text' suffice.[67]

At first the authorities seem to have left the Wycliffite translators to their own devices. When faced with so radically democratizing a translation, however, and when faced with it in what must have been a burgeoning number of manuscripts, they could not but react.[68] Knighton can speak for them all; he well conveys his caste's sense of outrage as well as its sense that it had been betrayed from within:

Through [Wyclif the gospel] is become common and more open to laymen and women who can read, than it has customarily been even to lettered clerks able to understand well. Thus the pearl of the gospel is scattered abroad and trampled underfoot by swine, so that what before was customarily the treasure both of clerks and laymen is now become the plaything of both, and the jewel of clerks is turned into the sport of the laity, so that what was once entrusted from on high to the clergy and the doctors of the church should be held for ever in common with laity. ([P]er ipsum fit uulgare et magis apertum laicis et mulieribus legere scientibus, quam solet esse clericis admodum literatis et bene intelligentibus, et sic euangelica margarita spargitur et a porcis conculcatur. Et sic quod solet esse carum clericis et laicis iam redditur quasi iocositas communis utriusque, et gemma clericorum uertitur in ludum laicorum, ut laicis sit commune eternum quod ante fuerat clericis et ecclesie doctoribus talentum supernum.)[69]

As Knighton was probably writing in the late 1380s he may have been objecting to works containing translated biblical texts rather than to the Bible translation itself. But his words are of just the kind that would regularly be used against biblical translation in general.[70]

As clerks, indeed as very learned clerks, the Wycliffites would have appreciated the force of words like these. Some may have got cold feet relatively early.[71] Others marshalled arguments in support of such translation, often by simply appropriating what had been said before attitudes hardened and polarized.[72] As pointed out by Hudson, for example, the eleventh tract in support of biblical translation in Cambridge, University Library, MS Ii. 6. 26, a collection that surely circulated in a Wycliffite environment, appropriates part of the prologue to the English translation of Robert of Gretham's late-thirteenth-century *Mirror*, a translation that does not seem particularly associable with the Wycliffites.[73] And *Agens hem that seyn that hooli wrigt schulde not or may not be drawun into Engliche* takes over a determination by Richard Ullerston, otherwise known as a defender of orthodoxy against Lollard attacks.[74] These texts very often simply appeal to the precedent set by earlier translations, or to how Christ sent out the disciples to preach God's Law in the people's own language.[75] But when the writer of the first tract in CUL MS Ii. 6. 26 counters the idea that the faith should not be taught to the laity because it surpasses their wits by applying the same point to clerks, he sounds not unlike a Wycliffite (though as we shall see his views concerning the laity are on the whole conservative).[76] And when the appropriator of the prologue to the *Mirror* comments on how wicked living deprives people of the grace required to understand Holy Scripture, he is relying on an ideology that the Wycliffites made very much their own.[77]

The Wycliffites inherited their ideology from Wyclif; it traces to his idiosyncratic blend of philosophical realism (that is, a belief in the real existence of the abstractions into which we organize our perceptions of temporal being) and determined biblicism (that is, the acceptance of Scripture as ultimate authority). His realism enabled his followers to assume a continuity between temporal being and the more conceptual forms of being that for Wyclif had their source in God.[78] And his biblicism meant that they could then infer how certain of these conceptual forms must manifest themselves in their temporal beings.[79] In particular, the Bible's description of the historical Christ and his early followers meant they could infer how members of the Church of Christ must manifest themselves at any time in human history. And this, they decided, was not in the form of the obviously corrupt officers of the institutional church of their own time. Rather, it was in the form of all those who in their Christ-like poverty and simplicity gave promise that they eternally belonged in the true Church, or what the Wycliffites regularly termed the *Congregatio Praedestinorum*.[80]

The Wycliffites must have varied in the extent to which they espoused this ideology; it is also one that they preferred to assume than to explicate. But their conviction that the institutional church no longer had much to do with the Church of Christ did mean that they could assume that the biblical swine – the swine of the sensualists according to Wyclif – were far more likely to be composed of Knighton's 'lettered clerks' than of his 'laymen and women who can read'.[81] They could not, of course, be sure there were no modern equivalents of the swine in their mainly lay audience – the first tract in CUL MS Ii. 6. 26 continues to associate certain kinds of illiterate laymen with 'hem þat lyuen in synne an hoggis lijf ne han no lykynge in gostly þingis but al in þe lust of þe fleisch redy to turne aȝen to synne as houndis to her uomyth', for example.[82] But here too the Wycliffites didn't finally have to worry. For if the members of the *Congregatio Praedestinorum* were indeed those who eternally emulated Christ, then the Word could not but already be partly known to them. And by the same token, if those who would finally be excluded from this congregation were indeed those who eternally failed to emulate Christ, then the Word could not but remain largely obscure to them. Such persons might read and read, but like the Saducees they would never find God: 'Gessist thou that prestis of Saduceis redden not scripturis? but thei mygte not fynde God in hem, for thei wolde not lyue worthili to God,' observes the author of another tract on Bible translation.[83] The Wycliffites may have sometimes risked casting the Bible's words before the contemporary equivalent of the swine, but this did not mean that they should curtail their labours. Rather, they could point with Wyclif to Augustine on Matt. 7. 6:

Our Lord is found to have spoken many truths which many of his hearers did not receive, for they either resisted those truths or despised them. Nevertheless, we are not to think that He gave a holy thing to dogs or cast pearls before swine, for He did not give those truths to those who were unable to receive them. He delivered those truths to those who were able to receive them, and who, although they were assembled with the others, could not rightly be neglected because of the uncleanness of those others. (Quod autem Dominus et magister noster quedam dixisse invenitur, que multi qui aderant vel resistendo vel contempnendo non acceperunt, non putandus est sanctum dare canibus aut margaritas misisse ante porcos: Non enim eis dedit qui capere non poterant, sed eis qui poterant et simul aderant; quos propter aliorum inmundiciam negligi non oportebat.)[84]

For as Wyclif put it as he commented on these words:

From this we are taught not to hide the truth because of the obstacle of those incapable of understanding, when we plausibly believe we are strengthening the church by sowing the truths of the faith to others who are capable of understanding. (Ex quo docemur, non celare veritatem ex scandalo incapacium, dum probabiliter credimus aliis capacibus veritates fidei ad edificacionem ecclesie seminare.)[85]

Such a belief in what Janel M. Mueller has termed 'the self-revelatory character of the living Word', especially when combined with the Wycliffites' indignation against the institutions that had traditionally controlled learning, undoubtedly provided a powerful means of answering words like Knighton's.[86] But it also threatened to leave the Wycliffites sounding markedly anti-intellectual. Even Wyclif was not immune, more than once writing off his own university's learning as pagan and useless, for example.[87] And his followers were more than ready to take the cue. In the *General Prologue* their argument is still mainly with the wrong sorts of human learning:

But alas! alas! alas! the moost abomynacoun that euer was herd among cristen clerkis is now purposid in Yngelond, bi worldly clerkis and feyned religiouse, and in the cheef vniuersitee of oure reume, as manye trewe men tellen with greet weylyng. This orrible and deuelis cursednesse is purposid of Cristis enemyes and traytouris of alle cristen puple, that no man schal lerne dyuynite, neither hooly writ, no but he that hath doon his fourme in art [...]. This semith vttirly the deuelis purpos, that fewe men either noon schulen lerne and kunne Goddis lawe [...]. Lord! whether Oxunford drinke blood and birlith blood, bi sleeinge of quyke men, and bi doinge of sodomye [...]. But wite 3e, worldly clerkis and feyned relygiouse, that God bothe can and may, if it lykith hym, speede symple men out of the vniuersitee, as myche to kunne hooly writ, as maistris in the vniuersite.[88]

But wrong sorts of human learning could easily become human learning in general. When in 1430 John Skylan confesses to having held that the doctors Augustine, Ambrose, Gregory, and Jerome were heretics, or when in 1443 Thomas Bikenore dismisses all glosses of Holy Writ by any doctor approved by the church, they sound suspiciously like advocates of *scriptura sola*.[89] Wycliffism could easily have resolved itself into what A. J. Minnis has termed 'anti-intellectualist Bible-thumping'.[90]

The secret of the Wycliffites' success – and the more than 250 extant manuscripts of their Bible translation attest to their success – could perhaps have lain in just this kind of anti-intellectualism.[91] But the Wycliffites also catered to an age that was far more interested in laying claim to learning than it was in rejecting it. We have long known that Wyclif and his followers democratized God's Law. What we are only now learning is the extent to which they made their biblical translation only part of a much broader educational programme.[92] No one can say that they were not ambitious: in a country with only two universities they proposed establishing a further fifteen.[93] But they were also quite prepared to work from the bottom up, busily organizing what their opponents scathingly referred to as their 'schools and conventicles', sometimes in places like abandoned chapels, more often in people's homes.[94] Instruction in these schools may at times have been in little more than how to read;[95] in later years it sometimes consisted mainly of the simple memorization of stretches of the Bible.[96] But in its heyday their programme seems to have been conceptually sophisticated and very well organized. At the very least it involved visiting preachers and teachers and the distribution of specially prepared books.[97] It involved also intense group discussions at what can seem an impressively high level, the kind of level that had previously belonged almost exclusively in the universities.[98]

The Wycliffites may have been hopelessly idealistic when they replaced the institutional church with a congregation known only to God. But when they democratized learning, and especially when they democratized God's Law, they were challenging this institutional church in a very practical way. It was a challenge the church took very seriously. At first its officers struck mainly at particular tenets of Lollard belief. But they gradually seem to have realized that a major part of the Wycliffites' threat lay in the effectiveness with which they were educating the people.[99] In 1388 commissions were set up around the country to suppress not just the particular tenets of Wyclif's teaching but his writings in general, as well as those of the early Lollards Aston, Hereford, and Purvey; in 1389-90 we get our first datable Wycliffite text written from prison.[100] In 1401 the statute *De heretico comburendo* meant that relapsed or obdurate heretics might be burned; among other things this statute complained of usurpers who were holding schools, writing books, and generally inciting the people to insurrection.[101] And the first burning, of a priest by the name of William Sawtry, took place a few days before the statute was passed.[102]

The measures continued. In 1407 Archbishop Arundel drafted his legislation against biblical translation; this legislation became law in January 1409. Its effect was to cast a century-long pall on just about all religious writing in English.[103] 1408 saw the first burning of a layman, a tailor by the name of John Badby.[104] In 1414 – I will mention only a few representative events – a statute was passed ordering secular officials to investigate all suspected sources of heresy, including sermons, schools, conventicles, congregations, and confederacies.[105] In 1415 a London leather-dresser, John Claydon, was burned together with his books; the case is the more striking because Claydon could not read.[106] In 1416 it was objected against Ralph Mungin, a priest, that he had been dispersing books in London, including 'the gospels of John Wicliff'.[107] In 1429 John Burrell was in trouble partly because his brother had taught him the Pater Noster, Ave, and Credo in English.[108] In the same year William Wright made a deposition against Nicholas Belward for having bought a New Testament in London and spent a year teaching the same William and his wife Margery from it (that Belward purchased this manuscript for four marks and forty pence, sufficient for a curate's annual stipend, is noted in a modern hand on a flyleaf in VK MS 638).[109] Gradually the mere possession of vernacular books by certain classes of people became so suspect that in 1464 John Baron had to account for Chaucer's *Canterbury Tales*.[110] As we approach the end of the fifteenth century prosecutions increase, leading to what are indeed some horrifying stories, about Joan Clerk, for example, who in 1511 had to light the fire around her father, William Tylesworth, while her husband and others did penance on the sidelines.[111] In 1514 Richard Hun was declared a heretic – posthumously, after being found strangled in prison – partly because he had defended translating the Bible into English.[112] And as late as 1519 persons were apprehended in Coventry principally for having taught their families the Lord's Prayer and Ten Commandments in English.[113] Prosecutions would continue until the eve of England's break with Rome in 1534.

Those inspired by Wyclif's views were not directly responsible for the Protestant Reformation in England; rather they were responsible for what Anne Hudson has aptly termed the 'premature reformation'.[114] Very many of their books were destroyed, either by the authorities or by those like John Phip, who in about 1520 said he 'had rather burn his books, than that his books should burn him'.[115] Their Bible would not be printed until it reached the hands of scholars in a much later age; in its own time it would be quickly superseded by translations that looked behind the Latin to the Greek and Hebrew.[116] But the Wycliffites' story was not finally one of near-success followed by complete failure. Their thinking had a profound effect on various foreign reforming movements, most notably in Hussite Bohemia. They maintained their own communities long enough to welcome the new reformist ideas that came from abroad in the sixteenth century.[117] And even without the printing press they prepared and circulated so many copies of their Bible that even today we seldom have to travel very far – at least within the English-speaking world – to be able to see one.

On the cover of VK MS 641 is a note in an early modern hand. It reads: 'Imperfect at the Beginning and End; nevertheless a great curiosity'. Today VK MSS 637-42 represent valuable collectors' items. They must once have counted among their owners' most precious – and their most compromising – possessions.

NOTES

* I am grateful to Professors Jay Schleusener and Kostas Kazazis and to Dr Kimberly L. Molinari for commenting on drafts of this paper. Its shortcomings are my own.

1 170 manuscripts of this translation are listed in *The Holy Bible, [...] made from the Latin Vulgate by John Wycliffe and his Followers*, ed. by J. Forshall & F. Madden, 4 vols (Oxford: University Press, 1850), 1: xxxix-lxiv; 230 manuscripts are listed by Conrad Lindberg, 'The Manuscripts and Versions of the Wycliffite Bible: a Preliminary Survey', *Studia Neophilologica* 42 (1970), 333-47.

2 VK MS 637, a New Testament bought from the Goyder Trust at Sotheby's, 22 June 1993, is Forshall & Madden's and Lindberg's no. 163 (the same as Lindberg's no. 215); VK MS 638, of the gospels, which once belonged to Thomas Kerslake of Bristol, is Lindberg's no. 175.

3 The table is printed in *Holy Bible*, ed. Forshall & Madden, 4: 683-98; see pp. 685-8 for the section contained in the present manuscript (from the Epistle for the first Friday in Lent to the second lesson for the Saturday after Whitsun). A version referring only to the gospel readings for the year is contained in VK MS 638, fols 1-4.

4 Other manuscripts containing a version of the table with Old Testament readings in full include, for example, Oxford, Bodleian Library, MS 531 (SC 2249 – very similar to the present manuscript in size and layout); and Longleat MS 5 (on this manuscript see H. Hargreaves, 'The Marginal Glosses to the Wycliffite New Testament', *Studia Neophilologica* 33 (1961), 294). On such lectionaries see A. Hudson, *The Premature Reformation: Wycliffite Texts and Lollard History* (Oxford: Clarendon Press, 1988), 198-9; Hudson, 'Lollard Book Production', in *Book Production and Publishing in Britain 1375-1475*, ed. by J. Griffiths & D. Pearsall (Cambridge: University Press, 1989), 130-2.

5 As remarked in the Sotheby's Sales catalogue for 22 June 1993: 'There are no fewer than three Wycliffite Bibles in the present sale. This calls for comment. Such books are extremely rare. All three belong to different owners. Since 1960, only four other portions of Wycliffite Bibles have been sold at auction, three in our rooms and one in Basel. Probably never since the Middle Ages – and probably not even then, given the nature of the text – have three copies appeared for public sale at once, and it will certainly never happen again' (84).

6 As Hudson points out, the nearest rival is the *Prick of Conscience*, with 117 copies, while only 64 are known of Chaucer's *Canterbury Tales* (*Premature Reformation*, 231).

7 The estimate is D. Zaret's (*The Heavenly Contract: Ideology and Organization in Pre-Revolutionary Puritanism* (Chicago: University Press, 1985), 35, n. 17); see also H. E. Bell, 'The Price of Books in Medieval England', *The Library*, Fourth Series 17 (1936-7), 312-32; for the sums paid by some Lollards for Bible manuscripts see M. Aston, *Lollards and Reformers: Images and Literacy in Late Medieval Religion* (London: Hambledon Press, 1984), 200; Hudson, 'Lollard Book Production', 132.

8 On developments in the book trade see M. B. Parkes, 'The Literacy of the Laity', in *The Mediaeval World*, ed by D. Daiches & A. Thorlby (London: Aldus Books, 1973), 555-77, esp. pp. 563-4; C. P. Christianson, 'Evidence for the Study of London's Late Medieval Manuscript-Book Trade', in *Book Production and Publishing*, ed. by Griffiths & Pearsall, 87-108.

9 On the spread of literacy in the fourteenth and fifteenth centuries see Aston, *Lollards and Reformers*, 193-217; Jo Ann Hoeppner Moran, *The Growth of English Schooling 1340-1548: Learning, Literacy, and Laicization in Pre-Reformation York Diocese* (Princeton: University Press, 1985), 150-84; M. Keen, *English Society in the Later Middle Ages 1348-1500* (London: Penguin Books, 1990), 217-39.

10 On literacy in fifteenth-century England, see Moran, *Growth of English Schooling*, 17-20; Moran estimates it at 'just slightly less than 15 percent of the lay population' in York diocese on the eve of the Reformation (223).

11 *Growth of English Schooling*, 19.

12 On the texts containing spiritual information that were becoming available see A. I. Doyle, 'A Survey of the Origins and Circulation of Theological Writings in English in the Fourteenth, Fifteenth, and Early Sixteenth Centuries, with Special Consideration of the Part of the Clergy Therein', Ph.D. dissertation (2 vols; University of Cambridge, 1953); M. G. Sargent, 'Minor Devotional Writings', in *Middle English Prose: a Critical Guide to Major Authors and Genres*, ed. by A. S. G. Edwards (New Brunswick, NJ: Rutgers University Press), 147-75; V. Gillespie, 'Vernacular Books of Religion', in *Book Production and Publishing*, ed. by Griffiths & Pearsall, 317-44.

13 On the continuing importance of the concept of the three estates to this society see Keen, *English Society*, 1-5; on the history of the model see G. Duby, *Les trois ordres ou l'imaginaire du féodalisme* (Paris: Gallimard, 1978; translated by Arthur Goldhammer as *The Three Orders: Feudal Society Imagined*, Chicago: University Press, 1980); on how refractory the model could be see D. Aers, *Chaucer, Langland and the Creative Imagination* (London: Routledge & Kegan Paul, 1980), 1-61.

14 For the terms see Keen, *English Society*, 1.

15 On this limited spread, see M. Deanesly, *The Lollard Bible and Other Medieval Biblical Versions* (Cambridge: University Press, 1920), 205-24.

16 On the scarcity of Latin Bibles see Aston, *Lollards and Reformers*, 108-10.

17 On French translations see C. A. Robson, 'Vernacular Scriptures in France', in *The Cambridge History of the Bible*, vol. 2, *The West from the Fathers to the Reformation*, ed. by G. W. H. Lampe (Cambridge: University Press, 1969), 436-52; on the Anglo-Norman translation, see Deanesly, *Lollard Bible*, 142-3.

18 For vernacular texts containing biblical material see L. Muir, 'Translations and Paraphrases of the Bible, and Commentaries', in *A Manual of the Writings in Middle English 1050-1500*, ed. by J. Burke Severs (Hamden CT: Connecticut Academy of Arts and Sciences, 1970), vol. 2, 381-409, 534-52.

19 *Canterbury Tales* I (A) 3538-43, in *The Riverside Chaucer*, ed. by L. D. Benson et al. (3rd edn; Boston: Houghton Mifflin Co., 1987), 73.

20 On the terms *Wycliffite* and *Lollard* see Hudson, *Premature Reformation*, 2-4.

21 On Wyclif's life see H. B. Workman, *John Wyclif: a Study of the English Medieval Church* (2 vols; Oxford: Clarendon Press, 1926); K. B. McFarlane, *John Wycliffe and the Beginnings of English Nonconformity* (London: English Universities Press, 1952).

22 *Knighton's Chronicle 1337-1396*, ed. and trans. by G. H. Martin (Oxford: Clarendon Press, 1995), 242-4, and p. xvii on Knighton. Knighton places this passage under 1382, but he was probably writing a few years after this (xxiii-xxix). Some modern scholars have also attempted to see Wyclif's hand in the translation: see S. L. Fristedt, 'The Authorship of the Lollard Bible', *Studier i modern språkvetenskap* (=*Stockholm Studies in Modern Philology*) 19 (1956), 40-1; Fristedt, 'New Light on John Wycliffe and the First Full English Bible', *Studier i modern språkvetenskap*, n.s. 3 (1968), 78, 84-6; *MS. Bodley 959: Genesis-Baruch 3.20 in the Earlier Version of the Wycliffite Bible*, ed. by C. Lindberg (5 vols; *Stockholm Studies in English* 6 (1959), 8 (1961), 10 (1963), 13 (1965), 20 (1969)), 5: 90-8; Lindberg, 'The Language of the Wyclif Bible', in *Medieval Studies Conference, Aachen 1983: Language and Literature*, ed. by W.-D. Bald & H. Weinstock (Frankfurt am Main: Lang, 1984), 103-10. Caxton associated John Trevisa with the translation, an association that has been revised by D. C. Fowler, 'John Trevisa and the English Bible', *Modern Philology* 58 (1960), 81-98; Fowler, *The Life and Times of John Trevisa, Medieval Scholar* (Seattle & London: University of Washington Press, 1995), 213-34. Wycliffites who have been associated with the translation are Nicholas Hereford, on the basis of a rubric at Baruch 3. 20 in Oxford, Bodleian Library, MS Douce 369 that reads 'Explicit translacionem Nicholay de Herford' (fol. 250ʳ), and John Purvey; on the flimsiness of this latter association see A. Hudson, *Lollards and their Books* (London & Ronceverte: Hambledon Press, 1985), 101-8; Lindberg has recently suggested that we add John Aston to the list ('Language of the Wyclif Bible', 106).

23 *Knighton's Chronicle*, 242-3, trans. Martin.

24 On Wyclif's concern with the Bible see Workman, *John Wyclif*, 2: 149-55; G. Leff, *Heresy in the Later Middle Ages* (2 vols; Manchester: University Press, 1967), 2: 511-16.

25 For references see M. Wilks, 'Misleading Manuscripts: Wyclif and the Non-Wycliffite Bible', *Studies in Church History* 11 (1975), 155, and further Hudson, *Lollards and their Books*, 144-5.

26 On the Wycliffite movement in England see Leff, *Heresy*, 2: 559-605; M. Lambert, *Medieval Heresy: Popular Movements from the Gregorian Reform to the Reformation* (2nd edn; Oxford: Blackwell, 1992), 243-83; on Wyclif's influence abroad see F. Šmahel, '"Doctor evangelicus super omnes evangelistas": Wyclif's Fortune in Hussite Bohemia', *Bulletin of the Institute of Historical Research* 43 (1970), 16-34; R. R. Betts, *Essays in Czech History* (London: Athlone Press, 1969), 132-59, 236-46; Leff, *Heresy*, 2: 606-707; Lambert, *Medieval Heresy*, 284-300. Thomas Netter of Walden, in his anti-Wycliffite *Doctrinale Fidei Catholicae*, suggests that Wyclif's 'perversos pastores' penetrated regions of Spain and Portugal (ed. by F. B. Blanciotti, 3 vols (Venice, 1757-9; repr. Farnborough, Hants: Gregg Press, 1967), 1: 505).

27 On the early history of the Bible in English see G. Shepherd, 'English Versions of the Scriptures before Wyclif', in *The Cambridge History of the Bible*, 2: 362-87; Hargreaves, 'The Wycliffite Versions', ibid., 387-415.

28 The comment on the language is from *Agens hem that seyn that hooli wrigt schulde not or may not be drawun in to Engliche*, ed. by Deanesly in her *Lollard Bible*, 441; this tract has also been ed. by C. F. Bühler, 'A Lollard Tract: On Translating the Bible into English', *Medium Ævum* 7 (1938), 167-83. For further references to early translations see *Holy Bible*, ed. Forshall & Madden, 1: 59.

29 *Agens hem that seyn*, ed. by Deanesly in her *Lollard Bible*, 442. For Rolle's Psalter translation, see *The Psalter (...) With a Translation and Exposition in English by Richard Rolle of Hampole*, ed. by H. R. Bramley (Oxford: Clarendon Press, 1884); N. Watson, *Richard Rolle and the Invention of Authority* (Cambridge: University Press, 1991), 242-8; on Lollard treatments see Hudson, *Premature Reformation*, 259-64; M. P. Kuczynski, *Prophetic Song: the Psalms as Moral Discourse in Late Medieval England* (Philadelphia: University of Pennsylvania Press, 1995), 165-88.

30 *Agens hem that seyn*, ed. by Deanesly in her *Lollard Bible*, 441. The northern Bible was most likely an Old English translation, although it may have been related to one of the texts edited by A. C. Paues (*A Fourteenth Century English Biblical Version* (rev. edn; Cambridge: University Press, 1904), or to the Pauline Epistles edited by M. J. Powell (*The Pauline Epistles Contained in MS. Parker 32*, Early English Text Society, e. s. 116 (London: Kegan Paul, Trench, Trübner & Co., 1916). We could add further Middle English translations, including one of the Apocalypse perhaps related to the Wycliffite translations; on this translation see Hudson, *Premature Reformation*, 267 and n. 196.

31 Their translation includes the Old and New Testaments and the Apocrypha; III Esdras is not normally included in the translation's Later Version. As is made clear by its prologue, the uncanonical *Letter to the Laodiceans* was added after the main translating had been completed (*Holy Bible*, ed. Forshall & Madden, 4: 438); this letter appears in a few manuscripts including VK MS 637 (fols 205^v-206^v) and VK MS 640 (fol. 98^v, incomplete owing to the loss of a leaf).

32 Most recently Fristedt and Lindberg, Fristedt arguing for a complete literal translation that was then revised twice, Lindberg for a New Testament antedating the Old Testament, with both being then revised into the versions we know: see Wilks, 'Misleading Manuscripts', 151-3.

33 It is disputed when work on the translation began. Fowler argues for the 1370s on the ground that Trevisa was involved (*Life and Times*, 225-32); Fristedt similarly argues for such a date, although he believes this work took place at Lutterworth ('New Light', 84); Lindberg argues that work started about 1370 on the ground that Wyclif himself evolved the translational principles articulated in the *General Prologue* ('Language of the Wyclif Bible', 106-7). Wilks argues for an independent translation made probably in the later 1370s that was then taken over by the Wycliffites in the decade or so after Wyclif's death ('Misleading Manuscripts', 159-60).

34 On early theories about translation and in particular biblical translation see H. Hargreaves, 'From Bede to Wyclif: Medieval English Bible Translations', *Bulletin of the John Rylands Library* 48 (1965-6), 123-4.

35 As pointed out by Beryl Smalley, review of M. Deanesly's *The Significance of the Lollard Bible* (1951), in *Medium Ævum* 22 (1953), 49-52; on such translation in a Wycliffite text see *The Middle English Translation of the Rosarium theologie*, ed. by C. von Nolcken, Middle English Texts 10 (Heidelberg: Carl Winter, Universitätsverlag, 1979), 42-6.

36 EV has been printed in *Holy Bible*, ed. Forshall & Madden, and by Lindberg from the manuscript containing its most literal extant form (*MS Bodley 959*, 5 vols) and, after this manuscript ends incomplete, from Oxford, Christ Church, MS 145 (*Stockholm Studies in English* 29 (1973), 81 (1994)).

37 D. Wilkins, *Concilia Magnae Britanniae et Hiberniae* (4 vols; London, 1737), 3: 317; the

legislation is translated by J. Foxe, *Acts and Monuments*, ed. by G. Townsend (8 vols; London: Seeley, Burnside, & Seeley, 1843-9), 3: 245. For discussion of how this legislation was understood see Hudson, *Lollards and their Books*, 146-9. The dates at which the Wycliffite versions were completed remain disputed; the earliest datable manuscript containing EV, British Library, Egerton MS 617/618, was probably made before 1397 since it seems to have belonged to Thomas Duke of Gloucester who was killed in this year (but see S. L. Fristedt, 'A Weird Manuscript Enigma in the British Museum', *Studier i Modern Språkvetenskap*, n.s. 2 (1964), 116-21). Lindberg argues that the work behind EV was finished about 1390 ('Language of the Wyclif Bible', 107).

38 Hudson, *Premature Reformation*, 238.

39 *Holy Bible*, ed. Forshall & Madden, 1: 56-60. This section has also been edited and annotated by A. Hudson, *Selections from English Wycliffite Writings* (Cambridge: University Press, 1978), 67-72, 173-7. For discussion of the translational processes it describes see Deanesly, *Lollard Bible*, 256-67; Hudson, *Premature Reformation*, 243-6.

40 On some results of the Wycliffite translators' effort to establish a good original see H. Hargreaves, 'The Latin Text of Purvey's Psalter', *Medium Ævum* 24 (1955), 73-90.

41 *Holy Bible*, ed. Forshall & Madden, 1: 57. The translators especially consulted the *Glossa Ordinaria*, the standard collection of patristic authorities assembled around the biblical text, and a fourteenth-century work that was to become equally standard, Nicholas of Lyra's commentary on the Old Testament. On the importance of Lyra to the Wycliffites see A. J. Minnis, '"Authorial Intention" and "Literal Sense" in the Exegetical Theories of Richard Fitzralph and John Wyclif: an Essay in the Medieval History of Biblical Hermeneutics', *Proceedings of the Royal Irish Academy* 75, section C, no. 1 (1975), 1-31.

42 *Holy Bible*, ed. Forshall & Madden, 1: 57.

43 ibid.

44 Although the New Testament text this table refers to seems closer in places to EV: for example, the entry for the Saturday in the first week of Lent (fol. 1ᵛ) reads *fro deed men* (EV *fro dead*, or *fro deed men*; LV *fro deeth*); that for the Monday in the second week of Lent (fol. 2ʳ) reads *plesaunt* (EV *plesaunt*, LV *plesynge*); that for the Wednesday in the second week of Lent (fol. 2ᵛ) reads *stiynge* (EV *steyinge*, LV *wente*); on the other hand, the entry for the Tuesday in the fourth week of Lent (fol. 8ʳ) reads *þe myddil* (EV *medlinge*, LV *the myddil*); and that for Palm Sunday (fol. 11ᵛ) reads *peple* (EV *cumpany*, LV *puple*). For EV and LV readings, see *Holy Bible*, ed. Forshall & Madden, 4: 46, 260, 54, 255, 272. Hargreaves describes a similar situation in Longleat MS 5 ('Marginal Glosses', 294 and n. 2); the lectionary printed by Forshall & Madden (*Holy Bible*, 4: 683-98) also does not altogether correspond with either EV or LV. LV has been printed in *Holy Bible*, ed. Forshall & Madden.

45 Commentators usually date it between 1395 and 1397 on the basis of internal references in the *General Prologue*; its earliest datable manuscript, Bodleian Library, MS Fairfax 2, was originally dated to 1408 (though the date was subsequently altered to 1308). Lindberg argues that work on this version lasted from about 1375 to 1395, partly because he wants to attribute the *General Prologue* to Wyclif ('Language of the Wyclif Bible', 107-10).

46 Such as those edited by A. Hudson & P. Gradon in *English Wycliffite Sermons* (5 vols; Oxford: Clarendon Press, 1983-96); see P. A. Knapp, *The Style of John Wyclif's English Sermons* (The Hague & Paris: Mouton, 1977), 93.

47 *Holy Bible*, ed. Forshall & Madden, 4: 16.

48 On the church's attitude towards Bible translation see Hargreaves, 'The Wycliffite Versions', 391-2. That some firmly orthodox members of the church were not implacably against translating the Bible into English even as late as 1401 is indicated by a debate in Oxford; on this debate see Hudson, *Lollards and their Books*, 67-84; N. Watson, 'Censorship and

Cultural Change in Late-Medieval England: Vernacular Theology, the Oxford Translation Debate, and Arundel's Constitutions of 1409', *Speculum* 70 (1995), 840-6.

49 As observed by Deanesly: 'Had Wycliffe never lived, parts of the Bible would have been translated into English at about this time, and have found a place in the libraries of royal dukes and other noble bibliophiles' (*Lollard Bible*, 227).

50 On such 'safe' readers see Deanesly, *Lollard Bible*, 278-80, 288, 319, 336-42; as the author of *De Officio Pastorali* notes, the lords of England already have the Bible in French (*The English Works of Wyclif Hitherto Unprinted*, ed. by F. D. Matthew, Early English Text Society, o. s. 74 (rev. edn; London: Kegan Paul, Trench, Trübner & Co., 1902), 429/27-28).

51 For the arrangement of Rolle's Psalter translation and its commentary in a mid-fifteenth-century manuscript see M. Parkes, *English Cursive Bookhands 1250-1500* (rev. edn; Berkeley & Los Angeles: University of California Press, 1980), plate 19 (ii).

52 As K. D. Bülbring explains, this contains the Latin text followed verse by verse by the English translation (*The Earliest Complete English Prose Psalter [...]*, Early English Text Society, o. s. 97 (London: Kegan Paul, Trench, Trübner & Co., 1891), x-xii). The Latin has been interpolated with Latin glosses following the words explained (underlined in one of the manuscripts) and in the English text the glosses have been substituted for the text. For example, the last clause of Ps. 1. 1 ('Et in cathedra pestilentiae non sedit' reads in one of the two manuscripts Bülbring treats (British Library, Additional MS 17376) 'ne sat nauȝt in fals iugement' (rendering only the gloss), and in the other (Dublin, Trinity College, MS A. 4. 4.) '& haþ not syt in þe chayer of pestilence, þat is to seyne, of vengeaunce, or of fals iuggement' (rendering both text and gloss), because of a gloss in the Latin (recorded in the British Library manuscript, omitted in the Dublin manuscript) 'et in cathedra .i. iudicio pestilencie .i. falsitatis non sedit'.

53 The case is noted by L. Staley, *Margery Kempe's Dissenting Fictions* (University Park: Pennsylvania State University Press, 1994), 136.

54 *Holy Bible*, ed. Forshall & Madden, 1: 57.

55 In the explicitly Lollard *Pierce the Ploughman's Crede*, for example, it is the poverty-stricken ploughman, not the sophisticated friars, who has access to the Word (*The Piers Plowman Tradition*, ed. by Helen Barr (London: Dent; Rutland VT: Tuttle, 1993), 60-97). On Wyclif's emphasis on the poor as constituting the political presence of the evangelical Christ, see S. Justice, *Writing and Rebellion: England in 1381* (Berkeley & Los Angeles: University of California Press, 1994), 83-101.

56 'The Wycliffite Versions', 388-9; for observations on two elaborate copies as well as suggestions about how and where the Bible was copied see A. I. Doyle, 'English Books In and Out of Court from Edward III to Henry VII', in *English Court Culture in the Later Middle Ages*, ed. by V. J. Scattergood & J. W. Sherborne (New York: St Martin's Press, 1983), 168-9. On the standardized dialect of most Wycliffite Bibles see M. L. Samuels, 'Some Applications of Middle English Dialectology', *English Studies* 44 (1963), 84-7.

57 See, for example, their complaints that the friars gloss God's Law as they like in *Fifty Heresies and Errors of Friars* (*Select English Works of John Wyclif*, ed. by T. Arnold (3 vols; Oxford: Clarendon Press, 1869-71), 3: 384/21-21).

58 *Holy Bible*, ed. Forshall & Madden, 1: 57.

59 See, for example, statements attributed to William Butler and Thomas Palmer (ed. by Deanesly in her *Lollard Bible*, 401, 427-8).

60 *Holy Bible*, ed. Forshall & Madden, 1: 60; see also, for example, Wyclif, *De Veritate Sacrae Scripturae* (ed. by R. Buddensieg, Wyclif Society (3 vols; London: Trübner & Co., 1905-7), 1: 194/18-25).

61 On these prologues see Hudson, *Premature Reformation*, 237-8; they are printed at appropriate points in *Holy Bible*, ed. Forshall & Madden.

62 *Holy Bible*, ed. Forshall & Madden, 1: 37, 41, 58; see further Hudson, *Premature Reformation*, 235-7. On glossed manuscripts see *Holy Bible*, 1: xxx-xxxi; Hargreaves, 'Marginal Glosses'; Hargreaves, 'The Wycliffite Versions', 411-13.

63 In the table, underlined words include non-biblical introductions to the readings: 'In þo daies salomon seide to þe sones of Israel' (introducing Wisd. 1. 1-7, for the Wednesday after Whitsun); 'Þe lord god seiþ þese þingis' (introducing Joel 2. 28-32, which in LV is placed at the beginning of Joel 3), for the first lesson on the Saturday after Whitsun); 'In þo daies' (introducing Lev. 23. 10-14) for the second lesson on the same Saturday. Also underlined, however, are 'man' at Wisd. 1. 5 ('the man' is normally here underlined in LV manuscripts), and 'eþer reuelaciouns' glossing 'visiouns' at Joel 2. 28 (an alternative reading that appears with underlining in many LV manuscripts).

64 On the Wycliffites' biblical exegesis and in particular their understanding of Lyra's 'sense intended by the author' see A. Hudson, 'Biblical Exegesis in Wycliffite Writings', in *John Wyclif e la tradizione degli studi biblici in Inghilterra* (Genoa: il melangolo, 1987), 61-79.

65 London, Lambeth Palace, MS 1033, quoted by Hargreaves, 'The Wycliffite Versions', 413.

66 On medieval owners of the Wyclif Bible, by no means all of whom were Wycliffite, see Deanesly, *Lollard Bible*, 333-6; Hudson, *Premature Reformation*, 23-4 and n. 93, 232-4; to this list can perhaps be added the Cotton family, which may have owned VK MS 640 (see further T. Graham, *The Bible as Book: the Earliest Printed Editions. An Exhibition of Items from the Van Kampen Collection* (Grand Haven, Michigan: The Scriptorium, 1996), 24-5).

67 On nakedness in relation to the Bible see S. Delany, *The Naked Text: Chaucer's Legend of Good Women* (Berkeley & Los Angeles: University of California Press, 1994), 120-1.

68 The term 'democratisation' in this context is Deanesly's (*Lollard Bible*, 227, 262).

69 *Knighton's Chronicle*, ed. Martin, 242-4; translation my own.

70 As in the determination attributed to Palmer, ed. by Deanesly in her *Lollard Bible*, 429, 434. On the seemingly classic status of Matt. 7. 6 in such contexts see *Lollard Bible*, 32, 245; note, however, that Deanesly's claim that Innocent III used the text with reference to biblical translation has been challenged by L. E. Boyle, 'Innocent III and Vernacular Versions of Scripture', in *The Bible in the Medieval World: Essays in Memory of Beryl Smalley*, ed. K. Walsh & D. Wood, *Studies in Church History*, subsidia 4 (Oxford: Basil Blackwell, 1985), 97-107.

71 Like Hereford, who abandoned his Lollardy by 1391 and went on to hold a number of clerical offices (*Two Wycliffite Texts: The Sermon of William Taylor, 1406; The Testimony of William Thorpe, 1407*, ed. by A. Hudson, Early English Text Society, o. s. 301 (Oxford: University Press, 1993), 109-10, note to lines 499-501); or Philip Repingdon, who submitted in 1382 and went on to become abbot of the Augustinian canons in Leicester, Chancellor of Oxford University, and Bishop of Lincoln (ibid., 111-12).

72 On such writings see S. Hunt, 'An Edition of Tracts in Favour of Scriptural Translation and of Some Texts Connected with Lollard Vernacular Biblical Scholarship' (D.Phil. diss., University of Oxford, 1994), a work I have not yet seen.

73 *Lollards and their Books*, 107. As it appears in the Cambridge manuscript this text has undergone considerable modification, however (I compared it with the prologue accompanying the translated *Mirror* in Cambridge, Magdalene College, Pepys Library, MS 2498, pp. 45-50). On Gretham's *Mirror* and its English translation see Deanesly, *Lollard Bible*, 149-51, 315-17. On the tracts in Cambridge, University Library, MS Ii. 6. 26 see *Holy Bible*, ed. Forshall & Madden, 1: xiv-xv; Deanesly, *Lollard Bible*, 270-4, corrected by Hudson, *Lollards and their Books*, 106-7; *English Wycliffite Writings*, ed. Hudson, 107-9, 189-91.

74 As also pointed out by Hudson, *Lollards and their Books*, 67-84, esp. pp. 75-8.

75 For appeals to precedent see, for example, CUL, MS Ii. 6. 26, fol. 7^r; *Agens hem that seyn*, ed. by Deanesly in her *Lollard Bible*, 441-2; for the argument that Christ sent out the

disciples to preach God's Law in the people's own language see, for example, CUL, MS Ii. 6. 26, fols 5^r-5^v, 43^r-43^v.

76 CUL, MS Ii. 6. 26, fol. 20^r.

77 ibid., fol. 52^r.

78 On Wyclif's realism see Leff, *Heresy*, 2: 500-10 and, for example, J. A. Robson, *Wyclif and the Oxford Schools: the Relation of the 'Summa de ente' to Scholastic Debates at Oxford in the Later Fourteenth Century* (Cambridge: University Press, 1961), 141-95; A. Kenny, *Wyclif* (Oxford: University Press, 1985), 1-30; Kenny, 'The Realism of the *De Universalibus*', in *Wyclif in his Times*, ed. by A. Kenny (Oxford: Clarendon Press, 1986), 17-29; J. I. Catto, 'Wyclif and Wycliffism at Oxford 1356-1430', in *The History of the University of Oxford*, vol. 2, *Late Medieval Oxford*, ed. by J. I. Catto & R. Evans (Oxford: Clarendon Press, 1992), 190-3.

79 On Wyclif's biblicism see Robson, *Wyclif and the Oxford Schools*, 163-4; B. Smalley, 'The Bible and Eternity: John Wyclif's Dilemma', *Journal of the Warburg and Courtauld Institutes* 27 (1964), 73-89; Leff, *Heresy*, 2: 511-16; Minnis, 'Authorial Intention', 13-16; Kenny, *Wyclif*, 56-67; Catto, 'Wyclif and Wycliffism', 195-8, 209.

80 See G. Lechler, trans. by P. Lorimer, *John Wycliffe and his English Precursors* (London: Religious Tract Society, 1884), 287-96; Workman, *John Wyclif*, 2: 6-20; Leff, *Heresy*, 2: 516-21. For the Wycliffite definition of the Church as 'þe congregacion of juste men for whom Jesus Crist schedde his blood' see, for example, *Þe Grete Sentence of Curs Expouned* (*Select English Works of Wyclif*, ed. Arnold, 3: 273/14-15), or for them as 'alle þylke þat schulleþ be in blysse after þe dome' see *Þe Pater Noster* (ibid., 101/37-8).

81 The pro-vernacular-Bible rejoinder takes a different approach in the debate recorded by Palmer, however (ed. by Deanesly in her *Lollard Bible*, 432-3); for Wyclif's definition of the swine see his *Opus Evangelicum* (ed. by J. Loserth, Wyclif Society (2 vols; London: Trübner & Co., 1895-6), 1: 387/37-388/1: '(M)ulti sunt voluptuosi viventes bestialiter tanquam porci, qui non sapiunt subtilitatem veritatis evangelice'; in his *De Veritate Sacrae Scripturae* they are 'sophistas, hereticos et voluptuosos carnales' (ed. Buddensieg (cited above, n. 60), 1: 312/14-15). The Wycliffites regularly refer to those who read the Law of God in a worldly way as trampling it: see, for example, *Hou þe office of curatis is ordeyned of god* (*English Works of Wyclif*, ed. Matthew, 157/1-16); *The Lanterne of Liȝt*, ed. by L. M. Swinburn, Early English Text Society, o. s. 151, London: Kegan Paul, Trench, Trübner & Co., 1917), 56/24-26; for a complete identification of swine and corrupt priests see the passage appropriated from Odo of Cheriton in *An Apology for Lollard Doctrines*, ed. by J. H. Todd, Camden Society 14 (London: John Bowyer Nichols and Son, 1842), 58.

82 fol. 9^v.

83 *The holi prophete Dauid seith [...]*, ed. by Deanesly in her *Lollard Bible*, 450/13-15. For Wyclif's attempts to avoid the rigid dualism that was the logical outcome of such thinking, see Lechler, *Wycliffe and his English Precursors*, 290-6; Workman, *John Wyclif*, 2: 9-11; Catto, 'Wyclif and Wycliffism', 193.

84 *De Sermone Domini in Monte*, ii, ch. 20, trans. by D. J. Kavanagh, *Saint Augustine, Commentary on the Lord's Sermon on the Mount with Seventeen Related Sermons* (New York: Fathers of the Church, 1951), 179; the Latin here is the text quoted by Wyclif, *Opus Evangelicum* (ed. Loserth, I: 385/21-27). This passage is also quoted in Thomas Aquinas' *Catena Aurea in Quatuor Evangelia* (ed. by P. A. Guarienti (2 vols; Rome: Marsetti, 1953), I: 122-3), as well as in the Wycliffite Glossed Gospels (I consulted the versions in BL, Add. MSS 28026, fols 36^v-37^v, and 41175, fol. 24^v, and Bodleian Library, MS Laud misc. 235, fols 50^v-51^v; on these versions see Hudson, *Premature Reformation*, 249-59, esp. p. 249.

85 *De Veritate Sacrae Scripturae* (ed. Buddensieg, 1: 313/13-16), translation my own.

86 J. M. Mueller, *The Native Tongue and the Word: Developments in English Prose Style, 1380-1580* (Chicago: University Press, 1984), 43.

87 *Dialogus sive Speculum Ecclesie Militantis*, ed. by A. W. Pollard, Wyclif Society (London: Trübner & Co., 1886), 53-5; see also *Exposicio textus Matthei xxiii* (*Opera Minora*, ed. by J. Loserth, Wyclif Society (London: C. K. Paul & Co., 1913), 323-5; for further examples see M. Hurley, '"Scriptura Sola": Wyclif and his Critics', *Traditio* 16 (1960), 306-7.

88 *General Prologue* (*Holy Bible*, ed. Forshall & Madden, 1: 51-2).

89 *Heresy Trials in the Diocese of Norwich, 1428-31*, ed. by N. P. Tanner, Camden Society, 4th ser. 20 (London: Royal Historical Society, 1977), 148; Salisbury, Diocesan Registry, *Register of Bishop William Aiscough*, 2, fol. 53ᵛ. On how some Lollards dismissed all books except the Bible see R. Pecock, *The Reule of Crysten Religioun*, ed. W. Cabell Greet, Early English Text Society, o.s. 171 (London: Oxford University Press, 1927), 17. The question of whether the Wycliffites were advocates of *scriptura sola* has been examined by P. de Vooght, *Les Sources de la Doctrine chrétienne d'après les Théologiens du XIVe siècle et du début du XVe.* [...] (Bruges: Desclée De Brouwer, 1954), 168-200, and Hurley, '"Scriptura Sola"': 275-352; see also B. Smalley's review of the latter in *English Historical Review* 78 (1963), 161-2; Hudson, *Premature Reformation*, 228-31, 375-8.

90 Minnis 'Authorial Intention', 25.

91 On some of those who rejected learning see the passage quoted by R. B. Dobson, *The Peasants' Revolt of 1381* (London: Macmillan, 1970), 364.

92 On this programme see Aston, *Lollards and Reformers*, 193-217; Hudson, *Premature Reformation*, 174-227.

93 *The Lollard Disendowment Bill* (*English Wycliffite Writings*, ed. Hudson, 136/68); as Hudson points out (p. 204), this bill was probably presented in 1410, although the idea about the universities must have circulated amongst the Lollards for some time. Wilks suggests that Wyclif established just such a rival *universitas* or 'Centre for Lollard Studies' in the Leicestershire area after his virtual expulsion from Oxford in 1381 ('Misleading Manuscripts', 160). Five is the number of planned universities in the *St Albans Chronicle* (Hudson, *Premature Reformation*, 174, n. 2).

94 On the gradated nature of their education see, for example, *English Wycliffite Sermons*, ed. Hudson & Gradon, 1: 466/50-59; on their schools and conventicles see Hudson, *Premature Reformation*, 174-200.

95 As suggested by Aston, *Lollards and Reformers*, 201-2.

96 On Lollards memorizing texts see Aston, *Lollards and Reformers*, 201; Hudson, *Premature Reformation*, 190-2.

97 For overviews of the Wycliffites' books see A. Hudson, 'Wycliffite Prose', in *Middle English Prose*, ed. Edwards, 249-70; C. von Nolcken, 'Wycliffite Texts', in *Medieval England: an Encyclopedia*, ed. by M. T. Tavormina (New York: Garland Publishing, forthcoming 1997(?)); E. W. Talbert & S. Harrison Thomson, 'Wyclyf and his Followers', in *A Manual*, ed. Severs, vol. 2, 354-80, 517-33, provides a bibliography, supplemented by Hudson, *Lollards and their Books*, 1-12, 249-52. For a visiting preacher distributing such books see Hudson, *Premature Reformation*, 184-5.

98 On these discussions see Hudson, *Premature Reformation*, 192-5, 208-17. Richard Wyche's assumption that those he addressed in a letter in 1403 would understand his argumentation even when he does not give it in full supports the idea that discussions could be at a fairly high level: on this letter see C. von Nolcken, 'Richard Wyche, a Certain Knight, and the Beginning of the End', in *Lollardy and the Gentry in the Later Middle Ages*, ed. by M. Aston & C. Richmond (Stroud: Sutton Publishing, 1997), 127-54.

99 On the stages whereby suspicion of Lollardy embraced its use of the vernacular see Aston, *Lollards and Reformers*, 206-9; Hudson, *Lollards and their Books*, 141-63; on the stages

whereby the Lollards realized the importance of the vernacular see A. Hudson, 'Wyclif and the English Language', in *Wyclif in his Times*, ed. Kenny, 94-103.

100 Leff, *Heresy*, 2: 587, 593-4 and refs; the text is the *Opus Arduum*, a Latin Apocalypse commentary written between Christmas 1389 and Easter 1390: on this text see Hudson, *Lollards and their Books*, 43-66.

101 Wilkins, *Concilia*, 3: 252.

102 Foxe, *Acts and Monuments*, 3: 221-9; P. McNiven, *Heresy and Politics in the Reign of Henry IV: the Burning of John Badby* (Woodbridge, Suffolk: Boydell, 1987), 79-92.

103 Above, n. 37; on how this legislation affected many writers besides those aligned with the Lollards see H. L. Spencer, *English Preaching in the Late Middle Ages* (Oxford: Clarendon Press, 1993), 163-88; Watson, 'Censorship and Cultural Change', esp. pp. 830-5, 851-9.

104 Foxe, *Acts and Monuments*, 3: 235-9; McNiven, *Heresy and Politics*, 199-219.

105 Wilkins, *Concilia*, 3: 359; Leff, *Heresy*, 2: 597.

106 On Claydon and his books see Swinburn, ed., *Lantern of Liȝt*, vii-xv; Hudson, *Premature Reformation*, 211-14; Hudson, 'Lollard Book Production', 125-6.

107 John Foxe, *Acts and Monuments*, 3: 539; Deanesly, *Lollard Bible*, 356.

108 *Heresy Trials*, ed. Tanner, 73; Hudson, *Lollards and their Books*, 161.

109 Foxe, *Acts and Monuments*, 3: 597; Deanesly, *Lollard Bible*, 358.

110 Deanesly, *Lollard Bible*, 363.

111 Foxe, *Acts and Monuments*, 4: 123-4, 245; J. A. F. Thomson, *The Later Lollards 1414-1520* (Oxford: University Press, 1965), 87.

112 Foxe, *Acts and Monuments*, 4: 186; Deanesly, *Lollard Bible*, 369-70.

113 Foxe, *Acts and Monuments*, 4: 557; Aston, *Lollards and Reformers*, 216-17.

114 In the title of her 1988 book (above, n. 4).

115 Foxe, *Acts and Monuments*, 4: 237; Deanesly, *Lollard Bible*, 367.

116 The first printing of any part of the Wycliffite Bible was John Lewis's *The New Testament by John Wiclif* (London, 1731); the first of the whole Bible was Forshall & Madden's *Holy Bible*; see their 1: i for other early printings.

117 On Lollardy's links with the Reformation, see A. G. Dickens, *The English Reformation* (2nd edn; London: Batsford, 1989), 59-60; Dickens, *Lollards and Protestants in the Diocese of York 1509-1588* (2nd edn; London: Hambledon Press, 1982), 1-15; J. F. Davis, *Heresy and Reformation in the South East of England 1520-1559* (London: Royal Historical Society, 1983).

SOME REPRESENTATIONS OF THE BOOK AND BOOK-MAKING, FROM THE EARLIEST CODEX FORMS TO JOST AMMAN

Christopher Clarkson

INTRODUCTION BY JOHN SHARPE

THE EARLIEST REPRESENTATIONS OF THE CODEX are of the Christian book. Whether in frescoes, mosaics, or manuscripts, the codex for Christians is a symbol of their faith in that it represents the Word made flesh. It is variously depicted closed in the hands of the Pantocrator in the vault of a basilica or open before an evangelist busily copying the text.

Although the codex was born in the ancient near east as a set of wooden or ivory, waxed infilled leaves used by several civilizations including the Hittites, Assyrians, and Greeks, it was the Romans, according to Martial,[1] who adapted flexible, foldable materials – papyrus or parchment – to the purpose of a handy day-to-day notebook. Unfortunately none of these *pugillares* survive. A number of the wooden and ivory books do exist. Fragments of papyrus codices from the early second century and some complete examples from before the fifth have also been preserved by the hospitable sands of Egypt.

The earliest surviving codices are Christian. Their leaves are of papyrus and their texts are in Greek. The codex came to be identified as the earthly vessel of the Word and hence is represented so in Christian art. As an object full of meaning for the believing community, it was depicted together with the Evangelists who heeded the Great Commission to go and spread the Gospel to all the world. As a portable object, it was also a gathering of artistic, literary, and cultural ideas. And when it was copied and bound in its new home, it accrued characteristics identifiable with its rebirth. Hence the study of the history of the transmission and evolution of binding techniques becomes an important adjunct to understanding the cultural diversities of the communities where it originated and through which it passed.

By combining both an examination of the book's representation in art and a study of its existing structures, Christopher Clarkson broadens our vision and understanding of the communities where these books were produced and preserved. The story of its shape and construction cannot be separated from the early record of the propagation of the Gospel and its transmission in the form of the book. From the most simply

---

1 See S. P. Fowler, 'Martial and the Book', *Romus Roman Literature and Ideology II: Essays in Honor of J. P. Sullivan*, XXIV: 1 (1995), 31-58.

constructed codices in the earliest Christian community in Egypt through to the work of printers in the sixteenth century, Clarkson tells the story of the progress of shaping and forming the codex, of reading and copying the text, adapting forms as they were received and passing them on to the next community and generation. As each subsequent audience read, recopied, illuminated, bound, and rebound their books, they added a bit of their own history and art in the construction and materials they used. Carried in hand, bag, or pocket, the codex travelled easily throughout the literate world, from Africa to northern Europe, changing in shape, construction, and materials, but never in format: a gathering of leaves of which both sides were usable, fastened together along one side and wrapped in a protective covering. Clarkson's expertise as a binder and conservator illuminates the story of the Christian book as it reveals itself materially within its own covers.   JS

*

IT IS STILL TRUE TO SAY that the history of bookbinding is mainly viewed as the history of a two-dimensional decorative art. But I regard bookbinding as a fascinating, three-dimensional mechanical craft and one which should be held in higher regard within the general history of medieval technology. It is a subject which boasts numerous surviving examples for the Romanesque and medieval periods and, as these examples demonstrate, it is a subject full of material and structural variation.

In my terminology, 'binding' simply means taking an ordered (collated) number of sheets and connecting them together along one side, creating a 'spine' and thus producing a 'codex'. The foundation to the character of a codex is the style and technique of this connection, which until the twentieth century has been a system of sewing or tacketting. (In this paper I am going to concentrate only upon multi-quired text-blocks within stiff boards.)

In the Middle East, by the fourth and early fifth centuries AD, sheets were being folded and sewn through the spine fold onto some kind of support (such as the cover). There is evidence to suggest that quires were linked to one another by the sewing thread, creating a multi-quired text-block. Soon after this fully developed, link or 'chain-stitch' sewing appears and continued through to modern times (in Ethiopian bindings, for example [Pl. 19]). This term describes a family of sewing methods in which the thread or threads run along the inside the spine-fold of each quire. Every time it exits at a sewing station (passes from inside the fold to the outside), the thread loops round that from a previously sewn quire. The result gives the appearance of thread chains running at right angles to the spine folds. There usually is no support material contained within these thread links. Boards were attached to the text block either by utilizing the same thread (thus being incorporated in the 'primary' sewing system) or by pre-working both boards with thread 'bridles' opposite the sewing stations, and then attaching the primary sewing to these bridles.

Without any material covering the spine, this type of sewing allowed the book to open easily and quite flat. Viewed from the tail of the fully open book, the spine-folds can be seen to touch 'back-to-back'. This type of binding actually relaxes on opening, a characteristic directly opposite to that of western bindings going back to the Carolingian period, in which quires are sewn to supporting bands. Another example shows a similar shape of the open book, this one from the church of San Vitale in Ravenna which was consecrated in 547 or 548 (Pl. 20). Note that the two parts of the open text-block fall backwards, a characteristic one would never observe in representations of the western codex of the ninth century or later.

Another characteristic of the chain-stitch family of bindings is the triangular-shaped space or void formed at the spine of the half-open book, often represented by contemporary artists. An example dating from the sixth century is the familiar full-page painting (said to be Italian) inserted in the Codex Amiatinus, which shows the prophet Ezra seated in front of an armarium (Pl. 21). A triangular-shaped void is formed by the spine of the half-open book which has fallen to the floor.

Yet, the hanging ties and so-called markers with arrowheads seen in Pl. 19 call into question the type of attachment of the book's covering material. Is the cover firmly attached, or is it some form of loose wrapper? Is it a type of chemise, possibly held on the book boards by means of 'envelope pockets' similar to the later medieval chemise?

The two symbols of the Great Registers bound in codex form, as illustrated on two different pages in the Roman *Notitia Dignitatum* (Pl. 22 & 23), are most interesting in this regard. The manuscript shown here is a Renaissance copy of a ninth- or tenth-century copy, now lost, of an original Roman manuscript composed at the end of the fourth century AD, also lost. Note how one of the covers appears like an untrimmed skin (Pl. 22). Is it a loose wrapper over bound codices, or a form of chemise? The brick-like appearance of the text-blocks appears to represent multi-quired bindings. Even in these third-hand copies the Renaissance artist has been interested in accurately portraying the codex. Compare his careful drawing of these objects with the thought-less way he has represented the rolls in both illustrations. Accepting a certain loss of understanding of early codex construction by both later artists, this surely reflects the fascination which the late Classical artist had shown in these complex objects. He has carefully drawn the extensions to the cover, the folding marks and the fastenings. It is my opinion that what have been referred to as the 'emblems' on the covers are, in fact, closing systems of some kind, perhaps incorporating furry animals' tails. Even with this copy of a copy, they exactly line up with the holes in the flaps. That on folio 104^v has nine holes and seven ties (Pl. 22), but possibly the ties at the two tail corners served two holes, closing both the sides and tail flaps. The second example of a codex, fol. 146^r, has eighteen holes and eighteen ties (Pl. 23). Note that the two illustrations appear to reflect various fashions and are indicative of separate and distinct styles.

To the modern observer the pure chain-stitch has a certain looseness, and it is diffi-cult to imagine large parchment tomes such as Vaticanus, Sinaiticus, and Alexandrinus being well enough supported by such a sewing. Perhaps they originally included some form of support – such as threads or cords – in the chains of stitches, and support at the ends of the spine, a mechanically important region. Although there is no evidence among the extremely scarce primary sources to suggest that this happened until much later, perhaps other means (which we can only guess at) were used to strengthen such structures.

In northern Europe we first find the chains being formed around double cords, the thread creating a repeated chevron pattern now called 'herring-bone', a term which well describes its appearance (Pl. 24). Once finished, the cords were laced in a variety of ways into wooden covers and anchored. Such a technique causes slight tensions when the book is opened, inducing the leaves to curve; we notice this characteristic in northern European representations of the open book as early as the later eighth century. (Some examples are the Gospel-Book of Ada, c. 780s; the Gospel-Book of Saint Médard of Soissons, 827; and the Evangelist Luke in a ninth-century manuscript at Fulda.)

The Romanesque period is the first from which a reasonable number of manuscripts, still within their contemporary bindings, have survived. The great majority are books from monastic libraries, which at first look similar in appearance and technique. On closer acquaintance, however, we find that they differ considerably in certain respects. It is a sobering thought that today, just when we are beginning to realize how much Romanesque bookbinding has to teach us, such survivors are being destroyed through over-use and crude and uneducated library and rebinding practices.

The typical stiff-board monastic bindings of the Romanesque period in north-western Europe consisted of calfskin or sheepskin parchment quires sewn in a herring-bone style on two or three heavy, slit, whittawed bands, a change from the Carolingian/Anglo-Saxon double cords. In the last fifteen years I have been recording other, quite different, sewing systems as well as herring-bone, coming from the same monastic order and period.[1] Wooden boards were attached via simpler, straight lacing-paths, probably dictated by this heavier band material. Invariably the bands entered tunnels in the edge of the boards and emerged into a channel cut in the exterior face. Then either they were anchored with a wedge ('short lacing' [Pl. 25]), or they passed back through the board and ran along a channel cut into the inner face before being anchored ('long lacing').[2] This sewing system was reinforced and a mechanism achieved that allowed the book to open wide by the addition of heavy pieces of hide – 'tab stiffeners' at either end of the spine. These extended beyond the ends of the spine and were often cut in a curve and decorated with coloured threads, embroidered textiles, etc. So characteristic of Roman-esque binding were endband tabs that seemingly no book, however sketchily drawn, was shown without them.

A lighter-weight cover of whittawed skin was pasted on and turned in around the board edges, but at the spine it was left extending and connected to the tab stiffeners and 'facing' fabric. The fore-edge corners, where the covering material was turned in on the inner face of each board, show a mixture of techniques: tongued, lapped or mitred, and stuck with paste. In England these corners were often beautifully sewn, the mitred edges of the covering leather being closed in such a way that the thread is hidden. Is it possible that these practices are remnants from the great stitchery traditions of the Anglo-Saxons? Such corners disappear from use by the mid-twelfth century.

The appearance of the finished bookbinding is square and block-like; the spine is flat in cross-section and not convex, as in later binding. It was common practice to add a heavy whittawed chemise to all working books. This extra protection had 'skirts' extending at head- and tail-edges and a generous fore-edge flap. All was usually edged with a skin piping. The chemise was attached by envelope pockets which fitted tightly over the fore-edge half of the boards. A strap (two straps on large books) wrapped around the fore-edge and caught on a side pin protruding from the centre of the other board. The pin was located on the lower board in England, but on the upper board in the Germanic countries, a fashion which appears to have caught on in the late Anglo-Saxon period. The fore-edge flap of the chemise was tacketted to the strap so that when the book was closed the strap brought the fore-edge flap with it. Attaching the medieval chemise via envelope pockets allowed the chemise skirts to extend any amount beyond the book-edges, and in the fourteenth and fifteenth centuries this advantage led to the development of the so-called lappen binding and girdle book (Pl. 26).

The frontispiece to a manuscript of the works of St Ambrose, in the Bamberg Staats-bibliothek (Pl. 27), contains the earliest known illustrations representing the stages in Romanesque bookmaking; it dates from the first half of the twelfth century. Under Hermann I (1123-47) the library of the Benedictine Abbey of St Michelsberg in Bam-berg was greatly enlarged and the scriptorium reached a high point of activity. The full-page picture (a singleton), drawn in light orange and dark brown ink, depicts the Archangel Michael surrounded by ten roundels illustrating various processes involved in the manufacture of books. Starting in the top left-hand corner and proceeding anti-clockwise we are shown (not in order of the processes, or at least as we would now perceive them) the following:

1) 'Nibbling' a quill: note the shape of the knife, the complete removal of the barbs of the quill and the fact that one scoop only has been created (unless a second is about to be formed).

2) Although this drawing has been described as boring holes in the wooden cover boards to receive the spine bands, or else depicting a monk at work on a diptych (which is the more likely of the two suggestions), I feel that it simply shows a monk with wax tablet and stylus; note the point at one end and flat bar for erasure at the other. Various twelfth-century European representations of tablets are shown with the same round heads (and Sotheby's recently sold a fifteenth-century German hinged tablet of similar shape[3]). If this suggestion is the correct one, then it would appear to be exceptional in the series, unless it depicts the sketching out of ideas or instructions.

3) The manufacture of vellum: note the rectangular frame or 'herse', the possible indication of wooden tightening pegs as used in northern Europe today, and the shape and construction of the lunar knife.

4) Probably depicts the making of the wooden cover boards. A cabinet-maker's axe, here used for shaping, was a common tool from early times.

5) This roundel (bottom centre) may show a finished volume in use, or possibly a scribe being corrected or taught.

6) This drawing has been described as representing a monk making the clasps, bosses or other metal fittings for the binding. Certainly there is a hammer and possibly some type of anvil, but it is difficult to determine what is in his left hand.

7) Probably represents vellum being cut into sheets, if the implements are a knife and straight-edge. The knife is exactly similar to that used for quill cutting.

8) The earliest representation I know of a sewing frame. Luckily it is well observed and described by the artist. The uprights, which are probably attached directly to the edge of a table, are not threaded but end in forks(?) which support the horizontal bar. The artist has tilted this bar so that one can observe that it is slotted exactly like the modern German sewing frame, and that some type of key device is used to support the bands. The monk is in the process of sewing folded quires on three bands. Probably because these drawings are very small, only single lines are used to represent the heavy double whittawed bands used at the period.

9) One of the more difficult roundels to interpret. It has even been described in a recent publication as showing a monk who has placed the pen behind his ear and is busy painting the manuscript. Perhaps the author of this interpretation thought that the

monk was holding a bowl or dish of paint in his left hand, but surely it is nothing like the bowl held by the monk decorating the arch under the feet of St Michael. I think either that the monk is folding sheets into quires with a bone folder, ready for binding; or that he has his hand inside an already bound book and is at a particular stage in covering. The implement in his right hand could be a knife, as it has a similar curved and notched end to the knife shown in the first roundel described.

10) A monk uses, or proudly shows off, the finished volume.

The following centuries in western Europe utilised a wide variety of binding structures, often made by or for the layman. Some appear to be developments of the ancient chain-stitch, in which quires are simply sewn through a limp cover of heavy whittawed skin. The growth of universities stimulated much of this variety which I find so difficult to categorize: sewn with or without the use of the sewing frame, sewn to inflexible spine support, semi-flexible or indeed no support, simply tacketted in various ways, etc. But limited time here forces me to concentrate on wooden-board bindings.

In the thirteenth century a fashion developed of sewing quires on numerous bands. Such bands became lighter in weight and were usually pre-rolled whittawed thongs. By the mid-fifteenth century the number of bands had reduced again to what we would consider a more reasonable number.

The earliest binding I know in which the bands do not enter tunnels in the edge of the board, but lie in a channel on the cushioned exterior before passing through the board to the inner face, can possibly be dated to the 1220s. Although the spine is still flat in cross-section, the lacing-path pattern is totally different. The fact that the bands enter the boards from the exterior face points to a development which resulted by the late fifteenth century in the hand-bound book as we know it today, with features such as a convex spine with raised bands.

This late Gothic wooden-boarded binding was produced by sewing the quires to double thongs or cords using a sewing frame. The thread created a swelling at the spine, accommodated by the shaping of the wooden boards. The boards were laced on so that on closing the book a convex spine was produced (Pl. 25). A leather cover was then pasted around this structure and turned-in around the board edges. The cover was held down with thread on each side of the raised bands and the ends of the spine, and left to dry. Tying-up boards and a lying press were utilised for this purpose; consequently indentations from the thread show across the spine.

The Book of Trades (Ständebuch) by Jost Amman and Hans Sachs was originally published in 1568, and the woodcuts each have a poem below. That for the bookbinder, translated literally, reads: 'The bookbinder binds large and small books on all subjects in parchment or planed boards which are fitted with clasps and ornamented. Some books are gilded on the edges.' This is not very informative, but luckily the woodcut is more so and worth describing.

The sewing frame appears as part of the table; at its leading edge a clamping device to anchor the band material is possibly depicted. The bands are held vertically by hangers attached to a crossbar. In the foreground a figure is shown ploughing a book-edge. Another method of trimming employed a drawknife and such a tool is shown near his foot. (The draw-knife is still shown in use in eighteenth-century bookbinding manuals.)

A text-block hammer lies on the floor under the lying-press. A bow-saw and plane appear in the right fore-ground. Hanging on the wall are a cabinet-maker's axe and rasps for shaping the wooden boards. Alongside is a gimlet, possibly for boring holes through the boards for the band slips. Above hang tying-up boards, spools of thread and a ball of cord. Hanging from a rack by the window are two rolls and possibly a creaser – all used for decorative embossing of leather covers. In the left foreground is a lying-press with the spine of a leather-covered binding protruding. It is most interesting that the woodcut does not show tying-up boards in use.

On the shelf under the tools are finished bound books, one with fore-edge clasps fitted. These books are shown standing on end, a very new fashion for the mid-sixteenth century, and one which causes direct stress on the sewing structure. From this period when the shape and style of the Western book had already been established, the bookbinder has grappled with the problem of structural stress. He has never been able to resolve it very well. Adopting such techniques as artificial rounding and backing or gluing and overlining of the spine have not proven particularly successful. These stiffen the spine's convex shape but unfortunately inhibit the book's opening.

Dirk de Bray, in his instruction book of 1658, mentions that a wedge-shape to the finished binding is desirable, so that the fore-edge clasps catch firmly. Such a comment is an archaism from the time before the bookshelf demanded books with parallel boards.

NOTES

1 See C. Clarkson, 'A Hitherto Unrecorded English Romanesque Book Sewing Technique', *Bibliologia volume* 14, Brepols, Turnhout, 1996, 215-239, and 'English Monastic Bookbinding in the 12th Century'. Post Print of ERICE (ITALY) Conference September, 1992.

2 See C. Clarkson, 'Further Studies in Anglo-Saxon to Norman Binding Techniques of Manuscripts in The Bodleian Library, *Bibliologia volume* 14, Brepols, Turnhout, 1996, 154-214; bindings X-XIV.

3 See Sotheby Catalogue, 'Western Manuscripts and Miniatures', Tuesday 21st June 1994, Lot 81.

THE ARMENIAN BOOKMAKING TRADITION IN THE CHRISTIAN EAST

A COMPARISON WITH THE SYRIAC AND GREEK TRADITIONS

Sylvie L. Merian

THE STUDY OF BOOKBINDING TECHNIQUES of different cultures has, regrettably, often been neglected in medieval studies. This is unfortunate, since the close examination of a book as an archaeological object can reveal a wealth of information not otherwise obvious to scholars. The characteristic techniques used by literate societies to construct their books, as well as the materials and methods used, may reveal cultural interactions and relationships not necessarily evident by other means. These book-objects form distinctive, easily recognizable symbols to each national culture and some of the traditional methods used for constructing them lasted for centuries.

This article will briefly describe the traditional Armenian methods of crafting books, comparing and contrasting these techniques with those of the bookmaking traditions of Armenia's close neighbours, the Greeks and Syrians. The Armenian techniques have been studied by the present author.[1] The comparative material presented here to describe the Greek/Byzantine methods has been obtained primarily from previously published works.[2] Until now, very little codicological material on Syriac manuscripts has been published.[3] The Syriac material presented here is based on the author's examination of 96 Syriac manuscripts from 14 different collections.[4]

This Armenian gospel-book (Pl. 28) can be easily identified as a medieval Armenian religious manuscript. It is distinctive, and its form endured for centuries. The production of these manuscripts was a laborious and complicated task accomplished through the co-operation of numerous skilled craftsmen, usually priests or monks in monasteries. The traditions were passed down from master to student for generations. However, calling it a 'medieval' object can be somewhat misleading – the methods used by Armenian bookbinders to produce this book-form lasted well into the eighteenth century, and there are even a few extant examples from the early nineteenth century.[5]

Even though the Armenian method of producing books is distinctive, Armenians and Armenian culture did not exist in a vacuum. A close examination of the bookbinding craft will provide us with evidence of the manifold contacts that this nation had with other cultures, its aesthetic sensibilities, its trade relations, and perhaps even the origins of this craft in Armenian society. As we shall see, there are clear links with Greek and Syriac bookmaking traditions, and even with some western European bindings up to the twelfth century.

Sylvie L. Merian

In most Western and Near Eastern bookmaking traditions, before the scribe could begin copying a text there were numerous complicated preparatory steps. The writing material, as well as the inks, pigments, and pens had to be manufactured. Someone (the scribe, an assistant, or a professional paper-maker) had to first produce the handmade paper, or acquire it by importation. It is not yet clear whether Armenians manufactured their own paper before the seventeenth century, but they certainly bought paper from Islamic paper production centres, such as Tabriz or Damascus, as this is specifically mentioned in some colophons.[6] Imported European paper was also bought.[7] Especially in later periods, European paper was also used by both Syriac and Greek scribes.[8] If using parchment, someone had to undertake the complex, time-consuming and malodorous task of producing the parchment from animal skin.[9] He then had to prepare the paper or parchment by cutting it to the desired size, polishing it with a smooth stone or shell (if paper), and folding it into quires. Polishing paper was a preparatory step commonly performed in the Near East, but was apparently not part of the European tradition.[10] Sometimes an assistant or relative would be given this monotonous task – in some Armenian colophons, scribes have even thanked their wives for undertaking this work.[11]

The scribe or an assistant would next rule the paper or parchment to produce discreet horizontal lines so that he could write neatly on the page. This was commonly done by evenly pricking the edges of the leaf with a pin or the point of a knife; the space between pin-points indicated how wide a writing margin or line was desired. The horizontal ruling lines would be made by connecting the parallel pricking marks with a straight edge by using a hard point or with a light carbon or lead line.[12] Vertical ruling lines were also made to divide the columns of writing. Another method for producing ruling lines used in the Near East was by use of a ruling frame (called *toghashar* in Armenian, or *mastara* in Arabic), a board with parallel strings or wires stretched across it.[13] Paper or parchment, perhaps slightly dampened, would be pressed against the frame. The strings or wires caused protrusions or raised ridges, forming parallel ruling lines for writing. Armenians occasionally ruled both paper and parchment manuscripts with a ruling frame.[14] At least one researcher has identified Greek manuscripts in which the paper was ruled by the use of a ruling frame.[15] None of the Syriac manuscripts in this sample showed any evidence of having been ruled by using a ruling frame, but it is probable that such frames were used at least occasionally.[16]

After copying the text, the scribe would pass it to the artist for decoration (unless, of course, he were also the artist, not an uncommon occurrence). Although the focus of this discussion is the construction of these manuscripts and not their decoration, it should be mentioned that the production of illuminated Armenian and Greek manuscripts, especially in books of Sacred Scripture, was a highly developed art. In the case of Armenian manuscripts, the tradition persisted until the eighteenth century.[17] The majority of Syriac manuscripts examined for this study were either not decorated at all, or only crudely illustrated, although finer Syriac illumination has been studied and published.[18]

The quires (the packets of folded leaves of paper or parchment which will make up the text block) would now have to be prepared for sewing. In the Armenian and Greek traditions, the first step in this process was to cut V-shaped notches in the folds of each quire at each sewing station in order to facilitate the passing of the needle and thread.

These notches are so common in Greek bindings that they were given the name *grecquage* by bookbinders.[19] Curiously, however, V-notches have not been observed in any Syriac manuscripts so far. An unusual feature seen in a few Armenian bindings, but not reported in any other traditions, is a variation of the V-notch: some were made with W-notches (the most common modification), but sometimes round or even square-shaped notches were used.[20] The notches in both Armenian and Greek bookbinding served also to recess the sewing, producing a book with a smooth spine; that is, there are no raised bands visible on the spine of the book.

For covers, Armenian binders used very thin wooden boards, only 2 to 5 mm thick.[21] The wooden boards used for Greek bindings were much thicker, usually ranging anywhere from 5 to 24 mm, and averaging about 8 to 10 mm.[22] The boards used in Syriac bindings were generally thick also, ranging from 4 to 14 mm in my sample. In all three traditions, the boards were cut the same size as the text block; i.e. they were made without squares.[23]

Armenian binders placed the grain of the boards horizontally, that is, perpendicular to the spine. This is highly unusual – in almost all other traditions, including the Greek and the Syriac, the grain runs parallel to the spine.[24] The Armenian method was apparently done for a specific reason: several holes were pierced through the thin boards, a few centimetres away from the spine side, equal to the number and positions of the notches. These holes were used to attach the boards to the text block with the support cords. If the grain of the wood were placed parallel to the spine it would risk vertical cracking at the weakened vertical line formed by the holes in the thin boards. Placing the grain horizontally prevented this potential problem.[25] Even if the thin board cracked horizontally, it could not become detached from the rest of the text, while a vertically cracked cover could fall off.

To secure the quires and form the text block, Armenian binders used a method of 'supported' sewing, where the sewing is attached to double cords for support. A herringbone stitch was commonly employed. It is unusual to find supported sewing used in the Near East. Byzantine, Syriac, Coptic, Ethiopian, and Islamic bookbinders all used 'unsupported' sewing.[26] Armenian binders seem to be the only ones in this part of the world to construct their books with supported sewing. However, most western European manuscripts bound after the mid-eighth century used some form of supported sewing.[27] Although it is not precisely clear when Armenian binders began using sewing supports, they may have learned the technique through contact with Europeans who came to the Armenian kingdom of Cilicia between the eleventh and thirteenth centuries during the Crusades, when Armenians definitely had access to Latin manuscripts.[28]

Different cultures developed their own specific ways of attaching the boards to the sewn text block. The board-attachment method used by bookbinders is an important identifying characteristic which distinguishes one bookmaking tradition from another. In the Armenian tradition, the support cords are looped in a certain way to the holes previously drilled into the thin wooden boards. They form double cords attached to the boards, and the signatures are sewn around these cords. This 'loop board attachment' is seen with amazing consistency in Armenian bindings dating from at least the fourteenth to the eighteenth centuries.[29]

A number of board-attachment methods are found in Greek and Byzantine bindings.

One published study has documented at least fourteen different types used by Greek bookbinders, all of them unsupported.[30] The thicker boards permitted the development of channels and tunnels to be gouged into the wood, allowing this wide variety of different board-attachment methods to develop.

The majority of Syriac bindings which I have examined seemed to have been constructed using one method to attach the text block to the boards. It consists of a type of cord 'anchor' which was wound into the first hole in the board, and then, without cutting the cord, wound into the next one, and so on. The text block was then attached to these wound 'anchors' (Pl. 29a).

After the text block was securely attached to the boards, Armenian, Greek, and Syrian bookbinders all lined the spine of the text block with a mull, a piece of rough tabby-weave cloth which was glued or pasted around the spine and reached about a third of the way on each wooden board. Greek and Armenian binders usually used only one layer of fabric.[31] The majority of Syriac manuscripts examined for this study, however, were made with multiple layers of cloth, anywhere from two to five layers of fabric.

The binder's next step would have been to work the headbands. These are a form of decorative sewing found at the head and tail of the spine of the book, which have an important structural function in that they form yet another attachment between the text block and the covers. In Armenian, Greek, and Syriac manuscripts, the headbands form raised bumps at the head and tail, because they are also sewn down into the boards as well as into the centre of each quire. They are consequently called 'raised' headbands, for obvious reasons. Again, the method of working the headbands is particular to each bookmaking tradition. Note, however, that raised headbands were not made in any European tradition, nor by Islamic bookbinders.[32]

There are various steps to producing these headbands, the first of which is the attachment of a primary cord core, done in the same way in the Armenian and Syriac traditions.[33] Again, Greek manuscripts are found with a greater variety of primary cores for working their headbands; at least three types have been documented.[34] The decorative colourful secondary sewing is distinct in each tradition. Even though Armenian, Greek, and Syriac headbands are all raised, each one developed its own clearly distinct type or types. The majority of Syriac manuscripts I have examined so far were made with one particular type of headband, as seen in Union Theological Seminary, New York, Syr. MS 12, a book of Nestorian theological writings dated 1696[35] (Pl. 29b).

The Greek binders developed a wider range of raised headband types, although these are all peculiar only to Greek manuscripts.[36] It is certainly possible that these may be particular to certain regions or monasteries, but unfortunately the majority of Greek manuscripts do not include colophons giving us the date or place of manufacture, so it has been difficult to identify a specific style with a region or period thus far.

Armenian binders generally lined the inside of the wooden covers with some type of dyed or printed cloth. The loop board attachment cords mentioned above are usually visible below the fabric.[37] San Lazzaro MS 569 is an example in a collection of sermons and homilies copied in Palu in 1538. Many of the Syriac manuscripts examined in this study were also made with cloth doublures; however, Greek binders seem not to have bothered with this step, leaving the inside of the wooden boards uncovered.[38]

Next, the binders would have covered the books with leather. Armenian bindings were generally covered with goatskin or calfskin, while Greek binders seem to have primarily used goatskin or sheepskin.[39] It is likely that Syrian binders also used the skins of goat, sheep, and/or calf, but unfortunately most of the extant leather bindings examined in this study were too damaged to be able to determine the leather type with any certainty.

The Armenian binders added an interesting feature to their manuscripts: a separate leather, fabric-lined, rectangular flap at the fore-edge of the book. These flaps were glued or pasted to the inside back covers, and were often blind-tooled.[40] They were probably added to protect the fore-edge of the book. Neither Greek nor Syriac manuscripts include this feature.[41]

Armenian binders generally blind-tooled the leather covers and the fore-edge flap, that is, stamped the leather without gold.[42] A common decoration is a blind-tooled stepped cross (Pl. 28). The decoration of bindings will not be discussed in this article (an extensive study in itself) other than to mention that the Greeks also blind-tooled their bindings.[43] It does not seem to have been as important to Syrian bookbinders to decorate their covers; most of the manuscripts examined in this sample with surviving leather were not decorated at all.[44] The few which were decorated had been blind-tooled with unrefined geometric designs.[45]

This detailed examination of the bookbinding traditions and techniques of these three East Christian cultures has indicated that there are a number of similarities as well as some notable differences in their bookmaking traditions. What historical and cultural circumstances might have allowed these similarities and differences to develop?

Although ties between Armenians, Greeks, and Syrians can be found extremely early, the literary evidence dates from the earliest period of the invention of the Armenian alphabet in the fifth century AD by the scholar and cleric Mashtots'. In his fifth-century biography, written by his student Koriwn, there is abundant testimony to these connections.[46] The need for an alphabet was clear to Mashtots', since the Armenian people could not understand the Christian services which were given in either Syriac or Greek, depending on whether they were in Persarmenia or in Byzantine Armenia. Mashtots' himself was learned in the Greek language and in Greek literature, and eventually travelled to Syria to learn Syriac. He sent some of his students to study in a Syriac school in Edessa and others to Samosata to learn Greek. After inventing the Armenian alphabet, he sent more students to Edessa to translate works of the Syriac Fathers into Armenian, as well as others to Greek regions to translate Greek writings. The Bible was translated into Armenian from the Greek version of the Septuagint and from Syriac texts. He also instructed his students to bring back authentic copies of religious books. Clearly, the earliest Armenian scribes were unquestionably exposed to Greek and Syriac manuscripts, and must have learned the craft of bookmaking from those contacts. Although we may never know precisely what fifth-century Greek, Syriac, or Armenian bindings looked like (since it is unlikely that any have survived), it would be logical that they should have closely resembled each other at first, and developed their own special character as time passed.

Intriguing questions remain. It has been determined that Armenian binding methods persisted for at least four centuries in various geographic regions.[47] Why is there so much more variety in Greek and Byzantine bindings? Greek manuscripts have been

constructed with at least fourteen variations of board-attachment methods and numerous types of raised headbands, while Armenian bindings were consistently made with
one type of attachment and one style of raised headband. The preliminary research on
Syriac manuscripts presented here indicates that Syrian binders probably also used one
consistent type of board attachment method, and one or perhaps two styles of raised
headbands.[48] One possible reason may be that Armenian bookmaking was generally
confined to conservative monasteries, where the traditions were passed down carefully
from master to student. Armenians and their monasteries were situated in a fairly wide
range of geographic areas, since the people were often compelled to move because of
political circumstances or forced deportations. However, this geographic distribution
cannot compare to the vastness of the Byzantine empire throughout history. The
expansiveness of the empire probably contributed to the development of more
individualistic methods in the Greek monasteries.

This examination of manuscripts of Sacred Scripture of these three East Christian
traditions has identified similarities as well as differences in their characteristics and
in the techniques used to construct them. The next step would be to interpret these
observations further in view of the historical, religious, and political contexts in which
these cultures found themselves, which could have had an important effect on the final
form of their holy books. Only then will we be able to more fully comprehend the
cultures which produced these sacred words, as well as be permitted a glimpse into the
lives of the thousands of scribes, artists, and bookbinders who produced them. In this
way we might eventually truly understand the spirituality and reverence which their
makers sought to convey through their books.

NOTES

1 S. L. Merian, 'The Structure of Armenian Bookbinding and Its Relation to Near Eastern
Bookmaking Traditions' (Ph.D. diss., Columbia University, 1993); S. L. Merian, T. F.
Mathews, & M. V. Orna, 'The Making of an Armenian Manuscript', in *Treasures in Heaven:
Armenian Illuminated Manuscripts*, ed. by T. F. Mathews & R. S. Wieck (New York: The
Pierpont Morgan Library, 1994), 124-34; Merian, 'Cilicia as the Locus of European Influence
on Medieval Armenian Book Production', *Armenian Review* (Winter 1992, 45, no. 4/180),
61-72; Merian, 'Characteristics and Techniques of Armenian Bookbinding: Report on
Research in Progress', in *Atti del Quinto Simposio Internazionale di Arte Armena* (Venice:
San Lazzaro Press, 1991), 413-23; Merian, 'From Venice to Isfahan and Back: The Making
of an Armenian Manuscript in Early 18th Century Persia', in *Roger Powell: The Compleat
Binder*, ed. by J. L. Sharpe [Bibliologia 14] (Turnhout: Brepols, 1996), 280-91. Important
introductory research on Armenian binding techniques was published by B. van Regemorter,
a pioneer in the study of binding structures: 'La reliure arménienne', *Bazmavep*, 111, no. 8-
10 (1953), 200-4. She mentions Armenian bindings also in: 'La reliure byzantine', *Revue
belge d'archéologie et d'histoire de l'art* XXXVI (1967): 122-4.
2 B. van Regemorter, 'La reliure des manuscrits grecs', *Scriptorium* VIII (1954), 3-23, and 'La
reliure byzantine', 99-162. C. Federici & K. Houlis, *Legature Bizantine Vaticane* (Rome:
Fratelli Palombi Editori, 1988) is a study of 112 Greek bindings from the Vatican Library,
whose texts date from *c.* thirteenth to the seventeenth centuries. See also: A. di Febo,
K. Houlis, G. Mazzuco, & S. J. Voicu, *Legature Bizantine Vaticane e Marciane*, Exhibition

catalogue, 9 Sept.-30 Oct. 1989 at the Biblioteca Nazionale Marciana (Venice, 1989).

3 Some information on writing materials, inks, quires, etc. of Syriac manuscripts is available in the following: W. H. P. Hatch, *Album of Dated Syriac Manuscripts* (Boston: American Academy of Sciences, 1946), 3-24; W. Wright, *Catalogue of the Syriac Manuscripts in the British Museum* (London, 1872), 3, pp. xxv-xxix.

4 I would like to thank the Bibliographic Society of America for their 1993 Fellowship award, which enabled me to travel and undertake the research for this project. My thanks go to Dana Josephson for reading and correcting my typescript.

5 For example, UCLA Special Collections, Armenian MSS 28 and 29, two Rituals copied and bound in 1814 and 1817 respectively. They were bound using the traditional methods.

6 A. K. Sanjian, *Colophons of Armenian Manuscripts 1301-1480* (Cambridge, Mass.: Harvard University Press, 1969), 11.

7 The papers of many Armenian manuscripts examined were watermarked, indicating European origin. See: Merian, 'From Venice to Isfahan and Back' (cited above, n. 1) for a discussion of the Venetian paper used in an Armenian manuscript copied in Isfahan (San Lazzaro, Venice, MS 1571).

8 J. Irigoin, 'Papiers orientaux et papiers occidentaux', *La paléographie grecque et byzantine: Paris 21-25 octobre 1974* (Paris: Editions du CNRS, 1977), 45-54. Prof. Robert Allison of Bates University (Lewiston, Maine) is undertaking a long-term database project on water-marks and paper from the Philotheon Monastery. I examined many Syriac manuscripts with watermarked paper, mostly seventeenth-century and later; one example is Union Theological Seminary MS Syr. 6, a Nestorian book of prayers and services dated 1658, whose paper was watermarked with three crescent moons ('tre lune', a watermark common in papers produced in the Veneto and exported eastward).

9 For a description of parchment making, see C. de Hamel, *Scribes and Illuminators* (London: The British Museum and Toronto: University of Toronto Press, 1992), 8-16.

10 I. Mattozzi, *Produzione e commercio della carta nello stato veneziano settecentesco* (Bologna, 1975), p. 49, n. 90, discusses a method of burnishing paper by scribes in the Ottoman empire. A Mughal illustration from an album of Jahangir, c. 1600-1610, depicts book craftsmen at work, including a paper polisher (Freer Gallery of Art, acq. 54.116); for a reproduction of this illustration, see: M. C. Beach, *The Imperial Image* (Washington, D.C.: The Freer Gallery of Art, 1981), 159. In the late nineteenth to early twentieth century, Syriac scribes were described as polishing paper in preparation for copying manuscripts. See E. A. Wallis Budge, *By Nile and Tigris: a Narrative of Journeys in Egypt and Mesopotamia on Behalf of the British Museum Between the Years 1886-1913* (London, 1920), II, p. 72. I would like to thank Prof. James Coakley of Harvard University for indicating this reference to me.

11 In the colophon of a manuscript dated 1401 (Erevan, Matenadaran MS 4670), copied and illustrated by the famed artist and scribe Tserun, he thanks his wife Arghun for having laboured in polishing the paper. See *XV Dari Hayeren Tseragreri Hishatakaranner*, ed. by L. S. Khach'ikyan (Erevan, 1950), I (1401-50), p. 7, colophon no. 4.

12 Ruling lines of Greek manuscripts have been extensively studied by J. Leroy, *Les types de réglure des manuscrits grecs* (Paris: Editions du CNRS, 1976).

13 Ruling frames were used by many cultures in the Near East: Islamic, Hebrew, and Armenian, among others. For Islamic manuscripts see: G. Bosch, J. Carswell, & G. Petherbridge, *Islamic Bindings and Bookmaking: a Catalogue of an Exhibition*, The Oriental Institute, University of Chicago, 18 May-18 August 1981 (Chicago: University of Chicago, 1981), 41. The Metropolitan Museum of Art in New York has a seventeenth-eighteenth-century Islamic ruling frame in the collection of the Islamic Department, acc. no. 1973.1; see *Treasures in Heaven*, ed. Mathews & Wieck, fig. 88. For Hebrew manuscripts see M. Dukan, *La réglure des manuscrits hébreux au moyen age* (Paris: Editions du CNRS, 1988), 16; and Dukan, 'De

la difficulté à reconnaître des instruments de réglure: planche à régler (mastara) et cadre-patron', *Scriptorium* 40, no. 2 (1986), 257-61. For Armenian manuscripts see Merian, Ph.D. diss., 27-8.

14 Two examples: A paper Ritual made in New Julfa, Iran, between 1704 and 1709 (San Lazzaro, Venice, MS 1571); a parchment Hymnal from Cafay, Crimea, dated 1646 (Union Theological Seminary, New York, Arm. MS 1). In these examples, one can be certain that the ruling lines were made with a string ruling frame because the twist of the string was clearly impressed in the paper or parchment and was visible under magnification.

15 J. P. Gumbert, 'Ruling by Rake and Board', in *The Role of the Book in Medieval Culture*, ed. by P. Ganz [Bibliologia 3 and 4], (Turnhout: Brepols, 1986), I, p. 51, note 22.

16 Many of the Syriac manuscripts examined for this study were damaged and worn; a delicate mark such as that made by a string indented into paper could easily have worn away. According to Prof. S. Peter Cowe of U.C.L.A., Syrian monks in Jerusalem (whom he has observed), as well as in Tur Abdin (eastern Turkey) and the Monastery of Mar Ephrem in Glane, Holland, still use a ruling frame today for ruling leaves. Ruling frames are also used by scribes of the Old Believers in Siberia; see N. N. Pokrovskii, 'Western Siberian Scriptoria and Binderies: Ancient Traditions Among the Old Believers', transl. by J. S. G. Simmons, *The Book Collector* XX (Spring 1971), 20-1 and pl. 1.

17 For works on Armenian manuscript illumination, see *Treasure in Heaven*, ed. Mathews & Wieck, and its bibliography (cited above, n. 1); T. F. Mathews & A. K. Sanjian, *Armenian Gospel Iconography: the Tradition of the Glajor Gospel* (Washington, D.C.: Dumbarton Oaks, 1991); as well as the many books, articles, and manuscript catalogues written by the late Sirarpie Der Nersessian, especially *Armenian Art* (Paris: Arts & Metiers Graphiques, 1978). For Greek illuminations, see *Illuminated Greek Manuscripts from American Collections: an Exhibition in Honor of Kurt Weitzmann*, ed. by G. Vikan (Princeton, NJ: Princeton University Press, 1973), and *The Glory of Byzantium: Art and Culture of the Middle Byzantine Era A.D. 843-1261*, ed. by H. C. Evans and W. D. Wixom (New York: The Metropolitan Museum of Art, 1997).

18 J. Leroy, *Les manuscrits syriaques à peinture conservés dans les bibliothèques d'Europe et d'Orient*, 2 vols. (Paris: Librairie Orientaliste Paul Geuthner, 1964).

19 Van Regemorter, 'La reliure des manuscrits grecs', 5-6; Federici & Houlis, 23.

20 Merian, Ph.D. diss., 38-40. An example of a manuscript with square notches: London, British Library, Or. MS 2668, a Gospel copied in AD 1437 and now rebound; round (half-circle) notches: Vatican Library, Borg. Arm. 85, a Gospel copied in AD 1635 in Amida.

21 Merian, Ph.D. diss., 42.

22 Federici & Houlis, 71-2.

23 'Squares' are the small portion of the covers of a book which extend beyond the height and width of the pages, as we see on modern hard-cover books today.

24 Federici & Houlis, 27, 79-80. The wooden boards of the majority of Syriac manuscripts examined in this study with extant boards were cut with a vertical grain. Most western European binding traditions also use wooden boards cut with a vertical grain. In: L. Gilissen, *La reliure occidentale antérieure à 1400* [Bibliologia 1], (Turnhout: Brepols, 1983), all photographs of wooden boards show the grain running vertically.

25 Merian, Ph.D. diss., 40-3.

26 Merian, Ph.D. diss., 43-6, 221. 'Unsupported' sewing means that the gatherings are attached to each other by thread only, using some type of link stitch. There is no additional support (such as cords or leather thongs) for the sewing to go around.

27 J. A. Szirmai, 'Old Bookbinding Techniques and their Significance for Book Restoration', in *Preprints: Seventh International Congress of Restorers of Graphic Art, 26th-30th August*

1991, Uppsala, Sweden, ed. by K. J. Palm & M. S. Koch (Uppsala, 1991), 3; B. van Rege-morter, 'Evolution de la technique de la reliure du VIIIe au XII siècle', *Scriptorium* 2 (1948), 275-7, 282.

28 Merian, 'Cilicia as the Locus of European Influence on Medieval Armenia Book Production' (cited above, n. 1), 61-72.

29 For a detailed description of this board attachment method, see Merian, Ph.D. diss., 47-51, figs. 6-7; also *Treasures in Heaven*, ed. Mathews & Wieck, 131-2 and figs. 90a-90b; Merian, 'From Venice to Isfahan and Back' (cited above, n. 1), fig. 5.

30 Federici & Houlis, 28-32, and fig. 21.

31 ibid., 33; Merian, Ph.D. diss., 52-3.

32 This does not include 'alla greca' bindings, where Greek books printed in Europe were bound in a Greek manner by or for their customers. P. Quilici, 'Legature greche, "alla greca", per la Grecia', *Accademie e Biblioteche d'Italia* 52 (1984), 99-111. Islamic headbands are described in Bosch et al., 53-5; and in D. M. Evetts, 'Traditional Islamic Chevron Headband', *Guild of Book Workers Journal* 19 (1980-81), 30-5. For a late Armenian example on a Ritual copied and bound between 1704 and 1709 in Isfahan see San Lazzaro, Venice, MS 1571, in Merian, 'From Venice to Isfahan and Back ...' (cited above, n. 1), fig. 6. These headbands are also found in much earlier manuscripts. Note the distinctive Armenian black, white and red silk chevron design. Merian, Ph.D. diss., 53-7. For a step-by-step description of how to work an Armenian headband see *Les tranchefiles brodées: étude historique et technique* (Paris: Biblio-thèque Nationale, 1989), 78-9.

33 For a description on how the Armenian and Syriac primary cores were sewn, as well as a photograph of one, see *Les tranchefiles brodées*, 76-7.

34 Federici & Houlis, 33-5 and fig. 26.

35 *Les tranchefiles brodées*, 80-1, describes how to work this Syriac headband.

36 Federici & Houlis, 123.

37 Merian, Ph.D. diss., 57-9. Merian, 'Characteristics and Techniques of Armenian Book-binding' (cited above, n. 1), fig. 3, p. 422.

38 Neither the van Regemorter articles nor the study by Federici & Houlis mention any kind of cloth doublure in their descriptions.

39 Merian, Ph.D. diss., 59; Federici & Houlis, 35.

40 Merian, Ph.D. diss., 61-4, and figs. 10-12; *Treasures in Heaven*, ed. Mathews & Wieck, 132-3, figs. 87 and 91; Merian, 'From Venice to Isfahan and Back' (cited above, n. 1), figs. 5, 7, 8 and 9.

41 Although Islamic bindings usually include a type of fore-edge flap, they are very different from the Armenian ones. The flaps (called a *lisan* in Arabic) were made of leather-covered pasteboard (Armenian flaps are constructed of leather and fabric only), which consisted of a rectangular piece the height and width of the fore-edge of the book, and a pentagonal portion which reached over and covered a part of the front board. Bosch et al., *Islamic Bookbindings*, 55-6).

42 For a discussion of Armenian binding decoration, see B. Aṛakʻelyan, 'The Art of Decorative Bookbinding in Medieval Armenia' [in Armenian], *Banber Matenadarani* IV (1958): 183-203; D. Kouymjian, 'Inscribed Armenian Manuscript Bindings: a Preliminary General Survey', in *Armenian Texts, Tasks, and Tools*, ed. by H. Lehmann & J. J. S. Weitenberg (Aarhus, Denmark, 1993), 101-9; Merian, Ph.D. diss., 67-76.

43 Federici & Houlis, 41-68, discusses the decoration of Greek manuscripts.

44 Many of the manuscripts examined were damaged and either missing their covers completely or lacking the leather.

45 Two exceptions are BL, MSS Or. 8729 (a lectionary copied in 1230) and Or. 13465 (a New

Testament with homilies copied in 1475). Both of these were rebound, but it appears that the binder re-used the original leather. See *The Christian Orient* (London: The British Library, 1978), 76, nos. 150-1.

46 Koriun, *The Life of Mashtots*, transl. by B. Norehad (New York, 1965). Reprinted in *Vark' Mashtots'i—Koriwn* (Delmar, NY: Caravan Books, 1985).

47 Merian, Ph.D. diss., 170-1.

48 Additional research on a larger sample of extant Syriac bindings will be necessary to substantiate this claim.

THE IMAGE AS EXEGETICAL TOOL

PAINTINGS IN MEDIEVAL HEBREW MANUSCRIPTS OF THE BIBLE

Gabrielle Sed-Rajna

IN MEDIEVAL MANUSCRIPTS IN GENERAL, in Hebrew manuscripts in particular, ornaments and illustrations were not considered merely aesthetical components, with the sole aim of enhancing the artistic value of the book. Visual complements often had an intellectual function as well, one which varied according to the nature of these complements.

Visual additions can be divided into two main categories: non-significant decoration, generally called ornaments, on the one hand; and significant decoration, including all types of illustrations, on the other. The function of the ornaments is to organize the book, to define the literary units which compose the book, and to organize the layout of the text. The hierarchical graduation of the ornaments distinguishes the first page of the text and the beginnings of the chapters and the paragraphs. They operate as 'codes' destined to guide the reader and to facilitate the use of the manuscript. Although non-significant in themselves, these visual complements often provide valuable information concerning the history of the book. The most important criteria are provided by the style of the ornaments. When they exhibit affinities with the style of contemporary artefacts created in the same milieu, the ornaments offer evidence of the activity of well-integrated craftsmen working in harmony with their cultural environment. On the other hand, ornaments having no stylistic relation with contemporary works of art are often the products of a hermetic community, living on inherited traditions and lacking a professional relationship with the surrounding society. In both cases, the information provided by the non-significant visual elements concern only the manuscript as artefact; they have no relationship to the text to which they were added.

On the other hand, significant decorations, e.g. illustrations, offer far more complex material. Here, the main aspect to be analysed is the relationship between the text and its illustrations in a wide range of possible situations. Some images illustrate the text directly and may have been planned by the author himself. They then appear in all later copies of the text. In the course of time, these illustrations included in the successive copies of the text become altered as a consequence of the skill – or lack of skill – of the copying artist or because he used a different visual language. By a slow procedure, the illustrations gradually are updated stylistically. However, these modifications have no bearing on the content, which remains conformed to that of the model. Hence the relation between the image and the text remains unchanged.

At times, the image does not illustrate the text directly, but illustrates a commentary joined to the text at a later stage of its history. In that case, the stylistic criteria of the illustrations provide useful information in order to determine the period when the image was created. The style of the illustrations may also reveal whether they were created in the same place where the commentary was composed, whether they reflect contemporary local traditions or, perhaps, are derived from earlier, imported models. A group of paintings joined to the biblical text in a series of medieval Hebrew manuscripts will allow us to illustrate some of these abstract principles and show the complexity of the problem.

In Hebrew biblical manuscripts of Castile and Catalonia, between the end of the thirteenth and the end of the fifteenth centuries, it became a steady tradition to display paintings representing the implements and objects of the Tabernacle in the wilderness, as described in chapters 25 to 38 of Exodus, on two facing pages placed at the head of the text.[1] The earliest known example, dated 1277 (Parma, Bibl. pal., MS parm. 2668, fols 6ᵛ-7ʳ [Pl. 30]), is signed by Hayim b. Israel, member of a known family of professional scribes of Toledo. The codicological criteria of the manuscript and the style of the script confirm that the codex was produced in Toledo, as do the paintings since the bifolium where they appear belongs to the original manuscript.[2] That the paintings were not meant to illustrate the text directly is already shown by their placement at the head of the volume as opposed to being joined to the corresponding passage of Exodus. Moreover, an analysis of the iconography proves that the biblical description was not the only literary source used for the composition.

The two paintings represent an assemblage of objects, placed on the plain parchment in a geometric distribution, without any device which would intend to reconstitute their volume or their situation in the space. Among the objects displayed on the first page is the seven-branched candelabrum, called *menorah*, with the knops, bowls, and flowers decorating each of the branches and the central shaft, its seven lamps (flames turned towards the centre), its tripod base flanked by an *even*, 'stepping-stone' on each side for the priest, who stood on them when trimming the lamps. On the lowest branches of the candelabrum are hung two pairs of instruments needed for the upkeeping of the candelabrum: snuff shovels (*mahtot*) for raking the ashes, and tongs (*melqahayim*) to take the wicks out of the oil. Some of these objects, such as the 'stepping-stones', as well as several other details are not mentioned in the descriptions of Exodus.

The left-hand side of the composition is divided into two parts. At the bottom is the shew-bread table, standing on four legs with two piles of six moulds containing the twelve loaves of bread resting on the table. A spoon for frankincense is placed above each row of bread. In the upper half of the page are displayed the two tablets of the Law, with the first word of each of the ten commandments inscribed on them. The tables are topped by a plain rectangle – the mercy seat or *kapporet* – above which are two winged cherubim, turning their heads one toward the other. Only the wings of the cherubim can be distinguished and the heads without any facial features. Tablets, mercy seat, and cherubim are surrounded by a painted frame, in order to indicate that what is displayed here is the Ark of the Covenant with its contents – the Tablets of the Law. All the objects are outlined in black and covered with gold leaf, except for the stone steps and the outer frame of the Ark, which are painted in green. Next to each object is its name inscribed in red ink.

The Image as Exegetical Tool

The opposite page is divided vertically into two compartments by an ornamental frame. In the compartment on the right is the altar of incense represented as a golden cube with horns, following Exodus 25 and 30; beneath is the jar where the manna was kept, flanked by two rods, one barren, the other one bearing flowers and leaves (Numbers 17. 17-24). Beneath this group of objects are two silver trumpets blown on solemn occasions (Numbers 10. 2-10). In the left compartment is the altar of sacrifice, with the brazen network at its base. It has three steps (the one on the top having served as a walking circuit for the priests) and horns on the four corners, two of which only are visible. The ramp on the left side was used to ascend to the altar, as the priests were not authorized to use stairs. Beneath the altar is a laver (*kiyyor*), depicted as an amphora with two zoomorphic spouts and standing on its base. The last object found on the page is the ram's horn, the *shofar*, blown on the Day of Atonement (Leviticus 25. 9). Again, all the objects are outlined in black and filled with gold leaf, except for the trumpets painted in silver. All the names are inscribed in green or red ink.

The double-page composition of the Toledo Bible raises several questions. Which is the text that gave rise to the extra-biblical elements of the illustration? What was the intention in displaying these paintings at the head of the biblical text? When and where was this iconography created? As for textual sources of the paintings, most of the precisions added to the biblical descriptions derive from two medieval works: the commentary on Exodus of the illustrious French scholar Rabbi Salomon ben Isaac (1040-1105), better known by the name of Rashi, and the legal compendium (*Mishneh Torah*) of the Cordoba-born philosopher and exegete Moses Maïmonides (1135-1204), who lived during the second part of his life in Fostat, Egypt. The two exegetical works, widely used in the Middle Ages, are different in character. Rashi's philological explanations were the most popular intellectual tools among Jewish scholars for the understanding of the Bible. His precisions on the description of the Tabernacle and the cult objects were indispensable for understanding the text, and many ornaments in the paintings show that his commentary has been used for the elaboration of these visual representations. Maïmonides' work dealt mainly with the Temple of Jerusalem. He presented a systematic exploration of the sanctuary and, in order to enable the reader to visualize it, he added diagrams to the literal account. However, Maïmonides' Temple referred not only to the Sanctuary of the past which was destroyed by the Romans. His purpose was to evoke the Temple as it will be reconstructed in the future, during the messianic age. While Rashi remained within the frame of a historical description, to which he added mainly linguistic precisions and glosses, Maïmonides transformed the biblical account into a message of hope: he elaborated on the descriptions of the Bible in order to shape the image of the Temple of the future.

Maïmonides wrote his legal compendium during his stay in Fostat, Old Cairo, around 1185. The iconography of the double page of the Toledo Bible suggests that this text was familiar also to the painter who created the composition. This statement allows us to draw two conclusions. The first concerns the meaning of the paintings. Indeed, Maïmonides' text provides an explanation of why the paintings are at the opening of the volume rather than next to the relevant descriptions within the text. This iconography was not meant to describe any physical reality: it was proposed as an intellectual tool, inviting the reader and enabling him to meditate on the features of the Sanctuary of the messianic times, which, according to the author's conception, will resemble the building of the past. The paintings were also meant to recall that Scripture, which once was housed in the Sanctuary, became itself the abode of the presence of God, since the Temple had been destroyed. Hence the double-page frontispiece replaces the portal of the Sanctuary which in the past gave access to God's holy abode. Scripture also has the function of recalling the features of the Sanctuary of the past in order to prepare the model for the Temple of the future.

The second conclusion concerns the date of the composition. If the suggestion is correct that Maïmonides' text influenced the iconography of the paintings, the date of this text would necessarily have to be considered as the *terminus a quo* for the creation of the composition. The problem is complex. The tradition of placing the image of the Sanctuary at the frontispiece to the Bible was inaugurated in the Orient, well before Maïmonides composed his work. Evidence of this is provided by biblical manuscripts of the tenth century, from either Egypt or Palestine, with frontispieces representing the Tabernacle.[3] The iconography of these paintings is fundamentally different from that of the Toledo Bible and no direct relationship can be established between the two. Yet the symbolical idea was present already at that early date, according to the preserved evidence. The iconography of the Toledo paintings represents a parallel tradition, which may have been created at the very end of the twelfth century or at the beginning of the thirteenth under the influence of Maïmonides' commentary. This tradition may have reached the Iberian peninsula some time between the creation of the composition and 1277 when the painter of the Toledo Bible used it as a model for his frontispieces. The stylistic criteria of the Toledo paintings clearly indicate the oriental provenance of their model: the flat representation of the objects and avoidance of all devices which would create the illusion of space or volume, the geometrical division of the page, the use of gold as sole colour against a plain parchment ground, the frieze-ornaments painted on the jars and amphorae, as well as the zoomorphic spouts, belong to the most characteristic elements of book painting in the Middle East. Hence it appears that the paintings of the Toledo Bible provide the earliest preserved record of an iconographical tradition created probably in Egypt at the end of the twelfth, or the beginning of the thirteenth century, some time after Maïmonides had written the *Mishneh Torah* and his commentary on the Temple. At an unknown date, but certainly before 1277, this tradition was transported to Castile where it was used as a model for local manuscript production.

The double page composition of the Sanctuary implements continued in northern Spain for more than two centuries. Chronologically the closest to the Toledo Bible is a manuscript executed in 1299 in Perpignan, at that time part of the kingdom of Aragon (Paris, Bibliothèque Nationale de France, MS Hébreu 7, fols 12ᵛ-13ʳ [Pl. 31-2].[4] Presented in a much more precise and refined technique, the paintings of the Perpignan Bible are an exact replica of those of the Toledo manuscript. In order to adapt the composition to the new dimensions of the pages, which are taller in this manuscript than they were in the Toledo Bible, some modifications were necessary in the placement of the objects. For instance, on the first page the jar of the manna flanked by the two rods were placed beneath the candelabrum. On the second page, the space left vacant by the jar was filled by the group of musical instruments and some new objects (pots, amphorae). Finally, a second register containing spoons, forks, and shovels was added as a space filler. Except for these minor changes, conditioned by the new format, the paintings faith-fully replicate the model, including the oriental features of the style and the ornaments.

These stylistic features, which prevailed until the end of the thirteenth century, were progressively superseded by a pictorial language which was adapted to the requirements of contemporary local gothic art. The first evidence of such stylistic updating is seen in a Bible copied in the same atelier of Perpignan, in 1301 (Copenhagen, Kong. Bibl., Cod. hebr. II).[5] The composition and layout of this second Perpignan Bible are identical to those of the preceding manuscript except for the blank parchment background, which is here replaced by a typical gothic red and blue chequered ground. The Bible of Copenhagen is a rare and precious record: it is the witness of the turning-point of a process of acclimatization which began in order to adapt Jewish iconography, brought from oriental sources, to the requirements of its new cultural environment. The process itself is a frequent phenomenon in the history of art; it is less frequent, indeed even exceptional, that a single work of art should offer the possibility to point out precisely its beginning.

Harmonization and adaptation to the contemporary stylistic features went on for several decades. The symbolical composition and the message it represented have been carefully preserved and even accentuated. In the second half of the fourteenth century, the strict symmetry of the composition was abandoned, the framed space was filled more freely. In the Duke of Sussex Catalan Bible (London, British Library, Add. MS 15250 [Pl. 33])[6] from the third quarter of the fourteenth century, the candelabrum occupies the entire first page. On the second page all the other implements are re-grouped: the altar of incense, the altar of sacrifice, the tables of the Law, the jar of the manna, the shew-bread table with minor objects – silver trumpets, *shofar*, basins, pestles – filling the space. In the bottom left corner a new element appears: a small hill with a tree on its top. No such element is mentioned in any of the literary sources which gave rise to the original composition. This new element refers to the vision of Zachariah (14. 1-4) where the prophecy evokes 'the day of the Lord ... when his feet shall stand ... upon the mount of Olives which is before Jerusalem ... and the mount of Olives shall cleave in the midst ... By alluding to this prophecy, the symbolism of the paintings received a clear messianic orientation. Towards the end of the fourteenth century, the expression of messianic hopes was the response of the leaders of the Jewish communities of Castile and Catalonia to the increasing hostility of the political authorities and the gradual deterioration of the situation. Although the literary works were the main media of these messages of hope, messianic speculations also had an impact on the artistic creations, among them the iconography of the paintings inserted in the biblical manuscripts.

From the beginning of the fourteenth century until the last quarter of the fifteenth, paintings displaying Sanctuary implements continued to be used as frontispieces of the Hebrew Bibles made in Catalonia. The placement of the implements underwent further modifications, the main innovation being the extension of the composition to three, even at times to four, pages. In a Bible executed probably in Barcelona in the years 1360 to 1380 (Paris, Bibliothèque de la Compagnie des prêtres de Saint Sulpice, MS 1933, fols 5ᵛ, 6ʳ, 7ᵛ [Pl. 34-6],[7] the composition fills three pages. On the first page is displayed a full-page candelabrum with the tongs and shovels hanging from the branches, flanked by the two stone steps, on top of which are found two pestles; Aaron's flowering rod is on the right and the jar of manna on the left. The objects are in gold leaf on a chequered red and blue background, the shape of the jar of the manna has kept its oriental features. The centre of the second page is dominated by the altar of incense with its steps, horns and ramp, surrounded by different basins and jars; the tree on top of the Mount of Olives has been moved to the centre, a more prominent place. The top register of the third page is occupied by the ark of the Covenant, topped by a trilobed tympanum with the winged cherubim on both sides. It is flanked by an oriental amphora-like container, opposed to a chalice under a gothic canopy. The shew-bread table is on the right in the bipartite lower register, with the altar of incense on the left. In spite of the survival of many oriental features – mainly the use of gold for the objects and the form of the jars and the containers – a clear shift towards the gothic style is noticeable in the canopy on top of the ark and above the chalice, the chalice itself having a characteristic gothic form. However, the most noticeable innovation in this triptych is the central position of the tree on the top of the Mount of Olives. This became a steady part of the composition, echoing the increasing importance of the messianic speculations expressed in literary works.

A further step in this direction can be seen in the paintings in a Bible executed in Saragossa in 1404 (Paris, Bibliothèque Nationale de France, MS hébreu 31).[8] Here the composition occupies four pages, each of which has an emphasis on its centre. The first page (fol. 1[v]) is dominated by a monumental candelabrum with the shovels, tongs, and raking instruments hanging from its branches, the two stepping-stones on the sides. The bipartite red and blue ground is decorated by fine pen scrolls. On the second page (fol. 3[r], Pl. 37) are the two superimposed tablets of the Law, inscribed with the incipit of the ten commandments. In the lower register are the altar of sacrifice with multiple steps and horns on top, and its ramp on the side. On the third page (fol. 2[v], Pl. 37), the shew-bread table occupies the central position; below it stands an oversized chalice for the jar of manna. Smaller basins and containers fill the space on both sides. The fourth page (fol. 4[r], Pl. 38) portrays only one element: a full-page three-branched tree on top of a rocky hill. The inscription framing the painting provides the key for understanding the image by quoting the prophecy of Zachariah 14. The new prominence of this illustration clearly demonstrates the increasing influence of the messianic commentaries and the role of the composition as a visual support. Striking, also, is the realistic depiction of the tree and the almost modern style of the painting.

During the fifteenth century, under the pressure of the hostile politics of the ruling classes, the cultural activity of the Jewish communities in Catalonia declined. The production of illuminated manuscripts reflects this phenomenon by the lack of innovation, in spite of the high level of technical execution. This lack of inspiration means not only the absence of new subjects, of new trends. It also means that the traditional repertoire of subjects is repeated without a deeper understanding. The relationship between the development of technical skill – which attained its highest level during this final period of the handwritten book, just before being superseded by the new procedures of printing – and the absence of authentic creativity, is perceptible in the few known examples of the representations of the Sanctuary implements for this period. The paintings inserted in the Kennicott Bible (Oxford, Bodleian Library, MS Kennicott 1), made in La Coruna, 1476, illustrate this evolution.[9] The first page, on fol. 120[r], as usual, shows the full-page candelabrum with tongs and censers hanging from the branches. All the other objects are grouped on the opposite page, fol. 121^r.[10] But these objects have lost their functional shape: they are reduced to be mere silhouettes on a painted background. The cherubim are on top of the shew-bread table, the stepping-stones are separated from the altar, and the instruments, jars, and amphorae are grouped without any allusion to their function. All are presented as ornaments, their meaning as symbols or as visual complements of an exegesis seemingly lost. The curve of evolution has reached its final point; the didactic compositions gave place to a decorative carpet-like painting without any intellectual pretensions.

The paintings of the Sanctuary implements, as presented in the Hebrew manuscripts mentioned above, offer an example of the use of visual complements as pedagogical tools which reflect the major exegetical trends of the period of their creation. They offer also an example of the complexity of these visual documents and show that, in a manuscript, text and image form an indivisible unit.

NOTES

1 Some aspects of these paintings have been evoked by Cecil Roth in 'Jewish Antecedents of Christ Art', *Journal of the Warburg and Courtauld Institutes*, XVI (1953), 24-36; C. O. Nordström, 'Some Miniatures In Hebrew Bibles', *Synthronon*, Paris (1968), 85-105; Th. Metzger 'Les objets du culte, le sanctuaire du désert et le temple de Jérusalem dans les bibles hébraïques médiévales enluminés en Orient et en Espagne', *Bulletin of the John Rylands Library* 52 (1970), 408-15; 53 (1971) 167-209; and by M. Garel, 'The Foa Bible', *Journal of Jewish Art* (1979), 78-85.

2 Information communicated orally by Prof. Beit Arié, who has checked the codicology of the manuscript on my request.

3 B. Narkiss, *Illuminations from Hebrew Bibles of Leningrad* (Jerusalem: Mosad Byalik, 1990).

4 G. Sed-Rajna, *Les manuscrits hébreux enluminés des Bibliothèques de France* (Leuven: Peeters, 1994), 12.

5 U. Haxen, *Kings and Citizens*, Exhibition Catalogue of the Jewish Museum, New York (1963), vol. II, p. 5.

6 B. Narkiss, in collaboration with A. Cohen-Mushlin & A. Tcherikover, *Hebrew Illuminated Manuscripts in the British Isles. I. Spanish and Portuguese Manuscripts* (New York: Oxford University Press for the Israel Academy of Sciences and Humanities and the British Academy, 1982), 19.

7 Garel, 'The Foa Bible' (cited above, n. 1); G. Sed-Rajna, *Les manuscrits hébreux enluminés* (cited above, no. 4), 22.

8 ibid., 32.

9 B. Narkiss (cited above, n. 6), 48.

10 Reproduced in B. Narkiss (as above), pl. CLIV.

THE THEOLOGY OF THE WORD MADE FLESH

Andrew Louth

FROM THE BEGINNING, Christianity was a religion of a book, but with a difference. It was a religion of a book because the earliest Christians were Jews who already had, of course, a sacred book – the Torah – as well as other scriptural writings. Such writings, as it were, surrounded and supported the core of the Torah, the book of the Law, the Pentateuch. But these early Christians were Jews with a difference. They believed that the Messiah had come and was indeed the one called Jesus of Nazareth. He had been crucified by the Romans at Jerusalem and had appeared alive again, risen from the dead, to his disciples three days later. This difference led to a distinctively Christian way of interpreting the Scriptural writings of the Jewish people. More simply: Jews had traditionally understood their Scriptures as the Law – the declaration of God's will for humankind and especially for themselves as his chosen people; Christians came to understand the Scriptures as essentially prophetic – the Scriptures foretold the coming of the Messiah.

This is manifest in several ways. For instance, if one compares the use of the Old Testament in the New Testament letters of St Paul and in the Gospels, one will discover that Paul, the traditionally-trained rabbi, argues, for the most part, from the books of the Law, using the Prophetic writings as supplementary. However, in the Gospels it is the prophetic writings that are quoted and alluded to, rather than the core of the Jewish Scriptures, the Torah. Along with Christians altering the balance between the Law and the Prophets, there emerges a growing tendency to interpret the Law itself prophetically – the most obvious example being the way in which the regulations about sacrifice in the books of the Law are interpreted as pointing forward to Christ's sacrifice on the cross and its celebration in the Eucharist, a process already under way in the Epistle to the Hebrews.

It is because Christians made the Jewish Scriptures their own – as the *Old* Testament – that it is tempting to see the culmination of this process of Christianization in the order of the books of the Old Testament.[1] This is best exemplified in the fourth-century *Codex Vaticanus*. In that codex, the books of the Old Testament begins with the Pentateuch and end with the prophetic books (in fact with the four major prophets, Isaiah, Jeremiah, Ezechiel, and Daniel). The account of creation is followed by the account of the series of covenants that God made with humankind after the Fall, the covenants themselves culminating in the Law of the covenant made through Moses on Mount Sinai; this merges into an account of the history of Israel, presented as the nation from which the prophets came, who foretold the coming of the Messiah. The Old Testament, then, forms a kind of ascending gradient, leading from creation to the formation of the Messianic hope: something fulfilled in the New Testament which follows. The New

Testament thus supplements the Old Testament – the New to be interpreted in terms of the Old and itself providing the key to the understanding of the Old. It contains writings that document the apostolic witness to the fulfilment of the ancient promises about the coming of the Messiah. These writings were never self-consciously intended as 'scriptures' (in contrast to the 'gnostic scriptures' that emerged in imitation, once the notion of recent scriptures got off the ground). Written by the apostles, or their close followers, and gradually (by the end of the second century) recognized by virtually all the Christian churches as preserving the apostolic witness, the writings were to be placed after the prophetic witness of the Old Testament as the 'New' Testament (a terminology and distinction that also emerges towards the end of the second century).[2]

I have begun with this brief account of the emergence of the Christian canon of Scripture because I believe that this is more than an innocent list of books: it is an implicit programme of interpretation. For Christians, their Scriptures contain the prophetic and the apostolic witness to Christ – 'the light to lighten the Gentiles, and the glory of [God's] people Israel' (Luke 2. 32) – the heart and fulfilment of God's loving will for humankind. These Scriptures are to be read in the light of this programme of promise and fulfilment – or, more concretely, are to be read in the light of the Church's own summary of the essentials of the Christian faith, the 'rule of faith', as the summary of the baptismal faith came to be called in the second century, or the 'creed', or symbol of faith, as it later came to be called.[3] The whole of the Scriptures – all its teaching and all its symbolism – finds its true Christian orientation in what the poet Paul Claudel once called the 'magnetic field' of the rule of faith.[4]

But if the Scriptures are to be read as the prophetic and apostolic witness to Christ, then there is another factor to be borne in mind: and that is that, for Christians, Christ is not primarily a figure of the past. To quote the Easter troparion that Orthodox Christians repeat over and over again during the Easter season, 'Christ has risen from the dead, by death he has trampled on death, and to those in the graves given life'. The Scriptures are to be read as witness to the historical manifestation of the living Christ. In reading the Scriptures, Christians encounter Christ. The Scriptures are then the visible means for an invisible, spiritual encounter: they are, to use a term that is very important to Orthodox Christians, 'theophanic' – in the Scriptures, God is manifest.

The great Christian theologian Origen speaks of interpretation of the Scriptures as an encounter with God. In a striking passage from his *Commentary on the Song of Songs*, he talks of the problem of interpreting difficult passages in Scripture, and sees the solution as an encounter with the Word of God:

... at such a time riddles and obscure sayings of the Law and the Prophets hem in the soul, and if then she should chance to perceive him to be present, and from afar should catch the sound of his voice, forthwith she is uplifted. And when he has begun more and more to draw near to her senses and to illuminate the things that are obscure, then she sees him 'leaping upon the mountains and the hills'; that is to say, he then suggests to her interpretations of a high and lofty sort, so that this soul can rightly say: 'Behold, he comes leaping upon the mountains, skipping over the hills.[5]

Manifestation, unfolding of meaning: this sort of terminology is at the heart of the Christian religion, perhaps of any religion. In sacred texts, sacred events, sacred places, sacred ceremonies, the meaning of existence is communicated, made manifest. But for Christians, the most profound meaning is expressed in a human life embraced and experienced by God Himself – the Incarnation. The Greek word for 'meaning' is *logos*, which can also be translated 'reason', and is often translated 'word'. Very early on, Christians came to use the word, *logos*, of the one who is Christ. Quite why is no longer clear: I suspect that its background lies in the Jewish idea of *Memra*, an Aramaic word, used in the Targumim, to express the sacred presence of God.[6] But whatever its background, the use of this word tapped a rich vein in the Greek philosophical tradition, where the word, *logos*, was widely used to express the ultimate meaning of things. Relatively quickly, again by the end of the second century, the idea of Jesus as the Christ, the Messiah, the anointed one – something that made sense only to Jews – was virtually supplanted by the idea of Jesus as the 'Word made flesh' – something that made much more immediate sense in the intellectual world of late antiquity.

The 'Word made flesh' was the expression in a human life of the divine meaning of the world, but a meaning that was no code or formula, but the creative source of the universe itself. We would see this as something at least personal, but this way of thinking had not yet developed in late antiquity. And this 'Word made flesh' was foreshadowed in the prophecies of the Old Testament, and attested in the apostolic witness of the New Testament. If the Scriptures, as we have seen, are theophanic, then so too, even more so, is 'Word made flesh' – the 'Theophany' is the most ancient title in the East for the feast of the birth of Christ – and these two theophanies mutually illuminate and interpret each other.

In the Byzantine tradition, the close analogy between the interpretation of Scripture and the theology of the Word made flesh was boldly grasped and strikingly developed – by no one so much, perhaps, as by the greatest of Byzantine theologians, St Maximus the Confessor. Born in 580, St Maximus first emerges on the stage of history, briefly, as the first secretary of the Imperial Chancellery, the *protoasecretis*, to the Byzantine Emperor, Heraclius, when he deposed the usurper, Phocas, in 610. But within a few years Maximus resigned to become a monk. As a result of the upheavals caused by, first, the Persian and, second, the Arab invasions of the Byzantine Empire, Maximus found himself from about 630 in North Africa, then still a Byzantine province. There he became known as the defender of Orthodox Christology against the imperial religious compromises called monenergism and monothelitism.[7] He was involved in the papal repudiation of these heresies at the Lateran Council in 649, as a result of which he was arrested by Imperial forces, tried, exiled, and eventually mutilated, as a result of which sufferings he died, in exile in Lazica (Western Georgia) in 662, a confessor of Orthodoxy. In his often varied and difficult writings, he gives expression to a supremely coherent and profound vision of the Orthodox Faith.[8]

Maximus is fond of pointing out a quite direct parallel between the Word made flesh as a human being, and the Word expressing himself in 'syllables and letters'. He often draws this parallel by remarking on the way in which the Word made flesh preached in parables. 'When he is present to human beings, ... he converses in a way familiar to them in a variety of stories, enigmas, parables, and dark sayings, then he becomes flesh' (*Chapters on Theology*, II.60).[9] In other words, the Word becomes flesh, not just in the physical incarnation, but also through the way in which he expresses himself in words and stories. He compares this to the way in which teachers use simple stories and illustrations to convey ideas and concepts that their students would not be able to grasp directly (*Amb.* 33: PG 91.1285C–1288A).[10] Scripture – at the heart of which are the words of the Word made flesh, and other words helping us to understand and encounter him – and the Incarnation are in this way placed in direct juxtaposition: they are both ways in which naked spiritual reality (as he puts it) is put within reach of material beings of flesh and blood.

But this parallel – between the Word in words and the Word made flesh – is only the beginning of a series of correspondences developed by Maximus. There are two places, in particular, where he explores this. In what is perhaps his most important work, the early *Book of Difficulties* (so called because it discusses difficult passages in the writings of St Gregory the Theologian, one of the most revered fourth-century Cappadocian Fathers), he discusses the transfiguration of Christ, the event in the Gospels when, on a mountain (traditionally Mount Tabor) with three of his disciples, Christ appeared transfigured in light, accompanied by the great Old Testament prophets, Moses and Elijah. Maximus observes that not only was Christ's face transfigured with light, but his clothes became radiant: the light from Christ's transfigured body streamed out through his clothes. He suggests two interpretations of this: one which takes its cue, so to speak, from the presence of Moses, who received the Law on Mount Sinai, the other of which takes its cue from Elijah, to whom God revealed himself through the elements of creation – a storm, an earthquake, lightning, and a gentle breeze (3 Kingdoms 19. 11-12). The first is that the 'whitened clothes' are 'a symbol of the words of Holy Scripture, which became shining and clear and limpid to them'; the second is that they are a symbol of creation itself, through which the purified mind can engage in 'natural contemplation of reality' (*Amb.* 10. 17: PG 91.1128B-D).[11] He then goes on to suggest that the natural law of creation can be regarded as a kind of book – with letters and syllables that together express a meaning – just as creation consists of elements that together form the 'harmonious web of the whole'. Put the other way about, the law (the written law) can be regarded as a '*cosmos*' – a Greek word which conveys the sense, not just of the universe, but also of harmony. Both Scripture and the created order, then, point to and express the transfiguration of the Word made flesh (in other words, the revelation of the reality of the Word made flesh). The Word made flesh is the ultimate theophany; but reflecting it is the theophany of the Word in the words (of Scripture), and also the theophany of the created order, which was brought into being by the Word.

There is a further place where Maximus explores these mutually-referring words or *kosmoi*. For Maximus also wrote a commentary on the Byzantine liturgy, called the *Mystagogia*.[12] This is prefaced by several chapters on the symbolism of the church building, in which he gives early expression to the idea that came to govern the structure and decoration of churches from the ninth century onwards, according to which the church building mirrors the cosmos, reflecting in its structure the division between heaven and earth (not just vertically, with the dome as heaven, but horizontally, with the sanctuary, to which the rest of the church leads, also representing the heavenly court). The last two chapters of the preface (ch. 6 and 7) explore the wider implications of the division of the church building into nave and sanctuary. The penultimate chapter sees this division mirrored in the Scriptures and in the human person (the bulk of the preface has, in fact, explored at length the way in which the soul-body distinction mirrors the distinction of sanctuary and nave). Here he suggests that the sanctuary-nave distinction is mirrored in the distinction between the Old and the New Testaments, in the distinction between body and soul in humankind, and in the distinction between a text and its meaning: each distinction takes one onwards and inwards. But this is true because each division is the division within a cosmos.

Scripture is a cosmos, as we have seen; the human person is a cosmos, a little cosmos, *mikros kosmos*, from which the philosophers of the Renaissance coined the term 'microcosm'; and the relation of text to meaning is found in any cosmos, for it is an ordered whole, the order (text) being an expression of its inner meaning. The final chapter of the preface sums this up in a discussion of three worlds or *kosmoi*, or, as he also puts it, of three 'human beings' – the universe, Scripture, and the 'human being who is ourselves'. And all these worlds, or cosmoi, themselves point to and reflect the unique example of the human microcosm, the Word made flesh, that, as Maximus argues elsewhere (*Amb.* 41),[13] alone fulfils the role that is implicit in the human person's being a microcosm, namely that of being the bond that holds the whole creation together, a role forfeited by the Fall of humankind and the introduction of chaos into what was meant to be cosmos, but recapitulated by the absorption of the destructive powers of chaos in history on the cross, and symbolically in the power of the cross to bind together height and depth, and one extreme with another.

The genius of Orthodoxy – not just Byzantine Orthodoxy, though that was the cradle of Orthodoxy – is the way in which all these worlds are held together. All these worlds – Scripture, creation, the human person – lead back to the Word made flesh, through whom and for whom they are: interpretation of the interlocking meanings of Scripture, contemplation of the inner coherence of the created *cosmos*, and the recovery in each human being, through an ascetic purification of love, of the image of God in which we were created and which is our true reality – these all lead to contemplation of and communion with the Word made flesh, and it is his being made flesh that makes all of these possible.

But there is a further factor that is relevant to the Byzantine attitude to the Scriptures. The Scriptures exist as physical objects: and as physical objects, because they contain the words of Scripture, they are objects of veneration. In the public worship of the Church, the Scriptures are read from books – rarely containing the whole Bible, sometimes containing just the Gospels, more usually containing the passages used liturgically, from the Gospels or the Epistles – and these books are venerated. When the Gospel is read, we stand to hear the words of the Saviour. The Gospel book, especially, is treated with great reverence, including being honoured by being kissed. Such veneration was defined as entailed by Orthodox teaching, especially the Orthodox understanding of the Person of Christ, in relation to visual images – icons – at the Seventh Ecumenical Council, held in Nicaea in 787, and reaffirmed at the Triumph of Orthodoxy in 843. If one reads the defenders of veneration of icons – both those contemporary with the controversy and later writers – one finds that the Scriptures are often presented as a premise, on the basis of which icons are postulated, and this in relation both to their existence (the existence of Scriptures entails the existence of icons) and to their veneration (the veneration of Scriptures entails the veneration of icons). So St Theodore the Studite says, 'What is written on paper and with ink is depicted on an icon through colours and various other materials' (*Antirrheticus* I.10: PG 99: 340D). Rather later on, in the fourteenth century, we find St Symeon of Thessalonika affirming: 'To represent with colours which conform to Tradition is true painting; it is analogous to a faithful copy of the Scriptures: and divine grace rests upon it, since what is represented is holy' (*Against Heresies* 13: PG 155: 113D). Icons and the scriptures belong together: they both express revealed truth in accessible form, they both lead humankind to communion with the Word made flesh. What was defined in relation to icons is equally true in relation to the Scriptures.

The Byzantine understanding of Scripture is therefore multi-faceted: embracing both the interlocking pattern of meanings of the words of the Word and also its relationship to the Word revealed in the created order and in the human person – all of which revelations are summed up in the Word made flesh.

NOTES

1 There are very few early codices that survive: very soon Christians made the Old Testament scriptures serve their purposes more drastically, by excerpting the Scriptures to produce lectionaries, rather than copying out the Scriptures as a whole.

2 On the formation of the Christian canon of scripture see R. M. Grant, 'The New Testament Canon', *The Cambridge History of the Bible* (3 vols.; Cambridge: University Press, 1963-70), 1, 284-308; and especially H. von Campenhausen, *The Formation of the Christian Bible* (London: Black, 1972; German original, Tübingen: J. C. B. Mohr (Paul Siebeck), 1968).

3 On the development of the Christian Creed see J. N. D. Kelly, *Early Christian Creeds*, 3rd edn (London: Longman, 1972).

4 '*Un champ magnétique*': in his preface to the reprint of Abbé Tardif de Moidrey, *Introduction au Livre de Ruth* (Paris: Desclée de Brouwer, 1938). Reprinted as 'Du sens figuré de l'Ecriture', *Oeuvres complètes de Paul Claudel*, vol. 21 (*Commentaires et Exégèses*), 7-90 (20).

5 Origen, *Commentary on the Song of Songs*, III.11; English trans.: Origen, *The Song of Songs: Commentary and Homilies*, ed. & trans. by R. P. Lawson (Westminster, Maryland: The Newman Press, 1957), 209-10.

6 For this theory see C. T. R. Hayward, 'The Holy Name of Moses and the Prologue of St John's Gospel', *NTS* 25 (1978-9), 16-32.

7 For a reliable account of this period of the history of the Church see J. Meyendorff, *Imperial Unity and Christian Divisions* (Crestwood, NY: St Vladimir's Seminary Press, 1989), 251-92, 333-73.

8 For an introduction to St Maximus, see A. Louth, *Maximus the Confessor* (London: Routledge, 1996).

9 Maximus' *Chapters on Theology [and the Incarnate Dispensation]* can be found in PG (*Patrologia Graeca*, ed. by J. Migne (Paris, 1865)) 90.1084-1173. There is an English translation in *The Philokalia*, trans. G. E. H. Palmer, P. Sherrard, & K. Ware, vol. 2 (London: Faber, 1981), 114-63.

10 Maximus' *Ambigua*, or 'Books of Difficulties', can be found in PG 91.1032-1417. Several of these *ambigua* are translated in Louth, *Maximus the Confessor*.

11 *Amb.* 10 is translated in Louth, *Maximus the Confessor*, 94-154.

12 PG 91.657-717. English translation in Maximus Confessor, *Selected Writings*, trans. by G. C. Berthold (London: SPCK, 1985), 181-225.

13 Translated in Louth, *Maximus the Confessor*, 163-8.

1. The Book of Kells. Dublin, Trinity College Library, MS 58, fol. 34ʳ

2. The Lindisfarne Gospels. London, British Library, Cotton MSS, Nero D. iv, fol. 27ʳ

3. The Lindisfarne Gospels. London, British Library, Cotton MSS, Nero D. iv, fol. 29[r]

4. The Book of Kells. Dublin, Trinity College Library, MS 58, fol. 28ᵛ

5. The Book of Kells. Dublin, Trinity College Library, MS 58, fol. 29^r

genuit acham	tionem babylo
achash genuit	nis · apostra
ezechiameze	nis migratione
chias autem	babilonis le
genuit manas	chonias genuit
sen manasses	salathiel sala
h genuit am	thiel h genui
os amos autez	sorobabel so
genuit iosiam	robabel autez
iosias h genuit	genuit abiud
ieconiam &	abiud autem
fratres eius	genuit eliachi
matus migra	eliachim

6. The Book of Kells. Dublin, Trinity College Library, MS 58, fol. 30ᵛ

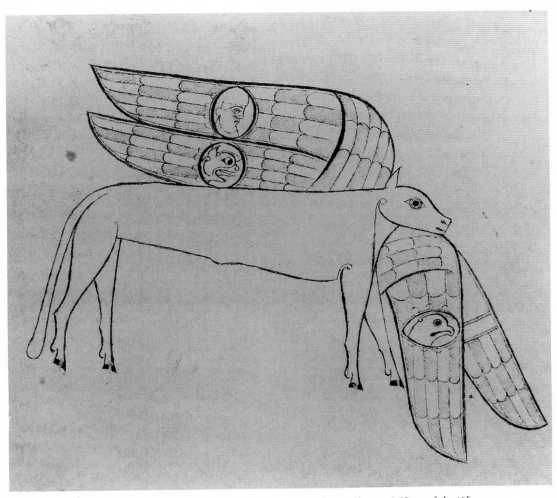

7. The Book of Armagh. Dublin, Trinity College Library, MS 52, fol. 68^v

8. The Echternach Gospels. Paris, Bibliothèque Nationale de France, MS lat. 9389, fol. 18ᵛ

9. The Book of Kells. Dublin, Trinity College Library, MS 58, fol. 290^v

10. Finispiece with Ankh Cross. New York, Pierpont Morgan Library, William S. Glazier Collection, G. 67, fols 155ᵛ–156ʳ

11. Virgin and Child. The Book of Kells. Dublin, Trinity College Library, MS 58, fol. 7ᵛ

12. Canon 1. Rabbula Gospels. Florence, Laurentian Library, Plut. I, 56, fol. 3ᵛ

13. St Mark. Coptic Gospels. Oxford, Bodleian Library, MS Huntington 17, fol. 120ᵛ

14. Double frontispiece to St Matthew's Gospel. Arabic Gospels. London, British Library, Add. MS 11856, fols 1ᵛ-2ʳ

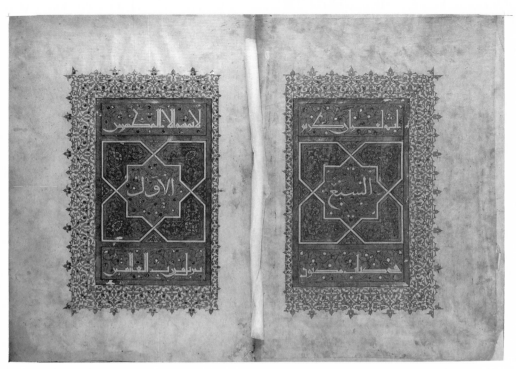

15. Double frontispiece to the Qur'an of Baybars al-Jashnagar, volume VII. London, British Library, Add. MS 22406-13, fol. 59ᵛ

16. Deisis and title-page to Arabic Gospels. Istanbul, Topkapi Sarayi Library, Ahmet III 3519, fols 1ᵛ-2ʳ

18. Wycliffite Gospels. Grand Haven, The Scriptorium, VK MS 638

17. Wycliffite Gospels.
Grand Haven, The Scriptorium, VK MS 637

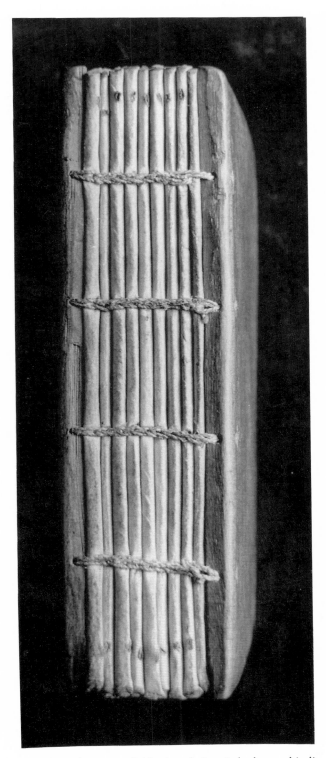

19. Nineteenth-century Ethiopian chain-stitched sewn binding

20. Church of San Vitale, Ravenna

27. Bamberg Staatsbibliothek (Msc. Patr. 5, fol. iv^r)

28. Typical Armenian gospel-book, blind-tooled with an interlaced stepped cross. Text copied in Kan village (Karin canton) in AD 1283; rebound. The Library of the Mekhitarist Congregation of San Lazzaro, Venice, MS 1313

29a. Syriac board attachment (below cloth). Nestorian theological writings, AD 1696. Burke Library of the Union Theological Seminary in the City of New York, Syriac MS 12

29b. Syriac headband. Nestorian theological writings, AD 1696. Burke Library of the Union Theological Seminary in the City of New York, Syriac MS 12

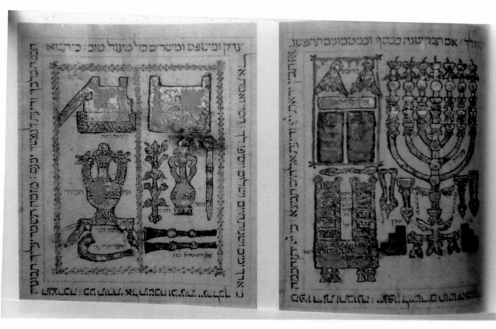

30. Parma, Bibl. pal., MS parm. 2668, fols 6ᵛ-7ʳ

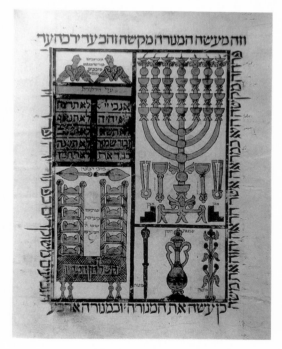

31. Paris, Bibliothèque nationale de France,
MS Hébreu 7, fol. 12ᵛ

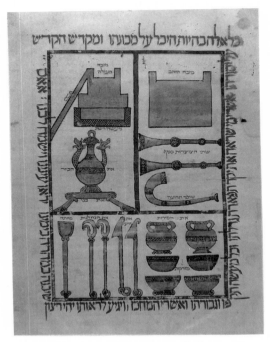

32. Paris, Bibliothèque nationale de France,
MS Hébreu 7, fol. 13ʳ

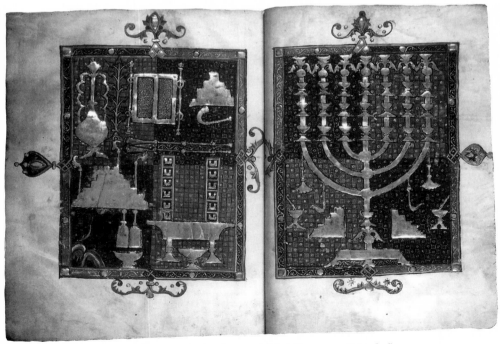

33. London, British Library, Add. MS 15250, fols 1ʳ-2ᵛ

34. Paris, Bibliothèque de la Compagnie des prêtres de Saint Sulpice, MS 1933, fol. 5^v

35. Paris, Bibliothèque de la Compagnie des prêtres de Saint Sulpice, MS 1933, fol. 6^r

36. Paris, Bibliothèque de la Compagnie des prêtres de Saint Sulpice, MS 1933, fol. 7ᵛ

37. Paris, Bibliothèque nationale de France, MS Hébreu 31, fols 2ᵛ-3ʳ

38. Paris, Bibliothèque nationale de France, MS Hébreu 31, fol. 4ʳ

BIBLIOGRAPHY

ABBREVIATIONS

ASOR	*American Schools of Oriental Research*
BA	*Biblical Archaeologist*
BAR	*Biblical Archaelogy Review*
BASOR	*Bulletin of the American Schools of Oriental Research*
DJD	*Discoveries in the Judaean Desert* (Clarendon Press: Oxford)
DSD	*Dead Sea Discoveries*
ErIsr	*Eretz Israel*
HUCA	*Hebrew Union College Annual*
IEJ	*Israel Exploration Journal*
JJS	*Journal of Jewish Studies*
JNES	*Journal of Near Eastern Studies*
JQR	*Jewish Quarterly Review*
JSOT	*Journal for the Study of the Old Testament*
OBO	Orbis biblicus et orientalis
PEQ	*Palestine Exploration Quarterly*
RB	*Revue biblique*
RevQ	*Revue de Qumran*
SBL	Society of Biblical Literature
VT	*Vetus Testamentum*

Åberg, Nils, *The Occident and the Orient in the Art of the Seventh Century*, 3 parts (Stockholm: Wahlström & Widstrand, 1943-7).

Abullif, Wadî, 'Vita e Opera del Pensatore Copto al-Safî Ibn al-'Assâl' (sec. XIII)', *Studia Orientalia Christiana Collectanea* xx (1987).

Adriaen, M., ed., *Sancti Gregorii Magni: Homiliae in Hiezechihelem prophetam* (Corpus Christianorum 142, Turnhout: Brepols, 1971).

Aers, David, *Chaucer, Langland and the Creative Imagination* (London: Routledge & Kegan Paul, 1980).

Ahroni, Reuben, *Yemenite Jewry, Origins, Culture, and Literature* (Bloomington: Indiana University Press, 1986).

Aland, K., *Kurgefasste Liste der griechischen Handschriften des Neuen Testaments* (Berlin: De Gruyter, 2nd edn, 1994).

Aland, K. & B. Aland, *The Text of the New Testament*, 2nd edn, trans. by E. F. Rhodes (Grand Rapids: Eerdmans, 1989).

Alexander, J. J. G., *The Decorated Letter* (New York: George Braziller, 1978).

Alexander, J. J. G., *Insular Manuscripts: 6th to the 9th Century* (London: Harvey Miller, 1978).

Alexander, J J. G., *Medieval Illuminators and their Methods of Work* (New Haven and London: Yale University Press, 1992).

Alexander, Michael, *Old English Literature* (New York: Schocken Books, 1983).

Anchor Bible Dictionary, The, ed. by D. N. Freedman (New York: Doubleday, 1992).

Anderson, A. O., & M. O. Anderson, *Adomnan's Life of Columba* (London: Nelson, 1961).

Anderson, T., *Studies in Samaritan Manuscripts and Artifacts – The Chamberlain–Warren*

Bibliography

Collection (American Schools of Oriental Research Monograph Series 1; Cambridge, Mass., 1978).

Anglo-Saxon Poetry, 2nd edn trans. by S. A. J. Bradley (Everyman: London, 1995).

Aquinas, Thomas, *Catena Aurea in Quatuor Evangelia*, ed. by P. Angelici Guarienti, 2 vols (Rome: Marsetti, 1953).

Aṛak 'elyan, B., 'The Art of Decorative Bookbinding in Medieval Armenia' (in Armenian), *Banber Matenadarani* IV (1958).

Astle, Thomas, *The Origins and Progress of Writing* (London, 1784).

Aston, Margaret, *Lollards and Reformers: Images and Literacy in Late Medieval Religion* (London: Hambledon Press, 1984).

Aston, Margaret, *Faith and Fire: Popular and Unpopular Religion, 1350-1600* (London & Rio Grande: Hambledon Press, 1993).

Attridge, H. & others, in consultation with J. VanderKam, 'Qumran Cave 4.VIII, Parabiblical Texts, Part 1', *DJD* XIII (1994).

Attridge, H. W. & others, eds, *Of Scribes and Scrolls, Studies on the Hebrew Bible Intertestamental Judaism, and Christian Origins Presented to John Strugnell* (College Theology Society Resources in Religion 5; Lanham, Md., 1990).

Augustine, *The City of God* (Harmondsworth, England: Penguin Books, 1972).

Augustine, Saint, Commentary on the Lord's Sermon on the Mount with Seventeen Related Sermons, trans. Denis J. Kavanagh (New York: Fathers of the Church, 1951).

Augustine, St, *In Johannis evangelium*, ed. by R. Willems (Corpus Christianorum 36, Turnhout: Brepols, 1954).

Avrin, Leila, Malla Carl & Noah Ophir, *Scribes, Script, and Books: the Book Arts from Antiquity to the Renaissance* (Chicago: American Library Association; London: British Library, 1991).

Backhouse, J., D. H. Turner, L. Webster et al., eds, *The Golden Age of Anglo-Saxon Art: 966-1066* (London: British Museum Publications, 1984).

Backhouse, Janet, *Books of Hours* (London: The British Library, 1985).

Backhouse, Janet, *The Lindisfarne Gospels* (London: Phaidon Press, 1981).

Baillet, M., 'Qumrân grotte 4.III (4Q482-4Q520)', *DJD* VII (1982).

Bald, Wolf-Dietrich, & Horst Weinstock, eds, *Medieval Studies Conference, Aachen 1983: Language and Literature* (Frankfurt-am-Main: Peter Lang, 1984).

Barker, N. J., ed., *The York Gospels: a facsimile with introductory essays by Jonathon Alexander ...[et al.]* (London: Printed for presentation to the members of the Roxburghe Club, 1986).

Barns, J. W. B., G. M. Browne, & J. C. Shelton, *Nag Hammadi Codices: Greek and Coptic Papyri from the Cartonnage of the Covers* (Nag Hammadi Studies XVI; Leiden: Brill, 1981).

Barns, J. W. B., et al., *Nag Hammadi Library in English*, rev. edn, ed. by J. M. Robinson & M. Meyer (San Francisco: Harper & Row, 1990).

Barr, Helen, ed., *The Piers Plowman Tradition* (London: J. M. Dent; Rutland Vt.: Charles E. Tuttle Co., 1993).

Barthélemy, D. & J. T. Milik, 'Qumran Cave 1', *DJD* I (1955).

Bartz, G. & E. König, 'Die Illustration des Totenoffiziums in Studenbüchern', *Liturgie als Sterbe-und Trauerhilfe, Ein interdisziplinäres Kompendium*, ed. H. Becker, B. Einig and P. O. Ullrich, *Pietas Liturgica*, III-IV, (Berlin: Kupferstichkabinett, 1987).

Battiscombe, C. F., ed., *The Relics of St Cuthbert* (Oxford: University Press, 1956).

Beach, Milo Cleveland, *The Imperial Image* (Washington, D.C.: The Freer Gallery of Art, 1981).

Becker, H., B. Einig, & P. O. Ullrich, eds, *Liturgie als Sterbe- und Trauerhilfe, Ein interdisziplinares Kompendium* (1987).

Bede, *Ecclesiastical history of the English people*, ed. by B. Colgrave & R. A. B. Mynors (Oxford: Clarendon Press, 1969, repr. 1991).

Bibliography

Bede, *A History of the English Church and People*, trans. by Leo Sherley-Price and rev. R. E. Latham (Harmondsworth, England: Penguin Books, 1955, revised 1968).

Bede, *On the Tabernacle*, trans. with notes and intro. by Arthur G. Holder (Liverpool: University Press, 1994).

Bede, *De doctrina christiana*, ed. by J. Martin (Corpus Christianorum 32, Turnhout: Brepols, 1962).

Bede, *Ecclesiastical history of the English people*, ed. by B. Colgrave & R. A. B. Mynors (Oxford: Clarendon Press, 1969, repr. 1991).

Bede, *Homilies on the Gospels*, trans. by L. T. Martin & D. Hurst, 2 vols (Kalamazoo: Cistercian Publications, 1991).

Bede, *In Lucae evangelium expositio*, ed. by D. Hurst (Corpus Christianorum 120, Turnhout: Brepols, 1960).

Bede, *The exposition of the Apocalypse by the Venerable Bede*, trans. by E. Marshall (Oxford & London, 1878).

Bede, *The exposition of the Apocolypse*, trans. by E. Marshall (Oxford & London, 1878).

Beit-Arié, Malachi and Colette Sirat et al., *Manuscripts Médiévaux en caractères Hébraïques, portant des indications de date jusqu'a 1540* (Jérusalem: Académie Nationale des Sciences et des Lettres d'Israël; Paris: Centre National de la Recherche Scientifique, 1979).

Beit-Arié, M., 'Some Technical Practices Employed in Hebrew Dated Medieval Manuscripts', *Litterae textuales, Codicologica 2, Eléments pour une codicology comparée* (Leiden, 1978).

Bell, H. E., 'The Price of Books in Medieval England', *The Library*, Fourth Series 17 (1936-7).

Benoit, P. and others, 'Les grottes de Murabba'at', *DJD* II (1961).

Berger, Samuel, *Histoire de la Vulgate pendant les premieres siècles du Moyen Age* (Paris, 1893; repr. New York, 1956).

Betts, R. R., *Essays in Czech History* (London: Athlone Press, 1969).

Biggs, F. M., T. D. Hill, & P. E. Szarmach, eds, *The Sources of Anglo-Saxon Literary Culture: a Trial Version* (Binghampton, New York, 1990).

Biller, Peter, & Anne Hudson, eds, *Heresy and Literacy, 1000-1530* (Cambridge: University Press, 1994).

Birnbaum, Solomon A., *The Hebrew Scripts* (Leiden: E. J. Brill, 1954-7, 1971).

Birt, Th., *Das antike Buchwesen in seinem Verhältniss zur Litteratur* (Berlin: Hertz, 1882).

Birt, Th., *Kritik und Hermeneutik nebst Abriss des Antiken Buchwesens* (München, 1913).

Bischoff, Bernhard, *Manuscripts and Libraries in the Age of Charlemagne*, trans. & ed. by M. Gorman, Cambridge Studies in Palaeography and Codicology 1 (Cambridge: University Press, 1994).

Bishop, T. A. M., 'The Copenhagen Gospel-book', *Nordisc Tidskrist för Bok- och Biblioteksväsen* 54 (1967).

Blair, Peter Hunter, *An Introduction to Anglo-Saxon England* (2nd edn; Cambridge: University Press, 1977).

Blair, Peter Hunter, *Northumbria in the Days of Bede* (London: Gollancz, 1976).

Blair, Peter Hunter, *The World of Bede* (New York: St Martin's Press, 1970).

Blake, Norman, ed., *The Cambridge History of the English Language, Vol. 2, 1066-1476* (Cambridge: University Press, 1992).

Bonani, G., M. Broshi, I. Carmi, S. Ivy, J. Strugnell & W. Wölfli, 'Radiocarbon Dating of the Dead Sea Scrolls', *Atiqot* 20 (1991).

Bonner, G., ed., *Famulus Christi: Essays in Commemoration of the Thirteenth Centenary of the Birth of the Venerable Bede* (London: SPCK, 1976).

Bonner, Gerald, David Rollason, & Clare Stancliffe, *St Cuthbert, his Cult and his Community* (Woodbridge: Boydell Press, 1989).

Bibliography

Book of Kells, MS 58, Trinity College Library Dublin, ed. by P. Fox (Lucerne: Faksimile Verlag, 1990).

Bosch, Gulnar, John Carswell, & Guy Petherbridge, *Islamic Bindings and Bookmaking: Catalogue of an Exhibition, The Oriental Institute, The University of Chicago, 18 May-18 August 1981* (Chicago: The University of Chicago, 1981).

Brauer, Erich, *Ethnologie der jemenitischen Juden* (Heidelberg: Winters, 1934).

Braunfels, W., ed., *Karl der Grosse, Lebenswerk und Nachleben* (Düsseldorf: Schwamm- Bagel Verlag, 1965).

Brooks, N., *The Early History of the Church of Canterbury: Christ Church from 597 to 1066* (Leicester: University Press, 1984).

Brou, L., 'Etudes sur les Collectes du Psautier', *Sacris Erudiri* 6 (1954).

Brown, R. E., *The Birth of the Messiah* (London: Geoffrey Chapman, 1977).

Brown, T. J., 'The Irish Element in the Insular System of Scripts,' reprinted in *A Palaeographer's View: the Selected Writings of Julian Brown*, ed. by Janet Bately, Michelle P. Brown, & Jane Roberts (London: Harvey Miller, 1993).

Brown, T. J., ed., *The Stonyhurst Gospel of St John* (Oxford: University Press for the Roxburghe Club, 1969).

Brown, T. J., 'Northumbria and the Book of Kells', *Anglo-Saxon England*, 1 (Cambridge: University Press, 1972).

Bruce-Mitford, R. L. S., *The Art of the Codex Amiatinus*, Jarrow Lecture 1967 (Jarrow: Parish of Jarrow, [1968]), repr. *Journal of the British Archaeological Association*, 3rd ser. 32 (1969).

Buchthal, Hugo & O. Kurz, *A Hand List of Illuminated Oriental Christian Manuscripts* (repr. Nendeln: Kraus, 1968).

Buchthal, Hugo, 'The Painting of the Syrian Jacobites in its Relation to Byzantine and Islamic Art', *Syria* xx (1939).

Budge, Sir E. A. Wallis, *By Nile and Tigris: a Narrative of Journeys in Egypt and Mesopotamia on Behalf of the British Museum Between the Years 1886-1913* (London, 1920).

Bühler, Curt, ed., 'A Lollard Tract: On Translating the Bible into English', *Medium Ævum* 7 (1938).

Bülbring, Karl D., *The Earliest Complete English Prose Psalter [...]*, Early English Text Society o. s. 97 (London: Kegan Paul, Trench, Trübner & Co., 1891).

Burkitt, F. C., 'Kells, Durrow and Lindisfarne', *Antiquity* ix (1935).

Burrows, M., *The Dead Sea Scrolls of St. Mark's Monastery* (New Haven: American Schools of Oriental Research, 1950).

Calder, D. G., & M. J. B. Allen, *Sources and Analogues of Old English Poetry: the Major Latin Texts in Translation* (Cambridge: Brewer, 1976).

Camille, Michael, *Image on the Edge: the Margins of Medieval Art* (Cambridge, Mass.: Harvard University Press, 1992).

Carlini, A. & R. Kasser, *Papyrus XXXVIII: I1 Pastore (Ia-IIIa visione) Erma* (Cologny-Geneva: Fondation Martin Bodmer, 1991).

Carr, Annemarie Weyl, *Byzantine Illumination 1150-1250: the Study of a Provincial Tradition* (Chicago and London: The University of Chicago Press, 1987).

Carswell, J., 'Fastenings on the Qumran Manuscripts', *DJD* vi (1977).

Catalogue of Additions to the Manuscripts 1931-1935 (London: British Museum, 1967).

Catalogue of the Harleian Manuscripts in the British Museum, with Indexes of Persons, Places and Matters (Hildesheim & New York, Olms, 1973).

Catalogus Codicum Manuscriptorum Orientalium qui in Museo Brittanico asservantur. Pars Secunda: Codices Arabicos Amplectens I (London, 1846).

Catto, J. I., & Ralph Evans, eds, *The History of the University of Oxford*, vol. 2, *Late Medieval Oxford* (Oxford: Clarendon Press, 1992).

Bibliography

Cavallo, Guglielmo, *Ricerche sulla maiuscola biblica* (Florence: Le Monnier, 1967).

Cecchelli, C., G. Furlani, & M. Salmi, *The Rabbula Gospels: Facsimile Edition of the Miniatures of the Syriac Manuscript Plut. I. 56 in the Medicaean-Lauretian Library* (Olten & Lausanne: Urs Graf Verlag, 1959).

Černý, Jaroslav, *Paper and Books in Ancient Egypt: an Inaugural Lecture Delivered at University College London 29 May 1947* (London: H. K. Lewis, 1952).

Chadwick, Owen, *John Cassian: a Study in Primitive Monasticism* (Cambridge: University Press, 2nd edn, 1968).

Chapman, J., *Notes on the early history of the Vulgate Gospels* (Oxford: Clarendon Press, 1908).

Chaucer, G., *The Riverside Chaucer*, ed. by Larry D. Benson et al., 3rd edn (Boston: Houghton Mifflin Co., 1987).

The Christian Orient (London: The British Library, 1978).

The Church Historians of England, vol III, ii, *containing the Historical Works of Symeon of Durham*, trans. by J. Stevenson (London: Seeleys, 1855).

Churches Built in Ancient Times: Recent Studies in Early Christian Archaeology, ed. by Kenneth Painter, Vol. 16 of Occasional Papers from The Society of Antiquaries of London, Vol. 1, Specialist Studies of the Mediterranean (London: The Society of Antiquaries/The Acordia Research Centre, University of London, 1994).

Clanchy, M. T., *From Memory to Written Record, England 1066-1307* (2nd edn; Oxford: Blackwell, 1993).

Clark, K. W., 'The Posture of the Ancient Scribe', *BA* 26 (1963).

Codex Sinaiticus Petropolitanus. The Old Testament ... now reproduced in facsimile from photographs by Helen and Kirsopp Lake with a description and introduction to the history of the Codex by Kirsopp Lake (Oxford: Clarendon Press, 1911), New Testament (1922).

Colgrave, B., ed., *The Life of Bishop Wilfred by Eddius Stephanus* (with parallel translation) (Cambridge: University Press, 1927).

Conneely, D., *The Letters of St Patrick* (Maynooth: An Sagart, 1993).

Copeland, Rita, *Rhetoric, Hermeneutics, and Translation in the Middle Ages: Academic Traditions and Vernacular Texts* (Cambridge: University Press, 1991).

Coptic Encyclopedia, ed. by Aziz S. Atiya (New York: Macmillan, 1991).

Cordoliani, A., 'Le texte de la Bible en Irlande du Ve au IXe siècle', *Revue Biblique* 57 (1950).

Crawford, S. J., *The Old English Version of the Heptateuch, Ælfric's Treatise on the Old and New Testament and his Preface to Genesis*, Early English Text Society 160 (London: Oxford University Press, 1922; repr. 1969).

Cross, Clare, *Church and People 1450-1660: The Triumph of the Laity in the English Church* (Glasgow: Fontana/Collins, 1976).

Cross, F. L. & E. A. Livingstone, eds, *The Oxford Dictionary of the Christian Church* (2nd edn; Oxford: University Press, 1983).

Cross, F. M., 'Epigraphic Notes on Hebrew Documents of the Eighth-Sixth Centuries B.C. II. The Murabba> at Papyrus and the Letter Found near Yabneh-Yam', *BASOR* 165 (1962).

Cross, F. M., 'Le travail d'édition des fragments manuscrits de Qumrân', *RB* 63 (1956).

Crowfoot, G. M., *DJD* I (1955).

Crum, W. E., *Catalogue of the Coptic Manuscripts in the British Museum* (London: British Museum, 1905).

Curran, M., *The Antiphonary of Bangor* (Dublin: Irish Academic Press, 1984).

Daiches, David & Anthony Thorlby, eds, *The Mediaeval World* (London: Aldus Books, 1973).

Davis, John F., *Heresy and Reformation in the South East of England 1520-1559* (London: Royal Historical Society, 1983).

Deanesly, Margaret, *The Lollard Bible and Other Medieval Biblical Versions* (Cambridge: University Press, 1920).

Bibliography

DeBruyne, Donatien, *Sommaires, Divisions et Rubriques de la Bible latine* (Namur: Auguste Godenne, 1914).

De doctrina christiana 3.35-6., ed. by J. Martin (*Corpus Christianorum* 32, Turnhout: Brepols, 1962).

de Hamel, Christopher, *A History of Illuminated Manuscripts* (London: Phaidon, 1994).

de Hamel, Christopher, *Scribes and Illuminators* (London: The British Library & Toronto: University of Toronto Press, 1992).

de Jerphanion, G., *Les miniatures du manuscrit syriaque no. 559 de la Bibl. Vat.* (Città del Vaticano, 1940).

Delaissé, L. M. J., 'The Importance of Books of Hours for the History of the Medieval Book', *Gatherings in Honor of Dorothy Miner* (Baltimore, 1974).

Delany, Sheila, *The Naked Text: Chaucer's Legend of Good Women* (Berkeley & Los Angeles: University of California Press, 1994).

del Medico, H. E., *L'énigme des manuscrits de la Mer Morte* (Paris: Plon, 1957).

Demirez, Yildiz, 'Topkapi Sarayi III. Ahmed Kutuphanesinde bir Arapca Incil', *Sanat Tarihi Yillige* (1966-8).

Depuydt, Leo, *Catalogue of Coptic Manuscripts in the Pierpont Morgan Library*, 2 vols, Corpus of Illuminated Manuscripts 4-5 (Oriental Series 1-2) (Louvain: Peeters, 1993).

Der Nersessian, Sirarpie, *Armenian Art* (Paris: Arts & Metiers Graphiques, 1978).

de Vaux, R., 'Fouilles de Feshkha', *RB* 66 (1959).

de Vaux, R., 'Fouilles au Khirbet Qumran: Rapport préliminaire sur la dernière campagne', *RB* 61 (1954).

de Vooght, P., *Les Sources de la Doctrine chrétienne d'après les Theologiens du XIVe siècle et du début du Xve* (Bruges: Desclée De Brouwer, 1954).

Dickens, A. G., *The English Reformation* (2nd edn; London: Batsford, 1989).

Dickens, A. G., *Lollards and Protestants in the Diocese of York 1509-1588* (2nd edn; London: Hambledon Press, 1982).

di Febo, Assunta, Kostantinos Houlis, Gabriele Mazzuco, & Sever J. Voicu, *Legature Bizantine Vaticane e Marciane*, exhibition catalogue, 9 Sept.-30 Oct. 1989 at the Biblioteca Nazionale Marciana (Venice, 1989).

Dobson, R. B., *The Peasants' Revolt of 1381* (London: Macmillan, 1970).

Dodwell, C. R., & P. Clemoes, *The Old English Illustrated Hexateuch. British Museum Cotton Claudius B. IV*, Early English Manuscripts in Facsimile 18 (Copenhagen: Rosenkilde & Bagger, 1974).

Doyle, A. I., 'A Survey of the Origins and Circulation of Theological Writings in English in the Fourteenth, Fifteenth and Early Sixteenth Centuries, with Special Consideration of the Part of the Clergy Therein', Ph.D. dissertation (2 vols; University of Cambridge, 1953).

Duby, G., *Les trois ordres ou l'imaginaire du féodalisme* (Paris: Gallimard, 1978; trans. by Arthur Goldhammer as *The Three Orders: Feudal Society Imagined*, Chicago: University Press, 1980).

Dukan, Michèle, *La réglure des manuscrits hébreux au moyen age* (Paris: Editions du CNRS, 1988).

Dukan, Michèle, 'De la difficulté à reconnaître des instruments de réglure: planche à régler (mastara) et cadre-patron,' *Scriptorium* 40, no. 2 (1986).

Eales, R., & R. Sharpe, eds, *Canterbury and the Norman Conquest: Churches, Saints and Scholars, 1066-1109* (London: Hambledon Press, 1995).

Edwards, A. S. G., ed., *Middle English Prose: a Critical Guide to Major Authors and Genres* (New Brunswick, N.J.: Rutgers University Press).

Elbogen, Ismar, *Jewish Liturgy: a Comprehensive History*, transl. by Raymond P. Scheindlin (Philadelphia: Jewish Publication Society; New York: Jewish Theological Seminary of America (5753-1993).

Bibliography

Elliot, J. K., *A Bibliography of Greek New Testament Manuscripts* (Cambridge: University Press, 1989).

Emmel, Stephen, 'Shenoute's Literary Corpus' (Ph.D. diss.; Yale University, 1993).

Encyclopedia Judaica (New York: Macmillan; Jerusalem: Keter, 1971).

English, Edward, ed., *Reading and Wisdom: the De Doctrina of Augustine in the Middle Ages* (Notre Dame, Ind.: University of Notre Dame Press, 1995).

Eshel, E., H. Eshel, & A. Yardeni, 'A Qumran Composition Containing Part of Ps. 154 and a Prayer for the Welfare of King Jonathan and his Kingdom', *IEJ* 42 (1992).

Ettinghausen, Richard, *Arab Painting* (repr. London & Basingstoke: Skira, 1977).

Ettinghausen, R., 'Foundation-moulded Leatherwork – a Rare Egyptian Technique also used in Britain', *Studies in Islamic Art and Architecture in Honour of Professor K. A. C. Cresswell* (Cairo: The American University in Cairo, 1965).

Ettinghausen, R., 'Near Eastern Covers and their Influence on European Bindings', *Ars Orientalis* III (1959).

Evangeliorum Quattuor Codex Durmachensis (2 vols; Olten, Lausanne, & Freiburg: Urs Graf Verlag, 1960).

Evetts, Deborah M., 'Traditional Islamic Chevron Headband', *Guild of Book Workers Journal* 19 (1980-1).

Fadda, A. M. Fuiselli, & E. Ó. Carragáin, eds, *Quadetui di Romano-Barbaica* 1 (Rome, in press).

Farmer, D. H., & J. F. Webb, *The Age of Bede* (Harmondsworth, England: Penguin Books, 1965, 1983).

Federici, Carlo, & Kostantinos Houlis, *Legature Bizantine Vaticane* (Rome: Fratelli Palombi Editori, 1988).

Fields, W., 'Qumran Scribal Practices and the Size of the Column Block in the Scrolls from the Judean Desert', Unpublished seminar paper, Hebrew University (Jerusalem, 1987).

Fischer, B., *Lateinische Bibelhandschriften im Frühen Mittelalter* (Freiburg: Herder, 1985).

Fischer, Bonifatius, *Die lateinischen Evangelien bis zum 10. Jahrhundert* (Aus der Geschichte der lateinischen Bibel 13, 15, 17, 18; Freiburg im Breisgau: Herder, 1988, 1989, 1990, 1991).

Fitzmyer, J. A., *The Dead Sea Scrolls, Major Publications and Tools for Study*, rev. edn (SBL Resources for Biblical Study 20; Atlanta, GA: Scholars Press, 1990).

Fletcher, Alan J., 'The Faith of a Simple Man: Carpenter John's Creed in the Miller's Tale', *Medium Ævum* 61 (1992).

Fowler, David C., 'John Trevisa and the English Bible', *Modern Philology* 58 (1960).

Fowler, David C., *The Life and Times of John Trevisa, Medieval Scholar* (Seattle & London: University of Washington Press, 1995).

Foxe, John, *Acts and Monuments*, ed. by George Townsend, 8 vols (London: Seeley, Burnside & Seeley, 1843-9).

Frantzen, A. J., *King Alfred* (Boston, Mass.: Twayne Publishers, 1986).

Freedman, D. N. & K. A. Mathews, *The Paleo-Hebrew Leviticus Scroll* (11QpaleoLev; Winona Lake, Ind.: Eisenbrauns, 1985).

Friedman, Florence, ed., *Beyond the Pharaohs: Egypt and the Copts in the 2nd to 7th Centuries A.D.*, Exhibition Catalogue, Museum of Art (Rhode Island School of Design, 1989).

Fristedt, Sven L., 'The Authorship of the Lollard Bible', *Studier i Modern Språkvetenskap (= Stockholm Studies in Modern Philology)* 19 (1956).

Fristedt, Sven L., 'A Weird Manuscript Enigma in the British Museum', *Studier i Modern Språkvetenskap*, n.s. 2 (1964).

Fristedt, Sven L., 'New Light on John Wycliffe and the First Full English Bible', *Studier i Modern Språkvetenskap*, n.s. 3 (1968).

Fristedt, Sven L., *MS. Bodley 959: Genesis-Baruch 3.20 in the Earlier Version of the Wycliffite Bible*, 5 vols, [Stockholm Studies in English 6 (1959), 8 (1961), 10 (1963), 13 (1965), 20 (1969)].

Bibliography

Furlani, Giuseppe and Mario Salmi, *The Rabbula Gospels: Facsimile Edition of the Miniatures of the Syriac Manuscript Plut. I. 56 in the Medicaean-Laurentian Library* (Olten & Lausanne: Urs Graf-Verlag, 1959).

Gallo, I., *Greek and Latin Papyrology*, Classical Handbook 1 (London: Institute of Classical Studies, 1986).

Gameson, Richard, ed., *The Early Medieval Bible: its Production, Decoration and Use*, Cambridge Studies in Palaeography and Codicology 2 (Cambridge: University Press, 1994).

Gamillscheg, Ernst & Dieter Harlfinger, *Repertorium der griechischen Kopisten 800-1600, 1. Teil. Handschriften aus Bibliotheken Grossbritanniens* (Vienna: Österreichischen Akademie der Wissenschaft, 1981).

Ganz, Peter, ed., *The Role of the Book in Medieval Culture* [*Bibliologia 3 and 4*] (Turnhout: Brepols, 1986).

Garel, M., 'The Foa Bible', *Journal of Jewish Art* (1979).

Gilissen, L., 'La composition des cahiers, le pliage du parchemin et l'imposition', *Scriptorium: International Review of Manuscript Studies* 26 (1972).

Gilissen, L., *La reliure occidentale antérieure a 1400*, Bibliogia 1 (Turnhout: Brepols, 1983).

Glatzer, M., 'The Aleppo Codex – Codicological and Paleographical Aspects', *Sefunot* 4 (1989).

Glickler-Chazon, E., 'New Liturgical Manuscripts from Qumran', *Proceedings of the Eleventh World Congress of Jewish Studies* A (Jerusalem, 1994).

Godden, Malcolm, & Michael Lapidge, eds, *The Cambridge Companion to Old English Literature* (Cambridge: University Press, 1991).

Godfrey, C. J., *The Church in Anglo-Saxon England* (Cambridge: University Press, 1962).

Godlewski, Wodzimierz, ed., *Coptic Studies: Acts of the Third International Congress of Coptic Studies, Warsaw, 20-25 August, 1984* (Warsaw: Państwowe Wydawnictwo Naukowe, 1990).

Goitein, S. D., *A Mediterranean Society: The Jewish Communities of the Arab World as Portrayed in the Documents of the Cairo Geniza* (Berkeley: University of California Press, 1971).

Golb, N., 'Khirbet Qumran and the Manuscripts of the Judaean Wilderness – Observations on the Logic of Their Investigation', *JNES* 49 (1990).

Golb, N., 'The Problem of Origin and Identification of the Dead Sea Scrolls', *Proc. Am. Phil. Soc.* 124 (1980).

Golb, N., 'Who Hid the Dead Sea Scrolls?' *BA* 48 (1985).

Golb, N., *Who Wrote the Dead Sea Scrolls – The Search for the Secret of Qumran* (New York: Scribner, 1994).

Goranson, S., 'Qumran: a Hub of Scribal Activity', *BAR* 20,5 (1994).

Goranson, S., 'An Inkwell from Qumran', *Michmanim* 6 (1992).

Graf, Georg, *Geschichte der Christlichen Arabischen Literatur* I [Città del Vaticano: Biblioteca Apostolica Vaticana, Studi e Testi CXVIII (1944), and II, Studi e Testi CXXXIII (1947)].

Graham, Timothy, *The Bible as Book: the Earliest Printed Editions. An Exhibition of Items from the Van Kampen Collection* (Grand Haven, Mich.: The Scriptorium, 1996).

Gregory, Casper René, *Canon and Text of the New Testament* (Edinburgh: T. & T. Clark, 1907).

Gregory, Casper René, *Texkritik des neuen Testamentes* (Leipzig: J. C. Hinrichs, 1900-9).

Gregory the Great, St, *Homilies on the Book of Ezekiel*, trans. by T. Gray (Etna, California: Center for Traditionalist Orthodox Studies, 1990).

Griffith, Sidney H., 'The Gospel in Arabic: an enquiry into its appearance in the first Abbasid century', *Oriens Christianus* 69 (1985), repr. in Griffith, *Arabic Christianity in the Monasteries of Ninth-Century Palestine* (Aldershot: Variorum, 1992).

Griffiths, Jeremy & Derek Pearsall, eds, *Book Production and Publishing in Britain 1375-1475* (Cambridge: University Press, 1989).

Grillmeier, Aloys, *Der Logos am Kreuz* (Munich: Max Hueber, 1956).

Bibliography

Guida e Storia Abbazia del SS. Salvatore al Monte Amiata (Abbazia SS. Salvatore, 1991).

Hamilton, N. E. S. A., ed., *Willelmi malmesbiriensis monachi de gestis pontificum anglorum*, Rolls Series 52 (London: Longman/Trübner, 1870).

Hanson, A. T., *The Pastoral Epistles* (Grand Rapids, Mich.: Eerdmans, 1982).

Haran, M., 'Bible Scrolls in Eastern and Western Jewish Communities from Qumran to the High Middle Ages', *HUCA* 56 91985).

Haran, M., 'Book-Scrolls in Israel in Pre-Exilic Times', *JJS* 33 (1982).

Haran, M., 'Scribal Workmanship in Biblical Times – The Scrolls and the Writing Implements', *Tarbiz* 50 (1981).

Hargreaves, Henry, 'From Bede to Wyclif: Medieval English Bible Translations', *Bulletin of the John Rylands Library* 48 (1965-6).

Hargreaves, Henry, 'The Latin Text of Purvey's Psalter', *Medium Ævum* 24 (1955).

Hargreaves, Henry, 'The Marginal Glosses to the Wycliffite New Testament', *Studia Neophilologica* 33 (1961).

Harthan, J., *Books of Hours and their Owners* (London, 1977).

Hatch, Edwin & Henry A. Redpath, *A Concordance to the Septuagint and the other Greek versions of the Old Testament* (Graz: Akademische Druck, 1954).

Hatch, W. H. P., *Album of Dated Syriac Manuscripts* (Boston: American Academy of Sciences, 1946).

Haxen, U., *Kings and Citizens*, Exhibition Catalogue of the Jewish Museum, New York, (1963).

Hayward, C. T. R., 'The Holy Name of Moses and the Prologue of St John's Gospel', *NTS* 25 (1978-9).

Henderson, George, *From Durrow to Kells: the Insular Gospel-books 650-800* (London: Thames & Hudson, 1987).

Henry, Françoise, *The Book of Kells* (London: Thames & Hudson, 1977).

Henry, Françoise, *The Book of Kells* (London: Thames & Hudson, 1974, repr. 1988).

Henry, Françoise & G. L. Marsh-Micheli, 'A Century of Irish Illumination', *Proceedings of the Royal Irish Academy* 62C (1961-2; published 1962).

Henry, Françoise, 'Remarks on the Decoration of Three Irish Psalters', *Proceedings of the Royal Irish Academy* 61C (1960-1; published 1960).

Herbert, E. D., *A New Method for Reconstructing Biblical Scrolls, and Its Application to the Reconstruction of 4QSam^a*, Unpubl. Diss., Cambridge, 1995).

Hiergemann, A., ed., *Festschrift Bernhard Bischoff* (Stuttgart, 1971).

Hilgarth, J. N., 'Ireland and Spain in the seventh century', *Peritia* 3 (1984).

Historica de la liturgia, vol. I, trans. by C. Urtasan Irisarri (Madrid: Biblioteca de Autores Cristianos, 1955).

The Holy Bible ... made from the Latin Vulgate by John Wycliffe and his Followers, ed. by Josiah Forshall & Frederic Madden, 4 vols (Oxford: University Press, 1850).

Horner, G., *The Coptic Version of the New Testament in the Northern Dialect*, 4 vols (Oxford: University Press, 1898-1905).

Hudson, Anne, *Lollards and their Books* (London & Ronceverte: Hambledon Press, 1985).

Hudson, Anne, *The Premature Reformation: Wycliffite Texts and Lollard History* (Oxford: Clarendon Press, 1988).

Hudson, Anne, *Selections from English Wycliffite Writings* (Cambridge: University Press, 1978).

Hudson, Anne, ed., *Two Wycliffite Texts: The Sermon of William Taylor, 1406; The Testimony of William Thorpe, 1407*, Early English Text Society, o. s. 301 (Oxford: University Press, 1993).

Hudson, Anne, & Pamela Gradon, eds, *English Wycliffite Sermons*, 5 vols (Oxford: Clarendon Press, 1983-96).

Bibliography

Huglo, M., 'Un Tonaire du Graduel de la fin du VIIIe siècle, Paris, B. N. lat. 13159', *Revue Grégorienne* 31 (1952).

Humbert, J. B., & A. Chambon, *Fouilles de Khirbet Qumrân et de Aïn Feshkha*, I, Novum Testamentum et Orbis Antiquus, Series Archaeologica 1 (Fribourg-Göttingen, 1994).

Hunt, Lucy-Anne, 'Art and Colonialism: the Mosaics of the Church of the Nativity in Bethlehem (1169) and the Problem of "Crusader" Art', *Dumbarton Oaks Papers* XLV (1991).

Hunt, Lucy-Anne, 'Christian-Muslim Relations in Egypt of the Twelfth to mid-Thirteenth Centuries: Sources of Wallpainting at Deir es-Suriani and the Illustration of the New Testament MS Paris, Copte-Arabe 1/Cairo, Bibl. 94', *Cahiers Archéologiques* XXXIII (1985).

Hunt, Lucy-Anne, 'The Syriac Buchanan Bible in Cambridge: Book Illumination in Syria, Cilicia and Jerusalem of the later Twelfth Century', *Orientalia Christiana Periodica* LVII, fasc. 2 (1991).

Hunt, Simon, 'An Edition of Tracts in Favour of Scriptural Translation and of Some Texts Connected with Lollard Vernacular Biblical Scholarship' (D.Phil. diss., University of Oxford, 1994).

Huppe, Bernard, *Doctrine and Poetry: Augustine's Influence on Old English Poetry* (New York: State University of New York, 1959).

Hurley, Michael, '"Scriptura Sola": Wyclif and his Critics', *Traditio* 16 (1960).

Hurst, A., O. Reverdin, & J. Rudhardt, *Papyrus Bodmer XXIX: Vision de Dorothéos* (Cologny-Geneva: Fondation Martin Bodmer, 1984).

Irenaeus, *Adversus haerses*, ed. by F. Saguard, *Sources chrétiennes* 34 (Paris: 1952).

Irigoin, Jean, 'Papiers orientaux et papiers occidentaux', *La paléographie grecque et byzantine: Paris 21-25 octobre 1974* (Paris: Editions de CNRS, 1977).

James, David, *Qur'âns of the Mamlûks* (London: Alexandria Press/Thames & Hudson, 1988).

James, M. R., *The Ancient Libraries of Canterbury and Dover: the Catalogues of the Libraries of Christ Church Priory and St Augustine's Abbey at Canterbury and of St Martin's Priory at Dover* (Cambridge: University Press, 1903).

Jellicoe, S., *The Septuagint and Modern Study* (Oxford: Clarendon Press, 1968).

Jerome, St, *Commentariorum in Matheum* (Corpus Christianorum 77, Turnhout: Brepols, 1969).

Johns, J. J., 'The Greek Church and the Conversion of Muslims in Norman Sicily', *Byzantinische Forschungen* 21 (1995).

Joüon, Paul, *A Grammar of Biblical Hebrew*, transl. and rev. by T. Muraoka (Roma: Editrice Pontificio Istituto Biblico, 1993).

Jull, A. J. T., D. J. Donahue, M. Broshi, & E. Tov, 'Radio-carbon Dating of Scrolls and Linen Fragments from the Judean Desert', *Radiocarbon* 37 (1995).

Justice, Steven, *Writing and Rebellion: England in 1381* (Berkeley & Los Angeles: University of California Press, 1994).

Kahle, Paul, *Masoreten des Ostens: Die ältesten punktierten Handschriften des Alten Testaments und der Targume* (Leipzig: Hinrichs'sche Buchhandlung, 1913).

Karkov, C., & R. Farrell, eds, *Studies in Insular Art and Archaeology* (Oxford, Ohio: American Early Medieval Studies and the Miami University School of Fine Arts, 1991).

Kasser, R., 'Bodmer Papyri', *Coptic Encyclopedia*, vol. 8, ed. by Aziz S. Atiya (New York: Macmillan, 1991).

Katalogos tôn neôn arabikôn cheirographôn tes hieras monês hagias aikaterinês tou orous sina (Athens: Epitalophos A.B.E.E., 1985).

Keen, Maurice, *English Society in the Later Middle Ages 1348-1500* (London: Penguin Books, 1990).

Kelly, J. N. D., *Early Christian Creeds*, 3rd edn (London: Longman, 1972).

Kendrick, T. D., T. J. Brown, R. L. S. Bruce-Mitford et al., eds, *Euangeliorum Quattuor Codex Lindisfarnensis*, 2 vols (Olten & Lausanne: Urs Graf-Verlag, 1956-60).

Bibliography

Kenney, J. F., *The Sources for the Early History of Ireland: Ecclesiastical. An Introduction and Guide*, with addenda by L. Bieler (New York: Octagon Books, 1996).

Kenny, Anthony, *Wyclif* (Oxford: University Press, 1985).

Kenny, Anthony, ed., *Wyclif in his Times* (Oxford: Clarendon Press, 1986).

Ker, N. R., *Catalogue of Manuscripts Containing Anglo-Saxon* (Oxford: Clarendon Press, 1957; re-issued with suppl., 1990).

Keynes, S., & M. Lapidge, *Alfred the Great* (Harmondsworth: Penguin, 1983).

Khach 'ikyan, L. S., ed., *XV Dari Hayeren Tseragreri Hishatakaranner*, vol. 1 [1401-1450] (Erevan, 1950).

Kitzinger, E., *The Mosaics of St Mary's of the Admiral in Palermo* (Washington: Dumbarton Oaks, 1990).

Knapp, P. A., *The Style of John Wyclif's English Sermons* (The Hague & Paris: Mouton, 1977).

Knighton, Henry, *Knighton's Chronicle 1337-1396*, ed. and trans. by G. H. Martin (Oxford: Clarendon Press).

Koriun, *The Life of Mashtots*, trans. by Bedros Norehad (New York, 1965). Reprinted in *Vark' Mashtots 'i—Koriwn* (Delmar, NY: Caravan Books, 1985).

Kranzberg, M., & W. H. Davenport, eds, *Technology and Culture: An Anthology* (New York, 1972).

Krapp, G. P. & E. V. K. Dobbie, eds, *The Exeter Book*, Anglo-Saxon Poetic Records 3 (New York: Columbia University Press, 1936).

Kuczynski, Michael P., *Prophetic Song: the Psalms as Moral Discourse in Late Medieval England* (Philadelphia: University of Pennsylvania Press, 1995).

Kuder, U., 'Die Initialen des Amienspsalters (Amiens, Bibliothèque municipale MS 18)' (unpublished Ph.D. dissertation, Ludwig-Maximilians-Universität, Munich, 1977).

Kuhl, C., 'Schreibereigentümlichkeiten – Bemerkun-gen zur Jesajarolle (DSIa)', *VT* 2 (1952).

Kuhn, S. M., *The Vespasian Psalter* (Ann Arbor: University of Michigan Press, 1965).

Laistner, M. L. W., *The Intellectual Heritage of the Early Middle Ages*, ed. by C. G. Starr (Ithaca, NY: Cornell University Press, 1957).

Lambert, Malcolm, *Medieval Heresy: Popular Movements from the Gregorian Reform to the Reformation* (2nd edn; Oxford: Blackwell, 1992).

Lampe, G. W. H., ed., *The Cambridge History of the Bible*, 3 vols (Cambridge: University Press, 1969).

Lapidge, Michael, 'The School of Theodore and Hadrian', *Anglo-Saxon England* 15 (1986).

Lapidge, M., ed., *Archbishop Theodore: Commemorative Studies on his Life and Influence*, Cambridge Studies in Anglo-Saxon England 11 (Cambridge: University Press, 1995).

Lapidge, Michael, & Bernhard Bischoff, eds, *Biblical Commentaries from the Canterbury School of Theodore and Hadrian* (Cambridge: University Press, 1994).

Lapidge, M., & H. Gneuss, eds, *Learning and Literature in Anglo-Saxon England: Studies Presented to Peter Clemoes on the Occasion of his Sixty-fifth Birthday* (Cambridge: University Press, 1985).

Lapidge, Michael, & M. Herren, eds, *Aldhelm: the Prose Works* (Ipswich: Brewer, 1979).

Lasko, P., *The Kingdom of the Franks* (London: Thames & Hudson, 1971).

Lawlor, H. J., 'The Cathach of St Columba', *Proceedings of the Royal Irish Academy* 23C, 1916.

Layton, Bentley, *The Gnostic Scriptures* (Garden City: Doubleday, 1987).

Lechler, G., *John Wycliffe and his English Precursors*, trans. by P. Lorimer (London: Religious Tract Society, 1884).

Leff, Gordon, *Heresy in the Later Middle Ages*, 2 vols (Manchester: University Press, 1967).

Lehmann, Henning, & J. J. S. Weitenberg, eds, *Armenian Texts, Tasks, and Tools* (Aarhus, Denmark, 1993).

Bibliography

Lehmann-Haupt, H., ed., *Homage to a Bookman: Essays on Manuscripts, Books and Printing written for Hans P. Kraus on his 60th. Birthday* (Berlin: Mann, 1967).

Leroquais, V., *Les Livres d'Heures Manuscrits de la Bibliothèque Nationale*, 3 vols (Paris, 1927, with supplement, 1943).

Leroquais, V., *Les psautiers manuscrits latins des bibliothèques publiques de France* (Macon: Protat Frères, 1940).

Leroy, Jules, 'Un Évangélaire arabe de la Bibliothèque de Topkapi Sarayi à décor Byzantin et Islamique', *Syria* XLIV (1967).

Leroy, Jules, *Les Manuscrits Coptes et Coptes-Arabes Illustrés*, Institut Français d'Archéologie de Beyrouth, Bibliothèque archéologique et historique, XCVI (Paris: Paul Geuthner, 1974).

Leroy, Jules, *Les Manuscrits syriaques à peintures conservés dans les bibliothèques d'Europe et d'Orient* (Paris: Geuthner, 1964).

Leroy, Jules, *Les types de réglure des manuscrits grecs* (Paris: Editions du CNRS, 1976).

Lewis, John, *The New Testament by John Wyclif* (London, 1731).

Lewis, Naphtali, *Papyrus in Classical Antiquity* (Oxford: University Press, 1974).

Lewis, S., 'Sacred calligraphy: the chi-rho page in the Book of Kells', *Traditio* 36 (1980).

Liber Psalmorum ex recensione Sancti Hieronimi (Biblia Sacra iuxta Latinam Vulgatam Versionem ad codicum fidem 10, Rome: Vatican Polyglot Press, 1953).

Lindberg, C., ed., *MS. Bodley 959: Genesis-Baruch 3.20 in the Earlier Version of the Wycliffite Bible*, 5 vols *(Stockholm Studies in English* 6 (1959), 8 (1961), 10 (1963), 13 (1965), 20 (1969).

Lindberg, Conrad, 'The Manuscripts and Versions of the Wycliffite Bible: a Preliminary Survey,' *Studia Neophilogica* 42 (1970).

Liuzza, R. M., *The Old English Version of the Gospels. Volume I. Text and Introduction*, Early English Text Society 304 (Oxford: University Press, 1994).

Llewelyn, S. R. & R. A. Kearsley, *New Documents Illustrating Early Christianity* (Macquarie: Macquarie University, 1992).

Louth, A., *Maximus the Confessor* (London: Routledge, 1996).

Lowden, John, *Illuminated Prophet Books: a Study of Byzantine Manuscripts of the Major and Minor Prophets* (University Park & London: Pennsylvania University Press, 1988).

Lowe, E. A., *Codices Latini Antiquiores* (12 parts; Oxford: University Press, 1934-71; second edition of part II, 1972).

Lowe, E. A., *Codices Latini Antiquiores* (Oxford: Clarendon Press, 1991).

Lowe, E. A., *English Uncial* (Oxford: University Press, 1960).

Lyon, H. R., *The Making of the English Nation: From the Anglo-Saxons to Edward I* (London: Thames & Hudson, 1991).

McCone, K., *Pagan Past and Christian Present in early Irish Literature* (Maynooth: An Sagart, 1991).

McCracken, V. E., L. M. C. Randall, & R. H. Randall, Jr, eds, *Gatherings in Honor of Dorothy Miner* (Baltimore, 1974).

McFarlane, K. B., *John Wycliffe and the Beginnings of English Nonconformity* (London: English Universities Press, 1952).

McGurk, Patrick, 'The Irish pocket Gospel Book', *Sacris Erudiri* 8 (1956).

McGurk, Patrick, *Latin Gospel Books from A.D. 400 to A.D. 800* (Les Publications de Scriptorium V; Paris & Brussels: Editions Erasme, 1961).

McGurk, Patrick, *The Book of Kells*, Commentary volume, ed. Peter Fox (Lucerne: Faksimile Verlag Luzern, 1990).

McNally, R., 'Der irische *Liber de numeris*: eine Quellenanalyse des *ps-isidorischen Liber de numeris*' (Dissertation, Munich 1957).

McNally, R., 'The *Tres Lingua Sacrae* in early Irish Bible exegesis', *Theological Studies* 19 (1958).

Bibliography

McNally, R., ed., *Scriptores Hiberniae Minores I*, Corpus Chritianorum 108 B (Turnhout: Brepols, 1973).

McNamara, Martin, 'Psalter Text and Psalter Study in the Early Irish Church (AD 600-1200)', *Proceedings of the Royal Irish Academy 73C* (1973).

McNamara, M., ed., *Biblical Studies: the Medieval Irish Contribution*, Proceedings of the Irish Biblical Association 1 (Dublin: Dominican Publications, 1976).

McNamara, M., ed., *Glossa in Psalmos: the Hiberno-Latin Gloss on the Psalms of Codex Palatinus Latinus 68 (Psalms 39:11-151:7)* (Studi e Testi 310, Vatican City: Biblioteca Apostolica Vaticana, 1986).

McNamara, Martin, 'The Celtic-Irish Mixed Gospel Text: some recent contributions and centennial reflections', *Filologia mediolatina*, II; Spoleto: Centro Italiano di Studi sull'Alto Medioevo, 1995.

McNiven, Peter, *Heresy and Politics in the Reign of Henry IV: the Burning of John Badby* (Woodbridge, Suffolk: Boydell, 1987).

Manafis, Konstantinos, gen. ed., *Sinai: Treasures of the Monastery of Saint Catherine* (Athens: Ekdotike Athenon S.A., 1990).

Manuscript, Society, and Belief on Early Christian Egypt (London: Oxford University Press, 1979).

Marsden, Richard, 'Job in his Place: the Ezra Miniature in the Codex Amiatinus', *Scriptorium* 49 (1995).

Marsden, Richard, *The Text of the Old Testament in Anglo-Saxon England*, Cambridge Studies in Anglo-Saxon England 15 (Cambridge: University Press, 1995).

Marsden, Richard, 'Cain's Face, and Other Problems: the Legacy of the Earliest English Bible Translations' (*Reformation*, January 1996).

Martin, M., *The Scribal Character of the Dead Sea Scrolls* I-II (Bibliothèque du Muséon 44, 45; Louvain, 1958).

Martínez, F. García, & A. S. van der Woude, 'A "Groningen" Hypothesis of Qumran Origins and Early History', *RevQ* 14 (1990).

Masai, François, *Essai sur les Origines de la Miniature dite irlandaise*, Publications de Scriptorium, I (Brussels & Antwerp, 1947).

Masai, François, 'Observations sur le psautier dit de Charlemagne (Paris lat. 13159)', *Scriptorium 6* (1952).

Mathews, Thomas F., & Avedis K. Sanjian, *Armenian Gospel Iconography: the Tradition of the Glajor Gospel* (Washington, D.C.: Dumbarton Oaks, 1991).

Mathews, Thomas F., & Roger S. Wieck, eds, *Treasures in Heaven: Armenian Illuminated Manuscripts* (New York: Pierpont Morgan Library, 1994).

Matozzi, Ivo, *Produzione e commercio della carta nello stato veneziano settecentesco* (Bologna, 1975).

Maximus Confessor, *Selected Writings*, trans. by G. C. Berthold (London: SPCK, 1985).

Maximus, *The Philokalia*, trans. by G. E. H. Palmer, P. Sherrard, K. Ware (London: Faber & Faber, 1981).

Mayr-Harting, Henry, *The Coming of Christianity to Anglo-Saxon England* (London: Batsford, 1972).

Medieval Reader, A (Harmondsworth, Penguin Books, 1977).

Meehan, B., *The Book of Kells* (London: Thames & Hudson, 1994).

Meiss, M., *French Painting in the Time of Jean de Berry, the Boucicaut Master* (London, 1968).

Mercati, Angelo, 'Per la storia del codice amiatino', *Biblica* III (1992).

Merian, Sylvie L., 'Characteristics and Techniques of Armenian Bookbinding: Report on Research in Progress', *Atti del Quinto Simposio Internazionale di Arte Armena* (Venice: San Lazzaro Press, 1991).

Bibliography

Merian Sylvie L., 'Cilicia as the Locus of European Influence on Medieval Armenian Book Production', *Armenian Review* Winter 1992.

Merian, Sylvie L., 'The Structure of Armenian Bookbinding and Its Relation to Near Eastern Bookmaking Traditions', Ph.D. diss., Columbia University, 1993).

Merkel, H., *Die Wiederspruche zwischen den Evangelien: Ihre polemische und apologetische Behandlung in der Alten Kirche bis zu Augustin* (Tübingen, 1971).

Metzger, Bruce M., 'The Furniture of the Scriptorium at Qumran', *RevQ* 1 (1958).

Metzger, Bruce M., *The Text of the New Testament* (New York: Oxford University Press, 1964; 3rd edn, 1992).

Metzger, Th., 'Les objets du culte, le sanctuaire du désert et le temple de Jérusalem dans le bibles hébraïques médiévals enluminés en Orient et en Espagne', *Bulletin of the John Rylands Library* 52 (1970, 1971).

Meyendorff, John, *Imperial Unity and Christian Divisions* (Crestwood, NY: St Vladimir's Seminary Press, 1989).

Meyvaert, P., 'Bede and the Church Paintings at Wearmouth-Jarrow', *Anglo-Saxon England* 8 (1979).

Meyvaert, P., 'Bede, Cassiodorus, and the Codex Amiatinus', *Speculum*, forthcoming.

Micheli, G. L., *L'Enluminature du haut Moyen Age et les influences irlandaises: Histoire d'une influence* (Brussels, 1939).

Milik, J. T., *Books of Enoch* (Oxford: Clarendon, 1976).

Milne, H. J. M., *Catalogue of the Literary Papyri in the British Museum* (London: British Museum, 1927).

Milne, H. J. M., & T. C. Skeat, *The Codex Sinaiticus and the Codex Alexandrinus* (London: British Museum, 1963 (1st edn 1938, 2nd edn 1955)).

Milne, H. J. M., & T. C. Skeat, *Scribes and Correctors of the Codex Sinaiticus* (London: British Museum, 1938).

Minnis, A. J., '"Authorial Intention" and "Literal Sense" in the Exegetical Theories of Richard Fitzralph and John Wyclif: an Essay in the Medieval History of Biblical Hermeneutics', *Proceedings of the Royal Irish Academy* 75, section C, no. 1 (1975).

The Mishna, trans. by H. Albeck (Jerusalem & Tel Aviv, 1958).

The Mishnah, trans. by H. Danby (Oxford, 1964).

Moran, Jo Ann Hoeppner, *The Growth of English Schooling 1340-1548: Learning, Literacy, and Laicization in Pre-Reformation York Diocese* (Princeton: University Press, 1985).

Moschonas, T. D., Καταⓦλογοι τηϡ πατριαρχικηϡ βιβλιοθηⓦκηΠ, ΤοⓦμοΠ Α, Χειροⓦγραφα (Alexandria, 1945; 2nd edn, Salt Lake City: University of Utah Press, 1965, Studies and Documents 26).

Mueller, Janel M., *The Native Tongue and the Word: Developments in English Prose Style 1380-1580* (Chicago: University Press, 1984).

Nag Hammadi Codices, Facsimile Edition (Leiden: Brill, 1972-84).

Narkiss, B., A. Cohen-Mushlin & A. Tcherikover, *Hebrew Illuminated Manuscripts in the British Isles. I. Spanish and Portuguese Manuscripts* (New York: Oxford University Press for the Israel Academy of Sciences and Humanities and the British Academy, 1982).

Narkiss, B., *Illuminations from Hebrew Bibles of Leningrad* (Jerusalem: Mosad Byalik, 1990).

Naveh, J., 'An Aramaic Tomb Inscription Written in Paleo-Hebrew Script', *IEJ* 23 (1973).

Nees, Lawrence, 'A Fifth-Century Book Cover and the Origin of the Four Evangelist Symbols Page in the Book of Durrow', *Gesta* XVII/1 (1978).

Nelson, R. S., 'An Icon at Mt Sinai and Christian Painting in Muslim Egypt during the Thirteenth and Fourteenth Centuries', *Art Bulletin* LXV/2 (June 1983).

Netter, Thomas, *Doctrinale Fidei Catholicae*, ed. by F. Bonaventura Blanciotti, 3 vols (Venice, 1757-9; repr. Farnborough, Hants.: Gregg Press, 1967).

Bibliography

Netzer, Nancy, *Cultural Interplay in the Eighth Century: the Trier Gospels and the Making of a Scriptorium at Echternach* (Cambridge: University Press, 1994).

Ní Chatháin, P., & M. Richter, eds, *Ireland and Europe* (Stuttgart: Klett Cotta, 1984).

Ní Chatháin, P., & M. Richter, eds, *Irland und die Christenheit: Bibelstudien und Mission* (Stuttgart: Klett Cotta, 1987).

Nir-El, Y. & M. Broshi, 'The Black Ink of the Qumran Scrolls', *DSD*, in press.

Nordenfalk, Carl, *Celtic and Anglo-Saxon Painting: Book Illumination in the British Isles, 600-800* (London: Chatto & Windus, 1977).

Nordenfalk, Carl, 'Corbie and Cassiodorus: a pattern page bearing on the early history of book-binding', *Pantheon* XXXII (1974).

Nordström, C. O., 'Some Miniatures In Hebrew Bibles', *Synthronon*, Paris (1968).

Nybey, T., I. Pio, P. Sorensen, & A. Trommer, eds, *History and heroic tale* (Odensee, 1985).

Ó Corráin, D., L. Breatnach, & A. Breen, 'The laws of the Irish', *Peritia* 3 (1984).

Ó Cróinín, Dáibhí, *Early medieval Ireland 400-1200* (London & New York: Longman, 1995).

Ó Cróinín, Dáibhí, 'Pride and Prejudice', *Peritia* 1 (1982).

Ó Cróinín, Dáibhí, *Psalterium Salabergae. Staatsbibliothek zu Berlin – Preussischer Kulturbesitz Ms. Hamilt. 555*, Codices illuminati medii aevi 30: colour microfiche edition (Munich: Edition Helga Lengenfelder, 1994).

Ó Cróinín, Dáibhí, 'Rath Melsigi, Willibrord, and the Earliest Echternach Manuscripts', *Peritia* 3 (1984).

Odo of Cheriton, *An Apology for Lollard Doctrines*, ed. by J. H. Todd, Camden Society 14 (London: John Bowyer Nichols & Son, 1842).

O'Donnell, J. R., ed., *Essays in Honour of Anton Charles Regis* (Toronto: Pontifical Institute of Mediaeval Studies, 1974).

Oesch, J. M., *Petucha und Setuma, Untersuchungen zu einer überlieferten Gliederung im hebräischen Text des Alten Testament* (OBO 27; Freiburg/Göttingen, 1979).

Oesch, J. M., 'Textgliederung im Alten Testament und in den Qumranhandschriften', *Henoch* 5 (1983).

O'Grady, S. H., *Catalogue of Irish Manuscripts in the British Museum* (vol. 1. London: British Museum, 1926) (repr. as *Catalogue of Irish Manuscripts in the British Library [formerly British Museum]* (Dublin Institute for Advanced Studies, 1992).

O'Mahony, Felicity, ed., *The Book of Kells, Proceedings of a conference at Trinity College Dublin, 6-9 September 1992* (Aldershot: Scolar Press, 1994).

Openshaw, K. M., 'Images, Texts and Contexts: the Iconography of the Tiberius Psalter, London, British Library, Cotton MSS, Tiberius C.vi' (unpublished doctoral dissertation; University of Toronto, 1990).

Openshaw, K. M., 'The Symbolic Illustration of the Psalter: An Insular Traditio', *Arte Medievale* 2 ser. 6 (n. 1, 1992).

O'Reilly, Jennifer, 'Patristic and Insular traditions on the Evangelists: exegesis and iconography', in *Quaderni di Romano-Barbarica* 1, ed. by A. M. Fuiselli Fadda & É. Ó. Carragáin (Rome, in press).

Origen, *The Song of Songs: Commentary and Homilies*, ed. & trans. by R. P. Lawson (Westminster, Md.: Newman Press, 1957).

Orlandi, Tito, 'The Corpus dei Manoscritti Copti Letterari', *Computers and the Humanities* 24 (1990).

Orlandi, Tito, 'Un projet milanais concernant les manuscrits coptes du Monastère Blanc', *Muséon* 85 (1972).

Orlandi, Tito, & David W. Johnson, eds, *Acts of the Fifth International Congress of Coptic Studies: Washington, 12-15 August 1992*, 2 vols (Rome: Centro Italiano Microfiches, 1993).

Ostrogorsky, George, *History of the Byzantine State* (Oxford: Blackwell, 1968).

Bibliography

O' Sullivan, A., 'The Colophon of the Cotton Psalter (Vitellius F. XI)', *Journal of the Royal Society of Antiquaries of Ireland* 96 (1966).

O' Sullivan, William, 'The Lindisfarne Scriptorium: For and Against', *Peritia* 8 (1994).

Palm, K. Jonas, & Mogens S. Koch, eds, *Preprints: Seventh International Congress of Restorers of Graphic Art 26th-30th August 1991, Uppsala, Sweden* (Uppsala, 1991).

Parkes, Malcolm B., *English Cursive Bookhands 1250-1500*, rev. edn (Berkeley & Los Angeles: University of California Press, 1980).

Parr, R., *The Life and Times of the Most Reverend James Usher late Lord Arch-Bishop of Armagh Primate and Metropolitan of All Ireland* (London, 1686).

Patterson, Lee, *Chaucer and the Subject of History* (Madison: University of Wisconsin Press, 1991).

Pattie, T. S., *Manuscripts of the Bible: Greek Bibles in the British Library* (London: The British Library, 1995).

Paues, Anna C., ed., *A Fourteenth Century English Biblical Version* (rev. edn; Cambridge: University Press, 1904).

Pearson, B. A. & J. A. Goehring, eds, *The Roots of Egyptian Christianity* (Philadelphia: Fortress, 1986).

Pecock, Reginald, *The Reule of Crysten Religioun*, ed. by Willaim Cabell Greet, Early English Text Society, o. s. 171 (London: Oxford University Press, 1927).

Pedley, K. G., 'The Library at Qumran', *RevQ* 2 (1959).

Peshitta Institute, Leiden, ed., *List of Old Testament Peshitta Manuscripts* (Leiden: 1961).

Peter of Celle, *Selected Works* (Kalamazoo, Mich.: Cistercian Publications, 1987).

Petersen, Theodore C., 'Early Islamic Bookbindings and their Coptic Relations', *Ars Orientalis* I (1954).

Pfann, S. J., '4Q298: The Masîl's Address to All Sons of Dawn', *JQR* 85 (1994).

Pietersma, A., *The Acts of Phileas, Bishop of Thmuis*, Cahiers d'Orientalisme VII (Geneva: Patrick Cramer, 1984).

Planta, J., *A Catalogue of the Manuscripts in the Cottonian Library deposited in the British Museum* (London, 1802).

Plummer, C., *Venerabilis Baedae Opera Historica*, 2 vols (Oxford: Clarendon Press, 1896).

Pokrovskii, N. N., 'Western Siberian Scriptoria and Binderies: Ancient Traditions Among the Old Believers', transl. by J. S. G. Simmons, *The Book Collector* xx (Spring 1971).

Poole, J. & R. Reed, 'The Preparation of Leather and Parchment by the Dead Sea Scrolls Community', *Technology and Culture* 3 (1962).

Poole, J. & R. Reed, 'A Study of Some Dead Sea Scroll and Leather Fragments from Cave 4 at Qumran: Part II, Chemical examination', *Proceedings of the Leeds Philosophical and Literary Society*, Scientific Section 9/6 (1964).

Poole, J. B. & R. Reed, 'The "Tannery" of >Ain Feshkha', *PEQ* 93 (1961).

Porcher, J., *Bibliothèque Nationale: les manuscrits à peinture en France du VIIe au XIIe siècle* (Paris: Bibliothèque Nationale, 1954).

Porten, B. & A. Yardeni: *Textbook of Aramaic Documents from Ancient Egypt*, 3 (Jerusalem: Academon, 1993).

Powell, Margaret Joyce, ed., *The Pauline Epistles Contained in MS. Parker 32*, Early English Society, e. s. 116 (London: Kegan, Trench, Trübner o., 1916).

The Psalter, (...) With a Translation and Exposition in English by Richard Rolle of Hampole, ed. by H. R. Bramley (Oxford: Clarendon Press, 1884).

Quilici, Piccarda, 'Legature greche, "alla greca", per la Grecia', *Accademie e Biblioteche d'Italia* 52 (1984).

Receuil d'études bollandiennes, Subsidia Hagiographica (Brussels, 1963).

Regul, Jurgen, *Die antimarcionitischen Evangelienprologe*, Aus der Geschichte der lateinischen

Bibliography

Bibel, 6 (Freiburg im Breisgau: Herder, 1969).

Rella, F. A., 'Continental Manuscripts acquired for English Centres in the Tenth and Early Eleventh Centuries: a Preliminary Checklist', *Anglia* 98 (1980).

Rengstorf, K. H., *Hirbet Qumrân und die Bibliothek vom Toten Meer* (Studia Delitzschiana 5; Stuttgart, 1960).

Reuter, T., ed., *The Greatest Englishman: Essays on St Boniface and the Church at Crediton* (Exeter: Paternoster Press, 1980).

Richardson, H., 'Number and Symbol in early Christian Irish Art', *Journal of the Royal Society of Antiquaries of Ireland* 114 (1984).

Richardson, S., ed., *The Negotiations of Sir T. Roe in his embassy to the Ottoman Porte from the year 1621 to 1628 Inclusive* (London: Society for the Encouragement of Learning, 1740).

Righetti, M., *Storia liturgica*, ed. 2 (Rome, 1950).

Roberts, Colin H., 'The Codex', *Proceedings of the British Academy* 40 (1954).

Roberts, Colin H., *Manuscript, Society, and Belief in Early Christian Egypt* (The Schweich Lectures of the British Academy 1977; London: Oxford University Press, 1979).

Roberts, Colin H. & T. C. Skeat, *The Birth of the Codex* (London: Oxford University Press for the British Academy, 1983, 2nd edn 1987).

Robertson, E., *Catalogue of Samaritan Manuscripts in the John Rylands Library of Manchester* (Manchester, 1938).

Robinson, J. A., *The Times of Dunstan* (Oxford: Clarendon Press, 1923), 71-80.

Robinson, James M., *The Pachomian Monastic Library at the Chester Beatty Library and the Bibiothèque Bodmer* (Occasional Papers of the Institute for Antiquity and Christianity 19; Claremont, Calif.: Institute for Antiquity and Christianity, 1990).

Robinson, James M. & B. Van Elderen, *Institute for Antiquity and Christianity Report 1972-1980* (Claremont, Calif.: Institute for Antiquity and Christianity, 1981).

Robson, J. A., *Wyclif and the Oxford Schools: the Relation of the 'Summa de ente' to Scholastic Debates at Oxford in the Later Fourteenth Century* (Cambridge: University Press, 1961).

Romaine, Suzanne, *Bilingualism* (Oxford, UK and Cambridge, Mass., USA: Blackwell).

Roth, Cecil, 'Jewish Antecedents of Christian Art', *Journal of Warburg and Courtauld Institutes* XVI (1953).

Rousseau, Phillip, *Pachomius: the Making of a Community in Fourth-century Egypt* (Berkeley: University of California Press, 1985).

Ryder, M. L., 'Follicle Arrangement in Skin from Wild Sheep, Primitive Domestic Sheep and in Parchment', *Nature* 182 (1958).

Safadi, Yasim Hamid, *Islamic Calligraphy* (London: Thames & Hudson, 1978).

Šagi, Janko, S. J., 'Problema historiae codicis B', *Divus Thomas* 75 (1972).

Salmon, P., *Les 'Tituli Psalmorum' des manuscrits latins*, Collectanea Biblica Latins 12 (Rome & Vatican City, 1959).

Salway, P., *Roman Britain* (Oxford: Clarendon Press, 1981).

Samuels, M. L., 'Some Applications of Middle English Dialectology', *English Studies* 44 (1963).

Sanders, J. A., 'The Psalms Scroll of Qumrân Cave 11 (11QPsª)', *DJD* IV (1965).

Sanjian, Avedis K., *Colophons of Armenian Manuscripts 1301-1480* (Cambridge, Mass.: Harvard University Press, 1969).

Sawyer, P. H., *Anglo-Saxon Charters: an Annotated List and Bibliography* (London: Royal Historical Society, 1968).

Scattergood, V. J., & J. W. Sherborne, eds, *English Court Culture in the Later Middle Ages* (New York: St Martin's Press, 1983).

Schaf, P., ed., *Augustine: Harmony of the Gospels* (New York: Library of Nicene and post-Nicene Fathers, 1888).

Schiffman, L. H., ed., *Archaeology and History in the Dead Sea Scrolls – The New York Uni-*

Bibliography

versity Conference in Memory of Yigael Yadin (*JSOT/ASOR* Monograph Series 2; Sheffield, 1990).

Schmidt, C., 'Die neuesten Bibelfunde aus Agypten', *Zeitschrift für dir neutestamentliche Wissenschaft* 30 (1931), 32 (1933).

Scholten, Clemens, 'Die Nag-Hammadi-Texte als Buchbesitz der Pachomianer', *Jahrbuch für Antike und Christentum* 31 (1988).

Schulz, R., & Manfred Görg, eds, *Lingua Restituta Orientalis: Festgabe für Julius Assfalg, Aegypten und Altes Testament* xx (Wiesbaden: Harrassowitz, 1990).

Sed-Rajna, G., *Les manuscrits hébreux enluminés des Bibliothèques de France* (Leuven: Peeters, 1994).

Seider, R., *Palaographie der lateinischen Papyri* (Stuttgart: Hiersemann, 1978).

Severin, Hans-Georg, 'Oströmische Plastik unter Valens und Theodosius I', *Jahrbuch der Berliner Museen* XII (1970).

Severs, J. Burke, ed., *A Manual of the Writings on Middle English 1050-1500*, ed. J. Burke Severs, vol. 2 (Hampden, Conn.: Connecticut Academy of Arts and Sciences, 1970).

Sharpe, John, III, ed., *The Compleat Binder: Studies in Book Making and Conservation in Honour of Roger Powell* to be published in the *Bibliologia* series, Brepols Publishers (in press).

Shepherd, G., *Poets and Prophets: Essays on Medieval Studies*, ed. by T. A. Shippey & J. Pickles (Woodbridge: Brewer, 1990).

Sidarus, Adel Y., 'Ibn ar-Râhibs Leben und Werke: ein koptisch-arabischer Encyclopädist des 7/13 Jahrhunderts', *Islamkundliche Untersuchen*, 36 (Freiburg: Klaus Schwarz, 1975).

Siegel, J. P., 'The Employment of Palaeo-Hebrew Characters for the Divine Names at Qumran in the Light of Tannaitic Sources,' *HUCA* 42 (1971).

Siegel. J. P., 'Final *Mem* in Medial Position and Medial *Mem* in Final Position in 11QPs^a – Some Observations', *RevQ* 7 (1969).

Siegel. J. P., 'The Scribes of Qumran: Studies in the Early History of Jewish Scribal Customs, with Special Reference to the Qumran Biblical Scrolls and to the Tannaitic Traditions of Massekheth Soferim', Unpubl. Diss., Brandeis University, 1971 (Ann Arbor: University Microfilms, 1972).

Skeat, T. C., '"Especially the Parchments": a note on 2 Timothy IV.13', *Journal of Theological Studies* 30 (1979).

Skeat, T. C., 'The Codex Vaticanus in the Fifteenth Century', *Journal of Theological Studies* 35 (1984).

Skeat, T. C., 'Irenaeus and the Four-Gospel Canon', *Novum Testamentum* XXXIV (Leiden: Brill, 1992).

Smahel, Frantisek, '"Doctor evangelicus super omnes evangelistas": Wyclif's Fortune in Hussite Bohemia', *Bulletin of the Institute of Historical Research* 43 (1970).

Smalley, Beryl, 'The Bible and Eternity: John Wyclif's Dilemma', *Journal of the Warburg and Courtauld Institutes* 27 (1964).

Smalley, Beryl, review of Margaret Deanesly's *The Significance of the Lollard Bible* (1951), *Medium Ævum* 22 (1953).

Smalley, Beryl, *The Study of the Bible in the Middle Ages* (2nd edn; Oxford: Basil Blackwell & Mott, 1952; repr. Notre Dame: University of Notre Dame Press, 1964).

Smid, H. R., *Protevangelium Jacobi* (Assen: Van Gorcum, 1965).

Sörries, Reiner, *Die Syrische Bibel von Paris: Paris Bibliothèque Nationale, syr. 341: Eine frühchristliche Bilderhandschrift aus dem 6. Jahrhundert* (Wiesbaden: Ludwig Reichert Verlag, 1991).

Sources, Les, de la Doctrine chrétienne d'après les Théologiens du XIVe siècle et du début du XVe. (...) (Bruges: Desclée De Brouwer, 1954).

Spencer, H. Leith, *English Preaching in the Late Middle Ages* (Oxford: Clarendon Press, 1993).

Bibliography

Staley, Lynn, *Margery Kempe's Dissenting Fictions* (University Park: Pennsylvania State University Press, 1994).

Steckoll, S. H., 'Investigations of the Inks Used in Writing the Dead Sea Scrolls', *Nature* 220 (1968).

Steckoll, S. H., 'Marginal Notes on the Qumran Excavations', *RevQ* 7 (1969).

Stegemann, H., *Die Essener, Qumran, Johannes der Taufer und Jesus: Ein Sachbuch*, 4th edn (Freiburg im Breisgau: Herder, 1994).

Stegemann, H., *KURIOS O QEOS KURIOS IHSOUS – Aufkommen und Ausbreitung des religiösen Gebrauchs von KURIOS und seine Verwendung im Neuen Testament* (Habilitationsschrift, Bonn, 1969).

Stenton, F., *Anglo-Saxon England* (Oxford: Clarendon Press, 3rd edn, 1971).

The Style of John Wyclif's English Sermons (The Hague and Paris: Mouton, 1977).

Swan, George R., *Photographs of the Washington Manuscript of the Psalms in the Freer Collection* (Ann Arbor: University of Michigan, 1919).

Swanton, Michael, *English Literature Before Chaucer* (London: Longman, 1987).

Swinburn, Lilian M., ed., *The Lanterne of Liȝt*, Early English Text Society, o. s. 151 (London: Kegan Paul, Trench, Trübner & Co., 1917).

Symeonis monachi Opera omnia, Rolls Society, 2 vols (London: Longman/Trübner, 1882-5).

Szerwiniack, Olivier, 'Des Recueils d'Interprétations de Noms Hébreux chez les Irlandais et le Wisigoth Théodulf', *Scriptorium* XLVIII (1994).

Talbot, C. H., *The Anglo-Saxon Missionaries in Germany* (New York: Sheed & Ward, 1954).

Talmon, S., 'Fragments of Two Scrolls of the Book of Leviticus from Masada', *ErIsr* 24 (Jerusalem, 1993).

Talmon, S., 'Some Unrecorded Fragments of the Hebrew Pentateuch in the Samaritan Version', *Textus* 3 (1963).

Tangl, M., ed., *Die Briefe des Heiligen Bonifatius und Lulius*, Monumenta Germaniae Historica, Epistulae selectae I (Berlin: Weidmannsche Buchhandlung, 1916).

Tanner, Norman P., ed., *Heresy Trials in the Diocese of Norwich, 1428-31*, Camden Society, 4th ser. 20 (London: Royal Historical Society, 1977).

Tavormina, M. Teresa, ed., *Medieval England: an Encyclopedia* (New York: Garland Publishing, forthcoming 1997).

Temple, E., *Anglo-Saxon Manuscripts 900-1066*, A Survey of Manuscripts Illuminated in the British Isles 2 (London: Harvey Miller, 1976).

Tov, Emmanuel, with the collaboration of S. J. Pfann, *Companion Volume to the Dead Sea Scrolls Microfiche Edition*, 2nd edn (Leiden: Brill, 1995).

Tov, Emmanuel, 'The Greek Minor Prophets Scroll from Naḥal Ḥever (8ḤevXIIgr) (The Seiyal Collection I)' *DJD* VIII (1990).

Les Tranchefiles brodées: étude historique et technique (Paris: Bibliothèque nationale, 1989).

'Travail, le, d'édition des fragments manuscrits de Qumrân,' *RB* 63 (1956).

Tsafrir, Yoram, ed., *Ancient Churches Revealed* (Jerusalem: Israel Exploration Society, 1993).

Turner, Eric G., *Greek Manuscripts of the Ancient World*, 2nd edn rev. by P. J. Parsons (London: Institute of Classical Studies, 1987).

Turner, Eric G., *Greek Papyri: an Introduction* (Oxford: Clarendon, 1968).

Turner, Eric G., *The Typology of the Early Codex*, Hanley Foundation Series 18 (Philadelphia: University of Pennsylvania Press, 1977).

Ulrich, E., 'An Index of the Passages in the Biblical Manuscripts from the Judean Desert (Part 1: Genesis-Kings)', *DSD* 1 (1994).

Ulrich, E., 'An Index of the Passages in the Biblical Manuscripts from the Judean Desert (Part 2: Isaiah-Chronicles)', *DSD* 2 (1995).

Vaccari, A., 'Il genuino commento ea salmi di Remigio di Auxerre', *Biblica* 26 (1952).

Bibliography

van Regemorter, Berthe, 'Evolution de la technique de la reliure du VIIIe au XII siècle', *Scriptorium* 2 (1948).

van Regemorter, Berthe, 'La reliure arménienne', *Bazmavep*, 111, no. 8-10 (1953).

van Regemorter, Berthe, 'La reliure byzantine', *Revue belge d'archéologie et d'histoire de l'art* XXXVI (1967).

van Regemorter, Berthe, 'La reliure des manuscrits grecs', *Scriptorium* VIII (1954).

Verey, Christopher D., 'A Collation of the Gospel Texts contained in Durham Cathedral MSS A.II.10, A.II.16 and A.II.17' (unpublished M.A. thesis, University of Durham, 1969).

Verey, Christopher D., T. Julian Brown, & Elizabeth Coatsworth, eds, *The Durham Gospels* (Early English Manuscripts in Facsimile, 20; Copenhagen: Rosenkilde & Bagger, 1980).

Vikan, Gary, ed., *Illuminated Greek Manuscripts from American Collections: An Exhibition in Honor of Kurt Weitzmann* (Princeton: University Press, 1973).

von Campenhausen, H., *The Formation of the Christian Bible* (London: Adam & Charles Black, 1972; German original, Tübingen: J. C. B. Mohr (Paul Siebeck, 1968).

von Nolcken, Christina, ed., *The Middle English Translation of the Rosarium theologie*, Middle English Texts 10 (Heidelberg: Carl Winter, Universitätsverlag, 1979).

von Nolcken, C., 'Richard Wyche, a Certain Knight, and in the Beginning of the End' (forthcoming).

von Soden, Hermann, *Die Schriften des neuen Testaments in ihrer ältesten erreichbaren Textgestalt* (Berlin: Arthur Glaue, 1902).

Waddell, Helen, *More Latin Lyrics* (New York: Norton, 1977).

Walker, G. S. M., ed., *Sancti Columbani opera* (Dublin: Institute for Advanced Studies, 1970).

Walsh, Katherine, & Diana Wood, eds, *The Bible in the Medieval World: Essays in Memory of Beryl Smalley, Studies in Church History*, subsidia 4 (Oxford: Basil Blackwell, 1985).

Walsh, M. & D. Ó Cróinín, *Cummian's letter De controversia paschali* (Toronto: Pontifical Institute of Medieval Studies, 1988).

Watson, Nicholas, 'Censorship and Cultural Change in Late-Medieval England: Vernacular Theology, the Oxford Translation Debate, and Arundel's Constitutions of 1409', *Speculum* 70 (1995).

Watson, Nicholas, *Richard Rolle and the Invention of Authority* (Cambridge Studies in Medieval Literature 13 (Cambridge: University Press, 1991)).

Webster, Leslie & J. Backhouse, eds, *The Making of England: Anglo-Saxon Art and Culture AD 600-900* (London: British Museum Press, 1991).

Weitzmann, Kurt, 'An Early Copto-Arabic Miniature in Leningrad', *Ars Islamica* IX (1942).

Weitzmann, Kurt, *Late Antique and Early Christian Book Illumination* (London: Chatto & Windus, 1977).

Weitzmann, K., ed., *Age of Spirituality: Late Antique and Early Christian Art, Third to Seventh Century: Catalogue of the exhibition at The Metropolitan Museum of Art, November 19, 1977, through February 12, 1978* (New York: The Metropolitan Museum of Art with Princeton University Press).

Weitzmann, Kurt, 'Loca Sancta and the Representational Arts of Palestine', *Dumbarton Oaks Papers* XXVIII (1974), reprinted in *Studies in the Arts at Sinai* (Princeton: University Press, 1982).

Werckmeister, O. K., *Irisch-northumbrische Buchmalerei des 8. Jahrhunderts und monastische Spiritualitat* (Berlin: Walter de Gruyter, 1967).

Werner, Martin, 'The Four Evangelist Symbols Page in the Book of Durrow', *Gesta* VIII (1969).

Werner, Martin, 'The Madonna and Child Miniature in the Book of Kells', part I *Art Bulletin* LIV/1 (March 1972), and part II *Art Bulletin* LIV/2 (June 1972).

Werner, Martin, 'The Durrow Four Evangelist Symbols Page Once Again', *Gesta* XX/1 (1981).

Westwood, J. O., 'On the Peculiarities exhibited by the Miniatures and Ornamentation of

Bibliography

Ancient Irish Illuminated Manuscripts', *Archaeological Journal* 7 (1850).

White L. Michael & O. Larry Yarbrough, eds, *The Social World of the First Christians: Essays in Honor of Wayne A. Meeks* (Minneapolis: Augsburg Fortress, 1995).

Whitelock, Dorothy, ed., *English Historical Documents, vol. I: c. 500-1042* (London: Eyre Methuen, 1955, 2nd edn 1979).

Wieck, R. S., *Time Sanctified: the Book of Hours in Medieval Arts and Life* (Baltimore & London, 1988).

Wilkins, David, *Concilia Magnae Britanniae et Hiberniae*, 4 vols (London, 1737).

Wilks, Michael, 'Misleading Manuscripts: Wyclif and the Non-Wycliffite Bible', *Studies in Church History* 11 (1975).

Williamson, C., *The Old English Riddles of the Exeter Book* (Chapel Hill, NC: University of North Carolina Press, 1977).

Williamson, C., *A Feast of Creatures: Anglo-Saxon Riddle-Songs* (Philadelphia: University of Pennsylvania Press, 1982).

Willibald, *Vitae Sancti Bonifatii archiepiscopi Moguntini*, ed. by W. Levison, Monumenta Germaniae Historica, Scriptores rerum Germanicarum 57 (Hanover & Leipzig: Hahn, 1905).

Wilmart, A. & L. Brou, *The Psalter Collects from V-VIth century Sources*, ed. with introduction, apparatus criticus and indexes by Louis Brou (Henry Bradshaw Society 83, London, 1949).

Wilson, R. McL., ed., *The Future of Coptic Studies*, Coptic Studies 1 (Leiden: E. J. Brill, 1978).

Winlock, H. E., W. E. Crum, & H. G. Evelyn-White, *The Monastery of Epiphanius at Thebes*, 2 vols (Publications of the Metropolitan Museum of Art Egyptian Expedition 3-4; New York: Metropolitan Museum of Art, 1926).

Wise, M. O., 'Thunder in Gemini, and Other Essays on the History, Language and Literature of Second Temple Palestine', *Journal for the Study of the Pseudepigrapha*, Suppl. Series 15 (Sheffield, 1994).

Wordsworth, C. & H. Littlehales, *The Old Service-Books of the English Church* (London, 1904).

Wordsworth, J. & H. J. White, eds, *Nouum Testamentum Domini Nostri Iesu Christi Latine secundum editionem Sancti Hieronymi: pars prior, Quattuor Euangelia* (Oxford: University Press, 1889-98).

Workman, Herbert B., *John Wyclif: a Study of the English Medieval Church*, 2 vols (Oxford: Clarendon Press, 1926).

Wormald, Francis, *Collected Writings, I, Studies in Medieval Art from the Sixth to the Twelfth Centuries*, ed. by J. J. G. Alexander, T. J. Brown, & J. Gibbs (London: Harvey Miller, 1984).

Wright, D. H. & A. Campbell, eds, *The Vespasian Psalter*, Early English Manuscripts in Facsimile 14 (Copenhagen: Rosenkilde & Bagger, 1967).

Wright, W., *Catalogue of the Syriac Manuscripts in the British Museum* (London, 1872).

Wright, W., *A Catalogue of the Syriac Manuscripts preserved in the Library of the University of Cambridge* (Cambridge: University Press, 1901).

Wyclif, John, *De Veritate Sacrae Scripturae*, ed. by Rudolf Buddenseig, Wyclif Society, 3 vols (London: Trübner & Co., 1905-7).

Wyclif, John, *Dialogus sive Speculum Ecclesie Militantis*, ed. by Alfred W. Pollard, Wyclif Society (London: Trübner & Co., 1886).

Wyclif, John, *The English Works of Wyclif Hitherto Unprinted*, ed. by F. D. Matthew, Early English Text Society, o. s. 74 (rev. edn; London: Kegan Paul, Trench, Trübner & Co., 1902).

Wyclif, John, *Exposicio textus Matthei xxiii, Opera Minora*, ed. by Johann Loserth, Wyclif Society (London: C. K. Paul & Co., 1913).

Wyclif, John, *Opus Evangelicum*, ed. by Johann Loserth, Wyclif Society, 2 vols (London: Trübner & Co., 1895-6).

Wyclif, John, *Select English Works*, ed. by Thomas Arnold, 3 vols (Oxford: Clarendon Press, 1869-71).

Bibliography

Wyclif, John, *Select English Works*, ed. by T. Arnold (London: Trübner & Co., 1905-7).

Wyclif, John, e la tradizione degli studi biblici in Inghilterra (Genoa: il melangolo, 1987).

Yadin, Y., *The Temple Scroll* (Israel Exploration Society: Jerusalem, 1983).

Yadin, Y., *The Scroll of the War of the Sons of Light against the Sons of Darkness* (Oxford: Clarendon, 1962).

Yeivin, Israel, *Geniza Bible Fragments With Babylonian Massorah and Vocalization, including Additional Bible Fragment with Babylonian Massorah and Vocalization, Together with a Description of the Manuscripts and Indices [Hebrew]* (Jerusalem: Makor, 1973).

Yeivin, Israel, *The Hebrew Language Tradition as Reflected in the Babylonian Vocalization [Hebrew]* (Jerusalem: The Academy of the Hebrew Language, 1985).

Zaret, David, *The Heavenly Contract: Ideology and Organization in Pre-Revolutionary Puritanism* (Chicago: University Press, 1985).

INDEX OF MANUSCRIPTS

Index of Manuscripts

GENERAL INDEX

Page numbers in **bold type** denote main treatments.
Further references will be found in the Index of Manuscripts.

General Index

General Index

General Index

General Index

Roberts, C. H. *and* Skeat, T. C. 36
Robinson, J. M. 51-2
roll *see* scrolls
Rolle, Richard 179, 180
Romans 53
Rome, Vatican Library 51, 65
Rouen, Double Psalter of St-Ouen 89, 90, 91, 95, 98
Royal Bible 161
Royal Gospels 158
rulings 13, 16-17, 21-2, 64, 206
    'blind' 17
    double 17, 64
    ruling frames 206
    vertical 16-17, 22-3, 64, 206
Ruth 20, 23, 24, 63
Ryder, M.L. 13

א *see* Codex Sinaiticus
Šagi, Janko 65
St Gall Gospels 78, 79
St Wilfrid's Gospels 147
Salaberga Psalter 99
Salmon, P. 97
Samaritan texts 16, 22, 23, 25
Samuel 24, 27, 61
Samuel, Archbishop 24
Sanctuary 217-21
Schmidt, Carl 46
scribal schools 10, 11
Scrivener, F. H. A. 67
scrolls/rolls 9-33, 61
    Bodmer Papyri 52
    in New Testament 45
    structure/layout 10, 13-27
        beginnings/ends 14, 23-5
        closures 14, 15
        damage/repair 25-7
        dimensions 18-19, 20, 38
        handling areas 24
        horizontal joins 14
        sheets 13-14, 18, 19-20, 38
    use declining 35-7, 62
Se'elim manuscripts 10
Septuagint (LXX) 18, 39, 66, 69, 209
    ἀδωναι 70
sewing 63, 64, 198-202, 206-7
    chain-stitching 198-200, 202
    frames 201-2
    scrolls 14, 19-20, 25-6
sheets
    codices 38-9, 64-5, 198, 201
    scrolls 13-14, 16, 19-20
        numbering 13
Shepherd of Hermas 53, 55, 68
sherds *see* ostraca
Simeon ben Eleazar, Rabbi 25-6
Simonides, Constantine 67
Skeat, T. C. 45, 62, 66
Skylan, John 184
Smid, H. R. 54

Smith, Thomas 93, 94, 96
Solomon, Odes of 53
Song of Songs 52, 61, 138, 139, 156, 160, 161
Southampton Psalter 90, 91-3, 94, 95
Spain, Hebrew Bibles 216-21
Speculum humanae salvationis 142
Steckoll, S. H. 16
Stegemann, H. 11, 13
Stephanus (Robert Estienne) 66
Strugnell, J. 26
Susanna 53
symbols *see* iconography
Symeon of Thessalonika 227-8
Syria 123-4, 126-8, 129, 131, 205ff
Syriac texts 35, 41, 64, 126-9

Tabernacle 152, 216-21
tackets 198, 200, 202
Talmud, biblical copying 'rules' 12, 16, 19, 24, 25-6
Thekla, Saint 69
Theodore of Canterbury 149
Theodore of Mopsuestia 90, 91
Theodore the Studite 227
Timothy 45, 65
Tischendorf, xx 67, 68
titles 25, 65, 66, 67, 70
    exegetic aspects 77, 78, 83, 90, 97
τίτλος 66
Titus 65
Tobit 53, 65
Toledo Bible 216-19
Torah 19, 217, 223
    copying 'rules' 21, 24, 26
Tregelles, S. P. 67
Trier Gospels 80, 106, 109, 110
Trinity Gospels 158
Turner, E. G. 51
Tyndale, William 180

Ullerston, Richard 182
Ulpian 35-6
Usserianus Primus Gospels 108
Ussher, Archbp James 93-4, 95
Utrecht Psalter 63

Van Haelst, J. 51
Van Kampen Collection 177, 180, 185, 186
VanderKam, J. *and* Milik, J. T. 26
de Vaux, R. 16
Vision of Dorotheos 53, 55
Vitruvius 15
volumina 36
Vulgate 75, 89, 105, 111, 112, 147, 148, 151, 157, 161, 179, 181

Wadi Murabba'at *see* Murabba'at
Walton, Bryan 69
Werckmeister, Otto 74
Westwood, J. O. 94, 95
Whitby, Synod of 147, 148

General Index